EMPIRES AND EXPLORATION

PITT LATIN AMERICAN SERIES
Catherine M. Conaghan, Editor

EMPIRES AND EXPLORATION

RICHARD FRANCIS BURTON'S
TRAVELS IN BRAZIL

MARSHALL C. EAKIN

UNIVERSITY OF PITTSBURGH PRESS

Published by the University of Pittsburgh Press, Pittsburgh, Pa., 15260
Copyright © 2025, University of Pittsburgh Press
All rights reserved
Manufactured in the United States of America
Printed on acid-free paper
10 9 8 7 6 5 4 3 2 1

Cataloging-in-Publication data is available from the Library of Congress

Hardcover: 978-0-8229-4872-8
Paperback: 978-0-8229-6785-9

Cover image: Richard Francis Burton in 1870s. Etching of painting by Lord Leighton.
Cover design: Melissa Dias-Mandoly

Publisher: University of Pittsburgh Press, 7500 Thomas Blvd., 4th floor, Pittsburgh, PA 15260, United States, www.upittpress.org
EU Authorized Representative: Easy Access System Europe, Mustamäe tee 50, 10621 Tallinn, Estonia, gpsr.requests@easproject.com

Ao grande amor da minha vida

All Faith is false, all Faith is true:
Truth is the shattered mirror strown
In myriad bits; while each believes
his little bit the whole to own.

—RICHARD FRANCIS BURTON, *THE KASIDAH*, 1880

CONTENTS

ACKNOWLEDGMENTS   XI

INTRODUCTION: KNOWLEDGE, PLACE, PERSPECTIVE   3

CHAPTER 1. A WILD LAWLESS CREATURE IN THE BRAZILIAN EMPIRE   25

CHAPTER 2. RIO DE JANEIRO, SÃO PAULO, SANTOS   46

CHAPTER 3. THE EXPEDITION BEGINS   61

CHAPTER 4. INTO THE MINING ZONE   78

CHAPTER 5. AN ENGLISH VILLAGE IN BRAZIL   102

CHAPTER 6. ENGLISHMEN, GOLD, AND IRON   129

CHAPTER 7. LIFE AND DEATH IN MARIANA   146

CHAPTER 8. TOWN OF TARNISHED GOLD   163

CHAPTER 9. A RAFT, A RIVER, AND A LONELY RIDE   183

CHAPTER 10. RIVER OF OLD WOMEN   195

CHAPTER 11. CITY OF DIAMONDS   214

CHAPTER 12. RIVER OF SAINT FRANCIS   231

CHAPTER 13. MYSTICISM AND VIOLENCE IN THE BACKLANDS   250

CHAPTER 14. DROUGHTS, DAMS, AND FALLS   268

EPILOGUE: BURTON, BRAZIL, AND THE SHATTERED MIRROR   285

NOTES   305

BIBLIOGRAPHY   333

INDEX   349

ACKNOWLEDGMENTS

My journey with this book began some ten years ago, but my association with Richard and Isabel Burton really began more than fifty years ago with a brief comment on the destruction of his papers by a fellow student (and future Rhodes Scholar) during my first year in college. (Here's to you, L. Lewis Wall!) I really began to learn about the extraordinary Richard Burton as I spent a year of dissertation research in Minas Gerais in 1979–1980. My most profound thanks go out to the many wonderful *mineiros* who helped me find my way through archives, libraries, and over the next few decades as I wrote two books on the economic, business, and social history of my favorite Brazilian state. Douglas Libby and Amilcar and Roberto Martins (in Belo Horizonte and Nova Lima) have been wonderful supporters and collaborators for over forty-five years. Decio Barbosa in Nova Lima has helped keep the history of the community alive, and I am grateful for the tours around the mining community with him and his brother, Elcio, in June 2022. A fond *abraço* to Maysa Gomes—poet, writer, artist—for the hikes through the old Morro Velho watershed, and for also working so hard to preserve the history of the community. In earlier decades, the leadership of Mineração Morro Velho graciously allowed me to scour the company archives, tour the facilities, go down thousands of feet into the mine, and even spend a night in the old Casa Grande. To the many descendants of the English community (*morrovelhenses*) who spoke and corresponded with

ACKNOWLEDGMENTS

me, and the dozens and dozens of *novalimenses* who assisted my work and told me their stories, I am eternally grateful.

Although they funded earlier book projects, grants from a number of sources made possible my work in Minas Gerais, São Paulo, and Rio de Janeiro over decades. All these projects, even if indirectly, prepared my way to write this book. With the assistance of a Fulbright Dissertation Fellowship (1979–1980), and a Fulbright Senior Scholar Fellowship (2009–2010), and a National Endowment for the Humanities Fellowship (2015), I was able to spend long periods in Brazil doing research and getting to know Brazil and the Brazilians. My home for forty-two years, Vanderbilt University, has very generously funded my research trips on many occasions, and granted me many funded sabbaticals. I am extraordinarily lucky to have spent four decades on the faculty before retiring at the end of 2024. In particular, I have benefited enormously from my collaborations with hundreds of Vanderbilt faculty in many schools and departments, but especially my colleagues in Latin American Studies and History. A special thanks to Celso Castilho, Eddie Wright-Rios, Frank Robinson, Paula Covington, and Jane Landers.

Archivists and librarians at many institutions have aided my research on Richard Burton in Brazil. A grant from the Huntington Library made possible an exceptionally stimulating month in the papers of Richard and Isabel Burton. A number of trips over four decades to the Nettie Lee Benson Library at the University of Texas at Austin have been extremely rewarding. My profound thanks to the staff of the Benson Collection for their curation and care for the London office archive of the St. John d'el Rey Mining Company. Several trips to the National Archives (Kew) and the British Library helped me delve into the Richard Burton's consular correspondence and Burton family history. The staff at the Wiltshire and Swindon History Centre aided me adeptly during a week in lovely Chippenham. The center also generously allowed me to use three photographs from the Isabel Burton papers in their care. I spent several wonderful afternoons at the Local Studies Library, Borough of Richmond, and I am thankful to the staff there as well as biographer of the Burtons Mary Lovell for her notes and files both there and in Chippenham. My appreciation as well to the Library of Congress in Washington, DC, and the Arquivo

ACKNOWLEDGMENTS

Nacional and Biblioteca Nacional in Rio de Janeiro for access to key papers, photographs, and publications.

Jim Schindling guided me through the process of creating a website that has accompanied my journey with Richard Burton. Bill Nelson did a wonderful job putting together the maps for this book, and I am especially thankful to Josh Shanholtzer and his editorial team at the University of Pittsburgh Press. Josh Hone played the key role in pointing me to Burton's verse about the shattered mirror of truth. Many thanks to Dane Kennedy, Douglas Libby, and Hendrik Kraay for their comments and help improving the manuscript. Luiz Nogueira captained me on his boat retracing Burton's across Guanabara Bay, and Jackson Rodrigues was a wonderful guide from Belo Horizonte to Aracajú. As always, I owe so much to Michelle Beatty-Eakin for her support and understanding as I have disappeared for long periods overseas in pursuit of Richard and Isabel Burton. *Um profundo agradecimento ao grande amor da minha vida.*

EMPIRES AND EXPLORATION

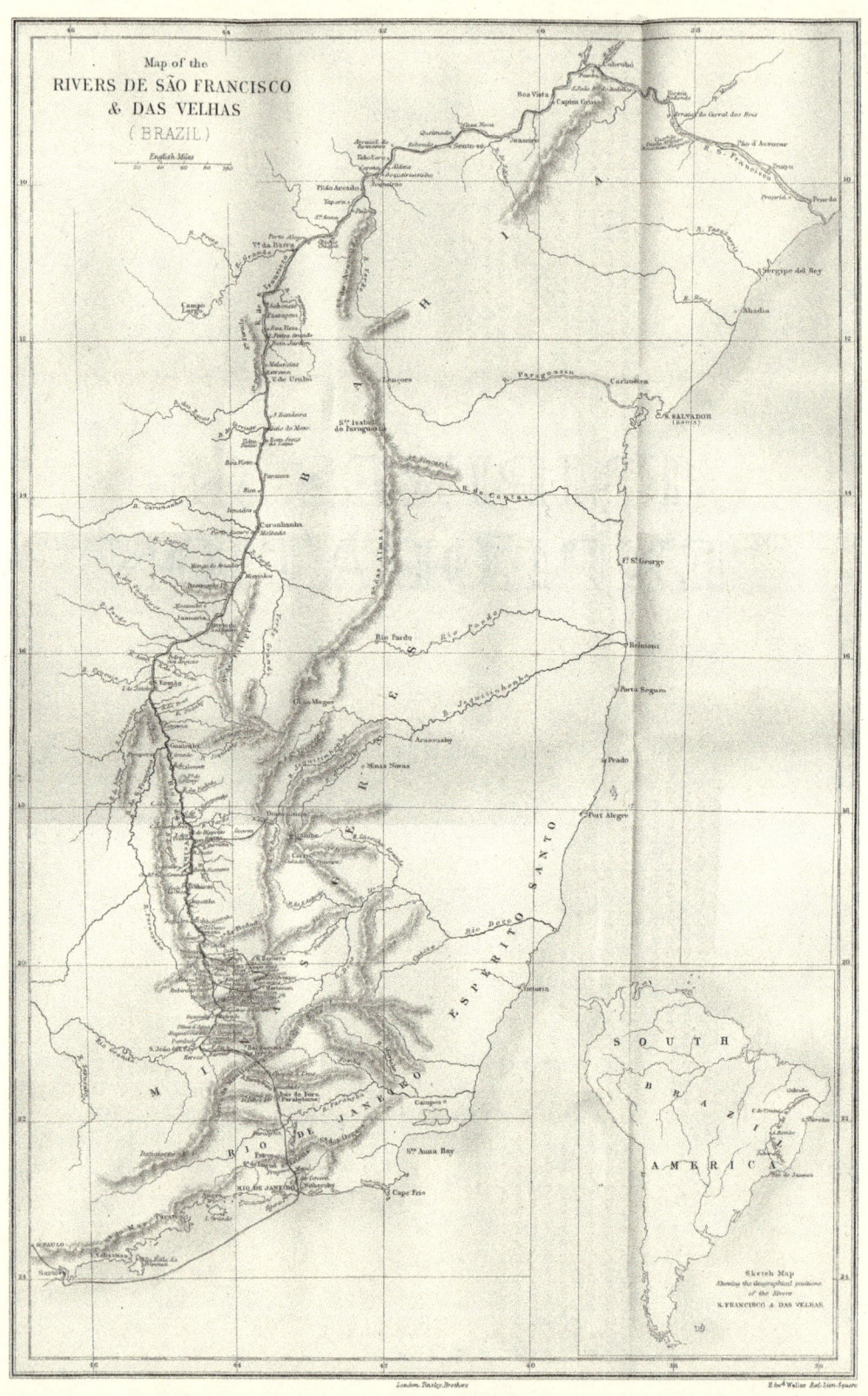

INTRODUCTION

KNOWLEDGE, PLACE, PERSPECTIVE

> The historian who visits a place writes a different history than the historian who stays home, satisfied to read about a place someone else once visited.
>
> —BARRY LOPEZ

A blinding tropical sun forces me to seek shade beneath the dense trees surrounding the shattered headstones of the British graves scattered atop this quiet Brazilian hill. These broken shards of once-stately burial markers offer visible yet silent testimony to once-mighty empires and fortunes now long gone. Nestled in the rugged, mountainous interior of the state of Minas Gerais (General Mines), the dead rest uncomfortably atop the exhausted gold mine that slices a mile and a half into the earth beneath them. On a small shelf of land jutting out to the east, just below the British graves, no gravestones—broken or intact—mark the resting place of the decaying bones of hundreds of enslaved women and men who once labored for the British mining company. The lives and deaths of these Africans and Afro-Brazilians left even fewer visible traces than the British miners and managers once interred more respectfully and ceremoniously just a few dozen yards up the hill above them.

FIGURE I.I. Morro Velho with mine reduction works (*bottom left*), Catholic church (*right*), and British cemetery (*in circle*). Image in the public domain. Auguste Riedel.

THE SOULS OF MORRO VELHO

Trudging through the thick brush and clumps of trees in the sweltering heat, I am acutely conscious of the difficulties of recovering the past, of even this small but poignant fragment of human history, of ever truly comprehending the lives of the people who once inhabited this centuries-old mining town. Multitudes of men and women came to their segregated, final resting places on this steep "old hill" (Morro Velho, pronounced *mohoo velyoo*) in southeastern Brazil. How is it, asks the historian, that we can come to understand people from such different times, places, and cultures—enslaved people from many parts of the African continent, men and women from the British Isles, Brazilian peasants, merchants, and wealthy landowners? Can we ever hope to come close to comprehending them and the worlds they once inhabited? Can we even truly make sense of those who are our contemporaries in the early twenty-first century, and who will one day be figures in a distant past for historians in future decades and centuries?

KNOWLEDGE, PLACE, PERSPECTIVE

One hundred and fifty-eight years ago, when Richard Francis Burton walked among these English graves, they numbered only a few dozen, and the cemetery of the enslaved, slightly down hill, probably contained some two hundred poorly marked burials. Most of this hill and the surrounding region had been stripped

FIGURE I.2. Morro Velho, British cemetery, 2022. Marshall C. Eakin.

of trees to supply fuel and timber for the deepening gold mine below. Today, these hillsides are lush, green, and heavily forested. Only the older inhabitants of this town would know that these neglected cemeteries sit in the middle of what was, for two centuries, a sprawling complex of industrial machinery, thousands of workers, and the constant din of massive stamping and rock-crushing machines. The final dismantling of the Morro Velho mine over the past two decades has largely stripped the valley below of most of the buildings and refining works. Scrubby grass and stunted trees have reclaimed the rusting industrial equipment, and the steady roar of the machinery has been silenced. The burial ground of the enslaved, an overgrown field of bushes and gnarled vines, has been completely forgotten. Vandals have gradually destroyed nearly all the once-impressive headstones in what was at one time a beautifully landscaped British graveyard.

More than four decades ago, in a previous century, I first began to intrude into the lives of the hundreds of people interred beneath the rocky soil on this hilltop, the gold mine that brought them to this mineral-rich state, and the country that took shape around them.[1] I began with the (perhaps naive) assumption that *we can* come to some reasonable understanding of those around us in our own society, those from cultures other than our own, and, by extension, those who inhabited the past. As an English novelist so famously once wrote, "The past is a foreign country: they do things differently there."[2] A historian, especially this historian of

Brazil, acts as a sort of cultural intermediary, much like an anthropologist, seeking an understanding of and an empathy for peoples other than his own, and strives to communicate this understanding to his own. Cultural translation is always imperfect, and its flaws increase not only with distance but also over time. My hope is that this multiple translation—of Richard Burton's Brazil, my reading of Burton, and Brazil—will reveal both the richness and the limits of the historian's empathetic efforts to bridge time and space.

I am a historian committed to my craft. I believe that the past matters, that it continues to shape the present and the future. Just as in the case of humans, nations bear the imprint of their birth, and the phases of their development—and Brazil is no exception. For nations today, threats to their survival were woven into the very fabric of their being as they first emerged and then developed over centuries. Some nations more than others are an amalgam of regions, ethnicities, religions, and classes. Their survival and ability to thrive have been built and depend on subsuming those many identities and interests below the surface of a cohesive, encompassing, and overarching sense of national identity an "imagined community," to use the inspired image of the late Benedict Anderson.[3] The story of the construction of nations has been the successful efforts to build these national identities, and persuade the multiplicity of groups within their borders that, despite all their differences, each inhabitant could lay claim to a place in the big tent of the national community. Richard Burton witnessed the very tentative efforts to bring the many groups in Brazil into an incipient nation-state in the late nineteenth century. My reading of nineteenth-century Brazil and Burton benefits from a century and a half of hindsight, and the specter of the possible implosion of Brazil's imagined community—and others—in the early twenty-first century.

A Rage to Live

Richard Francis Burton—travel writer, linguist, translator, ethnographer, explorer—is one of the most fascinating figures of the nineteenth century. In the words of one scholar of Victorian exploration and empire, he was a "furiously energetic multidisciplinarian."[4] Along with David Livingstone and Henry Morton

Stanley, he was one of the most famous explorers of the century, gaining initial recognition for his daring pilgrimage in 1853 to the inner sanctum of the Great Mosque at Mecca disguised as a Muslim.[5] His fame and notoriety increased as he tenaciously pursued the source of the Nile River in East Africa in the mid-1850s, leading to a deadly dispute with one of his former colleagues turned adversary, John Hanning Speke. As a British consul in West Africa, Brazil, Syria, and Trieste from 1861 to 1890, he continued to explore foreign regions, publish popular accounts of his travels, and edit and translate numerous works from Portuguese, German, Arabic, and Sanskrit. One of the two or three greatest linguists of his century (reputedly he mastered two dozen languages, including Arabic, Hindi, and Urdu), he gained even greater notoriety in the 1880s translating and publishing uncensored editions of the *Arabian Nights* (sixteen volumes), the *Kama Sutra*, and a major Arab treatise on sexuality. Richard published some of this work anonymously to avoid prosecution under Britain's strict obscenity laws.[6]

Richard Burton always made a strong and lasting impression on everyone he met. When fellow Brit Wilfrid Blunt encountered him in Buenos Aires in late 1868, the world-famous explorer had just finished his travels through Brazil and his three-year tour as British consul in Santos. He was at one of the lowest points in his life, depressed, and drinking heavily. Blunt later described Burton's face as "the most hideous I have ever seen, dark, cruel, treacherous, with eyes like a wild beast's. He reminded me of a black leopard, caged but unforgiving." Nevertheless, Blunt went on, "even the ferocity of his countenance gave place at times to more agreeable expressions, and I can just understand the infatuated fancy of his wife that in spite of his ugliness he was the most beautiful man alive."[7] On a "medical leave" after his posting in Brazil, he drank his way across the battlefields of Paraguay, the pampas of Argentina, and over the Andes to Chile and then Peru. In early 1869, while sitting in a café in Lima, Peru, a Foreign Office colleague spotted him and congratulated Burton on his appointment as consul in Damascus. Startled by this good news, he immediately boarded a ship to Buenos Aires via the Straits of Magellan—a five-thousand-mile voyage. In Buenos Aires he found months of accumulated mail from his wife, Isabel, and he immediately wrote

Figure 1.3. Richard Francis Burton in 1870s. Etching of painting by Lord Leighton. Image in the public domain. Léopold Flameng, after Frederic, Lord Leighton.

the Foreign Office to accept his appointment. The South American chapter of his life drew to a close, but only after one more visit to the battlefields of Paraguay.[8]

Although he worked on at least a half dozen book projects that he later published, Richard's years in Brazil form a gap in his enormous literary productivity. From 1850 to 1865, he published no less than seventeen books, most of them multiple volumes. He published another two dozen between 1870 and 1890 (and the *Arabian Nights* was sixteen volumes)! During his nearly four years in Brazil, no books appeared. *Travels in the Highlands of the Brazil* appeared shortly after his departure from South America in 1869.[9] He clearly did not stop writing during his years in Brazil. Short articles and essays appeared on a regular basis, and he formulated plans for several more books including a second (never written) book on the "lowlands" of Brazil. *Letters from the Battle-Fields of Paraguay* covering the months between his departure from Brazil and making his way across the pampas came out in 1870. We know very little, however, about Richard's peregrinations through Argentina, Chile, and Peru in 1869. As one biographer has noted, it is the most undocumented portion of his adult life.[10] Given Wilfrid Blunt's frank assessment during their meeting in Buenos Aires at the end of Richard's tour of duty in Santos, we can fairly well believe that he was at one of the lowest points in his life. The appointment to his dream job in Damascus, putting him back into the Middle East, no doubt reenergized him and snapped him out of his depression.

Richard's "midlife crisis" in Brazil marked a turning point, an interlude between the two great halves of his adult life. His expedition down the São Francisco River—however tame it might have been compared to his previous explorations—was his last. He would make other trips over the last twenty years of his life back to the Middle East and West Africa, but none of them came close to the explorations of the 1850s and 1860s. Just as his extraordinary travels would define the first half of his life, translations defined the second half. Richard's years in Brazil formed the transitional moment between the audacious explorer in his thirties and forties to the bold translator in his fifties and sixties.

Most of Richard's biographers spend very little space on his time in Brazil, dismissing its importance in comparison with his earlier explorations through the Middle East and Africa, and his later translations of Arabic and Indian works. One of his biographers, Byron Falwell, bitingly describes his Brazilian writing as "even duller and less popular than usual." An anonymous British reviewer quite rightly lambasted Richard for "letting his text tell only half of what he means to say, and adding the other half in

FIGURE I.4. Isabel Burton, 1864. Image in the public domain. From Isabel Burton's autobiography.

a note," forcing the reader "to break off two or three times in a page"![11] Richard's prose is often turgid and filled with the overwhelming detail that so often appeared in the travel accounts of the nineteenth century. At times, the approach of the ethnographer combined with the encyclopedist leads to minutiae that bore the reader.¹² A couple of his biographers have astutely pointed out that Richard was something of a mix of Montesquieu and Humboldt. He missed nothing "and can bring to bear on each unique experience a vast range of comparative instances." Burton, says Frank McLynn, "is always interesting."¹³ For the historian, however, this bounty of detail on everything from local food prices to the sartorial habits of rich and poor alike offers us some of the very rare glimpses into daily life that the mountains of government-produced, official documentation ignore.

Despite the infamous destruction of what was likely the most interesting material in Richard and his wife Isabel's personal papers, we do have an impressive amount of documentation on Richard Burton's time in Brazil. In addition to Richard's two-volume *Explorations in the Highlands of the Brazil* (dedicated to the "Right Hon. The Lord Stanley, P.C., M.P."), we have Isabel Burton's biography of Richard, her two-volume "autobiography," an extensive surviving correspondence for both Burtons that has been compiled on a website, Foreign Office records, surviving personal papers scattered from the Huntington Library in California to Chippenham, England, and a raft of biographies produced over more than a century. These sources, at times, allow us with the opportunity to cross-check information and opinions.¹⁴

To complicate matters, although we see Richard and Brazil in the 1860s through Richard's eyes, especially through his two-volume travel account, our view of Richard and the Brazil he experienced has also been shaped through Isabel's letters, her biography of Richard, her own autobiography, and her role in editing his works. The destruction of the couple's most personal journals and papers on Richard's death in 1890, and thereafter by her executors (following Isabel's detailed instructions), also profoundly shaped our view of both of them. For this chapter of their life, Isabel's editing and destroying shaped the surviving writings of Richard about Brazil. In particular, his deeply hypermasculine imperial gaze was consciously reframed and refined by Isabel's eyes and hands. This may be my interpretation of Richard's Brazil, but it is deeply inflected, in ways we cannot fully appreciate, by Isabel's role as his editor, publicist, and biographer.

A parade of foreign travelers moving through Brazil in the nineteenth century have left us with a profusion of rich and detailed information, in accounts that we must read with great care and the customary skepticism of the historian.[15] For several decades now, historians, anthropologists, and literary scholars have analyzed, deconstructed, and decolonized travel accounts of North Americans and Europeans who fanned out across Asia, Africa, the Middle East, and the Americas, especially in the nineteenth century.[16] We are now well sensitized to the biases and prejudices that so often accompanied the "imperial eyes" of travel writers, especially the British. At its heart, the historian's challenge in using these accounts lies at the core of the fundamental dilemma of all historians in their craft—how to recover the past through sources that are always tainted by the attitudes and beliefs of their creators. No information, by definition, is neutral. One of the most important skills of the historian is the ability to read closely, carefully, attuned to the circumstances surrounding the creation of the source material, whether it be a diary, letter, government document, photograph, or travel account. In the best of cases, we have multiple sources from a variety of perspectives that allow us to cross-check and build a stronger case for the historical narratives we create. Too often, however, especially the farther one moves back in the past, the number of sources shrink, and the ability to cross-reference diminishes.

Compounding the task of the historian is the enormous imbalance in sources. Not only do the victors write history, but elites generate most of the material for those narratives. One of the greatest challenges are the "silences" of not only the vanquished but also the non-elites, the vast majority of those who have lived on this earth. The historian of Brazil, for example, has dozens of accounts written by foreign visitors and ample material generated by government officials and wealthy Brazilians. For the nineteenth century, the voices of the so-called subalterns are rare, and those few that exist are almost always "mediated" through the hands of others—notaries, courts, police, clergy.[17] As Richard Burton condescendingly observes and records bits of the lives of the enslaved and the lower classes, we have no records of what they may have been thinking of the many foreign travelers moving through their world. (How surprising and rewarding it would be to have accounts of the enslaved and the peasants about their encounters with these foreign travelers and their hosts!) Unlike in the United States, we do not even have "slave narratives" for Brazil. How can the historian construct a reliable narrative in the face of the cacophony of elite voices and the almost complete silence of the poor and dispossessed?[18]

When Richard Burton traversed the Brazilian backlands (*sertão*), he was only a year older (forty-six) than the Brazilian nation that had declared its independence from Portugal in 1822. In the aftermath of the wars for independence across all the Americas (1770s–1830s) Brazil became the only new nation to follow the path of empire and monarchy.[19] Like the new American republics, the Empire of Brazil (1822–1889) faced the

FIGURE 1.5. Richard Francis Burton, 1864. Image in the public domain. Rischgitz.

daunting challenges of creating a new nation out of a former European colony. The Brazilian elites inherited a state apparatus (the instruments and institutions of power) from the Portuguese, but they would have to create a nation (an imagined community). On paper, Brazil was larger than what eventually became the forty-eight contiguous US states. In theory, it was six times the size of the young United States of America in 1822.

This Victorian empire in the tropics with its fair-haired, blue-eyed Emperor Pedro II was in some ways the most stable nation in the Americas for much of the nineteenth century. Bloody wars wracked much of North and South America, including the United States, and the old viceroyalties of Spain's American empire eventually fragmented into sixteen different countries. Brazil, a colony of truly continental dimensions, held together despite a series of internal rebellions from the 1820s to the 1840s. The long reign of Pedro II (1840–1889) made Brazil unlike any other country in the Americas.[20]

During his three years as a British consul in Brazil, Burton personally regaled the emperor (in fluent Portuguese and French) with tales of his Middle Eastern and African exploits. As he did everywhere he went, he read voraciously about local history, literature, economics, and politics, and he studied and wrote about the Brazilian nation in its youth with all its struggles, problems, and promise. With his excellent language skills in Portuguese, he stood out from so many of the foreign travelers who passed through Brazil in the nineteenth century, who were rarely able to speak the local language.

EMPIRES AND EXPLORATIONS

Richard Burton's arrival in Brazil in 1865 came just as Great Britain was reaching its peak as the most powerful and expansive empire in world history.²¹ A generation after Burton's death in 1890, World War I would mark the beginning of the end of four centuries of European global expansion and power. In the fifteenth and sixteenth centuries, many different peoples and polities had surged outward from Europe, initiating waves of conquest and colonization that would reach their peak in the late nineteenth century, eventually circling the entire globe. When he stumbled into the islands of the Caribbean in late 1492, Christopher Columbus unknowingly set the planet on an irreversible and ongoing process of globalization and integration. Columbus and those who followed him—westward across the Atlantic and eastward into the Indian and Pacific Oceans—connected the Old World (Europe, Africa, Asia) with the New (the Americas) to create a rudimentary but truly global economy. Powerful and long-developing historical forces drove the Europe-

FIGURE I.6. Brazilian royal family, 1864. *Left to right, standing:* Princess Isabel, Comte d'Eu, Princess Leopoldina, Duke of Saxe-Coburg; *seated*, Pedro II, Empress Teresa Cristina. Image in the public domain. Joaquim Insley Pacheco.

ans outward around the globe: the most advanced nautical technology, the revolutionary market forces of an emerging capitalist economy, and a cultural and religious worldview that envisioned the earth and its peoples as resources and souls that needed to be understood, subdued, and saved. The combination of these factors propelled Europeans outward in search of goods, souls, and conquest on a scale never seen before in world history.[22]

In the sixteenth century, the Spanish and the Portuguese formed the vanguard of this expansion. Over several centuries after the Columbian voyages, Spain built a colonial empire, primarily in the Americas, stretching from what today is the US Southwest and Southeast to Tierra del Fuego. Abundant silver extracted from the high deserts of northern Mexico and the Andes fueled the construction and maintenance of this empire, one that stretched its tentacles as far west as the Philippines (named after Philip II, 1556–1598) and southward into West Africa.[23] Unlike the Spanish, the Portuguese were primarily traders, not settlers. Between 1450 and 1550, they built the first truly global commercial empire that included coastal trading posts down the shores of Atlantic Africa, around the perimeter of the Indian Ocean, and into the Pacific to China (Macau) and Japan (Nagasaki). On the second Portuguese voyage to India in 1500, the fleet veered to the southwest in the Atlantic, stumbling upon what they believed was an island. Over the next century as the Portuguese profited immensely off trade with the East (trading spices and silver), this "island" played a very small part in their larger global and imperial ambitions.[24]

Increasing French incursions along the coast of South America compelled the Portuguese monarchy to pay more attention to the "Island of the True Cross," which gradually became known for the dense wood of the brazil tree that produced a deep red dye. In the last decades of the sixteenth century, the Portuguese planted sugar cane on the northeastern coast of Brazil in the new colonial captaincies of Bahia and Pernambuco. After all, they had more than a century of experience cultivating this luxury crop on the tiny islands of the eastern Atlantic: the Azores, Madeira, Cape Verde. Unable to cajole or compel the Native Americans to work on the rapidly expanding sugar plantations, the Portuguese began to import enslaved Africans, primarily from the areas that today

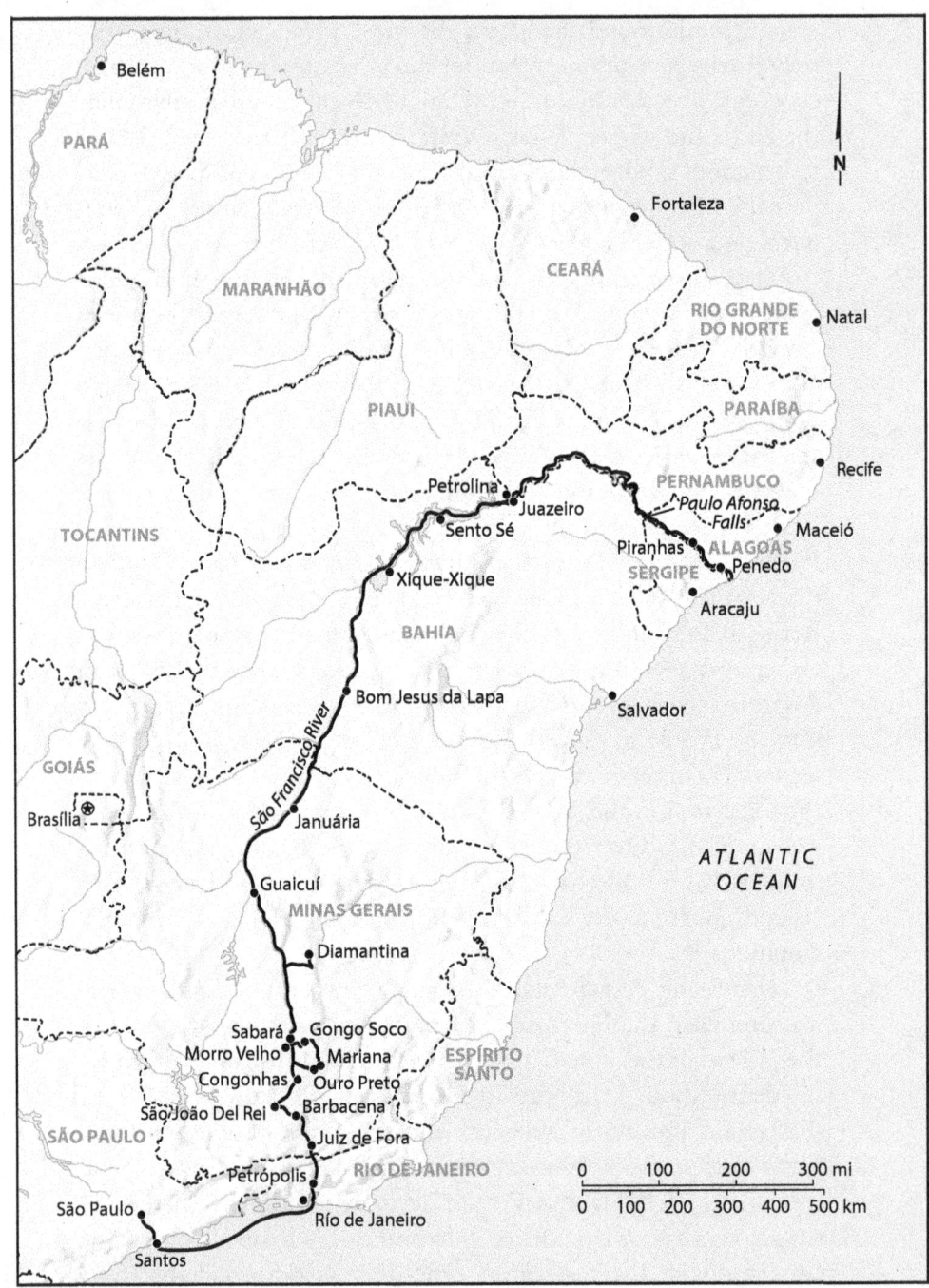

FIGURE I.7. Richard's route through eastern Brazil.

are coastal West Africa and Angola. Although enslaved Africans had been shipped to the Americas since the 1490s, the traffic to northeastern Brazil massively accelerated and consolidated a transatlantic slave trade that would forcibly transport millions of captive Africans and last until the second half of the nineteenth century.[25]

Sugar and slavery transformed Brazil into the heartland of the Portuguese world empire in the seventeenth century and created the plantation-slavery complex that the Spanish, English, French, and Dutch would reproduce in the islands of the Caribbean and the US South. The rise of the Dutch and English global navies after 1600 drastically challenged and weakened the Portuguese in the Indian Ocean and Asia, fueling the rise of new European world empires. The Dutch, French, and English moved into the Americas, challenging Spain and Portugal, and spread the sugar and slavery complex.[26]

The discovery of gold in the interior of Brazil around 1700, about 250 miles north of the small port of Rio de Janeiro, reinforced the central role of Brazil in the increasingly weak Portuguese empire.[27] The demand for labor in the region that the Crown called Minas Gerais again accelerated the Atlantic slave trade, shifting the major port of entry from Pernambuco and Bahia in the Northeast to Rio de Janeiro in the Southeast. Along with the rapid expansion of plantations in the French, Dutch, and English Caribbean, the gold rush in Brazil helped make the eighteenth century the most tragic for the Atlantic slave trade. Of the 11 million to 12 million enslaved Africans who arrived in the Americas between the late fifteenth century and the late nineteenth century, probably half crossed the Atlantic in the eighteenth century. Most of those captive souls endured the so-called Middle Passage—between Africa and the Americas—on British ships.[28]

With the defeat of Napoleon at Waterloo in 1815, the British emerged as the dominant power in Europe and around the globe. They constructed an empire on which the "sun never set." Although they lost their thirteen colonies on the Eastern Seaboard of North America to rebellious colonials in the 1770s, they retained control of Canada, parts of the Caribbean, and coastal settlements and islands around the globe. In the late eighteenth and early nineteenth centuries, the British began to move into the interior of Africa and India. On the South Asian subcontinent, they gradually gained greater control over peoples and terrains they had known and observed for centuries. For the British, and most of the world, the interior of Africa was a vast unknown. European explorers, especially British explorers, spread out across the globe in the nineteenth century in search of fame and fortune. They consciously followed in the tradition of Columbus, Magellan, and the great navigators of the fifteenth and sixteenth centuries. The earlier explorers had navigated and charted the seas. The great frontiers of the nineteenth century were the inland regions of Asia, Africa, and the Americas.[29]

Just as the voyages of the navigators in earlier centuries had expanded the scope and power of the emerging European empires, the explorers of the nineteenth century advanced imperial ambitions even when operating independently of governments and armies. As in Richard Burton's case, the lines between officially sanctioned and private expeditions often blurred.[30] The British Admiralty, for example, commissioned the "scientific" expeditions of Captain James Cook across the Pacific Ocean in the second half of the eighteenth century. Although he sought to advance understanding of currents, climates, flora, fauna, and peoples of the Pacific, Cook's work was clearly designed to further the commercial and military goals of the British Empire.[31] The fledgling naturalist Charles Darwin went along on the HMS *Beagle* in the 1830s as a private citizen, but Captain Robert FitzRoy's objective was to map his way around the world to ease the path of British ships—military or commercial.[32]

Richard Francis Burton began his career as a surveyor in the army of the British East India Company in the 1840s, to generate some of these maps of empire. When he sought out the source of the Nile River in East Africa in the 1850s, he was on leave as army officer, partially financed by the Royal Geographical Society in London.[33] Often critical of British society and mores, and much too independent to follow faithfully the orders of officers or bureaucrats, Burton nonetheless served the aims of empire in his explorations, even when he did not consciously mean to do so. After he became an employee of the Foreign Office in 1861, a consul for the next three decades, Burton rarely explored (or published) to fulfill official duties, yet his findings served the voracious needs of imperial expansion and control. As many British social anthropologists would come to realize in the twentieth century, any knowledge they generated not only helped the well-meaning to understand seemingly strange and exotic peoples, but that same knowledge could also be used to subdue, or eliminate, them.[34]

THE EXPEDITION, THE TRAVELER, AND THE HISTORIAN

In June 1867 Richard Burton headed north from Rio de Janeiro into the Brazilian interior on an expedition that would last five months. He had convinced his superiors that this foray would provide valuable information on economic assets of the interior, especially on mineral resources.[35] After thoroughly inspecting the mountainous mining region for nearly two months, he boarded an improvised riverboat with abundant supplies, several Brazilian crew members, an expatriate US Southerner, and a young enslaved man from Morro Velho to serve as his cook. Richard and his constantly changing crew navigated 1,300 miles north and east along the São Francisco River, through the arid northeastern backlands, eventually emerging on the lush, tropical Atlantic coast in early November. In June 2022, 155 years later, I set out in Burton's footsteps beginning from São Paulo (where he lived), through the port of Santos (where he was British consul), to Rio de Janeiro and then north into the mining zone. Difficult to navigate in the nineteenth century, large sections of the upper São Francisco (where Burton began his voyage) no longer allow even the smallest boat traffic. The last 1,300 miles of my "voyage" combined time on the river and on the roads alongside it through the arid backlands of the Northeast.

A seasoned and cosmopolitan explorer of South Asia, the Middle East, the Americas, and Africa, Burton provides us with a panoramic view of Brazil in mid-century, commenting on politics, economics, race relations, social structures, cultural norms, and the environment. Understandably, Richard embodied many of the conceits and prejudices of the Victorian Englishman, despite his highly unusual and truly cosmopolitan life.[36] His enormous curiosity and compulsion to provide detailed information on all that he observed made Richard something of a self-taught anthropologist. In fact, he became one of the founders of the Anthropological Society of London in 1863, an organization notorious among historians today for its explicitly racialized and racist view of humankind. Richard's incredibly detailed descriptions of the peoples he encountered on multiple continents—natives of India and Africa, Arab pilgrims, Mormons in Utah, Brazilians of all types—remain invaluable firsthand observations by an astute, observant, and highly opinionated Victorian Englishman.

As a citizen and diplomat of the world's most powerful empire, and one of the most seasoned travelers of his time, he provides us with a complex interlocutor for seeing Brazil from within and without, and in the larger context of the Americas and the world in the nineteenth century. As a citizen (but certainly not diplomat) of the most powerful empire of the twentieth century, I bring with me the some of the conceits and prejudices of the early twenty-first century native of the United States, profoundly tempered by fifty years studying, writing about, and traveling around Brazil and Latin America. My hope is that the reader will benefit from my analysis of Richard Burton's Brazil in the late 1860s—the perspective of the nineteenth-century British explorer via the twenty-first-century American historian. Along the way, I ponder Burton's view in his bit of the shattered mirror with my own, and what these reflections tell us about Brazil, Brazilians, and the pursuit of historical knowledge.

The River and Road Map

The allure of gold and diamonds drew Richard Burton into the heart of the eastern Brazilian Highlands. Just as the Morro Velho gold mine takes up half a dozen chapters and about seventy-five pages in volume 1 of *Explorations*, the reconnaissance of the diamond workings around Diamantina spans four chapters and sixty pages in volume 2. About one-third of the nine hundred pages of these two volumes focuses on detailed sketches of the gold mines and diamond deposits of Minas Gerais. About half of the first volume recounts the trek into the mining zone, and the second volume focuses entirely on the voyage down the São Francisco River—except for ten days at the beginning dedicated to the side trip overland to Diamantina. Burton's *Explorations*, then, tells three stories: the trek from Rio to gold mining zone, surveys of the gold and diamond mining zones, and then the river expedition to the Atlantic. Given Richard's view of the trip from Rio to Minas as a "holiday" excursion, the two-volume account offers two kinds of accounts—the first aimed at those interested in the economic opportunities of mining in Brazil, and the second at those who might see the potential of the São Francisco to become a vibrant economic corridor for the nation. In the first volume, Richard plays the role of the economic development promoter and in the second, the intrepid explorer.

The first chapter of *this* book summarizes Burton's extraordinarily full life to place his Brazilian experience within the larger context of five decades of travels on five continents. Richard's sojourn in Brazil came at roughly the middle of his seven decades of an eventful life (he arrived in Brazil at the age of forty-four and lived for another twenty-two years after his departure). For those uninitiated in things Brazilian, the second chapter provides a brief overview of the historical and geographical context of Brazil and the Burtonian moment in the 1860s. The next twelve chapters reconstruct each stage of his travel account, beginning with his principal residence (São Paulo), the port of Santos where he served as British consul, and the imperial court in Rio de Janeiro. This portion of his trip took a matter of days. Burton was already very familiar with these three cities, and his primary objective was to move into the rich gold mining zone of Minas Gerais before embarking on his long trek down the São Francisco River. Chapter 3 takes the Burtons from Rio through the summer imperial residence of Petrópolis and into southern Minas Gerais. Chapters 4–8 cover Richard and Isabel's weeks circuit through the mining zone. During these weeks, he and Isabel stayed at the most successful gold mining enterprise in nineteenth- and twentieth-century Brazil, the Morro Velho gold mine in the village of Congonhas de Sabará (today Nova Lima). Burton inspected and wrote in detail about the mine and the village, descending into the depths of the earth and walking amid the graves on the hill above the mine. By the time the Burtons arrived, the London-based St. John d'el Rey Mining Company had been burrowing ever deeper into the earth, following the rich vein of gold ore for more than three decades. The mine would continue to produce into the early twenty-first century, and the graves in both cemeteries atop the "old hill" would steadily increase.

In early August 1867, Burton began his river expedition at Sabará (a larger and more substantial town some fifteen miles north of Congonhas de Sabará). Initially, he made his way down the winding Rio das Velhas (River of the Old Women) that flows north into the São Francisco (Saint Francis) just northeast of the town of Pirapora. His keen interest in mining shows, as he paused his voyage for a week to cross overland to the diamond mining zone around (the appropriately named) Diamantina. After thoroughly studying the local diamond deposits, he returned to the river and, in mid-September, finally reached the São Francisco. Chapters 9–11 focus on this time on the Rio das Velhas. The final three chapters, 12–14, recount the two-month-long voyage down the São Francisco River. He and his crews (he changed them a half dozen times) carefully making their way through a series of rapids that made the river unnavigable for boats or ships of any serious size. Near the end of his trip, Richard abandoned his rough-hewn vessel and approached on foot the impressive Paulo Afonso Falls, one of the prime objectives of his expedition. His published account ends rather abruptly after his detailed description of the falls, as he made his way the short distance to the Atlantic coast and caught a steamer back to Rio de Janeiro in early November 1867.

Months later, Richard fell deathly ill. Gradually nursed back to health by a distraught Isabel, he resigned his consular position and took a medical leave, heading for Argentina and Paraguay hoping to witness firsthand the bloody war Argentina and Brazil had been waging for three years against Paraguay. Isabel packed up their belongings, including the manuscript of a book on his expedition. On her arrival in England, she was able to persuade the Foreign Secretary, Lord Stanley (a friend of her family), to appoint Richard as consul in Damascus. She also arranged publication of the book, but not before adding her own short preface complaining about Richard's "anti-Catholic" comments in the two-volume account![37] Although the Burtons would never return to Brazil, he took with him a project that he had been wrestling with during his time there, a translation of the epic poem *The Lusiads*. Written in the sixteenth century by Portugal's most legendary author, Luís de Camões, the saga captures Portugal at the moment of its greatest imperial reach, from Brazil to Japan. The Portuguese consider the epic a poetic rendering of the formation of their national identity. Richard would not finish and publish the six-volume translation until 1880.[38]

FIGURE I.8. Title page of *Explorations in the Highlands of the Brazil*, vol. 1. Image in the public domain.

Richard Burton carefully and enthusiastically scrutinized a Brazil in the 1860s that was just starting to become a nation, just beginning to construct the institutions and symbols of a national identity and community. The Brazil of the early twenty-first century, a nation that has come of age over the last century and a half, seemingly bears little resemblance to Richard Burton's Brazil. Nevertheless, to invoke the great novelist William Faulkner,

"The past is never dead. It's not even past."[39] All nations, like all individuals, bear the burdens of their history. Brazil is no different, and perhaps feels those burdens more acutely than most countries. As I retrace Richard Burton's steps in the following chapters, I seek to stress the particular historical moment that he witnessed in mid-nineteenth-century Brazil—its landed aristocracy, slave society, and coffee economy, with a monarchy attempting to bridge deep regional, racial, and cultural divides through the construction of national infrastructure, and early efforts to create some sense of national identity. In the epilogue I reflect on the Brazil of the 1860s, the nation it became, and the fragility of historical knowledge, place, and perspective.

CHAPTER 1

A WILD LAWLESS CREATURE IN THE BRAZILIAN EMPIRE

He unites the wild lawless creature and the gentleman.
—ISABEL BURTON, WRITING TO HER MOTHER IN 1859

Although they had been married for four years, the consular posting to Brazil marked the first time that Richard and Isabel had lived together in their own home. In late January 1861, shortly after returning to London from East Africa, Richard had married the twenty-nine-year-old Isabel Arundell in a small ceremony that she tried (and failed) to keep secret from her mother.[1] Theirs would be a strong and enduring marriage, with Isabel as Richard's confidante, staunch defender, and devoted caregiver for nearly three decades. Mary Lovell, the Burtons' best biographer, described Isabel as "warm-hearted, energetic, loyal and adventurous. She was also arrogant, pretentious, impulsive and capricious."[2] Isabel's Roman Catholic family belonged to a much more distinguished level of English society than Richard's, and she used all her personal connections to land an appointment for him in the Foreign Office. She wanted to help him secure a respectable profession, one that would also allow the great explorer to keep traveling the world and writing. In 1860, before his marriage, he had an income of around £350 a year from a small family inheritance and his salary with the army of the East India Company. Richard's income was at about the level of a white-collar clerk, far above the £50 a year salary of a manual laborer, and far below the more than £150,000 annual income of Edward Stanley (Lord Derby), one of the richest men in Britain.[3]

West Africa, Sex, and Brazil

Within months of his marriage, he was named consul to Fernando Pó (known today as Bioko), a tiny island in the Gulf of Guinea just west of modern-day Cameroon and south of Nigeria, a few degrees above the equator. At £700 per annum, he now had a more respectable income, and what he probably considered a promising start in the consular corps. Despite its obscurity, the island would give him access to explore West Africa, a logical continuation of his recent exploits in East Africa. Although he requested retirement and a pension from the Indian Army after nearly twenty years' service, the East India Company in Bombay retired him (at the rank of captain) without a pension, likely due to animosities his unorthodox path had provoked among his peers and superiors in India. (For the next quarter century, his name would appear in the press and publications as Captain Richard F. Burton.) Ignoring the retirement snub, the Burtons spent much of the next few months as guests of aristocratic patrons—the prime minister, Lord Palmerston, and the foreign secretary, Lord John Russell—and even made an appearance at the court of Queen Victoria.[4] Lord Russell, then on the verge of becoming prime minister, described Richard as "a very dark man, with a fierce and scowling eye, & a repulsive hard face, but exceedingly clever & amusing in conversation. He believes in no particular religion, though calling himself a Mussulman."[5]

In August, just seven months after their renegade wedding, Richard headed off to spend the next three years in West Africa. Seized by the Portuguese in the late fifteenth century (and named after a Portuguese navigator), Fernando Pó became an important transit point for the Atlantic slave trade. In the mid-nineteenth century, Spain controlled the island and allowed the British to use it as a staging point for naval vessels intent on halting the slave trade. By the time Richard arrived, the trade had nearly ended, and his duties largely dealt with observing and facilitating commercial shipping. He refused to allow Isabel to accompany him due to the "pestilential" environment (malaria and yellow fever). On several occasions, they met for holidays in the Canary Islands.[6]

A relentless and insatiable traveler, Richard paddled up the Congo River, made several visits to sites in present-day Nigeria and Cameroon, and spent extended time with the king of Dahomey (present-day Benin). Writing at what must have been a furious pace, he produced three books (each two volumes) with detailed descriptions of West Africa and its peoples.[7] He went in search of gorillas, confirmed their existence and habits, and became the first European to scale several mountains in the region.[8] The Kingdom of Dahomey had emerged in the eighteenth century as one of the most notorious for Europeans, and Burton made an extended trip to the court of its king, Gelele. Reputedly protecting his kingdom with army of Amazon women warriors and engaging in cannibalism and the sacrifice of thousands of captive victims, Gelele welcomed Burton and his expedition into his camp but refused for weeks to meet with him. Eventually, the king met with Richard several times, on one occasion forcing him to dance to entertain the court. Richard had timed his arrival to coincide with the arrival of the new year, a time noted for its large number of ritual executions.[9]

As it turned out, the army of Amazons consisted mainly of captive women, and Richard was not impressed. "An equal number of British charwomen," he wrote, "armed with the British broomstick, would . . . clear them off in a very few hours."[10] The tales of mass executions, it turned out, were true. Despite his disgust and English sense of superiority, Richard grasped that all that he witnessed was intimately wrapped up in a religious worldview with its own (non-European) logic. The level of meticulous detail and insight yielded an ethnographic account of the peoples of the region that would not be achieved again until the arrival of the great American anthropologist Melville Herskovits in the 1930s.[11]

In early 1865, after Isabel's insistent lobbying, Lord Russell finally came through with a new assignment, but not the coveted position in the Middle East that Isabel and Richard had hoped to secure. Instead, he was assigned to Santos, Brazil, the port for the town of São Paulo (slightly inland). Shortly after his arrival in Brazil, Richard described the town to his friend Richard

Monckton Milnes as "a wretched hole but with 40 miles lies S. Paulo a more tolerable place of exile."[12] Although we now know that both cities were on the verge of becoming great coffee-exporting centers for the world's largest coffee producer, their days of greatness were still in the near future. São Paulo and Santos in the 1860s remained secondary cities in the shadows of Brazil's social and political capital, Rio de Janeiro. Just over two hundred miles up the coast, Rio was by far Brazil's largest city, and home to the imperial court (and the British legation) with a population of more than 250,000.[13] Richard Burton was hardly the typical Victorian British consul. He knew his job was to advance British commerce and protect British citizens, but that mundane work became his means to travel and write. The position in Santos would allow the Burtons to live together and set up a household for the first time since their marriage. During those first four years, they had spent less than a year together during Richard's leaves, mostly in the Canary Islands and traveling around Britain.

Biographers and scholars have long speculated about the couple's relationship—and Richard's sexuality and sex life. From his own writings and the accounts of others, it is clear that Richard had various heterosexual relationships during his youth in Europe and India. During his time in India, he probably lived with a local woman, and his early writings speak of several affairs—from wishful fantasies to intimate relationships. He always projected the virile, martial masculine persona fascinated with the sexual appeal of the East, something he had in common with many fellow Orientalists.[14] His fascination with homosexuality was notorious, from his purported investigation of male brothels in Karachi to his later published writings "on pederasty" (the synonym for homosexuality in his day).[15] We do know that a British army physician diagnosed him with a case of secondary syphilis while he was in Aden nursing his wounds from the ill-fated expedition to Somaliland in 1855.[16] Burton's most rigorous biographer, Mary Lovell, makes the sound argument that he had recently contracted the disease in relationships with Somali women he described as having "rich brown complexions and round faces" and who "greatly resemble the stony beauties of Egypt."[17]

Richard remained fascinated with the sexual habits of all peoples, and the subject played a large role in his writings during the last thirty years of his life and his marriage to Isabel. None of their surviving writings provides any hint to the nature of their physical relationship. (He surely must have told her of his syphilis before they married.) The personal journals and correspondence that Isabel later (so notoriously) burned no doubt contained a great deal of information that would have helped resolve biographers' questions.[18] Isabel never became pregnant despite marrying Richard at the age of twenty-nine, but one or both of them may have been infertile. What we do know is that Isabel adored Richard and became his personal assistant, editor, publicist, and soulmate for three decades. No surviving document speaks to any aspect of their sexual relationship or sexuality. We can only speculate.

To prepare for the assignment in Santos, in May 1865 Isabel and Richard headed off for two months in Portugal, a chance for him to refresh the Portuguese he had first learned while in Goa in the late 1840s, and for her an intense immersion course. In the words of her first biographer, Richard took her to Portugal "probably to accustom her to the savage sights and sounds which might await her in the semi-civilized country whither they were bound"![19] Establishing a pattern that would continue in the coming years, Richard left Lisbon for Brazil in June, and Isabel immediately headed back to England to settle their affairs before heading to Brazil in August. In the following decades, as Richard normally preferred to take off on his next assignment alone, Isabel would (in his infamous words) "pack, pay, and follow."[20]

From the Foreign Office correspondence, we know that Richard kept postponing his arrival in Santos, much to the irritation of his superiors in London and Rio de Janeiro. In the months between his appointment and his arrival in Brazil, he had been negotiating vigorously to delay his departure for Santos to head back to Africa to explore the Niger River in search of its source. He had mobilized the support of Sir Roderick Murchison, an eminent geologist and president of the Royal Geographical Society, in his appeals to Lord Russell. In late 1864 Russell denied his request, but Richard then received a summons to give testimony in late April before a parliamentary committee investigating West Africa.[21] After time in Britain, then in Portugal, he finally arrived in Recife in July 1865. Rather than heading south to Santos, he wrote Lord Russell yet again, asking for permission to wait for Isabel because she would not "find it easy to reach Santos without me."[22] He finally sailed down the coast and—more than a year after departing Fernando Pó for home leave and nearly a year after his appointment as consul in Santos—officially arrived at his post on 8 September 1865. He did not stay long. After a quick reconnaissance of Santos and nearby São Paulo, he returned to Rio to await Isabel.[23]

With today's jumbo jets, the trip from London to Rio de Janeiro is a twelve-hour flight. In the 1860s, passenger steamships circulated between Southampton and Rio de Janeiro via Portugal and the Atlantic islands on a regular basis, normally taking three weeks to make the transatlantic crossing.[24] Before the arrival of a transatlantic submarine telegraph cable in the mid-1870s, the flow of information for British merchants and diplomats moved at the speed of ships and consisted of handwritten letters transported on these regular "mail packets." The Royal Mail Steam Packet Company was a private firm that held the government contract for delivering the mail in South America and the West Indies. These ships generally departed every two weeks (a fortnight), so the back-and-forth with London was slow. (Richard's letter of 8 September 1865 informing the Foreign Office that he had just arrived at his post was received in London on 4 November!)[25]

Once back in England, Isabel regularly sent letters to Richard about her own travel plans. Much to her dismay, on arrival in Recife in late September she discovered that all her letters had piled up in the post office there. They had not been forwarded to Richard in Santos. Despondent, she spent the next few days sailing to Bahia and then on to Rio. To her delight, he came aboard the ship for her early morning arrival in Guanabara Bay. The view of the mountains surrounding the bay entranced her, as it has many others for centuries: "It is about the most glorious sight that a human being can behold, at sunrise and at sunset, the mountains being of most fantastic shapes, and the colours that of an opal. Richard said that it beats all the scenery he had ever seen in his life—even the Bosphorus."[26] Their Brazilian adventure had begun.

The Geography of Empire

In the six decades between the signing of the Declaration of Independence of the United States of America in Philadelphia in 1776 and the creation of the Republic of Texas in 1836, nineteen new nations took shape across the Americas. In this age of Atlantic revolutions, nearly all these new nations followed the republican path forged in revolutionary France and the United States, rejecting the monarchical political systems that had created and exploited the European colonies from Canada to Argentina over three centuries. Mexico in the 1820s and then the 1860s and Haiti episodically over several decades experimented fitfully with monarchy and empire.[27] As most of the aspiring nations of the Americas produced republics and constitutions, Brazil alone forged a sustained experience with empire and constitutional monarchy. From independence in September 1822 to the sudden and dramatic collapse of the Braganza monarchy in November 1889, Brazilians constructed a country that aspired to be both an empire and a nation.[28]

The Empire of Brazil emerged out of three hundred years of Portuguese conquest and colonization of the eastern edge of the South American continent. Rather audaciously, both the Portuguese monarchy and its Brazilian successors laid claim to more than three million square miles, from the mouth of the Río de la Plata to the plains (*llanos*) of Venezuela, and from the long Atlantic coastline to the eastern slopes of the Andes some 2,500 miles west of the mouth of the Amazon River. Throughout the nineteenth century, the dimensions of the empire on official maps were aspirational rather than real.[29] The presence of any sort of official government authorities (much less control) across the vast interior of the continent was minimal or nonexistent. Although Brazil now shares borders with ten countries, not until the early twentieth century would Brazil's northern and western neighbors agree on the shared boundaries we recognize on maps today. And not until the last quarter of the twentieth century would the Brazilian government exercise even a semblance of authority over most of the northern and western expanses that the country had so long claimed. Access to the vast savannas, forests, and waterways of the continent challenged empire and nation builders for centuries. Until the arrival of the airplane in the early twentieth century, rivers provided the most important pathways into this immense and mostly uncharted inland terrain.

Brazil is a country of truly continental dimensions, accounting for half of all South America's landmass. Only Russia, China,

Canada, and the United States are larger. Brazil is three times the size of Argentina and four times the size of Mexico, the second- and third-largest countries in Latin America. All of Europe, from Scandinavia to the Mediterranean and from the Atlantic to the Urals, could fit inside Brazil, with room to spare. Tens of millions of years ago, when all the continents formed the single landmass of Gondwana, what today forms the eastern coastline of Brazil nestled up against what is now the west coast of Africa, from Liberia to South Africa. Over millions of years, as the continental landmasses slowly drifted apart across the crust of the earth, the Atlantic Ocean took shape. The collision of the tectonic plates of what is today western South America with the Nazca and Antarctic plates under the emerging Pacific Ocean thrust up the Andes Mountains about six to ten million years ago. Until then, what is now the Amazon River emptied into the Pacific Ocean *to the west*. Cut off by the rising Andes, the river reversed course and flow— into the equatorial Atlantic.[30]

In contrast with the young and rugged Andes, the eastern highlands of South America are old, worn down, and much lower in elevation. The Amazon basin splits them into two enormous massifs.[31] To the north are the Guiana Highlands (or Shield), and to the south are the Brazilian Highlands, which cover most of eastern Brazil. The Guiana Highlands are smaller in area and concentrated primarily in southern Venezuela, extending into northern Brazil on the borders with Venezuela, Guyana, Suriname, and French Guiana. Indeed, the Continental Divide serves as Brazil's border with these countries (and the French overseas department of Guiana). Covering a very sparsely inhabited million square miles, the dense jungles, lofty waterfalls, and stunning tablelands have tantalized writers such as Arthur Conan Doyle, who made it the setting for his novel *The Lost World* (1912). Richard Burton's Brazilian Highlands, extending over two million square miles, underlay most of Brazil south of the Amazon River Basin. The southern third of the "shield" contains most of Brazil's inhabitants (most importantly, the states of Minas Gerais, São Paulo, and Rio de Janeiro). Both highlands gradually decline in altitude as they move inland eventually disappearing into the Amazonian lowlands. At their high points (in the East), the Guiana and Brazilian Highlands reach only a few thousand feet above sea level.

Richard and Isabel Settle In

In 1865, at age forty-four, Richard Burton had already lived a full life as an explorer and ethnographer. He was one of the founders of the Anthropological Society of London in 1863, at a time when what we now call anthropology was just taking shape in Britain. One of the most famous members of the Royal Geographical Society, he had already published four books on India, the account of his pilgrimage to Mecca, a volume on his travels to a Mormon colony in the western United States, and nine studies of Africa—in other words, thirteen volumes, or more than 4,500 pages. He may have been the most knowledgeable European on Africa and was certainly one of the greatest linguists of his time. His accomplishments brought him fame and respect from many of his peers, while his bravado and rebellious personality appalled an equally important group of his Victorian compatriots. As one of Burton's biographers has astutely noted, he was simultaneously the classic nineteenth-century imperial British explorer and at once the wild-eyed savage rebel. He was both the civilized and the uncivilized man.[32]

After Isabel's arrival in early October 1865, the Burtons spent a month in Rio de Janeiro socializing with the British community and the Brazilian upper classes. Before leaving England, Isabel had written to Richard's close friend and confidant Lord Houghton (Monckton Milnes) asking for introductions to Princess Isabel (heir to the throne) and her recently wed French husband, the Count of Eu.[33] Always the devoted wife and principal publicist for Richard, Isabel never shied from using every means at her disposal to promote him through what we would call networking today. While in Britain, this meant a steady stream of visits to the homes of the aristocracy and the politically powerful. During their time in Brazil, the Burtons made regular visits to Rio de Janeiro and the summer residence of the royal family in Petrópolis to mingle with the rich and powerful, especially the royal family.

Shortly before leaving Rio, the Burtons hosted a dinner party at the Hotel dos Estrangeiros (Foreigners Hotel) in the Botafogo neighborhood. Richard talked their guests into a late moonlight walk in the royal botanical garden (Jardim Botânico) about four miles away. Finding the gates locked on their arrival, everyone clambered over the fence. Isabel developed a fever the next day and became delirious. Richard nursed her with hot baths, quinine, and hypnotism. (He apparently hypnotized her regularly, to the amusement of his friends.) At the docks, she had to be carried on board the ship to Santos. The two-day, 250-mile voyage took travelers along some of the most beautiful coastlines in Brazil, areas sparsely populated in 1865. They had wonderful vistas of Ilha Grande, Angra dos Reis, and Paraty, to name just a few of the waypoints that today are some of the most popular tourist and vacation destinations in Brazil.[34]

Finally, in early November, they arrived in Santos to much fanfare aboard the Royal Mail's HMS *Triton*. Richard suited up in his official consular uniform (complete with braids and a tricorn hat), a band played, cannons fired, and the consular corps and local notables officially received them. Much to the chagrin of these officials and Richard's fellow European consuls, the Burtons refused even to spend the night in Santos but headed up over the mountains to deposit Isabel in São Paulo! A British company had begun building a railway between Santos and São Paulo, one that would become exceptionally busy in the coming decades, but in late 1865 only short sections of the line had been completed, extending outward from each of the cities. Their substantial entourage spent the night on the *serra* (mountain range) at the end of the first section of the rail line. The next day they rode mules and walked most of the way into São Paulo before getting on to the final stretch of rail line to ride the last few miles into town. Richard headed back to his post in Santos the following day.[35]

Isabel spent a few weeks hunting for housing, eventually renting an old Carmelite convent near the center of town. A two-story structure with at least a half dozen rooms, the rear opened out on a bucolic scene of pastures gradually descending over a quarter mile to the Tamanduateí River. The main road to Rio de Janeiro ran past the Carmo (Carmel) Church just a block to the north, and to the east a sturdy wooden bridge (Ponte do Carmo) spanned the river at the bottom of the hill. A lovely watercolor (1821) by the French painter Arnaud Julien Pallière (fig. 1.1) provides us with a view of the Burton residence as seen from the opposite side of the river at what was the edge of town in 1865. (Today the neighborhood is in the inner city of the massive metropolis.) The artist stood on

A WILD LAWLESS CREATURE IN THE BRAZILIAN EMPIRE

FIGURE 1.1. View toward Carmo Church, São Paulo, 1820s. The Burtons' residence was in the old convent to the left behind the church. Image in the public domain. Arnaud Pallière.

the eastern banks of the river looking west. The road from Rio into São Paulo crosses two bridges rising a small hill between the Carmo Church and the Church of Our Lady of the Good Death (Nossa Senhora da Boa Morte). The road is dirt, and scrubby vegetation covers much of the hillside and riverbanks. Isabel assembled a team of workers to wash and paint the house, apparently shocking her Brazilian neighbors by joining in the work. The team also helped her unpack the fifty-nine(!) trunks she had brought with her. Despite sharing the typical British disdain for slavery, she had no qualms about renting enslaved workers from her neighbors as part of her crew to paint and fix up the convent quarters.[36]

Always the devout Catholic, Isabel constructed a small chapel in their home and described it to her mother as the "only pretty and refined part" of her house. She personally painted it white and blue, and always kept a lamp burning on the altar. After arranging to have the landlord's child christened there, she complained that they "brought a lot of friends, children, and n——s" and stayed for six hours running all over the house, eating and drinking, and spitting on the floors.[37] One of his correspondents reported that Richard had told him that his "n——r servant-boys at Santos" "had been good and honest" until "she (pointing at his wife) undertook to make them all Roman Catholics like herself and then they took to stealing my shirts and cigars!"[38]

During their travels through Ireland earlier that year, Isabel had hired a young woman, Kieran (or Kier as Isabel called her), as her personal maid, and eventually arranged for Kier's brother to work for the British railway company.[39] Within weeks of arriving, Isabel also hired a recently emancipated Black man, who became her personal servant and principal intermediary with the locals. Chico (a nickname for Francisco) was four feet tall, in his mid-thirties, and as Isabel described him, "as black as a coal, brimming full of intelligence, and could put his hand to anything."[40] A passage in Isabel's autobiography starkly reveals the classic hierarchies of race, class, and nationality that characterized the worldview of the privileged English in mid-nineteenth-century Brazil. She described Chico as "honest and sharp as a needle, and can do every thing. All the English here wanted him, and did their best to prevent his coming to me; but he ran away, and came to me for less than half the money he asked them; and he watches me like a dog, and flies for every thing I want. . . . There is something superior and refined in my dwarf, and I treat him with the same consideration as I would a white servant; I see that he has plenty of good food, a good bed, and proper exercise and sleep, and he works none the worse for it."[41] She even planned, she claimed at the time to her mother, to take him back with her to England.

A photograph of Chico has survived (fig. 1.2), sandwiched between those of prominent English and Brazilians, in one of Isabel's albums. She clearly took the time to have him pose in a Brazilian studio. Dressed in a bowler, shiny shoes, white pants and shirt, and shiny blazer, we have a tantalizingly brief glimpse of a once enslaved young man who, had he not worked for these "eminent Victorians," would be almost entirely lost to the historical record.[42] Chico stares blankly, directly into the camera. A photo of Kier also survives (fig. 1.3). With her hair pulled tightly onto her head, she is seen from the waist up, seated, facing left, with her head turned slightly toward the camera. Lips tightly pursed, she gazes intently into the camera lens, another fleeting figure from the past.

From Isabel's detailed notes we can glimpse the daily labors of her servants, which also included a cook and a "boy." Rising at 5 a.m., Kier brought in Isabel's "tea and bread and butter," stayed with her during her "morning toilette" to help with her hair and clothes, then arranged her room, did the shopping at the market, superintended the other servants, and stayed with Isabel while she was going to bed. She took care of Isabel and "Captain Burton's

FIGURE I.2. Isabel's valet, Chico. Isabel Burton Papers, Wiltshire History Centre.

FIGURE I.3. Isabel's Irish maid, Kier. Isabel Burton Papers, Wiltshire History Centre.

wardrobe" as well as all the needlework. Chico made the beds, washed rooms in the house, prepared the table for breakfast and dinner, answered the door, cleaned the cutlery, and served as the valet for "the consul."[43]

Richard's tenacious work habits required ample space to organize and write multiple books simultaneously. In their new home, the couple arranged a forty-foot-long room with tables for each of Richard's many book projects. Opening out onto a wide veranda facing east and overlooking the river, the couple also used the room and the veranda to exercise, practice fencing, and engage in target shooting! Isabel spent a good deal of time playing the piano and singing. She had private tutoring in Portuguese and apparently was able to communicate well. She kept a bevy of barnyard animals (chickens and goats) and rode daily on one of her two ("not very good") horses.[44] A determined and independent woman, Isabel was devoted to Richard, tolerating his frequent absences. Their biographer, Mary Lovell, succinctly summed up their relationship: "The Burtons' marriage worked because Richard was not confined or chafed. No other man could have given Isabel the adventure and freedom that came in abundance in her life with Richard; conversely, few women of her station would have found the life acceptable, let alone reveled in it."[45]

The Locomotive Gathering Steam

São Paulo had fewer than thirty thousand inhabitants in the 1860s (roughly the same size as contemporary Los Angeles). Richard and Isabel were able to rent a home near the center of the city yet remain close to the fruits of rural life. The city and province were on the verge of a massive coffee export boom at the very moment of the Burtons' stay in Brazil.[46] By the 1830s, coffee had become the country's leading export, and by the 1860s Brazil accounted for the majority of the world's coffee exports. Coffee exports also helped Brazil achieve trade surpluses for most of the last half of the nineteenth century.[47] From its founding in the 1550s until independence in the 1820s, São Paulo had been a small settlement of rough-and-tumble frontiersmen and women surviving off subsistence agriculture, enslaving expeditions, and plundering of the interior. In this world of Indians and Portuguese colonists, for three centuries most of the population consisted of racially and culturally mixed people often more comfortable speaking a mixture of Portuguese and indigenous languages (*lingua geral*, or general language). The mixed-race men and women who scoured the interior for gold and Indian slaves have been immortalized in Brazil as *bandeirantes* (frontiersmen). With the discovery of gold in the interior, to the northeast, at the end of the seventeenth century, São Paulo became one of the principal routes into the General Mines (Minas Gerais). The town of São Paulo remained a small backwater as the port of Rio de Janeiro boomed and became the main entry point for supplies and the enslaved into Minas Gerais and for the gold and diamonds leaving the mining zone.[48]

Although Brazil became, and remains, the world's largest exporter of coffee, the plant is not native to the Americas. Originating in the Horn of Africa (either in Ethiopia or the Arabian Peninsula), coffee trees were planted by colonists in French Guiana in the early eighteenth century. The Portuguese followed suit and transplanted trees to the northern coast of Brazil soon after. By the beginning of the nineteenth century, they were cultivating trees in the Paraíba River Valley just north of the city of Rio de Janeiro, in southern Minas Gerais, and westward into São Paulo.[49] The rise of coffee plantations reinforced the demand for enslaved labor, and the flow of captives into the port of Rio de Janeiro accelerated dramatically to about fifty thousand per year until British pressure forced the end of the legal trade in 1850.[50] When the Burtons arrived in the 1860s, the center of coffee production was already shifting into the interior of São Paulo, and Santos was just beginning the rapid ascent that would make it the busiest port in Brazil—and Latin America.

The 30,000 inhabitants of 1867, in a small radius around the Burton home, have exploded to more than 15 million today in the densely built metropolitan area of nearly 600 square miles. Waves of immigrants from Portugal, Spain, and Italy flooded into the city after 1870, followed in the twentieth century by streams of Japanese (mainly from Okinawa) and Arabs (mostly Christian) from the collapsing Ottoman Empire (principally Syria and Lebanon). The rapidly expanding coffee fields generated jobs and capital for investment in both agriculture and industry. By the 1930s, the city had surpassed Rio de Janeiro as the largest city and industrial center in Brazil. In the following decades, the state became the most populous in Brazil, home to nearly one of every five Brazilians. By the 1950s, São Paulo city and state had become the most powerful driver of the Brazilian economy accounting for more than half of the nation's gross domestic product. The country's principal financial, economic, media, and cultural center, São Paulo (the city and the state) is today something like Texas and New York City combined.[51]

With the rise of its economic power and the massive influx of southern Europeans, São Paulo came to see itself as the most advanced and progressive region of Brazil, often looking down on other regions, especially the impoverished and racially mixed Northeast. Ironically, it was an enormous flow of poor *nordestinos* into São Paulo that provided much of the labor force after 1930 and reinforced the racial and cultural stereotypes that mark Brazil today. A common refrain of the *paulistas* (residents of the state) has for decades compared Brazil to a train with São Paulo as the locomotive. In Richard's day, nonetheless São Paulo was still a frontier town, Santos a growing secondary port, and the *paulistas* mainly a rough-and-tumble country folk.

Emperors and Empires

The Burtons arrived in a Brazil profoundly shaped by centuries of monarchical rule, deeply embedded social hierarchies, and an economy powered by enslaved labor. The transition from a Portuguese king ruling over a South American colony to a Brazilian emperor in the tropics had provided Brazil with a stability unlike any other American nation in the nineteenth century, but at a very high social cost. Fleeing Portugal in 1807 in advance of Napoleon's armies, the Braganza royal family—and an entourage of thousands!—crossed the Atlantic escorted by British warships. For the first and only time in European history, a monarch ruled his empire from the Americas. When King João (John) VI finally returned to Lisbon in 1821, the wars for independence had been ravaging much of Latin America for a decade. He left behind his oldest son, the Crown Prince Pedro (born in Portugal in 1798), with some sound advice: Should the move for independence emerge in Brazil, do not oppose it—lead it.[52] When he declared Brazilian independence on 7 September 1822, the prince anointed himself Emperor Pedro I of Brazil, and eventually renounced his claims to the Portuguese Crown. When he abdicated in 1831, leaving Brazil to fight his brother (Miguel) and put his daughter (Maria) on the Portuguese throne, Pedro left behind his five-year-son, also named Pedro. When the Burtons arrived in Rio de Janeiro in 1865, Pedro II had ruled Brazil for a quarter century, and he would continue his reign for nearly a quarter century more.[53] Both Richard and Pedro were in their forties in the late 1860s.

João and the two Pedros created a Brazilian nobility, complete with titles (in ascending order—baron, viscount, count, marquis, duke) and Brazilian place-names.[54] Over roughly eight decades, the monarchy bestowed titles (but not lands) on about one thousand men and women, overwhelmingly powerful landowners and merchants. The landed class was Brazil's traditional aristocracy, and the wealthiest nobles were merchants, especially those engaged in international commerce. All received their titles for important services to the empire. In the case of the Duke of Caxias (the only duke), his contributions came on the battlefield, preserving Brazil's unity against many regional revolts. The mistress of Pedro I, Domitila de Castro, became the Marchioness of Santos as a reward for her passionate extramarital affair (and four pregnancies) with the emperor.[55]

During his nearly half century as emperor (1840–1889), Pedro II consciously modeled his monarchy on Victoria's Britain. As a constitutional monarch, he served both as the executive and a special fourth branch of government—the moderating power. In the mid-nineteenth century, two political groupings—Liberals and Conservatives—filled a senate of around 50, and a chamber of deputies of around 120. Pedro had a Council of State with a dozen men drawn from the Senate. As the moderating power and prudent monarch, Pedro would dissolve the Parliament when he believed politics to be at a deadlock. Often, the opposition party would win the (highly restricted) elections. In forty-nine years, power shifted hands between the two parties twenty-six times, a remarkable feat of conciliation and political consensus, even for nineteenth-century Europe. Pedro II reigned, but he did not rule. As two of the most distinguished historians of Brazil have observed, the 1850s and 1860s were a golden age of hierarchy and order, conciliation and little ideology.[56]

The great political divide in nineteenth-century Brazil (until the rise of the Republican Party in the 1870s) was between Liberals and Conservatives. Not really political parties in the modern sense of the term, Liberals and Conservatives really represented ideological groupings often underlaid by kinship networks and regional loyalties. At least in theory, Conservatives looked back to the past, hoping to preserve as much of the old colonial order as possible. They looked to Portugal for the cultural heritage and roots. Strong, central government ruled by a powerful executive (in this case the monarch) was their preference. Conservatives wanted to retain the traditional social structure, hold on to privileges and hierarchies, and maintain slavery, and they supported the Catholic church and its traditional cultural and religious primacy. Finally, they were wary of free trade and hoped to maintain strong government intervention in the economy (i.e., protectionism and monopolies).

Liberals, on the other hand, saw their future in the models provided by England, France, and the United States. In theory, they wanted decentralized government with a loose confederation of provinces. They called for liberty, equality, and the end of social hierarchy and the power of the Catholic church. They also wanted to open their economy to international commerce through free trade (Adam Smith's laissez-faire). I emphasize *in theory* because once Liberals gained power, they almost always maintained strong, central governments, and they rarely made any serious efforts to extend liberty and equality beyond their own small social networks. In a Brazil built on slavery, they also remained largely silent on abolition. Not until the rise of the Republican Party in the 1870s did the question of abolition become a serious debate in parliament, and the most important legislation on abolition—Law of the Free Womb (1871) and Sexagenarian Law (1885)—came under Conservative cabinets resisting full abolition. The "Golden Law" ending slavery (without compensation for the masters) finally came abruptly in May 1888, largely as a means to maintain social order in the wake of the flight of larger and larger numbers of enslaved people over the previous year.[57]

Elections at the municipal and provincial levels took place regularly, and (especially under Pedro II) the two major political "parties"—Liberals and Conservatives—alternated in power for decades.[58] Both parties drew their support from the same socioeconomic constituencies. Despite the facade of electoral representation, the empire was built on the politics of exclusion. The rights of citizenship were extended to very few. Only about 10 percent of the population could vote, and especially at the local level, powerful landowners determined the outcome of elections through coercion, force, and alliances.[59] In the 1880s, electoral legislation further restricted the vote. The Constitution of 1891, although modeled on that of the United States, severely restricted voting with requirements of wealth and literacy (even more so than in the United States). More important, those who controlled local politics determined who voted, whatever the official legal requirements.

Unlike in much of nineteenth-century Latin America, the military and the church did not figure prominently in Brazilian politics. Despite the social and cultural omnipresence of the Catholic Church, Pedro II made sure to constrain its administrative and political influence. By limiting the capacity of seminaries and multiplication of dioceses, the emperor ensured that the church's physical presence shrank as the population increased from around three million in the 1820s to around fifteen million at the end of the century. The military played a key role in putting down the regional revolts of the 1830s and 1840s, but its leadership, especially the Duke of Caxias, remained devoted to the monarchy, and the army remained small, with the exception of the 1860s, during the war against Paraguay. Disputes with the Vatican and disgruntled younger officers after 1870 would be crucial in the erosion of the support of the church and the military leading up to the overthrow of the monarchy in 1889.[60]

In the seventeenth century, sugar and slaves generated the great wealth of landowners and merchants. In the eighteenth century, it was gold and slaves. By independence in 1822, coffee cultivation and exports had begun to boom. Coffee and enslaved labor created the wealth of the Brazilian empire and its greatest fortunes. Gold and then coffee exports, and the import of enslaved Africans, made Rio de Janeiro the principal port and wealthiest city in nineteenth-century Brazil. British shipping accounted for more than half of the tonnage in the Rio and Santos harbors in the late nineteenth century, and half of all Brazilian imports.[61] Stationing a consul in Santos became essential for Brazil's major trade partners, and most important was Great Britain.[62]

British economic and political influence in Portugal and (later) Brazil dated back to the Middle Ages, when the English and

Portuguese monarchies began a centuries-long relationship of trade, intermarriage, and diplomatic collaboration. The Treaty of Methuen (1703) codified the economic relationship, and Brazilian gold in the eighteenth century flowed through Lisbon to London to pay a long-running trade deficit. With the rise of French power and France's close relationship with Spain, the Portuguese monarchy drew even closer to the British. Thus, the British navy and diplomats aided and abetted the flight of the Portuguese monarchy to Brazil in 1807 to thwart Napoleon's efforts to seize the Braganzas. Unsurprisingly, upon arrival in Brazil in early 1808, Prince Regent João declared Brazilian ports open to trade with the world, effectively meaning the British. Over the next few decades, the British negotiated special low tariffs for their goods entering Brazilian ports. Throughout the nineteenth century, Britain supplied the vast majority of foreign investment, and British firms built most of Brazil's infrastructure—ports, railways, docks, and public utilities.[63]

Brazilians both admired and resented the British. The Brazilian political system under Pedro II consciously styled itself as a tropical version of Victorian England.[64] While aspiring to imitate British economic success, the enormous asymmetrical power of the United Kingdom in the Brazilian economy and international politics regularly riled Brazilians. Imported textiles and manufactured goods drove locals out of the marketplace, and the Rothschild banking house in London monopolized the entire foreign debt of the Brazilian government. By 1860 British warships had forced Brazil to abandon a highly lucrative and thriving slave trade, originating primarily in Portuguese colonies in Angola and Mozambique.[65] Shortly before Burton's arrival in Santos, Brazil broke diplomatic relations with Great Britain.[66] The British minister in Rio, William Christie, ordered British naval vessels to seize five Brazilian ships near Rio after the cargo of a British shipwreck in southern Brazil was reportedly plundered, and after several British sailors were arrested in the city of Rio. Eventually, arbitration and negotiations reduced tensions. Christie went home, and Sir Edward Thornton replaced him as diplomatic relations resumed in early 1865, just as the Burtons arrived.

CHAPTER 2

RIO DE JANEIRO, SÃO PAULO, SANTOS

> I do hate Santos. The climate is beastly, the people fluffy. The stinks, the vermin, the food, the n——s are all of a piece. There are no walks; and if you go one way, you sink knee-deep in mangrove swamps; another you are covered with sand-flies; and a third is crawling up a steep mountain by a mule-path to get a glimpse of the sea beyond the lagoons which surround Santos.
>
> —ISABEL BURTON TO HER MOTHER, DECEMBER 1865

The Burtons both loved and hated Brazil. They resented Richard's assignment to a country that was not in his beloved Middle East or Africa, but they reveled in the opportunities for travel and exploration. Isabel especially enjoyed the opportunities to socialize with the Brazilian royal family and aristocracy. She told Richard's close friend Monckton Milnes that she did not like Brazilian Portuguese, found the language "a harsh, coarse sounding one[,] but then the literature repays the trouble." She went to say that she spoke the language only "so-so" but that Richard spoke it "perfectly." For "the first time in his life," she claimed, Richard had "nothing but pleasant things to say (he likes the Brazilians)." She marveled at Brazil's natural riches and then revealed her Victorian worldview, noting that "if the whole Empire were let out to a British company for 20 years there would be nothing like it."[1]

As he did everywhere he went, Richard thrived on forays into the interior. Richard, Isabel reported to his friend Milnes, "is as happy as possible. He leads a domestic life to the letter for 3 or 4 months & then suddenly tells me to pack up the saddle bags. Sometimes I go, sometimes am left in charge."[2] Ultimately, Richard formulated plans for an expedition that would take him across the vast Brazilian backlands and might even present him with opportunities for making some money. Isabel carved out a very independent and self-sufficient life in São Paulo, and she eagerly anticipated the expedition even though she would accompany Richard only as far as his point of embarkation on the São Francisco River. Although Isabel spent most of her time in São Paulo with an occasional visit to Rio or the beach at Santos, Richard constantly moved back and forth between the consulate and his home with Isabel. By mid-1867 their "commute" became much easier with the completion of the British-owned San Paulo Railway between the two cities.

Santos

Richard spent as little time in Santos as possible, calling it a "wretched hole" and preferring São Paulo as "a more tolerable place of exile."[3] Isabel's attitude toward Santos was even more vehement than her husband's. Unsurprisingly, she spent little time there, usually only visiting for the nearby beaches with Richard. In the mid-nineteenth century, the city spread across the northern and eastern part of São Vicente, an island of just over twenty (mostly flat) square miles. A line of hills runs down the center of the island from north to south. With a fine bay on the south (Atlantic) side of the island, and a deep channel running around the east side into a large estuary, increasingly sophisticated docks took shape on the north side of the city to accommodate the rapidly growing maritime economy.[4] The core of the city in Richard's day took shape near the docks on a short strip of land just north of the hills, a densely developed area of about six or seven square blocks. The two-story English consulate on the principal street running parallel to the waterfront faced the busy piers, ships, cargoes, and stevedores packing the bustling wharves. Just a few blocks down the street (to the west), the San Paulo Railway constructed the station that served as the terminus of the line coming down the mountains from São Paulo and the coffee hinterlands.[5]

Santos sits some forty miles southeast of São Paulo. An abrupt and dramatic coastal escarpment rises to more than 2,500 feet, separating the port and the town on the plateau above. The Portuguese Crown created the settlement of São Vicente (Saint Vincent) in the 1530s, while Jesuit priests founded São Paulo (Saint Paul) in the 1550s. Just a few miles south of the Tropic of Capricorn, Santos has a humid tropical rainforest climate. With more than eighty inches of rainfall per year, it is one of the wettest places in Brazil outside of Amazonia. Despite the complaints of the English residents, temperatures are moderate, averaging in the low eighties in midsummer (January), and the low seventies in midwinter (June).[6] The Burtons were wise to worry about tropical port pestilence. Surrounded by rainforest and mangrove swamps in the 1860s, the area was a breeding ground for mosquitoes and disease—especially yellow fever and malaria. As Brazil's busiest port, Santos also served as an entry point for bubonic plague in 1899. A global cholera pandemic reached Rio and Santos in late 1866. Isabel and Kier suddenly became ill. Isabel took confession and communion, thought she was dying, and "settled all her worldly affairs."[7] She and Kier both recovered quickly.

In the mid-sixteenth century, at a time when Portugal had barely established a few tentative settlements along thousands of miles of Brazil's coast, French incursions threatened these tiny outposts of empire. Hans Staden, a Germany mercenary in the employ of the Portuguese, fought with the French and their Indigenous allies in the swampy lowlands around the area of modern-day Santos. Captured by Tupinambá warriors, Staden spent months among the Natives near the modern town of Ubatuba under constant threat (if we can believe him) of being ritually sacrificed and eaten. When he finally managed to escape to a French ship in February 1555, he returned to his native Hesse. With the help of local university professor, he published a graphic account of his "true captivity" illustrated with lurid woodcuts of cannibalism. Whatever its flaws, Staden's account is but one of two firsthand European descriptions of life among the native peoples of Brazil in the earliest moments of the birth of the Brazilian colony.[8] Richard took a special interest in Staden and worked on a new translation and edition of his account during his time as consul.

As coffee production took off in the province, wagons filled with sixty-pound bags of beans clogged the winding, steep roads from the city of São Paulo down the mountains to Santos. Mule-drawn wagons on dirt roads were the only viable means of transport up and down the steep escarpment. Isabel complained about the mule carcasses littering the roadway. By the 1850s, local businessmen, led by the industrious Baron of Mauá, had contracted a Scottish engineer, James Brunlees, to survey a potential ninety-mile-long railway line to run from Santos through São Paulo to Jundiaí just north of the city in the heart of coffee country. Brunlees had extensive experience building rail lines in Britain, but after assuring Mauá and his partners that the line could be constructed for £200,000 (roughly $1 million in 1860), he declined to carry out the project himself. Instead, he recommended his thirty-year-old assistant, Daniel Makinson Fox, to build the railway line. The San Paulo Railway Company (complete with the hispanized misspelling), organized in London and contracted to build the railway, began work in March 1860. Built with British capital, contractors, and engineers, the completed railway was an engineering marvel, architectural testimony of British technical expertise in the age of iron.[9]

The line began two blocks from the English consulate, heading west and north over about eight miles across two rivers and a series of marshes before reaching the daunting mountains. Given the steep slopes of the Serra do Mar (Coastal Range), Fox designed a series of four inclined sections (about a mile each) with steam-powered hauling engines at the top of each. These powerhouses pulled the trains up each section and then handed them off to the next. A braking car rode on the lower end of each train to halt the train in case the hauling cable (located in the center of the two rails) ruptured. This route took the road northeast along the slopes of the Serra to the melodiously named Paranapiacaba (today a fascinating tourist town that has preserved the English village that surrounded the railway switching station). From there, locomotives took the trains over the next thirty-five miles to the center of São Paulo and the Estação da Luz (Light Station), the railway depot that continues to serve as a key hub for the city's extensive commuter rail lines.[10]

Britain's Consuls and Diplomats

The colonial-era convent was Richard and Isabel's first home together since their marriage nearly five years earlier. For the first time, they lived together—when the peripatetic Richard was not off on his travels in the interior or handling business at the consulate in Santos. He shuttled back and forth constantly between the two towns. By late 1866 the railway could take him back and forth, and he could avoid the rough-and-tumble mule-drawn coaches. Fortunately, he had an able and ambitious assistant, Charles Archibald Glennie, a British citizen who had lived in Brazil for decades and had married a Brazilian. Glennie longed to be named consul and seemed to be on the verge of this honor when Burton departed in early 1868, only to be tragically denied his wish.[11]

In his official position in Santos, Burton joined another half dozen British consuls in Brazil in the 1860s—in Rio Grande do Sul, Rio, Bahia, Recife, São Luís, and Belém do Pará. In a few places, vice consuls covered neighboring regions (Ceará in the north, Santa Catarina in the south), normally without pay. With one quirky exception (Morro Velho after the early 1870s), all the consuls and vice consuls resided in Brazil's main ports.[12] The system we take for granted today of a diplomatic and consular corps around the globe had gradually begun to take shape in eighteenth-century Europe, and to fully form after the Congress of Vienna (1814–1815) had reorganized Europe after the final defeat of Napoleon at Waterloo. A principal objective was to open lines of communication among the region's powers after the costly wars that had devastated Europe over the previous generation. With some notable exceptions around mid-century (Crimean War in the 1850s, Franco-Prussian War in the 1870s), peace prevailed among the European powers until the great cataclysm of 1914.[13]

As the world's preeminent power, the British led the way in building its corps of ambassadors and consuls around the globe. Nevertheless, it was a modest enterprise compared to other areas of Britain's government. One scholar has estimated that the creation of the new nations of Latin America (about a dozen) in the 1820s had likely doubled the workload of the consular corps! As late as 1914, the total staff of the Foreign Office was barely four hundred! The British upper class still dominated the diplomatic corps, while the consular corps continued to be men (never women) of less exalted social status. In a small number of countries or empires, a British aristocrat served as ambassador or minister plenipotentiary. In the mid-nineteenth century, this small group of countries included Brazil and Mexico. Across their global enterprise, the British stationed consuls where economic activity was most vibrant. In Brazil, that meant the Atlantic ports.[14]

In the north, Belém (capital of the province of Pará) served as the point of access inland to the lengthy Amazon River, only recently opened to international commerce and navigation.[15] São Luís (capital of the province of Maranhão, southeast of Belém) was the smallest of the ports and, no doubt, the quietest coastal consulate. Much busier and more prominent were the cities of Recife and Salvador, both on the northeastern coast, and the two main sugar plantation zones since the sixteenth century. A thousand miles (southeast and then south) farther down the coast from São Luís, and on the edge of Brazil's "bulge" into the Atlantic, Recife was often the first point of disembarkation for ships coming out of the North Atlantic from Europe and the United States. (It was the port of arrival for the Burtons.)

Some five hundred miles south-southwest of Recife, Salvador da Bahia had served as the capital of the Portuguese colony from 1549 until 1763, had been the largest city in Brazil until the 1820s, and was home to around one hundred thousand inhabitants in the 1860s. As one of the two main centers for the incoming slave trade for three centuries, the city and province of Bahia were the most Africanized region of Brazil. Modern-day racial activists refer to the city as Brazil's "Black Rome."[16] Rio Grande, a small port in the province of Rio Grande do Sul, had assumed increasing importance in the mid-nineteenth century, especially with the Paraguayan War. About 125 miles from the border with Uruguay, Rio Grande served as a key staging area for troops and supplies moving into and out of the war zone up the Rio de la Plata. In the late nineteenth century, the city would be eclipsed by the rise of Porto Alegre, about two hundred miles to the north. Cattle ranching, salted beef (*charqui*), mule production, and cowboy (*gaúcho*) culture were the hallmarks of southern Brazil.[17]

The city of Rio de Janeiro, the imperial court, dominated economic, social, and cultural life in the young nation, and the city's population of around 250,000 would grow to more than a million over the next five decades. For the Americas, Rio was a major urban center, roughly the same size as Mexico City, but less than half the size of Philadelphia and a quarter that of New York City in the 1860s. (London was the largest city in the world then, with more than 3 million inhabitants; Paris was about half that, and Liverpool was around 400,000.)[18] As the greatest importer of enslaved Africans right up until the end of the transatlantic trade, African peoples and cultures also profoundly shaped Rio de Janeiro's culture and society. Slave traders had transported some 1.5 million Africans through the port of Rio de Janeiro and nearby areas over nearly 300 years. About 50,000 captive Africans arrived each year in Brazil from 1800 to 1850, and the vast majority disembarked (before 1831) at the docks in Rio to be sold in the local slave market—the Valongo.[19] (In comparison, the estimated total of enslaved Africans entering what is now the United States—Baltimore to New Orleans—from 1500 to 1808 was likely less than half a million.)[20] British naval and diplomatic pressure had forced the end of the slave trade into Brazil in the early 1850s, not long before the Richard and Isabel's arrival. Rio had by far the largest population of urban enslaved people in all the Americas, probably one-third of the city's inhabitants when the Burtons arrived. European travelers regularly commented on the profound impact of Africa on the city.[21]

The British minister plenipotentiary resided in Rio (along with a consul), and for most of Richard and Isabel's time in Brazil they were on good terms with the aristocratic Sir Edward Thornton and his wife. Richard was certainly something of a celebrity, if a somewhat notorious one, but it was more likely Isabel's aristocratic family connections that gave them access to the Thorntons—and the Brazilian imperial family. (Thornton had served in Mexico in the 1840s and played a role in the treaty negotiations that formally ended the war with the United States. After serving in Brazil, he was ambassador to the United States for fourteen years and then ambassador in Russia.)[22] Isabel reveled in her time in Rio, remarking that "one of the great charms of Rio, was our little club, numbering about twenty-five intimates, all belonging to the

FIGURE 2.1. Isabel (*on the left*) with British friends in Rio Club. Sir Edward Thornton is seated to the left, facing Isabel. Isabel Burton Papers, Wiltshire History Centre.

Diplomatic corps or the Navy."²³ Much to her irritation, the consular corps were considered of lesser status than the ambassadors, and were given little access to socializing with the Brazilian aristocracy and the ambassadorial corps.²⁴ Consuls, after all, handled the mundane business affairs of commerce, shipping, and the legal problems of British citizens in Brazil, while ambassadors negotiated at the high level of international relations among their nations. Isabel's first biographer believed that the couple was completely mismatched for the consular life. "They were," he remarked, "too big for their position, in energy, in ability, in every way."²⁵

Both Thornton and Burton arrived in the country just as Brazil and Great Britain reestablished diplomatic relations after several years of conflict over what became known as the Christie Affair.²⁶ A British ship, the *Prince of Wales*, had wrecked on the coast of southern Brazil in 1861, and much of the cargo had been plundered by locals. The Brazilian government refused to compensate the ship owners. Then, in 1863, a police officer arrested some raucous (likely drunken) British sailors in Rio. The British minister in Rio, William Christie, demanded that the Brazilian government fire the police officers and pay compensation for the lost cargo of the *Prince of Wales*. When the government refused, Christie decided he would teach the Brazilians a lesson and ordered British naval vessels to seize several Brazilian ships. Emperor Pedro II broke off relations with the British and it appeared the two countries might even go to war. Christie stepped down as ambassador, and the Foreign Office brought in Thornton to negotiate a quiet resolution with Brazilian diplomats. (One historian has called Christie "impulsive, precipitate, and totally out of sympathy with the point of view of the Rio government.")[27] Relations were restored in mid-1865. For the Brazilians, the episode highlighted the arrogance of an empire whose powerful navy had essentially shut down the very lucrative slave trade into Brazil. It also demonstrated to both empires the importance of their economic relationship.[28] For Brazil, this meant access to foreign investment and markets for coffee, for Britain, the role of Brazil as a market for manufactured goods, machinery, and investment opportunities. Gold exports and slave imports had turned Rio into the busiest port in Brazil in the eighteenth century. It would soon be supplanted by Santos, the economic funnel into and out of São Paulo.

Richard the Consul

The Foreign Office stationed Richard in a busy port city, one that was already a vibrant entrepôt and would become the principal exit point for the vast majority of Brazil's coffee as the country became the world's largest coffee exporter in the last third of the century. It was also about to become the principal point of entry for an enormous wave of immigrants, primarily from Italy, Portugal, and Japan.[29] Burton's brief tour as consul in Santos came just as this transformative immigrant flow was about to explode. At mid-century, the flow of immigrants into Brazil had been averaging about five thousand to six thousand per year for nearly five decades. The government had encouraged European immigrants attracting small groups from Switzerland, Germany, and the Azores who settled mainly in areas from Rio de Janeiro to Rio Grande do Sul. German and Swiss immigrants founded and settled in what today are the towns of Petrópolis and Nova Friburgo (New Freyburg) in the mountains just north of Rio. In the late 1860s, the Brazilian government would also try to entice US Southerners to come to Brazil.[30]

Actively encouraged by the Brazilian monarchy, several enterprising recruiting agents moved across the US South in the immediate aftermath of the Civil War, enticing defeated Confederates with promises of cheap, fertile land. After the devastation of four years of war, the opportunity to start a new life in what was now the largest slaveholding society in the Americas must have seemed promising to the thousands of Southerners who boarded ships in New Orleans and Baltimore. Probably some five to ten thousand "Confederados" emigrated. Most of the land schemes proved illusory for people with few funds and the inability to purchase slaves once they arrived in Brazil. Two settlements, Santarém on the eastern Amazon River and Santa Bárbara do Oeste (Saint Barbara of the West) in the interior of São Paulo, eventually became thriving cities that expanded around the expatriate Southerners.[31] The Burtons would cross paths with these wandering Confederados on multiple occasions.

As consul, Richard carried out the mundane jobs of tracking commerce, ships, and the affairs of British citizens as they passed through this increasingly active port. The Foreign Office compelled consuls to focus primarily on economic activity (and how to promote British economic interests), and the affairs of British citizens.[32] The Portuguese empire had banned foreigners from Brazil throughout the colonial period, but the arrival of the royal family in 1808 (escorted by British warships) had opened Brazil to the outside world. British merchants streamed into Brazilian ports in the following decades, and Great Britain became the dominant foreign economic and diplomatic presence.[33] While the United States established its presence and power in Mexico, Central America, and the Caribbean, British "preeminence" was the rule in South America, especially in its two largest new nations—Argentina and Brazil. In the major Brazilian ports, the British eventually received the emperor's permission to build Protestant churches and consecrate their own cemeteries. (Protestants could not bury their dead in Catholic cemeteries.) The growing communities formed clubs, associations, and libraries, and consuls actively supervised these groups.[34]

The Foreign Office required consuls to register all births, marriages, and deaths in the British community. In the absence of an Anglican priest, the consul even had the authority to perform marriage ceremonies, something that must have amused Richard Burton, the unbeliever! Consuls spent a good deal of time assisting British citizens: repatriating the destitute, settling the estates of those who passed away in Brazil, and negotiating with local authorities over the problems of those who ran afoul of the law.[35] Richard's fellow consul in Trieste, Charles Lever, was also a witty novelist who had one of his fictional characters remark, "Isn't a consul a horrid creature that lives in a seaport, and worries merchant seamen, and imprisons people who have no passport?"[36]

Consuls had to file regular reports tabulating ships' entries and exits, especially military vessels. Richard exploited his government's interest in the state of the economy to range widely across the region, ostensibly to file reports on agriculture and mining. The Foreign Office complained about Richard's undecipherable handwriting, and Isabel appears to have spent a good deal of time writing up the final versions of Richard's reports.[37] (His cramped and compressed scrawl is the bane of the historians who have mined his archives!) Richard also sought out opportunities to invest his own funds, especially in gold mining, something he had to hide from his superiors. Engaging in personal "trading" directly violated his responsibilities as a Foreign Office employee. When Sir Edward Thornton discovered that Richard had purchased part interest in lead mines, he reported him to the foreign secretary, Lord Stanley, who eventually ruled that this investment did not violate the rule against "trading" as long as Richard did not profit from the venture![38] Burton had high hopes for the possibilities of Brazil's mines. He confided to a colleague in the Royal Geographical Society that his "great hope" was "to throw off the Government and become [a] free man." His close and extensive survey of the mining region did not arise out of purely official duties. He hoped to invest in gold or diamond mines to make his fortune and give him the freedom to pursue his own adventures.[39]

The Brazilian Archipelago

The early colonial settlements at São Paulo and Rio de Janeiro remained small until the eighteenth century, with the discovery of gold and diamonds in Minas Gerais. By 1800 Minas had the largest population of any province, and the largest concentration of enslaved labor, producing beef, dairy products, and coffee by the mid-nineteenth century. Vila Rica de Ouro Preto (Rich Town of Black Gold), its capital, perched precariously on small mountaintops, and had a population of about thirty thousand.[40] About the same size, the city of São Paulo was still a frontier town in the early nineteenth century, mainly significant as one means of access into the gold mining zone. The so-called Old Road (Caminho Velho) from São Paulo overland into the mining region was soon eclipsed by the New Road (Caminho Novo) from Rio northward. Shipping traffic along the Atlantic coast kept all the major population centers (except Minas Gerais) in contact with each other. No manageable roads connected São Paulo, Rio, Salvador, and Recife, much less Belém. The first railroad would not arrive in Brazil until the 1850s, and it would be a minor line largely to get the emperor from the court in Rio to his summer palace in Petrópolis.[41]

Brazilians today are acutely aware of regional differences, and they identify closely with their regional origins. Not simply a matter of geography and culture, regionalism in Brazil is a state of mind developed over centuries. In the second half of the twentieth century, government agencies divided the nation into five major regions based on long-standing historical and geographical patterns. Brazilian regionalization has deep roots in geography and patterns of colonization dating back to the beginning of the sixteenth century. The Portuguese constructed their colonial plantation society on the rich coastal plain in the *Northeast*, concentrated in what today are the states of Pernambuco and Bahia. With the discovery of gold and diamonds in the early eighteenth century, the axis of power and the focus of colonial development shifted to the *Southeast*, a region that today includes the states of Espirito Santo, Minas Gerais, Rio de Janeiro, and São Paulo. Effective settlement and development of the uplands and prairies of the *South* (Paraná, Santa Catarina, and Rio Grande do Sul) did not really take shape until the waves of European immigration in the last half of the nineteenth century. The Amazon basin in the *North* was sparsely settled until very recent times, and the *Center-West* has just begun to boom with Brazil's "westward movement" over the last two generations.[42]

The Northeast and Southeast, the two regions that Burton traversed, have the longest histories and a complicated relationship (and in the nineteenth century, they were really North and

South for Brazilians). Covering about a third of the country and home to about two-thirds of all Brazilians, the two form a sort of Brazilian equivalent to the North and South in the United States. The regional stereotypes of today had already begun to emerge by the 1860s, especially the negative view of the *nordestino*. This stereotype draws on the most prominent features of the Northeast: its economic backwardness, poverty, racial heritage, and traditional culture. In many ways, the Southeast, especially São Paulo in the twentieth century, has forged its own identity as a contrast to the Northeast and its people. Casting itself as economically successful and well educated, and emphasizing its European racial heritage, the *paulista* stereotype in its most egregious version is one of all that is "right" with Brazil—urban, civilized, educated, and white—versus all that is "wrong" with Brazil—rural, backward, ignorant, and dark-skinned.[43]

Preparing for the Expedition

By the second half of 1866, just a year after his arrival in Brazil, Richard had already begun to plan his lengthy trip across the backlands of eastern Brazil. During his first year as consul in Santos he had already made a series of weeks-long trips into the interior of the province of São Paulo.[44] After two decades exploring India, Arabia, Africa, and the US West, he was not about to sit still long in Brazil. Much to his irritation, each time he spent long periods away from the consulate in Santos, he had to request permission from his superiors in Rio de Janeiro and London to leave his post. He always couched these requests in terms that emphasized the need for field research on opportunities for economic development—for the Brazilians and the British.[45] In reality, Burton had two personal objectives for these "explorations"—his own desire to travel to new places *and* to search for opportunities to enrich himself by investing in mining. He was especially interested in Brazil's gold deposits. His investment in a local lead mining enterprise had brought him close to a rebuke from the Foreign Office even as he was planning his São Francisco River trip in late 1866. He would keep his gold mining interests hidden from his superiors.[46]

Richard's expedition would carry him across the length of the two most important regions in Brazil—the Southeast and the Northeast. Three objectives loomed large in Richard's planning for the expedition, and two of them focused on mining. The first part of the trip, covering some eight hundred miles, would take Richard and Isabel into Minas Gerais to thoroughly canvass mining operations, most of them financed and operated by English companies. He sold this stage of the trip to his superiors as a way to inspect economic possibilities for Britain, although he was clearly also interested in personal investment opportunities. This first section of the trip he even blithely referred to as "a holiday excursion" in *Explorations of the Highlands of the Brazil*.[47] He then planned to check out the diamond mines in Minas Gerais, again with an eye toward his own enrichment. Finally, he wanted to see the magnificent Paulo Afonso Falls near the end of the São Francisco River. Here, Burton the explorer prevailed over the potential investor anxious for riches.

His overarching aim, one he told the reader and sold to the Foreign Office, was "to visit the future seat of the Empire along the grand artery" of the São Francisco so that he could "make known the vastness of its wealth and the immense variety of its productions, which embrace all things, between salt and diamonds, that man can desire."[48] He would often compare the São Francisco to the Mississippi River and predicted that it would become as important to Brazil as the Mississippi had become to the United States. Richard's strong belief that this corridor would one day become so important for Brazil runs through the commentary of his account, especially the second volume. A tone of boosterism runs throughout his account as he constantly promotes and publicizes all kinds of potential economic opportunities, in the mining zone and along the São Francisco. At times, his suggestions and prognostications may be visionary and bold, but clearly Burton was not much of a prophet.

Sir Edward Thornton engaged in lengthy correspondence throughout 1866 with the foreign secretary, Lord Stanley, about Richard's proposed months-long trip into the interior. Thornton acknowledged that "the interior of Brazil is little known, and doubtless contains great undeveloped resources," and that "it would be decidedly advantageous to commercial interests that it should be visited and reported upon by an observant and intelligent traveler." Thornton, in understated British fashion, noted that Richard had "gained some reputation as a traveler." Thornton was particularly interested in cotton production, the possibilities for its expansion, statistics on slave populations, and attitudes toward abolition. Cotton for British textile factories and the continuing desire to end slavery in the Atlantic world clearly motivated the ambassador's agenda for the expedition. Lord Stanley informed Thornton that he was willing to allow the exploration, but Richard would have to pay his own expenses and find a substitute consul to work during his absence.[49]

With final approval in hand in late 1866, the Burtons resolved to depart in May or June 1867, completing the trip before the onset of the rainy season in November. Richard had already planned to employ Mr. Glennie as his substitute. After much preparation, the Burtons left Kier behind to take care of the house, and on 12 June 1867, along with the ever-present Chico, they left the old convent. Although Isabel gives the impression in her own writings that she was to accompany Richard down the São Francisco, it seems very unlikely this was Richard's plan, especially given the rough nature of the voyage over 1,300 miles and three months. In a letter to a fellow travel writer just before his departure, Richard says, "I am off for a few months trip to the Gold Mines & the Great Interior. My wife accompanies me part of the way."[50] In both her biography of Richard and her own autobiography, Isabel has another version of the story.

The entire expedition, it turned out, would last five months, from mid-June to mid-November. The bulk of the time (three months) would be Richard's voyage down the Rio das Velhas and São Francisco. From Rio they traveled by steamer, rail line, coaches, and then mules for two weeks to the English gold mine at Morro Velho. For the next month, they carefully scrutinized the impressive operations of the St. John d'el Rey Mining Company and crossed the mountainous region inspecting every significant gold mine. In early August, Richard boarded his river boat, and Isabel headed back to São Paulo via Rio. With planning concluded and permissions granted, in early June 1867, they left their personal convent in São Paulo to begin their "holiday excursion."

CHAPTER 3

THE EXPEDITION BEGINS

> We wanted to visit the gold-mines, and to report concerning the new railway—about the proper line of which two parties were contending—a question of private or public benefit. We also intended to go down the São Francisco River, the Brazilian Mississippi, from Sabará to the sea, and to visit the Paulo Affonso Rapids, the Niagara of Brazil.
>
> —ISABEL BURTON, IN HER AUTOBIOGRAPHY

On this trip to Rio, the Burtons did not tarry long but set out almost immediately northward into the interior.[1] For a century and a half, the principal route into Minas Gerais crossed the vast expanse of Guanabara Bay and then headed up through a series of mountain ranges into the gold mining zone. In the eighteenth century, tens of thousands of enslaved Africans in chains trudged north to the mines along this path, passing gold shipments on mules heading south from Minas Gerais to Rio de Janeiro. The route eventually became the Estrada Real (Royal Road) running from Rio to Vila Rica de Ouro Preto in the heart of the mining zone. In the 1720s and 1730s, with the discovery of diamonds north of Vila Rica, the Crown extended the road to Vila do Príncipe (Prince Town) and Tejuco, today known as Diamantina. This extension, the Caminho do Campo (Field Road), threaded through the Serro Frio (Cold Mountains). At strategic locations, inspection stations known as "registers" collected tolls and tariffs.[2]

In the last quarter of the century, gold and diamond production declined dramatically. By the early nineteenth century, small mining claims operated throughout the region but suffered from a lack of modern technology and investment. German mining engineer Wilhelm von Eschwege did an exhaustive survey of the mining region for the Crown in the second decade of the nineteenth century, providing historians with a baseline account of incredible detail and specificity.[3] His survey reveals an abundance of small-scale operators producing gold, diamonds, iron, and an assortment of other minerals. Despite the drastic decline in gold production, Minas had a very diverse economy of small mining operations, ranches, and farms producing (and in some cases exporting) gold, diamonds, leather, tallow, bacon, farinha, corn, and beans. At the beginning of the nineteenth century, the slave community in the province was eclipsed only by the size of the enslaved population in the United States (a little over one million in 1800).[4]

Leaving Rio de Janeiro

In the first half of the nineteenth century, coffee production steadily expanded northward from the province of Rio de Janeiro into southern Minas Gerais. Africans, primarily from Angola and Mozambique, continued to flow inland by the tens of thousands, but now largely to expanding plantations. Rather than gold bullion, hefty burlap bags of coffee beans moved south on mules to the port of Estrela dos Mares (Star of the Seas) on the north shore of Guanabara Bay. In 1867 Brazil's first modern business tycoon controlled the first two steps in the Burtons' expedition, a steamship across the bay, and then a rail journey of just eleven miles to the foot of the Serra dos Órgãos (Organs Range). This striking set of peaks runs eastward, parallel to the coast, shrouded by rainforest, and its jaggedly carved slopes jut into the skies, rising to nearly 7,500 feet above sea level. Apparently, early colonists thought the finger-like peaks resembled organ pipes. Coaches carried passengers from the end of the rail line up a winding mountain road in just two hours to Petrópolis, the summer residence of the royal family, at a cool and mild altitude of 2,700 feet. In the late 1860s, the passage from

Rio to Petrópolis would have been one of the fastest trips in Brazil, covering a little over forty miles in about five hours.[5]

The entrepreneur who controlled the dock, steamboat, and railway, Ireneu Evangelista de Sousa, was the richest man in Brazil in the mid-nineteenth century, and likely one of the richest in the world. Born in 1813 in Rio Grande do Sul in humble circumstances, as a child he followed an uncle to Rio, became an office clerk, hired on with a Scottish merchant, learned English, and eventually took over the firm. Sousa built a business empire worthy of the likes of a Cornelius Vanderbilt or an Andrew Carnegie. In the 1860s he controlled the eight largest private companies in Brazil (railways, steamships, gas lighting, shipyards, banks), and his total worth approached $750 million (roughly $20 billion today). Pedro II had begun to spend the hot, humid Rio summers (December to March) in the mountains in the 1840s, making the annual trek by boat and mule-drawn coach to Petrópolis. Sousa, always attentive to the monarch, proceeded to build the first rail line in South America from the edge of the bay to the foot of the mountains (Raiz da Serra). After the royal family and aristocracy packed the inaugural train trip in April 1854, the emperor elevated Sousa to the peerage as the Baron of Mauá (later viscount).[6]

Mauá stood out as a great exception in mid-nineteenth-century Brazil, a wealthy man whose fortune had come not from family and land but from creating new industries, banks, and transportation networks. Hundreds of thousands of enslaved laborers planted, cultivated, harvested, and processed the beans that fueled the economy of the world's largest coffee exporter. By the 1860s foreign investors and some local elites had created small industrial firms for textiles, food processing, and woodworking, but the economy remained overwhelmingly rural, agricultural, and dependent on captive labor. Capitalism in Brazil took shape around two sources of investment. Entrepreneurs like Mauá tapped into foreign investment, largely from Britain. Most Brazilian businesses, nevertheless, took shape around pooled capital from extended family networks. This pattern would continue well into the twentieth century. The state and foreign investors would provide the enormous sources of capital needed for large industrial firms while perennially scarce local, private capital funded the majority of domestic business enterprises.[7] Brazilian capitalism developed around networks of personal and political patronage, and all of the most prominent businessmen (especially Mauá) depended on the support of the state. Coffee exports created Brazil's greatest fortunes (with the prominent exception of Mauá) and generated the bulk of government tax revenues (from export duties). In the vast interior, as Richard would see, local and regional agricultural production created many different internal markets. Some connected to national and international commerce, but many did not. The farther from the coast, as a rule, the more these diverse internal commercial islands survived and went about their business independent of most of the rest of the Brazilian archipelago.[8]

On 12 June 1867, a Wednesday, Richard and Isabel boarded their steamship at the Mauá Wharf, about a mile north of the center of the city, a small "finger" of land jutting out northward into the bay. The trip across the bay took about an hour and a half threading between the lovely Paquetá Island on the starboard side and the very large Governor's Island on the port side. In 1867 the wharf sat in the middle of a two-mile-long span of docks stretching from the imperial palace to the east and the Morro da Saúde (Hill of Health) to the west. Just a few hundred yards west of the spot where the Burtons stood that June morning were the Docks of the Empress (Cais da Imperatriz). Hundreds of thousands of Africans disembarking from slave ships in the eighteenth and nineteenth centuries first stepped ashore on this series of wide stone stairs rising out of the bay. The slave market, Valongo, had been close by, as well as mass gravesites for those who expired soon after their arrival at the Brazilian end of the long and tragic Middle Passage. Just a half mile farther to the west, on a serene, forested hillside, the British cemetery looked down on the site of the old Valongo market and burial ground.[9]

Richard and Isabel departed Rio with a *portaria* (a special travel license) signed by the minister of foreign affairs and a pack full of "letters of introduction" to ease their way across the Brazilian interior. These letters, he noted, often proved "more valuable than banknotes."[10] Always ready to travel, Richard was anxious to get on the road after "eighteen dull months spent at Santos" (more likely he had spent only about half that much time in Santos).[11] Standing on the Mauá Wharf, he could both admire the grandeur of the natural beauty surrounding the bay and cynically bemoan

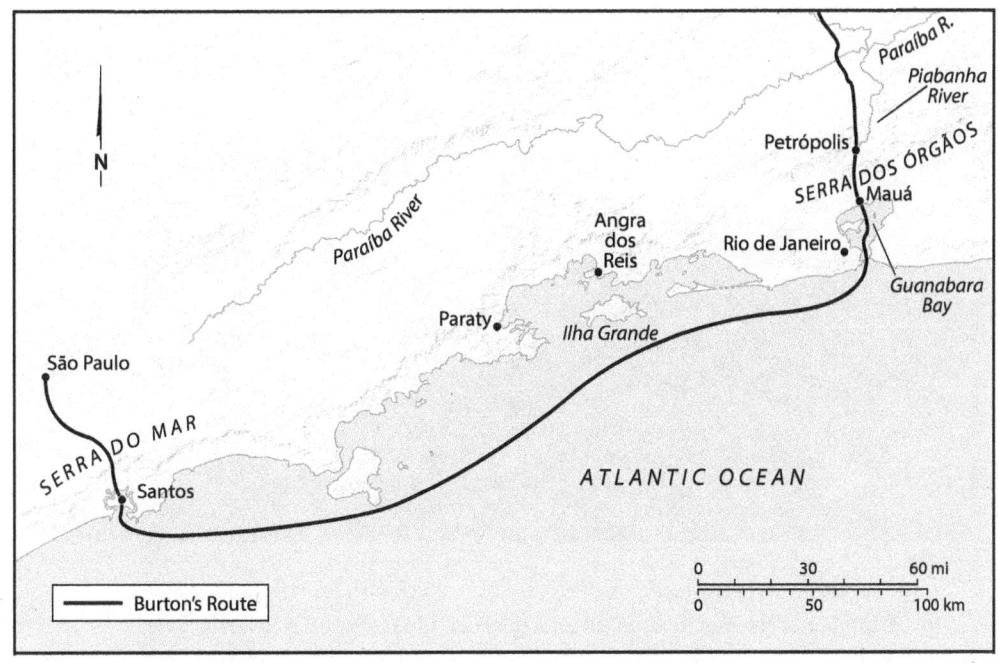

FIGURE 3.1. Richard's route through Southeastern Brazil.

the chaos and filth of the docks. Off in the distance he could see the Organ Mountains with "a power and a majesty born of the size and the abrupt grandeur of mountain and peak, of precipice and rock," while the area around the wharf reminded him "eye, nose, and ear of certain sites on the Thames which shall be nameless." The Burtons hustled "through a crowd of blacks," piles of coffee sacks, and beans scattered on the floor. "Near the coarse pier of creaking planks lie swamped canoes and floating boats, a red dredging craft, sundry little black steamers, a crowd of loading ships, and a scatter of crippled hulks; a dead dog floats lazily past us."[12] On a hill rising above the east side of the pier, the colonial monastery of São Bento (Saint Benedict) loomed above the shoreline—as it does today. The vast majority of the workers—on the docks and on the bay—were enslaved Africans or Afro-Brazilians, free and enslaved. For someone who had spent so much time in East and West Africa, Richard would not have been taken aback by the powerful and pervasive African influences in Rio, as were so many of his European fellow travelers.[13]

FIGURE 3.2. Mauá wharf (much enlarged) in 2022 with recently constructed Museum of the Future. Looking north across Guanabara Bay. Marshall C. Eakin.

The staggering inequalities in Brazilian society—deeply embedded and astonishingly persistent across centuries—likely also did not faze Richard in the least. As in the United States, slavery marks one of the great tragedies in the creation and construction of the Brazilian nation. Enslaved labor made possible the sugar boom of the seventeenth century, the gold rush of the eighteenth, and the coffee economy of the nineteenth. Without the hard labor of millions of enslaved Africans and Afro-descendants, the Brazil that we know today would not have been possible. One of the primary functions of the central state—under colony and empire—was to protect and maintain the rights of the slave masters and to keep the always restive population of the enslaved in their place.[14] Uprisings, runaways, and resistance constantly challenged this racist, hierarchical system from the 1500s until the abolition of slavery in 1888. A rising wave of the enslaved fleeing their plantations in 1887 and 1888, in fact, forced the Brazilian parliament to end three centuries of human bondage "with the stroke of a pen." In essence, as they faced the prospect of anarchy and the failure of the state to maintain the slave order, the Brazilian parliament chose to abolish the collapsing system on 13 May 1888.

FIGURE 3.3. View south from Alto da Serra toward Guanabara Bay and the Atlantic Ocean. Raiz da Serra station and path of old rail line at the foot of the mountains (*center*). Upper right in the distance is Corcovado Mountain. Marshall C. Eakin.

In the United States, the destruction of slavery came at the price of a bloody civil war and 600,000 dead, and the freedom of nearly 4 million enslaved people. In Brazil, thousands of the enslaved rose up spontaneously and, within a few months, forced the end of the last slave system in the Americas, liberating an enslaved community of around 700,000 men, women, and children.[15]

Across the Bay and into the Mountains

Mauá built his railway a couple of miles east of the old Estrela port, and by the time the Burtons came ashore at the "Mauá landing place," the ancient route and town had been completely abandoned and was "hopelessly ruined." After their transit across the bay, Richard and Isabel stepped onto a "shaky, creaky, little plank-jetty leading to the railway carriages" before boarding the train for the eleven-mile trip to its terminus at the "Root of the Range."[16] At the railway terminus, the Burtons loaded their luggage and Chico into a carriage pulled by four mules that took them up a winding, zigzag road for two hours, rising from near sea level to nearly three thousand feet above sea level. Paintings from the period and Richard and Isabel's accounts depict a well-paved macadam road through the Atlantic rainforest, lush with ferns, filled with "the soft rush and splash, and the silvery tinkle and

FIGURE 3.4. View of Petrópolis, 1860s. Image in the public domain. Revert Henrique Klumb.

murmur of falling water, make music in our ears."[17] This point in his narrative is one of those rare moments where Richard waxes lyrical about his surroundings. At the Alto da Serra (Mountaintop), the Burtons paused to look back southward across the bay. It was, and remains, despite massive urban growth, an astonishing view. "This is beautiful—a delight, an enchantment!" in Richard's words.[18] Directly below lay the large Governor's Island, sitting in the vast "inland sea" with the humps of Sugarloaf Mountain some forty miles off at the entrance to the bay. Just to the right sat the docks of Rio and, rising behind the city center, Corcovado Mountain (not yet with a Christ statue).

Emperor Pedro I passed along this route in 1822, and then again in late 1830, spending the night at the royal gunpowder factory in Raiz da Serra before heading up the mountain. The royal entourage included the Empress Amelia, a baroness, a cabinet minister, physician, chaplain, and a dozen servants. They spent New Year's Eve and New Year's Day at the farm of a local priest.[19] Impressed with the climate and scenery, Pedro purchased a nearby site and began plans to build a summer palace. Within months, he abdicated. It would be his son, Pedro II, who completed the project more than a decade later. He would also bring in a colony of German settlers to populate the town that became Petrópolis

(Petersburg). Much of the local architecture resembles European chalets. Over more than a half century, Pedro II moved the court to Petrópolis each summer, spending the three or four hottest months of the year in the cool confines of the mountain town. While Pedro constructed his palace, members of the aristocracy and wealthy imperial officials built their own summer homes along the few streets near the palace.[20]

The Burtons spent three nights in Petrópolis at the Hotel Inglez, run by a Mr. Morritt from Yorkshire who also managed the system of coaches between the city and Juiz de Fora, a hundred miles to the north. At 6 a.m. on Saturday, June 15, they sent the bulk of their luggage ahead on a coach carrying seventeen passengers and three tons of cargo! Richard and Isabel boarded a char-à-banc belonging to Morritt; the open carriage with four rows of two seats facing forward was pulled by "four fiery little mules."[21] Richard rarely reveals much about his companions on this expedition. From his account and Isabel's, we do know that they were accompanied on this day by Mr. Morritt and three more Englishmen. One Richard simply refers to as "Mr. L'pool." This twenty-nine-year-old Liverpudlian was Arthur Earle, the son of Sir Hardman Earle, a baronet and international merchant. He was engaged to the twenty-four-year-old Ida Euphemia Bertie Mathew, whose father Sir George Buckley-Mathew had arrived in Rio in 1867 for what was to be a twelve-year stint as the British minister, replacing Edward Thornton.[22] The other two Englishmen were a Major Newdigate and his brother "'on the rampage' from Canada." The major had served in the Crimean War, was working in the late 1860s in Canada, and would later become a general. The six sat in the back three rows while in front a "stout young German" driver had the diminutive Chico seated beside him.[23] Petrópolis's one main avenue followed the Piabanha River as it wound westward through the city. Paved on both sides of the river (really a large stream) and crossed by both carriage and pedestrian bridges at intervals, the imperial palace occupied a large area at the beginning of the avenue on the northeast end.[24]

From Petrópolis to Juiz de Fora

The road between Petrópolis and Juiz de Fora, some one hundred miles, was the finest in Brazil in the mid-nineteenth century.

Mariano Procópio Ferreira Lage, a businessman from Juiz de Fora and a sort of Mauá of the interior, invested much of his coffee fortune on local infrastructure hoping to modernize his small town. The two colonial routes, the Old Road from São Paulo and the New Road from Rio, connected at this small village in the eighteenth century. Tens of thousands of travelers flowing into the gold mining region from the coast converged at this key crossing point over the Paraibuna River. The town, however, only took shape in the mid-nineteenth century. (In the colonial period, a *juiz de fora* was a sort of circuit judge in the interior.)[25] Eventually, Juiz de Fora, a town 150 miles from the coast, would have its own textile factory and the first hydroelectric power plant in South America (1889). The boosterish locals liked to refer to it as the "Manchester of Minas" to liken it to England's industrial heartland.[26] Richard described the town "as a single dusty or muddy street, or rather road, across which palms are planted in pairs."[27]

In the 1850s Lage persuaded Pedro II to grant him a concession to build a toll road. Using the most advanced methods of the day, he crushed stone to pave the road, placing a dozen rest stops along the way to switch mule teams and to rest and feed the animals and passengers. Richard spotted, "in the virgin forest, French road-rollers" used to pack down the crushed rock. He also praised the French and Brazilian engineers who built and maintained the new road, "whose thoroughness of execution is admirable," no small praise from a man who found fault in just about everything.[28] Moving along at the brisk pace of about ten miles per hour, both Burtons pulled out their notebooks and peppered "poor Mr. Morritt" with questions about the road and the region. The biggest challenge for the Burtons was the heavy traffic of cargo mules, especially those heading in the opposite direction, toward Petrópolis and Rio.[29]

In 1867 long stretches of the route were still heavily forested, filled with toucans, acacias, mimosas, and lots of bamboo. The Burtons also saw before them the ongoing transformation of the landscape as fire and axes cleared forest and replaced it with fields lined with sugarcane and coffee trees. Densely forested when the Portuguese first began to move north from Rio, this southern region of Minas remains known as the Forest Zone (Zona da Mata) despite massive deforestation.[30] By the late nineteenth century,

THE EXPEDITION BEGINS

FIGURE 3.5. Enslaved workers on a coffee plantation, circa 1882. Image in the public domain. Marc Ferrez.

southern Minas had become one of the most important coffee producers in Brazil, as it still is today. Most of the mules passing the Burtons going south carried bags of coffee heading for the docks in Rio, and then ports of the North Atlantic.[31] The harvest season (July to November) roughly coincided with Richard's expedition.[32]

Every notable traveler through this region in the mid-nineteenth century made it a point to praise the first "macadamized" road in South America and to meet Commander (Comendador) Mariano Procópio Ferreira Lage.[33] Richard had met Lage earlier (probably in Rio), but the commander was in Europe when the Burtons passed through in June 1867. The hundred-mile trip along this exceptional road from Petrópolis to Juiz de Fora took about twelve hours, with about ten stops at rest stations along the way. Today, a major national highway between Rio de Janeiro and Belo Horizonte, BR-040, has taken over some sections of the old road, and the trip takes about two hours by car. A German entrepreneur, R. H. Klumb, traveled and photographed the route in the early 1870s, producing a guidebook for travelers complete with details on prices and places to stay.[34]

At roughly the halfway point between Petrópolis and Juiz de Fora, the Burtons briefly rested at the largest of Lage's mule-changing points. Entre Rios (now known as Três Rios) sits on the north banks of the Paraíba do Sul (Paraíba of the South) River, which flows from northeast to the southwest. Just east of the town, the Paraibuna River empties into the Paraíba do Sul, and the Piabanha splits off south toward Petrópolis. The Paraíba do Sul and the Paraibuna form the political boundary between southern Minas Gerais and the northern edge of the province (now state) of Rio de Janeiro. The town had long served as a crossroads between the commerce in the region, and up to a thousand mules grazed at Lage's station serving the coach and coffee traffic. Slightly to the northeast of Três Rios in a completely rural area, today two perfectly intact but rusting iron railway bridges span the Paraibuna River in silent testimony to the once proud and powerful English presence in this region. They are the sparse remains of one stretch of the railway line that the Burtons discuss in their own accounts.[35]

Much like the broken fences and shattered headstones in the English cemetery at Morro Velho, the rusting iron railway bridge, crumbling buildings, and reshaped landscapes provide the historian with some evidence, albeit silent and decayed, of those who came before, their achievements, and the limits of their power. Much like Shelley's "Ozymandias," these "lifeless" monuments to past glory now ironically bear witness to the hubris of British power—in Brazil and around the globe—a reminder that all glory is fleeting.[36] The surviving vestiges of this material culture provide the historian with a bit more information on the past with the help of archaeologists. The ruins of the many mines and surrounding villages in Minas Gerais, for example, provide us with another angle on slavery and mining, but very little archaeological work has been done at these sites where some of the largest enslaved communities in Brazil lived and worked.[37] None has been done at Morro Velho.

The detailed descriptions of travelers, along with the work of early photographers in Brazil and wonderful artists such as Jean-Baptiste Debret, Johan Moritz Rugendas, and Marianne North have left us glimpses of not only structures but also the natural landscapes. At times, the glimpses are astonishing, for both the change and the continuity. Today, the route up the mountain from Raiz da Serra to Petrópolis follows exactly the same path, although the paving may have actually been smoother in Burton's day. As impressive as the surrounding forest remains, houses fill up much of the way to the Alto da Cruz. The view is still astonishing, but it is now filled out with about ten million people, a bay surrounded by petrochemical plants and shipyards, and an international airport on Governor's Island, none of which the Burtons could have imagined. Yet these snapshots of a small number of locations at a few moments in time provide us with the perspective of (almost entirely) European travelers or settlers. We are left pondering the unresolvable question of what the artist actually saw versus what they chose to include in their painting. In the case of the photographer, we at least get to see an exact reproduction of the scene, but from the angle and gaze chosen by the photographer. Rather than these views of artists working for elites, what might the scenes have been had the enslaved or the peasants chosen the views? Despite the often lush and beautiful landscapes of North and Rugendas, some of these natural environments did not impress the Burtons.[38]

Richard did not like what he saw around Entre Rios. The air, he observed, "is bad, hot and damp, breeding fever like grubs; the water is worse." Every stream "is a sewer of liquid manure." (Quite likely, the hundreds of mules in the area had something to do with this!) The land, he added, "suffers from two especial curses,—the large proprietor" and an agricultural system "perpetuated by the slovenly methods of culture everywhere necessary when slave labour is employed."[39] Although he had little empathy (if any) for the enslaved, Richard here clearly sees the damage that a slave economy inflicted on Brazil. As a true Victorian Englishman, Richard was convinced that slavery was backward, outmoded, and inefficient, but his concern was economic. The more enduring legacy of three hundred years of slavery in Brazil was the entrenchment of a social system where a small elite controlled land and wealth while the majority lived in bondage or with their freedom in rural poverty.

Richard's account, like that of some of the other nineteenth-century travelers, provides us with incredible detail at the local level about the life, work, customs, and relationships of the Brazilian masses, especially the enslaved. Yet we have nothing like the participant observation of the best anthropological work of the twentieth century. As difficult as it is for the sensitive and astute ethnographer to immerse herself in the world of a different people, we have virtually nothing like this for the enslaved in Brazil. While we may dissect and deconstruct the worldview of the Burtons through their publications, correspondence, and unpublished writings, the closest we can ever get to the worldview of the enslaved is extremely limited and flawed. Inquisition records, court cases, notarial records, police files, and parish registers offer tantalizing tidbits of this world, but all through the mediation of public officials with their own agendas and translation of the voices of the enslaved.

When the Burtons reached the Paraibuna River, they paused briefly at the Serraria (Sawmill), today one of the last surviving stations from the old União e Indústria highway. Still standing but in disrepair, the old building also served as a railway depot in the years after Richard and Isabel passed through. More enduring than this human-made structure, the Rock of the Paraibuna towers over the south side of the river. This 1,500-hundred-foot-tall block of solid gneiss resembles the many hills that distinguish the topography of Rio de Janeiro, forged out of volcanic activity many millions of years ago. For Richard, the "vertical wall" gathered "up the sunbeams" and radiated "them like a furnace."[40] Directly across the river, on what is today a quiet country road, the 250-year-old Registro sits at the end of the bridge linking the states of Minas Gerais and Rio de Janeiro. Although an impressive stone marker, complete with engraved text, testifies to the historic importance of the location, the exterior walls and red tile roof are all that remains intact of this sizable wood and adobe building. Some two hundred feet long and forty feet wide, the old two-story customs house has likely survived because it is no longer on the beaten path. A major state highway now follows the south bank of the river, and the old União e Indústria road that once carried the Burtons and tens of thousands of wagons between Rio to Juiz de Fora has been relegated to local traffic and the trains that still run past the Registro between the road and the river. In Matias Barbosa, some twelve miles due north, an even older customs house, dating back to the early eighteenth century and the gold rush years, had collected the royal taxes on gold moving southward toward Rio. As always with government efforts to control and tax trade, these roads and

FIGURE 3.6. Ruins of Paraibuna Registro in 2022. Marshall C. Eakin.

registros compelled smugglers and those with gold to seek the trails and streams in the backwoods to avoid paying taxes.[41]

These customs houses speak to the lack of national integration in the late nineteenth century. In effect, they treated provincial borders like international ones, charging those entering the province tolls and duties as if they were passing through a coastal port heading abroad. As Richard, the nineteenth-century liberal, understood, "this outlandish system of inland" tariffs interfered with the creation of a truly national commerce and marketplace."[42] They may have been a clear and straightforward means to fund provincial governments, but they reflected the inability of the central and provincial governments to generate revenue by any other means than taxing transactions. Given the power of the landholding class in Brazil for centuries, taxes on income and on land would not be an option for Latin American governments until the late twentieth century.

For Richard, Juiz de Fora was "the usual mixture of misery and splendor."[43] He and Isabel stayed in a "chalet" with a group of English railway engineers who were surveying a potential route from Rio into the heart of the mining zone. The next morning the Burtons toured Lage's château and the surrounding arboretum and orchard while devouring tangerines from his trees. After declaring that their "fastidious English taste could find no fault in house or grounds," he went on to observe that the grounds were "a little fantastic."[44] The scientific expedition of Louis Agassiz had passed through two years earlier and received a grand reception. He and his wife found the grounds "exquisite" and like other foreign travelers heaped praise on Lage and his work.[45] The Burtons just happened to be in town on the same day as the festival of the local patron saint, Santo Antônio (Saint Anthony), and Richard depicted the crowds of revelers with his usually sardonic humor, noting that the cathedral "was a Black Hole of worshippers."[46]

While visiting Juiz de Fora, Richard met with one of the most important contacts he would have for his expedition, the elderly German emigré Heinrich Wilhelm Ferdinand Halfeld. Born in the Harz Mountains in the Kingdom of Hanover in 1797, Halfeld trained as a mining engineer, was wounded fighting Napoleon's armies at Waterloo, and then headed to Brazil in 1825 with his pregnant wife. For the next decade, he worked for English mining companies in São José (Tiradentes), Cocais, and Gongo Soco. The provincial president hired him in 1836 to build a road between the provincial capital of Ouro Preto and the crossing over the Paraibuna River where the old colonial roads from São Paulo and Rio de Janeiro converged. After bearing him eight children in fifteen years, his German wife passed away in 1839. With his road complete, he became a Brazilian citizen (becoming Henrique Guilherme Fernando Halfeld), married the daughter of a prominent local leader (she would bear him seven more children!), and settled near her family at the Paraibuna River crossing. He laid out the grid plan for a new city on the site, the city that became Juiz de Fora. A park and a statue on the main street now honor him as the founder of the city.[47]

In 1852 the imperial government commissioned Halfeld to survey the São Francisco River.[48] Fifteen years before Richard Burton, he traversed the length of the river, producing a detailed account of the route, league by league, with a map of the river consisting of thirty separate sections. Over the next two decades, every notable foreign traveler made an obligatory visit to "Commander"

THE EXPEDITION BEGINS

Halfeld, including Louis Agassiz in 1865 and Burton in 1867. As he made his way down the river in the coming months, Richard constantly consulted (and critiqued) Halfeld's work. When the two men met in mid-June, Halfeld was seventy and about to marry for the third time. His sixteen-year-old bride would bear him a sixteenth child in February 1873. While cleaning his gun, Halfeld accidentally shot himself and passed away in November 1873. Commander Lage may have been the great promoter and industrialist of Juiz de Fora, but Henrique Halfeld was truly its founder and patriarch.[49]

After their swift ride to Juiz de Fora along the best road in Brazil, the Burtons now prepared for their last coach ride, over rougher roads northward, to the edge of the mining zone and the town of Barbacena.

CHAPTER 4

INTO THE MINING ZONE

> The text may appear paradoxical to those, to the many, who still believe cannibalism and human sacrifice, slavery, and polygamy, abominations per se, the sum of all villainies and so forth. I look upon them as so many steps, or rather necessary conditions, by which civilized society rose to its present advanced state.... Without slavery how could the Antilles and the Southern States of the American Union have been cleared of jungle? White men could not, and free black men would not have done it.
>
> —RICHARD BURTON

As he moved deeper into the interior, Richard Burton's detailed observations reveal the structures and subtleties of profoundly unequal social hierarchies in mid-nineteenth-century Brazil. At the top stood the *fazendeiros*, the owners of substantial landed estates, or *fazendas*. In isolated rural areas, in the absence of the representatives of the central state, these men wielded enormous local power, often becoming the de facto authorities over their own fiefdoms. Although not always recipients of the official title, they were widely known throughout rural Brazil as colonels (*coronéis*). Local merchants and free persons with small holdings made up the next lower level of society. The poorest of rural laborers worked for themselves or for the fazendeiros (or both), often scratching out their own subsistence crops on small plots of land (*roças*). Enslaved Africans and Afro-Brazilians formed the enormous base of the social pyramid. Most Indigenous peoples who had once occupied eastern Brazil had been driven into the interior, culturally degraded, or eradicated. Some of the more powerful and productive landowning families branched into commerce, buying and selling goods beyond their own local communities. A very small number invested their family wealth in incipient textile factories in the second half of the nineteenth century. Nearly everyone with any discernible wealth owned slaves.[1]

SLAVERY, RACE, HIERARCHIES

Since the gold and diamond boom in the eighteenth century, Minas Gerais had been the most populous region of Brazil, and home to one of the largest slave societies in the Americas. As Richard moved through the heart of Minas in 1867, he navigated his way through an enormous population of close to four hundred thousand enslaved people, many of them born in Africa. In the history of Latin America, only Cuba (in the same period) and Saint Domingue/Haiti (before 1790) had larger enslaved communities than the province of Minas Gerais, and not by much. Another million enslaved lived and worked across Brazil, primarily in the provinces of São Paulo, Rio de Janeiro, and the northeast (Pernambuco and Bahia). Richard's travels in Brazil took him through all the principal slaveholding regions. He would acquire a detailed and ground-level knowledge of the intricacies of slavery in Brazil.[2] His descriptions and analysis are practical, detailed, and completely unsympathetic to the enslaved.

Although one key sign of the wealth of a large landowner was the number of slaves they owned, slaveholding was highly dispersed in Brazil. In Minas Gerais, around one-third of the free population owned slaves. About one-half of all the enslaved were in groups of 20 or more, about a quarter in clusters of 11 to 20, and the other quarter in groups of 10 or fewer. Seen from another angle, three-quarters of all slaveowners (or about 7 percent of the free population) controlled 10 or fewer enslaved workers, and the other quarter amassed enslaved communities of 11 or more.

Although large plantations and mines sometimes had enslaved communities in the hundreds, at least half of the enslaved population was dispersed in groups smaller than 20.[3] As Richard's narrative reveals, the enslaved engaged in virtually every type of occupation, and could be found everywhere. Like the majority of the rural population, most labored on the land. They also toiled as craftsmen, street vendors, domestic servants, and skilled workers. Much of the labor force on the many, many mule trains that passed the Burtons (in both directions) as they rode through Minas was enslaved muleteers (*tropeiros*).

By the time he arrived in Brazil in 1865, Richard had spent nearly a decade exploring both East and West Africa, working his way through what today are Ethiopia, Somalia, Tanzania, Cameroon, Nigeria, and Benin. He was one of a handful of white Europeans with sustained experience living among and closely observing very diverse peoples across equatorial Africa of many different skin tones, languages, and cultures. A previous decade or more spent in South Asia and the Middle East, before his African travels, also provided him with close exposure to many other ethnic and cultural groups as points of comparison. Unlike many of his British contemporaries, Richard did not engage in armchair anthropology in the comfort and security of a quiet English study. By the late 1860s, he had accumulated a quarter century of ethnographic fieldwork and probably could claim to have personally observed a wider range of non-European peoples than any of his contemporaries.

In his numerous books, we can see both his appreciation for the particular logics of the many different cultures he observed and his profoundly racist worldview. In his descriptions of Hindus, Muslims, Arabs, and the diverse peoples of East and West Africa, he constantly sought out local insiders to explain to him the logic and workings of their group. His insatiable curiosity drove him to comprehend their worlds. The incredibly detailed descriptions of the customs and habits of the people he encountered have left us with an ethnographic bounty that remains his most enduring contribution. He was a self-taught anthropologist—indeed, one of the founders of the field. Much more so than his fellow members of the Anthropological Society of London and similar groups in his own time, he could see that his own people (Irish, English,

Europeans) had their own customs and traditions that often seemed strange, illogical, even irrational to outsiders. In spite of this impressive erudition and his astonishingly vast cultural exposure, he never seriously questioned his own deeply rooted ideas of race and morality—that whites, especially northern Europeans, stood atop an evolutionary hierarchy of racial and moral superiority looking down on a descending hierarchy of peoples of color. It is one of the striking ironies of the early founders of anthropology that the fieldwork of so many of them recorded the cultural practices of peoples who would be completely lost to us today had not they encountered these white European men (and very occasionally women) who saw them as inferior races.[4]

The inability to make a distinction between biology and culture—genetic inheritance versus learned behavior—plagued the emerging discipline of anthropology until the classic work of Franz Boas at Columbia University in the early twentieth century.[5] This German immigrant, originally trained in physics, nurtured several generations of anthropologists—including Ruth Benedict and Margaret Mead—who transformed both the academic and public perception of race in the twentieth century. The Brazilian intellectual Gilberto Freyre did graduate work at Columbia in the 1920s, returned to his native Recife, and produced what is perhaps the most influential interpretation of Brazil over the last century, *The Masters and the Slaves* (*Casa-grande e senzala*, or "the big house and the slave quarters," in the Portuguese original).[6] In direct contrast to Burton and the prevailing social science of the previous century, Freyre glorified the racial and cultural mixing in Brazil. Unlike most Brazilian intellectuals, he argued that the biological mixing of Indians, Africans, and Portuguese toughened the Brazilians, allowing them to endure the harsh tropical environments. More important, the cultural mixing forged a unique, creative, and dynamic society. Brazilians, Freyre announced, should not be ashamed of their mixed-race heritage; they should celebrate it.[7] Yet when Richard cast his patronizing, racially superior gaze across Brazil in the 1860s, these debates lay decades ahead, arguments he would not have been able to imagine. His world, one dominated by his countrymen, looked very different from the world in the early twenty-first century.

The enormous success of the British in constructing the world's first industrial nation, the largest commercial and naval fleets, in conquering a truly global empire reinforced a sense of cultural and moral superiority, especially among the elites.[8] Riding a wave of economic, military, and political conquests, the British explorer, diplomat, or merchant felt a sense of entitlement and saw himself engaged in a "civilizing mission." The British would bring to the "less fortunate" peoples of the world the benefits of white, Anglo-Saxon civilization. They might look down on the French, North Americans, or other Europeans, but they still considered them as part of the most "civilized" race. They saw the darker races as incapable of achieving civilization on their own. Even with the "assistance" of the Europeans, they reasoned, the Africans and Asians would probably never be capable of attaining the culture and civility of the white race.[9]

Burton believed that the Black man "suffered from arrested physical development" and that "for the most part" was "born servile" and "mentally remains a child." Bluntly stated, he believed "in the inferior genesis of the negro, and in his incapability of improvement, individually and *en masse*." Writing about West Africa as the Civil War raged in the United States, he claimed to have "wandered through every State of the Anglo-American Republic" (a dubious assertion) and that he was "convinced that the serfs of the Southern plantation would not change lots with their free brethren." As Burton surveyed and probed the Brazilian interior, these experiences in Africa and the United States framed his observations of race and slavery in the young Brazilian nation.

Despite the enormous population of free people, around 80 percent of Brazilians in the 1860s, large landowners never paid wages attractive enough to fill their demand for labor without having to resort to slavery as an alternative.[10] The vast amounts of open land and the possibilities of subsistence agriculture likely dissuaded free people from hiring on at sugar plantations in the Northeast in the seventeenth century, gold mines in Minas Gerais in the eighteenth century, and coffee plantations in the nineteenth century. Like country people on many continents, they preferred to be left alone to carve out their own rural livelihoods. As an "enlightened" Englishman in the mid-nineteenth century, Richard regularly condemned slavery as a backward and inefficient form of labor, believed the end of slavery a necessity, and viewed enslaved Blacks as inferior people. Abolition would come, but under the "careful and wise guidance" of the landed class. Like many of his contemporaries, in England and Brazil, he envisioned European immigration to Brazil and abolition as the twin means to develop the country. In his words, "As slavery diminishes so immigration will increase, and it is good to bear in mind that the two cannot co-exist." For Richard, with the demise of slavery and increased immigration, Brazil would "follow in the path of the great Northern Republic."[11]

From Coaches to Mules

"At 6 a.m. on a raw, dark morning," 17 June, Richard, Isabel, Mr. L'pool, and Chico departed Juiz de Fora on the last coach ride of the trip into the interior. Alongside them in a separate coach, but headed south to Juiz de Fora, sat their compatriots Mr. Morritt and the Newdigates. With the Burtons in their "mail" coach sat an Austrian who had settled in Minas and a "Brazilian lady" with "two black girls" and "the normal two black babies." They relegated Chico and another servant to a sort of rumble seat in the rear while Isabel sat snugly between Richard and Mr. L'pool behind Godfrey, the German driver, and a guard. Over the next twelve hours, they made nine stops while going up and down over "infamous" roads that were "hard and caky" but would turn into sloppy stretches of mud pits once the rainy season began in November.[12] With the exception of the road from Petrópolis to Juiz de Fora, paved roads would not appear in this region until the twentieth century.

The Burtons' route to Barbacena in 1867 eventually became the path for the railway line in the last decades of the nineteenth century, and now lies to the west of BR-040, off the beaten track. The survey engineers who had so pleased the Burtons with their hospitality eventually laid out the path of the Dom Pedro II Railway in the 1870s and 1880s, along a route very different from the old mule trains and coaches.[13] The rail line left the center of Rio, headed northwest to take advantage of a pass through the Serra do Mar (at Japeri-Paracambi), then followed the old Paraíba River Valley in a northeasterly direction, reaching Três Rios only a few months after the Burtons passed through. The rail line would not reach Juiz de Fora until 1875, and Barbacena in 1880. After the fall of the monarchy in 1889, the government renamed the line the Central Railroad of Brazil (Estrada de Ferro Central do Brasil).[14]

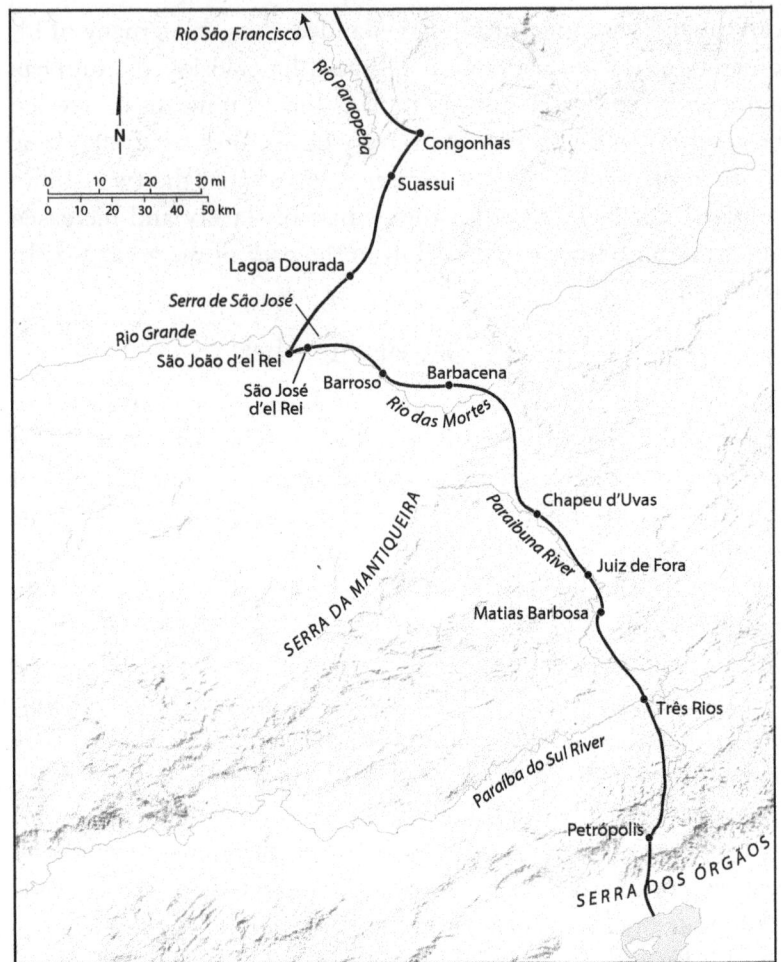

FIGURE 4.1. Richard's route through Minas Gerais.

For Richard, constructing modern roads held the key to the country's future. For "this Empire," he asserted, "about to be so mighty and magnificent, communication signifies civilization, prosperity, progress—everything. It is more important to national welfare even than the school or the newspaper, for these will follow where that proceeds."[15]

At Hat of Grapes (Chapeu d'Uvas), the Burtons caught their first glimpse of the Serra da Mantiqueira (an Indigenous Tupi word that means "mountains that cry"). Running from southwest to northeast, the range collides with the southern tip of the Serra do Espinhaço (Backbone Range) just east of where Richard was about to cross. Just before crossing the range, the Burtons passed through the small town of João Gomes consisting of a main square surrounded by palm trees. Richard pauses for a moment in his account to note that he now stood at the "eastern culminating plateau-point of the Brazilian Highlands, and from this radiate the headwater valleys of the Parahyba do Sul, the Rio Doce, and the Paraná, which becomes the mighty Plata." From this vantage point, Richard once again waxes lyrical about the Brazilian landscape. "Below us lay the land mapped out into an infinity of feature that ranged through the quadrant from south-east to south-west. There was the usual beautiful Brazilian perspective, tier after tier of mountain, hill, hillock, rise, and wavy horizon, whose arc was dotted with the forms familiar to Rio de Janeiro—sugar loaves, hunchbacks, topsails, and parrots' beaks."[16] The Paraibuna River originates on the southern slopes of the Mantiqueira just west of his crossing and flows south into the Atlantic, and the Rio das Mortes (River of the Dead) begins on the northern slopes just ahead of him, flowing west into the Rio Grande, Paraná, and eventually into the Rio de la Plata.

As the Burtons headed north through the mountains, they continued to gain altitude, reaching 3,800 feet above sea level at Barbacena. A thriving city of more than 100,000 inhabitants today, it was a small but prosperous town of about 5,000 in the 1860s. Like most of the towns founded during the gold rush in the early eighteenth century, the locals built churches honoring their favored saints, especially the Virgin Mary, and her many apparitions. Richard dutifully visited many of these churches as he made his way through the interior, probably at Isabel's instigation, and he nearly always gave them bad reviews. Three of these, all dedicated to Mary, framed the central area of Barbacena. Our Lady of Piety (Piedade), Our Lady of the Assumption or Good Death (Assunção, Boa Morte), and Our Lady of the Rosary (Rosário), historically the favorite of Black Brazilians, enslaved and free. In many of these churches throughout Minas, the builders used soapstone (steatite, a talc schist) to craft statuary or ornamentation. An easily carved soft rock, today soapstone provides local artisans in Minas with the material for an endless array of tourist souvenirs from sculptures to ashtrays.

In addition to curious European travelers like Richard Burton who crisscrossed the Brazilian interior in the nineteenth century, some of the foreign visitors (like Henrique Halfeld) settled down, married locals, led interesting lives, and sometimes sowed the seeds for large and enduring Brazilian family trees. In Barbacena, Richard delighted in meeting and conversing with French expatriate Pierre Victor Renault.[17] Born in 1811 in Metz, Renault made a halfhearted effort to train as an engineer at the school of mines in Saint-Etienne but could not seem to find a direction in life. He headed off to Brazil in 1832, apparently with the hope of a job in Minas Gerais. Arriving in Rio virtually penniless, he eventually made his way to Sabará, led several expeditions in the São Francisco and Mucuri River Basins for the provincial government, and acquired an intimate knowledge of hostile indigenous groups in the region. Taken seriously ill after his return from one of these expeditions, a physician in Barbacena nursed him back to health. The twenty-nine-year-old Renault then married the physician's eighteen-year-old daughter, and over two decades the couple produced many children. From the 1840s until his death in 1892 (at the age of eighty-one), he worked as a civil engineer and rancher, and ran his own school for a while. He gradually trained himself as a homeopathic physician with broad knowledge of the region's botanical riches. Renault became the local guide for many of the foreign travelers who made their way through Minas in the mid-nineteenth century, most of them speaking French. He impressed Richard as he showed him around, and Burton "felt sad when taking leave of him." He then observed that "a man living upon conversation and exchange of opinions, and to whom talk is bliss, he must find Barbacena as it now is, a penance, a purgatory."[18] Clearly, Richard could not envision settling down to a quiet rural life with a large family and deep local networks.

On their departure, Richard complained about the "unconscionable bill" from the Barbacense Hotel and suggested that the owner had been "excited by the abnormal appearance of Mr. L'pool." With a tall, broad-brimmed felt hat adorned with feathers, a threadbare shooting jacket and frayed waistcoat, a broad silk sash covered by a leather belt around the waist, and wooden clogs, his English compatriot carried a Colt six-shooter, a Bowie knife, and a coarse canvas pouch for his tobacco, flint, and steel. "Thus equipped," his traveling companion "was the model of an English traveling gentleman"![19] Richard does not say if they challenged the bill.

After sailing across Guanabara Bay, taking a train to the foot of the serra, and then riding in mule-drawn coaches to Petrópolis, Juiz de Fora, and Barbacena, the Burtons now shifted to riding mules over rough terrain with no real roads. Over the next month, from mid-June to mid-July, mules would be their principal means of travel on paths where even their local guides sometimes lost their way. As Richard put it, "We are now about to see the outer darkness of places to which mules are the only transport."[20] Fortunately, before beginning the expedition, Richard had been in contact with the superintendent of the British-owned and operated Morro Velho gold mine, and he had sent a team of ten mules and two enslaved men to guide them, supervised by James Fitzpatrick, an Irishman who worked at Morro Velho. Rather than take the standard route north from Barbacena. They headed west to São João del Rei (Saint John of the King). Numerous writers had traveled along and written about the 150-mile road north, so for Richard it was already "trodden to uninterestingness"![21]

Ranchos and Churches

As always, Richard carefully calculated and logged his travel distances and speed. On the route from Barbacena to Morro Velho via São João del Rei (nine stages) the group covered 163 miles at 3.5 miles per hour. Richard, Isabel, Fitzpatrick, Mr. L'pool, and Chico each rode mules, with three more beasts carrying their baggage. Although they had two spare mules, the two enslaved men, Miguel and Antonio, proceeded at the front of the caravan on foot as drivers and guides. Richard pointedly observed, "When I travel alone my men are always mounted, and thus we easily get over six to seven miles an hour."[22]

As they embarked on this mule-troop phase of the expedition, Richard laid out for the reader his advice for anyone who would like to be a "comfortable traveler." First, always look out for yourself. Second, do not let the age or sex of anyone get in the way of you taking "the strongest beast, the best room, the superior cut, the last glass of sherry." Third, "When riding lead the way, monopolise the path, and bump up against all who approach you—they will probably steer clear for the future." Fourth, in "the morning take care of No. 1; muffle your head, wrap up your throat, stuff your boots with cotton." Fifth, as the sun rises and the day heats up, gradually "unshell yourself," "open your umbrella and suck oranges." Sixth, "Never go to a hotel if there be a private house within a league, and above all keep accounts." "Finally," he concludes, "if you invite a man to dine, score up his liquor on the wall, staring him 'in the face,'" just to make sure to keep down your expenses.[23] Thus, the accumulated wisdom of the experienced world traveler in a nutshell.

In Petrópolis, Juiz de Fora, and Barbacena, the Burtons had the "luxury" of staying at country inns and "hotels." Now they would depend, quite literally, on the kindness of strangers to take them on to their fazendas. At times, this meant living the life of the *tropeiro*. Along well-traveled routes, landowners often built *ranchos*—enormous sheds, with a tile roof, sometimes with adobe walls, rooms, and a veranda. For a fee, travelers could pasture their mule teams, store their gear for the night, buy some provisions, and cook dinner over an open fire. Roast pork or chicken stew generally served as the main dish at these ranches. Across Brazil, beans and rice had become the staple diet. The most common flour came from the indigenous manioc plant, which when ground, dried, and lightly toasted, became *farinha*. In Minas, local cooks mashed up cooked brown beans and mixed them with *farinha*, bits of bacon and fried eggs, and chopped kale to produce *tutu à mineira*. A type of porridge made from boiled maize, sugar, milk, and cinnamon—*canjica*—was often served for dessert, along with very strong and heavily sweetened coffee. Not for those counting their calories or cholesterol, these dishes remain a staple of traditional *mineiro* (Minas) cuisine today. More developed stops might include a country store (*venda*) selling beans, lard, dried beef (*carne seca*), tobacco, rum, and essential supplies such as horseshoes, knives, pistols, and ammunition.[24]

Primed with a letter of introduction from Victor Renault, the Burtons' entourage spent the first night out from Barbacena at the fazenda of a Sr. Meirelles, with Isabel in her hammock in an inner room of the usual *tropeiro* shed and Richard wrapped in blankets on the veranda. Isabel described the place as "a shed like cottage" that "had one room with a ceiling of bamboo matting, whitewashed mud walls, no window, and a mud floor."²⁵ The fazenda had already become the core of the small community of Barroso on the northern banks of the Rio das Mortes. According to an early eighteenth-century chronicler and visitor to the region, the river took its name from the many dead generated from quarrels among the settlers over the division of the Indians they had enslaved. Richard noticed the abundant dolomite (calcium carbonate) deposits nearby, and how the locals crushed and fired it to produce lime. Today, a large Swiss-owned cement plant, as well as one controlled by the National Steel Company (Companhia Siderúrgica Nacional) just north of the old fazenda, consume the dolomite deposits and dominate the town's economy.²⁶

In their daily routine, the Burtons and their entourage rose very early to harness the mules, pack, and break camp, departing in darkness around 4:30 a.m. On this day, Thursday, 20 June 1867, they discovered that big brown vampire bats had fed on their troop of beasts, apparently with no harm to the mules, other than bloody spots around the puncture wounds. Their destination, São João del Rei, sits at the western end of the Serra de São José (Saint Joseph's Ridge), which rises up sharply some 1,400 feet, extending from southwest to northeast for several miles. With the rising sun at their backs, as they rode west from Barroso toward São João del Rei, the craggy line of the ridge jutted up dramatically on their right in the early morning light. "Its crest," Richard noted, "bristles with curious projections, stiff points, pikes, needles, and organ pipes."²⁷ Twenty-four miles down the road, they paused at a bridge over the Elvas River to breakfast. As they reached the outskirts of São João, a religious procession momentarily halted their progress. They had arrived on the feast of Corpus Christi, one of the most important religious festivals of the Catholic calendar celebrating the presence of the blood and body of Christ in the Eucharist. The ever-irreverent Richard described the pomp and pageantry as a "system of farces and masquerades."²⁸ Isabel no doubt cringed at his words later in England as she chaperoned his manuscript through publication.

Much to the delight of the Burtons, they encountered two more of their countrymen who provided them with expert guidance during their stay. Dr. William Cavendish Lee, from Kent, married a local woman and had resided for more than three decades in São

João, while Charles Copsy had studied at Cambridge with some of the Burtons' friends and relatives.[29] Small world. Once again showing his British sense of superiority, Richard expressed delight that despite their long and intimate experience in the country, the men had not become "Brazilianised." "Brazilian is good, and British is good," he asserted. "The mixture, as is said of other matters which shall be nameless, spoils two good things."[30]

Many of these baroque churches have been painstakingly restored in the past few decades as the state and local governments have worked to develop the tourism industry as a means of economic development. For most, the basic design is fairly straightforward and linear, a style Richard disparaged and ridiculed as "heavy and couthless." He blamed the Jesuits for introducing to Brazil a pattern that combined "the vertical lines of the Gothic with the horizontal length of classical architecture, and notably fails." While I am humbled and somewhat in awe in viewing the enormous interiors of these churches, Richard thought they lacked grandeur and, instead, gave the same effect as standing in a "large barn." He did concede that these colonial churches were "almost always built on the highest and prettiest site, and there is a fine open space in front for which St. Paul's and Westminster must sigh in vain."[31]

In spite of his disdain for the architecture, Richard carefully and in great detail described the São Francisco Church—in my opinion one of the most beautiful in Minas, with its rounded bell towers on each of the front corners, topped with domes that reminded Richard of ovens. On his visit the next day to the church of Our Lady of the Rosary, his disdain for Black people is evident. After commenting on its "tawdry coarseness in colour and form," he archly notes that he can tell that the church is the worship place of "Homo niger." True to the racist science of the day, he ascribed to the belief that each race had different shaped skulls, a theory long since discarded by scientists. He observes that a skull ("dolichocephalic") over the entrance to the adjacent cemetery could not be that of a Black man, and then notes snidely that "São João has not yet established a branch of the Anthropological Society of London."[32]

On his second full day in town, Richard hiked up the rising ridge on the northwest side with two objectives. At the top of a long flight of steps sat the Church of Our Lady of Mercy (Nossa Senhora das Mercês) and a "fine bird's-eye view" of the city and surrounding countryside.[33] Standing atop the steps he faced to the southeast and down below, slightly to his right, sat the Rosário Church, then a sizable stream, and a few blocks over the bridge, the large complex of the São Francisco Church. The spot, however, was but a midway point to his real objective—an examination of the abandoned mining works of the St. John d'el Rey Mining Company. The steep mountainside is now covered with houses, but the scars of mining excavations carved out nearly two hundred years ago remain visible across the plateau above.

Investors organized this company in a London tavern in 1830, purchased an existing gold mining operation on the western edge of São João d'el Rei (as it was then spelled), and took the anglicized name of the city for that of the company. In less than two years, the British superintendent and miners sent out to work the claim realized that the property had been completely oversold.[34] By 1834 the company's superintendent on the ground, Charles Herring, had located a promising and well established mine about a hundred miles to the northeast near the small village of Nossa Senhora da Conceição de Congonhas de Sabará (Our Lady of the Conception of Congonhas of Sabará). Known as Morro Velho (the old hill), the mine had already been worked with a low level of technology for more than a hundred years. After losing about half of their initial capital of £50,000 on the worthless property in São João del Rei, the investors raised more funds, and hoped the new claim would not be another dead end. It proved to be a very smart move. Despite the move to Morro Velho, the company name remained the same.

Early on 22 June, the group set out to visit the nearby town of São José del Rei (Saint Joseph of the King, now known as Tiradentes) just five miles to the east, at the base of the serra. Richard complained emphatically about the number of beggars, but then said that there was "with me a person who still believes in the Knightly and middle-aged legends about alms," clearly referring to Isabel. Mr. Copsy tagged along, and on bidding farewell, Dr. Lee gave Richard a puppy he called "Negra" (Black). With a "square head, broad shoulders, and huge hands and feet," the pup was a distinctly Brazilian breed known as *cão de fila*, a type of mastiff, and a very aggressive hunting dog used in colonial times to track down runaway slaves and hold them at bay.[35] Negra would be Richard's constant, if sometimes irritating, companion nearly to the end of his voyage down the São Francisco River.

Richard estimated that the village had some three hundred homes and 2,500 inhabitants. In this tiny village deep in the interior, "Nature, in one of her usual freaky moods," had produced one of Brazil's greatest poets, José Basílio da Gama. Born around 1740 at the height of the gold rush, da Gama wrote an epic poem, a "metrical romance," *O Uruguay*, a work that Richard was translating, though that translation would remain unpublished until 1982![36] Richard lamented that the town could build seven churches, but "not a slab to honour the greatest of Brazilian poets."[37] The local museum has now made up for this fault and has dedicated some of its space to honoring the poet Richard so admired.[38]

Smaller and more isolated than São João, Tiradentes has its own charm and appeal. Restaurants, bars, ateliers, craft breweries, and craft shops now fill the restored colonial buildings alongside the tiny rivulet of the Rio das Mortes. The view from the Santo Antônio Church facing the Serra de São José to the east is stunning. São José was also the birthplace of José Joaquim Xavier da Costa, better known to history as Tiradentes (the Toothpuller, for his apparent moonlighting in early dentistry). One of the leaders of a planned rebellion against the monarchy in 1789, the new republic made him into one of Brazil's best known national heroes in the decades after the overthrown of the Braganzas in 1889. To honor him, the founders of the republic renamed the city after him in 1889.[39]

Feasts and Saints

Unable to sleep and experiencing near freezing temperatures at an altitude of 2,700 feet in Brazilian midwinter, Richard and his companions stayed up all night talking and drinking while Isabel slung up her hammock and "slept the sleep of good conscience."[40] The group set out before 5 a.m., heading due north through a deep cut in the serra. By 8 a.m. they had made the crossing and paused at the Carandaí River to breakfast before heading northeast for eighteen miles along the old Estrada Real to the village of Lagoa Dourada (Golden Lake—Richard calls it Alagoa Dourada).

INTO THE MINING ZONE

Along the way, Isabel's startled mule jumped over a deep mud pit and her pistol fell out of her belt, disappearing forever into the muck. With some fifty one-story houses stretched along the road, the town reminded Richard of those he had seen in West Africa.

An arc of mountains running from northwest to southeast from the Serra da Canastra (Basket Range) to the north of São João del Rei never rises above four thousand feet but divides two of the great watersheds of South America. The Brumado River begins near Lagoa Dourada, flowing north into the Paraopeba River that empties into the São Francisco, whose origin point is two hundred miles to the northwest in the Serra da Canastra. The Rio Grande originates on the southwest slopes of the serra flowing into the Parnaíba River, forming the upper Paraná, one of the great tributaries of the La Plata River. As Richard's group moved northward from São João to Lagoa Dourada, they entered the southern limit of the São Francisco River Basin. Richard would spend the next five months moving north and east through it.

The group arrived in Lagoa Dourada on the afternoon of 23 June, the eve of Saint John's Day, one of the oldest Christian feast days. The early church fathers set it to coincide with Midsummer's Day in the northern hemisphere (20 or 21 June, midwinter in Brazil). With a number of important saints' days in June, in particular, Saint Anthony (13 June) and Saint Peter (29 June), over centuries the Brazilians gradually turned these European festivities into weeks of *festas juninas* (June festivals). In the mid-nineteenth century, these were largely rural celebrations of agricultural life. Like Europeans, the Brazilians built bonfires. In the Northeast, the festivities normally coincided with the end of the rainy season. Rural folk engaged in games and square dancing (*quadrilha*), and some attempted to walk barefoot across burning coals.[41] Today, these festivals serve as a powerful marker of Brazilian culture and identity, in particular, for those who nostalgically look back to a rural past.

Once again, at Lagoa Dourada, the Burtons met up with the team of English engineers scouting the future route of the Dom Pedro II Railway line. At noon on Saint John's Day, everyone headed to the outskirts of town "to lay the first chain" for the survey route northward. John Whittaker, the lead civil engineer, invited Isabel to strike the first blow on the survey peg with a bottle of champagne. After speeches, *vivas*, music, and many drinks, the entourage headed back to the surveyors' "ranch" for a bountiful feast of chicken, meat, beans, *farinha*, and peppers, along with beer and port. "The day ended," says Richard, "as great days always do amongst true Britons—with a grand dinner."[42] The singing, drinking, and "speechifying" must have been very satisfying, for he went on to say that he had "spent many a less merry Christmas in Merry England, and we shall not readily forget Midsummer Day at Alagoa Dourada, in the year of our grace 1867."[43]

Leaving behind his compatriots must have left Richard in a foul mood on his departure from the town the following day. He fills this section of his account with complaints about his guides, the locals, and even the ticks (*carrapatos*). Rising at 4 a.m., the group did not manage to depart until 9 a.m. The way forward, he grumbles, was "a mere bridle path, without commerce, communications, or comfort," and although "the few inhabitants are naturally intelligent . . . they never rise above semi-barbarism."[44] When they finally reached the small village of Campuã, the local fazendeiro, José Antonio de Azevedo, turned out to be the exception to the usual hospitality they had come to expect of ranchers. "His hovel was as filthy as his person, and his kitchen excelled the average pigstye, yet he was miserly not poor."[45] Isabel had to plead with Azevedo just to put up her hammock, and Richard slept on a wooden table. During the night, Isabel overheard Azevedo conversing with his "two negresses." No doubt due to her flawed Portuguese, she thought they were plotting to kill the visitors, and she armed herself in preparation. The next morning, they discovered that he was probably talking about killing some of his chickens!

Richard's mood improved as they moved toward Congonhas do Campo, and he even concedes at one point that "the ride was becoming delightful."[46] (Congonhas is a type of wild tea or *mate* found across the region. The city's name, then, is Tea of the Field.) Isabel took in the striking, mountainous landscape with both awe and a blasé attitude. Though "the scenery is magnificent," she observes, "it is so alike, that one description describes all, and what you see to-day you will see to-morrow and for the next three months, with the exception of every here and there a startling feature." At a brief stop for breakfast in the village of Suaçui, Isabel was "overcome with the luxury of being able to wash our hands

FIGURE 4.2. Church of Bom Jesus do Matozinhos, Congonhas, 2022. Marshall C. Eakin.

and faces *in a basin* (her emphasis)."⁴⁷ On their way out of Suaçui on the Estrada Real, they passed a band of Travelers (or "gypsies" in his language) at the Fazenda Covão, and Richard promised to write more about them in a future volume, noting that they are the "object of popular fear, disgust, and superstition."⁴⁸ The old fazenda buildings have survived and now serve as an events center. Whitewashed exterior walls, blue trim, and a red tile roof maintain the nineteenth-century look.

By mid-afternoon, they reached Alto Maranhão and had their first view of Congonhas, situated in "a charming valley" carved out by the Maranhão River. To the north, they saw the Serra da Boa Morte (Good Death Range) culminating in the Peak of Itabira, and to the east the Ouro Branco (White Gold) Range. They stood on the southern edge of ancient mountains that once contained some of the world's largest gold deposits and still contain enormous open-pit iron mining operations. The search for iron in the past half century has carved away mountaintops across Minas Gerais, leaving massive scars on the landscape the Burtons once viewed.

Congonhas has become one of the most famous and visited "historical cities" (*cidades históricas*) of Minas Gerais, as tourists and pilgrims flock to a religious complex designed and executed by Brazil's own racially mixed equivalent of Michelangelo. The illegitimate son of a Portuguese architect and his enslaved African, Antonio Francisco Lisboa was born in the 1730s in Vila Rica de Ouro Preto, grew up in his father's household, and learned his trade at the height of the gold boom. He also became an exceptionally talented sculptor of stone and wood. Legend has it he suffered from leprosy (or something like it), eventually losing the use of his fingers, hence his nickname, Aleijadinho ("the Little Cripple"). As the story is usually told, assistants strapped a hammer and chisel to his wrists, and he continued sculpting. (Although I have never seen any documented proof, it is a good story.) By the time he died in 1814, he had created a series of striking baroque churches, altars, carvings, and sculptures all over central Minas Gerais. His greatest achievement sits atop a hill in the middle of Congonhas do Campo.[49]

Every time I come to Congonhas (as it is known today), I am in awe of its striking complexity, scale, and stark beauty. A path leads up a steep hill with six small chapels, three on each side, the stations of the cross from the Passion of Christ. In the 1780s, Aleijadinho sculpted life-sized wooden figures for the chapels, illustrating in each one a scene from Jesus's path from the Last Supper to his crucifixion. The greatest artist of colonial Brazil, Manoel da Costa Ataíde, painted the sixty-six statues. At the top of the hill stands the Church of Bom Jesus de Matozinhos (Good Jesus of the Little Bushes), surrounded on all sides by a plaza with a panoramic view of the countryside, even today. An expansive, raised stone courtyard extends out from the front of the church and around its walls stand twelve life-sized (about five feet tall) soapstone statues of prophets from the Old Testament. Aleijadinho reportedly carved these prophets in the first five years of the nineteenth century. Oral tradition has it that he had to be helped on to ladders, supporting himself on his padded knees. At the feet of each of these prophets, he carved a short verse from their biblical book. On a sunny and crystal-clear winter day in June, even the most unreligious must find it hard not to be moved deeply by the scene.[50]

INTO THE MINING ZONE

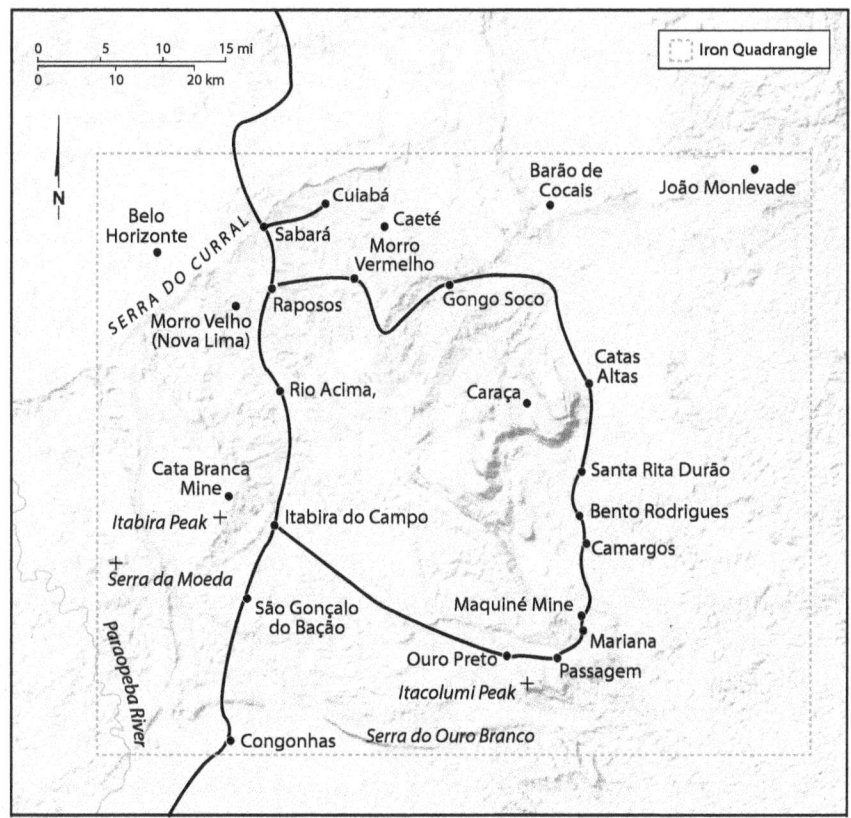

FIGURE 4.3. Richard's circuit around the mining zone.

Richard was not. His deeply rooted skepticism of all religion, and especially Catholicism, permeates his very detailed descriptions of the complex. (Surprisingly, the devout Isabel barely mentions the stop in her own account.) He describes the statuary in the chapels as "utterly vile works of art" and "wooden caricatures," and he highlights what is, I agree, one of their strangest features, very prominent noses.[51] The massive, carved wooden church doors did impress him, but he found the paintings inside to be "tawdry." Oddly, he does not react to the "miracle room" in a building on the east side of the church. Over the centuries, the devout have filled the room with *ex-votos*—letters, cards, and offerings in gratitude to the Good Jesus of Matozinhos for answering their prayers. Despite my decades of consciously cultivated religious toleration and empathy, the room continues to astonish me with its thousands of

FIGURE 4.4. Itabira Peak, 1820s. Image in the public domain. C. F. P. Von Martius.

artificial limbs, carvings, photographs, and testimonials. Perhaps it provokes my ancestral and visceral Calvinist indoctrination.

RIVER OF THE OLD WOMEN

As the Burtons departed Congonhas at noon on 27 June, they crossed the Serra de Ouro Branco and entered the southern edge of a massive iron ore zone (known today as the Quadrílatero Ferrífero, or Iron Quadrangle) and the headwaters of the Rio das Velhas. We "entered a land of iron, all black and red spangled with mica," declared Richard the geologist.[52] On a map, the quadrangle looks like an oddly shaped diamond. The Serra de Ouro Branco provides its southeast side, the Serra da Moeda (Money Range) the southwest, the Serra do Curral (Corral Range) its northwest, and the northeast side is the Serra do Espinhaço (Backbone Range), running from the old gold mining town of Cocais to Ouro Preto. These 2,700 square miles once contained some of the world's largest iron, gold, and diamond deposits—one of the richest mineral zones anywhere in the world. The gold and diamonds were already nearly exhausted by the time the Burtons passed through, but the iron ore was not to be seriously exploited until the late twentieth century.[53]

The Rio das Velhas originates just a few miles above Ouro Preto and moves north in the large basin between the Serra da Moeda to the west and the Serra do Espinhaço to the east. As the Burtons reached their destination for the day, São Gonçalo do Bação (Saint Gonzalo of the Basin), projecting up some four thousand feet to the north stood one of the iconic landmarks of the region, the Itabira Peak. Nearly 70 percent iron ore the peak thrusts up out of a large mound like a giant, craggy, broken tooth. Burton called it a "castled crag." On entering the basin, Richard reflected on the nearby Rio das Velhas and "the task which is to occupy me some three months of river navigation." "How many risks and hardships," he wonders, "are to be undergone, how many difficulties are to be conquered before the task can be accomplished, before we can see the scenes of what is about to be"?[54]

Congonhas sits at the bottom corner of the Iron Quadrangle, where the southern ends of the Serra do Ouro Branco and the Serra da Moeda converge. Like the ridges around the region today, the peaks on the northern and western edges of the town have been stripped away by open-pit iron mining. Massive scars in shades of brown, red, and gray cover the once green mountaintops. Richard did not realize it, but his path took him on top of and through rich iron deposits that would ultimately far more important to the region than the gold he so anxiously sought in these mountains. In recent decades, the largest mining company in the world, Brazil's own Vale, sliced away the slopes around the iconic Itabira Peak, leaving a distorted, yet somewhat intact, version of Richard's castled crag. Water has gradually pooled into a large lake in the immense crater the pit-mining operation carved into the adjacent slopes.[55]

Thirty-five years after the Burtons passed through Itabira do Campo (known today as Itabirito), Brazil's greatest poet of the twentieth century was born on the northeastern fringe of the Iron Quadrangle in Itabira de Mato Dentro (known today as Itabira). In the 1930s, Carlos Drummond de Andrade immortalized his hometown in the nostalgic poem, "Confession of an Itabiran," as he supported himself as a civil servant in Rio de Janeiro. Opening with the poignant lines, "For some years I lived in Itabira / Principally I was born in Itabira. / For this I am sad, proud: of iron. / Ninety percent iron in the sidewalks / Eighty percent iron in the souls." He goes on to say, "From Itabira I brought diverse gifts that now I offer you: / this rock of iron, future Brazilian steel." Drummond then mentions an Afro-Brazilian holy man (*santeiro*), Alfredo Duval, who he had known during his youth. Perhaps only the historian of gold mining would know that Alfredo was the grandson of enslaved Africans who worked for their owner, George Vincent Duval, at the Cata Branca gold mine.[56] Poetry and history converge.

Although Richard did not stop to climb the peak or spend time in Itabira do Campo, he did pause to recount the tale of one of the first (brief) successes among English gold mining companies in Minas. The Cata Branca (White Pit) mine sits on the eastern slope of this massive iron ore deposit less than a mile northeast of the Itabira Peak. Much like the mines at São João, in 1829 British investors raised £60,000 for the Brazilian Company, Limited. Unlike the mines at São João, this deposit quickly produced high yields and the company had some 400 enslaved laborers and dozens of British miners working the lode when it completely collapsed in 1844, killing some 15–20 enslaved African and free English workers trapped in the underground works. The St. John d'el Rey Mining Company bought up the property in 1845, primarily for its machinery and supplies. The board of directors in London also agreed to "rent" the nearly 400 Cata Branca slaves. The British Parliament, at that very moment passed legislation to make it illegal for British citizens to own or purchase slaves anywhere in the world. The agreement with the defunct Brazilian Company called for two "rental" payments, and the St. John agreed to free the slaves after 14 years. This added to the nearly 500 slaves the St. John had purchased between 1830 and 1845, before the ban on purchasing went into effect. British and Brazilian abolitionists, and intense British diplomatic pressure *finally* forced the company to free the 123 surviving Cata Branca slaves in 1879, some 20 years after the end of the "contract."[57]

The Burtons forged on northward along the winding Rio das Velhas, finally reaching a *rancho* surrounded by a few huts. They fortified themselves with one of the region's most famous products—*cachaça*. Although usually translated as "sugarcane brandy," to my unrefined and amateurish alcohol sensibilities it is closer to rum, but with a stronger kick. Richard believed it had the taste of "copper and smoke."[58] Brazil's most famous drink, constantly offered to tourists in Rio, is the *capirinha*, a concoction made from *cachaça*, sugar, limes, and crushed ice. When made well it is very smooth, and the strength of the *cachaça* will slowly but surely catch up with you. Much like Jack Daniel's from Tennessee or tequila from Jalisco, *cachaça* has been legally branded and is a big business today. Similar to craft-brewed beer in many parts of the world, Minas Gerais has numerous small and large distillers scattered all over the region, competing for market share.

After some pungent *cachaça*, dinner, and a few hours' rest, the

INTO THE MINING ZONE

Burton party arose at 3 a.m. and set out on the final stage of their ten-day mule train ride with Mr. Fitzpatrick to their home for the next five weeks—the Morro Velho gold mine and its bustling British expatriate community.

CHAPTER 5

AN ENGLISH VILLAGE IN BRAZIL

"N[oss]a S[enhor]a do Pilar de Congonhas de Sabará"—here names are long, apparently in direct inverse ratio to the importance of the place.

—RICHARD BURTON

Before sunrise on 29 June 1867, the Burtons saddled up for the final stage of their eighteen-day trek from Rio into the gold mining region. They would spend the next five weeks as guests of the St. John d'el Rey Mining Company at Morro Velho while they carefully scrutinized the large and successful operations around them and moved through the surrounding countryside touring many other gold mines, nearly all in English hands. Just over 112 years later, in October 1979, I arrived at the Morro Velho mine in search of a doctoral dissertation topic. I was completely unaware of how this mining town would shape my own life for decades. My only knowledge of Richard and Isabel Burton was a brief comment on the destruction of his papers by a fellow student (and future Rhodes Scholar) during my first year in college. On 24 June 2022, forty years after my first foray to Nova Lima, standing on a hilltop just south of the mine, I took in the view from the exact same location where Richard and Isabel Burton had first glimpsed the village more than 150 years ago. More than forty years, a long academic career, multiple books, and a lifelong fascination with Richard Burton and Brazil had brought me back to this vantage point.

In 1979 I wandered into Nova Lima with only a vague idea of a dissertation project. Over the next decade, the mine and the community became my obsession, first as a doctoral dissertation, then as I transformed it into my first book. I have returned many times to reconnect even as I moved on to other projects, other books, with a much larger scope. In 2022 I came back after decades spent researching, writing, and teaching about Brazil, years of living in Minas Gerais and Rio de Janeiro, and having traveled across nearly all of Brazil's twenty-six states (and Federal District). Uncomfortably close to the end of my professional life as a historian of Brazil, I came back to the place where I began that life. In many ways, Morro Velho is the birthplace of my life as a serious historian. The people and past of this small mining town initiated me into a lifelong pursuit to understand a vast country whose complexity and diversity continue to captivate and confound me nearly fifty years after my first tentative encounters with their language and culture.

Standing on this hilltop where Richard and Isabel had stood more than 150 years ago, and where I myself had first stood more than forty years ago, I was acutely aware of both how intimately I have come to know the language, people, and culture of Brazil—and the limits to my knowledge. Like Richard, I learned to speak Portuguese, then spent years living and working across much of southeastern Brazil. Unlike him, for me Brazil has not been one chapter in a life spent on many continents in multiple languages. Brazil has been the principal focus of my life as a historian, and this country and its people form many chapters in my life—and, unlike the small role they played in Richard's life, they are some of the most important chapters in mine. I find solace in knowing that I have brought to my work an empathy and cultural sensitivity that Richard experienced only in flashes throughout his life and work. At the same time, I am also keenly aware of the limits of my empathy, understanding, and ability to immerse myself in the language and culture of Brazil, or any people. Although I may have a longer and more intense experience of Brazil than Richard Burton, I will always be the outsider looking in, even when completely immersed in the Brazilian heartland.

Mining Town

Remarkably, the gold mine the Burtons visited in 1867 remained the dominant force in this city until very recently.[1] Mining operations expanded enormously at the beginning of the twentieth century reaching peak production at mid-century. The costs of extracting gold ore of declining quality finally shut down a mine that remained in English hands until 1960, then passed to Brazilian investors, and then to a South African company. When the operation finally closed down some fifteen years ago, the Morro Velho gold deposits had been exploited for nearly three hundred years, making it the longest continuously worked gold mine in the world. Today, AngloGold Ashanti has dismantled nearly all the old industrial plant, and there are very few visible signs of a mine that still slices eastward a mile and a half into the earth and once employed eight thousand people, in a town of some twenty-five thousand inhabitants. The headquarters for AngloGold Ashanti are still in the Casa Grande complex, and the old house has been converted into a beautiful museum and company archive.

In 1867 Nossa Senhora do Pilar (Our Lady of the Pillar) de Congonhas de Sabará, was one of some four hundred parishes in the most populous province in the Empire of Brazil, a province that contained just over two million people, one-fifth of Brazil's population.[2] With some five thousand inhabitants in Burton's time, Congonhas had tripled in size by 1900, and then tripled again by the time I first arrived in the late 1970s. When it became an autonomous municipality in the 1890s (escaping the jurisdiction of nearby Sabará), the locals renamed the town Villa Nova de Lima (New Town of Lima) to honor a local writer and politician, Augusto de Lima. They shortened the name in the 1930s to Nova Lima.[3] For close to two centuries, the company and the mine dominated local life as the single largest employer, taxpayer, and purchaser of goods, and—by far—the largest landowner and business enterprise in Minas Gerais.

In Richard Burton's day, the town and the mine faced each other on opposite sides of a broad basin, with the town square roughly a mile southeast of the entrance to the mine. In the twentieth century, blocked by the mine and the Curral Range on its north side, the city gradually spread out to the west and south. A classic working-class company town, by the 1950s its increasingly radicalized labor force, especially those who worked underground, made Nova Lima one of the most militant and unionized cities in all Brazil. As the mine gradually reduced operations over the last thirty years, the company sold off large stretches of its old landholdings to real estate developers. With the construction of expensive gated communities, Nova Lima has now become—ironically—the wealthiest municipality per capita in the state, and a bedroom community for the adjacent state capital, Belo Horizonte.[4]

The Burtons approached Morro Velho along the old Estrada Real that would continue to be the principal route south to Rio until the 1920s. Early on that June morning in 1867, their mule troop trudged along the east bank of the Rio das Velhas through the tiny parish of Santo Antônio do Rio Acima (Saint Anthony Upriver), and then to the even smaller Santa Rita, where several small mines caught Richard's attention, in particular one worked by Dona Florisbella da Horta. This lively widow lived in a substantial home, and she entertained many of the foreign travelers who passed through to visit Morro Velho. "Though already grey and aged," according to Isabel, "she was very buxom and clever, though deprived by circumstances of cultivation."[5] Another two miles farther along, a 270-foot-long bridge spanned the Rio das Velhas at what is now the small town of Honório Bicalho. Today, the old Royal Road on the east side of the river is a rarely used, narrow dirt lane, but the route into town from the river crossing follows the same path, now paved and densely packed with noisy cars, trucks, buses, and motorcycles. At this point, some three miles from the mine, the Burtons had already begun to traverse the St. John property, and to hear the "sturdy northern voices" of English miners.[6] After another mile, the road cut through a gap, and the town and the mine appeared straight ahead, then and today, with a wall of hills on the right side of the old road.

The town the Burtons entered contained a small dirt square with a one-story town council building on the south side. Rising on a fairly steep grade on the north side is an eighteenth-century church that has gone through extensive renovations for centuries.

It certainly does not have the baroque look of its contemporaries in Congonhas, Tiradentes, or São João del Rei. Atop the rising hill behind the cathedral (*matriz*) looms the Rosário Church, the most prominent landmark in Nova Lima even today. Richard disdained the "negro taste" of the structure, traditionally the church of free Blacks and the enslaved.[7] On the east side of the square one of the oldest theaters in Minas Gerais gave the town a small claim to cultural fame. In the 1860s, aside from the main square, one-story structures spread scattered across hillsides around the village and the mine.[8]

A densely constructed urban core around the mine and old square today is home to probably ten times the population of 1867. Although few structures rise more than three stories, nearly every inch of terrain has been covered by buildings, roads, bridges, and pavement. Imperial palms grace the plaza filled with vendors, taxi drivers, and a fair number of hustlers looking for opportunities. Town officials have regularly disfigured the square for decades, first with an ugly 1930s replacement for the colonial theater that harkens back to the brutal, authoritarian architectural styles of the age of fascism. To the right of the theater sits the union hall that once served as the focal point of dozens of demonstrations, debates, and strikes. Most disappointing is the three-story mayor's office on the west side of the square. With its concrete and right angles, it is, for me, the 1970s authoritarian version of public architecture. Fortunately, the old town council building on the south side of the plaza has survived, but its days, no doubt, are numbered.

During June and July (midwinter), a dense fog often settles over the town in the mornings and then burns off with clear, sunny days. The temperature in the mountains of Minas Gerais can drop down into the forties at night but rises into the high seventies in mid-afternoon. I love the bright, azure skies and dry days, but the nights sometimes chill me to the bone. The din of the old stamping works has given way to the chaotic cacophony of urban Brazil—bleating car horns, rumbling diesel trucks, the buzz of zooming motorcycles, mixed with crowing backyard roosters and barking dogs.

For three centuries, geology was destiny for Nova Lima. We will never know who first dug into the south side of Morro Velho, but it was likely in the first or second decade of the eighteenth century, in the early years of the first gold rush in the Americas. As tales of gold gradually streamed southward out of the mountains, thousands of Portuguese and settlers from the areas around the small towns of Rio de Janeiro and São Paulo flocked up rivers and streams into the mountains in search of fortune. By the 1720s, royal authorities began to establish a permanent presence, and crumbling records survive of the first mining claims. In the early nineteenth century, a priest, Antônio de Freitas, worked the Morro Velho mine with more than a hundred enslaved men and women and some simple machinery. A German mining engineer, Wilhelm Ludwig von Eschwege, visited the operations in the 1810s as he surveyed the mining zone for the Portuguese monarchy, and he scorned the priest for refusing to invest in more adequate and efficient machinery, despite the profits it could bring.[9] French naturalist Auguste de Saint-Hilaire passed through the town in 1817 with a severe judgment: "The precious metal is exhausted, the workings become more difficult, and Congonhas presently heralds only decadence and abandonment."[10] He could not have been more mistaken.

When the English investors realized that the property they had purchased at São João del Rei was barren, Superintendent George Herring suggested the company buy the Morro Velho estate, but not before it had been bought up by a handful of British speculators on the scene, one of them the original superintendent at Gongo Soco, George Francis Lyon.[11] The company paid just over $250,000 (£50,000) for the property, machinery, and several hundred enslaved workers. Over the next three decades, a series of British superintendents, dozens of Cornish miners, and hundreds of enslaved laborers steadily expanded the underground operation of the mine hundreds of feet downward and eastward into the old hill at a forty-five-degree angle. Superintendent James Newell Gordon, an Irishman with a Scottish wife, arrived in 1857 for what would be nearly twenty years in residence. The Burtons arrived at the midway point of his long tenure, when the operation was at a productive peak but only months away from a major tragedy.

Richard devotes more than half of the first volume of *Explorations in the Highlands of the Brazil* to describing Morro Velho and the gold mines in the surrounding area, a sure sign of his fascination with the prospects for British investors, especially for investing his own funds. The Burtons spent three of their five weeks in Minas as the exceptionally well-treated guests of Gordon and his large family at "the Queen of the Minas Geraes Mines."[12] In both their accounts, Richard and Isabel repeatedly praise Gordon's management and leadership. They also could not have been more mistaken.

Throughout its long history, the company regularly hosted foreign visitors, sometimes for months. Botanical painter and world traveler Marianne North spent eight months as a guest of the Gordons in 1872–1873. In the 1870s and 1880s, the intrepid North spent time in North America, the Caribbean, Brazil, Chile, Japan, Australia, Indonesia, and India, producing hundreds of botanical paintings and collecting specimens for the Royal Botanical Gardens (Kew). From an aristocratic and politically connected English family, North produced a series of striking paintings of local landscapes and several of the Morro Velho mine works.[13] Even more so than Isabel and Richard, she looked down on the enslaved Brazilians, complimented the company's treatment of them, and repeatedly noted how contented they seemed.[14] Eventually, she invested some of her personal fortune in building her own gallery at the Royal Botanical Gardens at Kew. Today, more than eight hundred of her boldly colored paintings cover the walls of the gallery, providing visitors with a botanical tour of the world.[15]

The Morro Velho rises up 2,657 feet on the north side of the old company grounds, bearing a massive scar on its southern slopes, an enormous pit, hundreds of feet deep, that three hundred years ago was, no doubt, a hillside meadow. Over many decades, dense vegetation has gradually returned to cover most of the sides of the old pit, except a few spots where small landslides have stripped away the hillside. This carved-out cavity—some several hundred yards wide and long, housed the main access tunnels and shafts into the mine until the late 1880s. To the south of the pit is another small valley, in the shape of an inverted U, with the opening of the U facing southeast and the bottom to the northwest. The Cardoso Stream (Ribeirão do Cardoso) runs from west to east coursing along the U, before heading off in a southeasterly direction and into the Rio das Velhas some three miles to the east. Until the 1880s, the industrial complex of the company covered the northern slopes of this valley, rising up from the stream on the northeast side of the U. On the southern side at the top of a small hill sat the Casa Grande (Big House) of Padre Freitas, the building that served as the home of company superintendents until the 1930s. Two wings have projected out the back (west) side of the original structure since the mid-nineteenth century, with a luxurious tropical garden in the middle. In the twentieth century, the company built many additions to the house, mostly for offices. In Burton's time, a two-story *sobrado* (townhouse) served as the guest quarters for visitors on the north side of the Casa Grande. In the early twentieth century, management replaced the old *sobrado* with a long three-story building to house the main company offices.

FIGURE 5.1. Morro Velho mine works, 1872. Image in the public domain. Marianne North.

Today, the South African company that owns the mine, AngloGold Ashanti, has converted the Casa Grande into a lovely museum and archive, and the company has its Brazilian headquarters in the old St. John offices alongside the house. In 1979–1980, I spent ten-hour days in the Casa Grande going through the St. John archives while seated at a table surrounded by the historic library, looking north out the open windows at the gardens and Morro Velho rising up in front of me. Marianne North left us a lovely painting from the exact same spot. Her view across the garden took in the back end of the north wing of the Casa Grande, and across the ravine, the water wheels, aqueducts, and refining machinery of the industrial plant. Framing the background of her painting rises the Morro Velho, already with an enormous scar on its slopes, and a tall black cross on its peak. On the left edge of this colorful vista, one glimpses just the corner of the enormous quarters for more than 1,500 enslaved workers. The English called this substantial *senzala* (enslaved quarters) Boa Vista and Timbuctoo.

A Little Bit of England in Brazil

More than three decades after purchasing the Morro Velho mine, the British company reigned over a business empire that would continue to grow for another eight decades. In 1867 the sleepy town that Saint-Hilaire had dismissed with contempt now formed the hub of a dynamic commercial network, as the mine consumed enormous quantities of timber, charcoal, gunpowder, candles, textiles, beef, corn, rice, sugar, and liquor from across the province to satisfy the company's ever-increasing needs. The population of the town (or more precisely the parish) of Congonhas de Sabará had tripled in size since 1820 to more than 5,000. The mine employed about 150 "Europeans" (overwhelming Brits), almost 1,000 free Brazilians, and nearly 1,500 enslaved—overwhelmingly Africans and first-generation Afro-Brazilians.

Morro Velho was but one of many British communities spread across the globe by the late nineteenth century. As the British formal and informal empires expanded, merchants and diplomats formed vibrant communities, especially in ports around the world. Many other communities took shape around British enterprises—some of them mining companies—from Malaysia to Latin America (such as the Rio Tinto copper mine in southern Spain). By the 1860s, similar English mining villages had taken shape in Mexico, Chile, and Peru.[16] In addition to the 150 company employees, another 200 family members shared an English school, club, Anglican church, and dozens of social clubs—from gardening to theater. Local graveyards were all consecrated Catholic ground, so the company had to petition the imperial government for permission to set up its own cemetery to bury Protestant dead. The first official burial was the chief commissioner from the Gongo Soco mine, J. K. A. Crickett, in 1844. In the 1860s, the British Parliament, after steady lobbying from the company, passed a special law to legitimize British marriages at Morro Velho—sanctified by the Anglican priest. Superintendent Gordon even persuaded the Foreign Office to appoint him as a vice consul (unpaid) to serve not only Morro Velho but also the many other British companies and citizens in the region. It was the only consular position outside the ports of the Atlantic coast.[17]

Within the British community, of course, a clear social

hierarchy prevailed. The "officers" who ran the mine's operations—two dozen men—stood at the top of social and economic pyramid, along with their families. James Newell Gordon, a man Burton could not have portrayed more positively, earned an annual salary of about $10,000 (£2,000) in the 1870s. (Burton earned £600 per annum as consul in Santos.) Heads of departments (mining, hospital, refining, mechanical, company store, for example) made annual salaries of $1,000–$1,500 (£200–£300). The English miners, carpenters, mechanics, and smiths took home monthly salaries of $50–$100 a month (£10–£20). (For comparison, the mason, bricklayer, or smith in London in the mid-nineteenth century made about £8–£12 per month.)[18]

The majority of the steady stream of British miners arriving at Morro Velho were refugees from the copper and tin mining industry of Cornwall, with some from the north country, especially around Durham. Stretching out from southwestern England into the Atlantic, Cornwall was one of the richest mining areas in the world, but one that went through cycles of boom and bust in the nineteenth century. Cornish miners in the nineteenth century circled the globe in search of work ending up in Malaysia, Australia, South Africa, Latin America, Colorado, and California. Some of these "hard-rock miners" settled in mining towns for good, while others eventually returned to Redruth, Camborne, Truro, or Penzance, rarely any wealthier than when they left home.[19]

At Morro Velho, a few Englishmen over the years married local women—much to the dismay of their British supervisors—and settled in. Others married within the British community but chose to stay in Brazil. With their own school, club, and church, some of these families maintained the English language, their Protestant religions (mainly Anglican and Methodist), and culture over generations, while spending only a few weeks in England every three or four years. When I first arrived in Nova Lima in 1979, Mary Gill, the exceptional secretary of the company president, greeted me with flawless British English. Her family went back four to five generations at Morro Velho, and, in my eyes, she was as English as could be. Born at Morro Velho, she had only occasionally visited her ancestral homeland over some four decades. With the closing of the English school in the 1960s, the institutions that had helped sustain British culture began to disappear. Mary's brother-in-law,

John Heslop, was another fifth-generation *morrovelhense* with flawless English, but his youngest children rarely spoke English. Their children speak little or none. Nevertheless, Heslop, Gill, Hodges, Edwards, Morgan, and other English surnames appear regularly today in Nova Lima and central Minas Gerais—living testimony to the once-global reach of the British Empire.

Africans in Brazil

Although the St. John investors and board of directors firmly believed in the superiority of freemen hiring on as wage labor, they would primarily rely on enslaved labor for five decades. The community of enslaved workers at Morro Velho may have been the largest concentration of its kind in Brazil in the mid-nineteenth century, in what was the largest slave community in the Americas for most of the century. The company purchased some five hundred enslaved Africans and Afro-Brazilians in the 1830s and 1840s. Most of them came with the purchase of the Morro Velho estate, but the superintendents bought the rest from slave traders based in Rio de Janeiro. Overwhelmingly, the company agents bought recent African arrivals, mostly adult men sold in the Rio de Janeiro slave market. After 1844 parliamentary legislation barred British citizens—regardless of their country of residence—from purchasing the enslaved. Intense lobbying in the British Parliament by the English gold mining companies in Minas Gerais produced a law that allowed the British companies in Brazil to keep the captive labor they already owned.[20]

For the next forty years, the St. John also engaged in subterfuge to add hundreds more workers to their enslaved community. The company, ironically, benefited from the failure of many of the other English mining enterprises in the surrounding region. When the Cata Branca and Gongo Soco mines collapsed in the 1840s and 1850s, the St. John "rented" hundreds of enslaved workers from companies that had ceased to exist. They leased hundreds more from Brazilian masters all over the surrounding region. The richest landowner in Minas, Francisco de Paula Santos, and his son-in-law Henrique Dumont took control of the hundreds of enslaved at Gongo Soco in 1856 and leased them to Superintendent Gordon.[21] Of the 1,500 enslaved at Morro Velho in 1867, nearly a thousand were rented.

The case of the Cata Branca slaves tragically illustrates the combination of paternalism, arrogance, and racism that pervaded the worldview of Burton and his British compatriots. When the "Brazilian Company" at Cata Branca failed in 1845, the board of the St. John signed a contract with the owners to pay them "rent" for their 385 captive workers on a contract that was supposed to last fourteen years and, at the end of that time, the St. John promised to free the surviving enslaved workers. In what was one of the most shameful actions of the company in its very long history, the Cata Branca workers remained enslaved for thirty-four years. Only after British and Brazilian abolitionists took up their cause, and a long and very public court battle, did the company, reluctantly, free the remaining 123 enslaved Cata Branca workers in 1879. The company's blatantly illegal tactics, and inhumanity, came under scathing attack from Brazil's most famous abolitionist, Joaquim Nabuco, and the British press. We know almost nothing about these forcibly freed men, women, and children, except that many apparently remained in the company's employ—now as paid wage workers.[22]

For the Burtons, and Marianne North a few years later, the St. John was a model master, providing its chattel with a nutritious diet, practical clothing, sturdy housing, attentive healthcare, and, most important, the discipline and training to become "productive and responsible" adults. In the 1850s the company set up a paternalistic system of gradual manumission. Every other Sunday, the hundreds of "Blacks" assembled in front of the Casa Grande, the men to one side, women to the other, decked out in clothing supplied especially for use on this occasion (a *revista* or review). "Meritorious" workers received special stripes and pins for "good conduct" to add to their skirts and shirts. Two striking photographs have survived of the fortnightly *revista*. The first is the frontispiece of the first volume of Burton's *Explorations*, the second, a much finer and up-close photograph the following year by the German photographer Auguste Riedel.

Burton does not reveal the author of his iconic photograph taken from the vantage point of the Blacks' church across the valley from the Casa Grande and looking to the south. More than a thousand enslaved people stand in formation in the foreground, with the Casa Grande to the right and eight company officers

FIGURE 5.2. Revista of the enslaved at Morro Velho, from *Explorations in the Highlands of the Brazil*, 1869. Image in the public domain.

in front of them. On the hill rising up in the background towers the massive two-story company store. Riedel's photograph is even more compelling. In 1868 he accompanied Luís Augusto, the Duke of Saxe-Coburg-Gotha and husband of Princess Leopoldina, on a tour of Minas Gerais and the Northeast. Riedel produced some exceptionally striking photographs, including a dozen of Congonhas de Sabará and Morro Velho.[23]

Unlike the long shot in Burton's book, Riedel planted his camera on the Casa Grande lawn, facing the house and the *sobrado* where the Burtons had resided only months earlier. Hundreds of the enslaved people face the camera, women to the right side, men to the left. The women wear "white petticoats, with narrow red band round the lower third; cotton shawls striped blue and white, and a bright kerchief, generally scarlet, bound round the wool." At the front are the "good-conduct women." To the left, an even larger group of men "are clothed in white shirts, loose blue woolen pants, red caps—Turkish or Glengarry—and cotton trousers."

FIGURE 5.3. Revista of the enslaved at Morro Velho, 1868. Image in the public domain. Auguste Riedel.

The "good-conduct men" also stand in front wearing "tailless coats of blue serge, bound with red cuffs and collars, white waistcoats, overalls with red stripes down the seams, and the usual bonnets."[24] As with all the enslaved people in Brazil, all the men and women are barefoot. A few of the company officers stand on the porch behind the crowd, but ten or so spread out along the front of the assembled multitude. In the middle, with a role of maps in his right hand, the jaunty James Newell Gordon stares directly into the camera. He and most of the officers are dressed in suits and vests with top hats. To Gordon's right is Father Francisco Petraglia, the priest hired to minister to the company's enslaved community. To his left is a dapper gentleman who must be the duke, in light pants, a dark waistcoat, and a dapper hat.

Riedel provided us with another priceless image in front of the Casa Grande on what must have been a blindingly sunny day. In the photograph, some two dozen enslaved men and boys pose arrayed in theatrical finery: white stockings, slippers, knee-length

FIGURE 5.4. Congado in front of Casa Grande, Morro Velho, 1868. Image in the public domain. Auguste Riedel.

satin skirts, long-sleeved white shirts, capes, and plumed headgear. What Riedel caught in a frozen still, Burton observed in motion—a *congada*. Richard had observed similar productions in Africa and Iberia: "A score of men, after promenading through the settlement, came to the Casa Grande . . . All were armed with sword and shield, except the king, who, in sign of dignity, carried his scepter, a stout and useful stick." For Richard, the "'play' was a representation of the scenes which most delight that mild and amiable negro race, orders for a slave hunt; the march, accompanied with much running about and clashing of swords, which all handled butcher knives; the surprise, dragging in prisoners, directions to put to death miscreant ministers and warriors, poisonings and administering antidotes."[25] Despite his vast erudition and previous experience with these "plays," Richard did not realize that what he was observing was a centuries-old recreation of the

Christianization of the Kongo, a performance that bore influences from Africa, Iberia, and the Americas.[26] Riedel's photograph captures the performers posed in front of the Casa Grande, with Gordon and the company officers and Father Petraglia posed on the veranda behind them.

Over four decades, I have come back to these photographs again and again, studying the faces of the English managers and the enslaved workers, wondering what could possibly be going through their minds. The historian has some limited access to the worldview of Superintendent Gordon through his correspondence to the board over two decades, telegraphic notes in his diary, and the accounts of visitors such as Burton. For the other officers, in their anonymity, we can at least make some suppositions, knowing a good deal about men like them through the written accounts of other nineteenth-century Brits abroad. For the enslaved men and women staring back at us from another century, another world, what they might have thought about this moment, or their lives, is almost entirely unrecoverable, as are the lives of most of the people who have lived and died since the rise of the human species. These two compelling photographs capture their existence and humanity and provide us with a rare and fleeting glimpse into their lives. For some of the enslaved, this photograph may be the one and only moment in their lives to have left visible traces.

Henry David Thoreau famously once wrote that the mass of men (and we would now include women) lead lives of "quiet desperation."[27] They certainly lived that desperation largely undocumented, unrecorded, and now inaccessible to historians. Although billions of us now generate massive amounts of electronic data about our habits and thoughts minute by minute, as we move back in time, the amount of data on individual lives, especially of the common person, trails off into emptiness. As much as Facebook or Google accumulates about each of us every day, we know almost nothing about the lives, and certainly the minds, of peasants in ancient Greece or the Maya in ninth-century Guatemala, apart from the archaeological and genetic traces they might have left behind. All the information we have managed to gather on the transatlantic slave trade and slavery in Brazil allows us to reconstruct the probable contours of their existence. Yet how can we ever really know the thoughts, hopes, dreams, and frustration of

FIGURE 5.5. Morro Velho mine works, 1868. Image in the public domain. Auguste Riedel.

the many hundreds of enslaved men and women, speaking many different languages, from multiple places in Africa and Brazil, brought together for this photograph in the Brazilian interior in 1868?

Of Riedel's dozen images of Morro Velho, my favorite is a sweeping, panoramic view from atop the mine plant looking south, the twin towers of the Rosário Church barely visible in the distance atop the hill between the Brazilian village and the English mine. Riedel's vantage point is Marianne North's in reverse. At the center of the photograph is the back wing of the Casa Grande and the veranda where North sat as she painted the Morro Velho and mine works five years later. It is the same spot where I sat for months, working my way through the archive of the St. John d'el Rey a century later. In the center foreground, standing atop an aqueduct (*rego*), a Cornish miner with flowing beard, leather hat, rolled up sleeves, and exposed paunch, points with his right hand off into the distance. Directly below and behind him are the rooftops of the refining plant with its many water wheels and aqueducts that form the centerpiece of North's painting.

Just barely visible in North's painting of the mineworks, in the upper left-hand corner, one glimpses the rooftop of the quarters for the company's enslaved workers. Eventually, two large communal buildings, Boa Vista and Timbuctoo, housed hundreds of enslaved people. Richard described the structures with their "white walls and heavy tiled roofs" with the interior "divided into courts." The few married couples had separate houses, and the unmarried were "divided into gangs of fifteen or twenty" with a place set aside for the girls. Four "black captains" surveilled the complex day and night.[28] Today, a small neighborhood sits on this ground on the western slopes of the Morro Velho with no trace of its past or the lives of the hundreds of enslaved Africans and Brazilians who once lived, loved, and died atop this hill.

Along with the daily, early morning muster for work in the courtyard of the slave quarters at Timbuctoo and Boa Vista, the fortnightly *revista* reminded these Africans and Brazilian-born children of Africans of their subservient, captive status, and of the power of their British masters. Occasionally, Gordon officially freed a few, although the records clearly show that these chosen few, invariably, were older, less useful workers. Over five decades, the company freed, on average, just five enslaved workers per year. After the ceremony, many trooped across the valley to the Catholic church across the ravine from the Casa Grande. Slightly higher up the hill sat the neatly trimmed English cemetery, and a few hundred feet past the church, the unmarked burial ground for the enslaved. Every time I have returned to Nova Lima over the decades, I have made my personal pilgrimage to this hilltop to contemplate the lives of the hundreds interred here. Standing on this cemetery hill with the white Europeans buried to my left, and enslaved African and Afro-Brazilians unceremoniously interred to my right, moves me to mourn the legacies of slavery and slave-owning in Brazil and my own society.

As someone with years of experience traveling through both East and West Africa, Richard Burton felt he had a special authority to speak about Black Africans and their descendants in the Americas. With his brief foray into the United States in 1860, and then two years in Brazil, he concluded that "emancipation will annihilate the African race." Nearly four decades after the abolition of slavery in the British West Indies, and two years after the emancipation of four million enslaved Blacks in the United States, he asserted that, "with very rare exceptions," the African "is viable as a slave recruited from home, not as a freeman in lands occupied by higher blood."[29] Burton's lengthy and extensive exposure to peoples across tropical Africa clearly had not generated any empathy or understanding for the descendants of enslaved Africans in Brazil.

Ever the ethnographer, but not a cultural relativist, Burton the unbeliever made the rounds of religious services on a Sunday morning at Morro Velho, beginning with the Anglican church, where the "mechanics sit on the right side, the miners on the left," and presumably, the company officers sat up front. After hearing singing much like that of a country church in Great Britain, he asked the rhetorical question, "why should men who cannot sing a song, sing psalms and hymns?" Burton quotes his contemporary, John Henry Newman, who left the Anglican priesthood to join the Catholic clergy: "Protestantism is the dreariest of all possible religions, and that the thought of the Anglican services makes man shudder." In a line that must have irritated Isabel when she did final edits on the manuscript, he wonders, "is there any middle term between the God-like gift of reason or the un-reason of Rome?"[30]

The devoutly Catholic Isabel did not attend the Anglican services, but she did accompany Richard to the "Blacks" church the following Sunday. Going into even greater detail, and disdain, he described the Italian priest, Father Petraglia, as "a retired Garibaldian." (Richard, no doubt, spoke in his own fluent Italian to the priest.) The congregation consisted mostly of Blacks with a few lighter-skinned free Brazilians, the whites standing in the front, "the blacks behind; men standing and women squatting on the floor." He found the conduct of the flock "in every way creditable, their singing was better in time and tune, and there was more fervor than in the rival establishment"! The always condescending Richard described the padre's sermon as filled with the severe inculcation of "Faith, Hope, and Charity." "Unhappily," he bemoaned, "the Reverend has forgotten Italian and has not learned Portuguese—here a common phenomenon, and not a little puzzling to Hamitic comprehension."[31] As so often with nineteenth-century ethnographers like Burton, they could describe in impressive detail the lives and customs of the peoples they observed, but they could not bring themselves to find much empathy or insight into their worldview.

Company management regularly bemoaned the "scarcity" of free labor and the inefficiency of the enslaved in their correspondence. Free labor, in fact, was not scarce. Free Brazilian peasants simply chose not to work in the horrendous underground conditions at the wages offered. Work aboveground in the refining works also presented its own dangers—slow poisoning from mercury and arsenic, and dangerous water wheels and rock-crushing machines. The St. John faced labor shortages for the first hundred years of its existence, turning to slavery (until its abolition in the 1880s), then importing labor from China, Japan, Italy, and Spain. The Chinese and the Japanese quickly fled, and the Asian labor experiment failed. Italians and Spaniards arrived in substantial numbers after 1890 but organized the workers and brought on decades of labor strife. Only with the Great Depression and then the labor reforms of Getúlio Vargas in the 1930s did the labor force of more than seven thousand stabilize. The appeal of access to healthcare benefits, minimum wage, vacations, and accrued seniority, ironically, brought the company the labor stability it had failed to achieve for nearly a century.[32]

Two Mine Disasters and a Rebirth

Richard's stay at Morro Velho would not be complete without a foray into the bowels of the mine for an exploration of "the huge Palace of Darkness" with its vast underground workings. In a bold move, Isabel chose to make the descent as well, accompanied by Mary Gordon. The superintendent's wife had been at the mine for some ten years, but had never gone underground, perhaps because of the miners' superstition, one that lasted well into the twentieth century. Although Saint Barbara was the patron saint of the miners, those who labored underground believed it unlucky for women and priests to go into the mine (both wore skirts). Richard descended into the depths with the ever-present Mr. L'pool, followed by Isabel and Mary Gordon. Superintendent Gordon went down the ladders. According to Isabel, Chico "wrung his hands, and implored me not to go, weeping piteously."[33]

There were only two ways down into the underground, via a complex system of wooden ladders or along a thousand-foot-long inclined plane inside an enormous iron bucket (a "kibble" for the Cornish miners, a *caçamba* in Portuguese) designed to haul up a ton of ore. Visitors could ride down the incline in the bucket on a "rough wooden seat" for fifteen bumpy, stop-and-start, anxious minutes. Mr. Gordon advised against using the ladders that the "miners run up and down like cats" (the round trip would have taken hours and physically exhausted them). A water wheel powered the winch (hauling wheel) that raised and lowered the tubular kibbles down a forty-five-degree incline, riding on a small carriage on a rail of iron-shod wood. An iron chain attached the winch to the kibble, and the safety of the trip depended on the strength of the weakest link in the chain. According to Richard, "should the chain snap, there is a catch, to which, however, one must not trust. The big tub careens helplessly forwards and downwards, 'with a surge,' till the strong rivets give way, and the affair becomes a ruin; the fate of a man dashed into this apparently fathomless abyss of darkness may be imagined."[34]

In preparation for the descent, the Burtons dressed in "old clothes," heavy boots, and "stiff leather hats to guard the head from falling stones," with a candle stuck to the hat in a lump of clay. In all his extensive travels, Richard had never seen anything like the huge underground caverns. The "mammoth cave," more than a hundred feet wide and rising up hundreds more, was "a huge stone quarry" illuminated by dozens of oil lamps "glittering like glow-worms." Richard marveled at the timber supports, and the "sight suggested a vast underground forest, but a forest torn up by terrible floods, and dashed about by cataracts in all directions, with the wildest confusion." He describes the scene: "Distinctly Dantesque was the gulf between the huge mountain sides, apparently threatening every moment to fall." In 1881 Pedro II and the Empress Teresa Cristina paid a visit to Morro Velho, descending to the depths of the mine (albeit in a more sophisticated elevator). The drawings of the royal couple in the enormous underground cavern by Angelo Agostini give us a sense of the scene Richard and Isabel took in.[35]

In his version, Richard launched into perhaps the most vivid prose in his two-volume account:

> The ear was struck by the sharp click and dull thud of the hammer upon boring iron, and this upon the stone; each blow invariably struck so as to keep time with the wild chaunt of the borer. The other definite sounds, curiously complicated by an echo, which seemed to be within reach, were the slush of water on the subterranean path, the rattling of the gold stone thrown into the kibbles, and the crash of chain and bucket. Through this Inferno gnomes and kobolds [sprites] glided about in ghostly fashion, half-naked figures muffled by the mist. Here dark bodies, gleaming with beaded heat-drops, hung by chains in what seemed frightful positions; there they swung like Leotard from place to place; there they swarmed up loose ropes like the Troglodytes; there they moved over scaffolds, which, even to look up at, would make a nervous temperament dizzy.

After two hours in this "inferno," the Burtons "left this cathedral'd cavern of thick-ribbed gold, and we were safely got like ore to grass."[36] Days later the chain broke, killing one of the enslaved miners. Mr. Gordon gave the broken link to Isabel as a "memento."

Just four months after the Burtons' visit, fire broke out in the lower levels of the mine and quickly spread throughout the works. The sea of timberwork that had awed Richard fueled the inferno and carried the flames into every area of the underground works. After fighting the blaze for days and eventually diverting water from the aqueducts into the mine, Gordon ordered the shafts sealed to cut off all oxygen. As the fire consumed the timberwork, the walls of the galleries came tumbling down, producing unsettling tremors on the surface and rendering the excavations completely unworkable. In a matter of days, three decades of financial success lay in ashes and rubble. Some two dozen men, free and enslaved, perished beneath the collapsing rock.[37]

Determined to reopen the mine, the company drove new shafts east of the old entrance down into the eastward-sloping vein. It took nearly seven years to return to regular gold production. Company directors then discovered that Gordon had been "milking" the mine of its best ore, and that he had been engaging for years in personal business ventures on the side. He had also refused to free some of the enslaved whose owners had legally emancipated them. The directors fired Gordon in 1876, after nearly twenty years on the job. James Newell Gordon remained a major stockholder and would occasionally show up at stockholder meetings in London to the dismay of the board. To add to Gordon's woes, only months before his dismissal, his twenty-nine-year-old son, Anderson, lost his footing while inspecting machinery, and one of the enormous rock-breaking machines brutally crushed him to death.[38] The Burtons would reencounter the Gordons once more during a visit to London in 1885.[39]

The Burtons' descent into the Morro Velho mine in 1867 bore almost no resemblance to my own foray into the bowels of the mine in 1980, primarily due to the heroic efforts of one exceptional man nearly a century before I arrived. In the late 1880s, the mine collapsed yet again, into complete ruin. Over a few days, the entire underground works came crashing down, burying two dozen workers on the night shift. Apparently, Gordon had not pursued a viable plan of excavation when he reopened the mine. Fortunately for investors, the board had hired a young superintendent, George Chalmers, who arrived in 1884. It proved to be one of the wisest decisions in the company's long history. A civil engineer with some mining experience in Cornwall, Chalmers had been on the job just two years when disaster struck in November 1886.

Undaunted, he drew up plans to reopen the mine and build a completely new industrial plant. He personally convinced the board to back his plan. The company dissolved itself, then reorganized, raising hundreds of thousands in new capital.[40]

Within a few years, the new underground works, located on the eastward-running lode just below the old mine at around 1,500 feet below the surface, began producing ore that then moved through the new refining plant. The 120 massive new stamps filled the valley and surrounding region with a constant din as they pulverized several thousand tons of ore into dust each day. Millions of gallons of water flowed through the refining plant as complex chemical and metallurgical processes separated the gold ore from the sludge. Chalmers gradually built an enormous operation while driving shafts and galleries thousands of feet below the surface, making the Morro Velho the deepest mine in the world by the

AN ENGLISH VILLAGE IN BRAZIL

FIGURE 5.6. Morro Velho mine works, early twentieth century, looking west. Note scarred hillside of old mine at center right. Author's collection. Carlos Gomes.

1920s. From the 1890s to the 1940s, through two world wars, a depression, and a brief civil war in Brazil, the St. John d'el Rey paid its stockholders steady dividends. Had it not been for George Chalmers, the St. John would have closed down in the late 1880s after a half century of operations. Instead, the English company would survive for another eight decades, crushing more than four hundred thousand tons of ore per year that generated one hundred thousand ounces of gold.

Like Richard Burton, Chalmers is one of those extraordinary characters produced by the British Empire in the nineteenth century, one to be admired for his enormous technical abilities but deplored for his attitudes toward those who were not his class or color.[41] He arrived in Brazil in 1884 at the age of twenty-seven with his young bride, who would die within months of tuberculosis, at the age of twenty-five. He then returned to Cornwall and married his deceased wife's sister, against the wishes of her parents. His new wife gave birth to two sons at Morro Velho, in 1887 and 1889, then, in 1900, she also died of tuberculosis. Raised at Morro Velho and schooled in England, the younger son became an electrical engineer and took up residence in the UK to run a consulting firm. George groomed the older son, Alexander George North (AGN), to succeed him as superintendent. George stepped aside in 1924, and AGN took charge, but he clearly did not have the managerial abilities his father had, and the board relieved him of his duties in 1930. George Chalmers died of a heart attack during a trip back to England in early 1928 at the age of seventy-one, just a few hundred yards from the Isabel Burton's old residence on Baker Street in the Marylebone district of London. AGN, and his two sons, John and William, remained in Brazil for the rest of their lives. In late 1980, shortly after I arrived at Morro Velho for the first time, John passed away. He was buried alongside his grandmother in the English cemetery at Morro Velho nearly a century after the arrival of his grandfather at Morro Velho. I was fortunate enough to spend some time with William and his wife at their home in one of the upscale communities built on the St. John's old reservoirs just south of Nova Lima.

The extraordinary richness and detail of the documentation on the British at Morro Velho, and on the life of the Burtons, contrasts starkly with the poverty of information on the many thousands of enslaved and free Brazilians that surrounded them. The historical record has always been skewed toward the upper levels of societies, toward those who are more literate and who have greater control over institutions and structures. The great majority of people throughout history have left little trace, and historians must engage in creative means to find the voices and actions of this vast silent majority. While these humble Brazilians move through the shadows of history, and we glimpse them sporadically and briefly, men like George Chalmers or Richard Burton confront us vividly and directly from the past. While we know very little of the lives, loves, and attitudes of these Brazilians, we have volumes of the words of Chalmers and Burton, along with the testimonies of many of their close friends and enemies. The few photographs of the enslaved people at Morro Velho contrast with the dozens of images of Chalmers and Burton, the latter taken across decades and continents. The mine Chalmers designed may have been his genius and vision, but many thousands of working-class Brazilians built it with their hard labor, just as hundreds of enslaved people excavated and processed the gold in the earlier incarnations of the St. John d'el Rey.

In the polarized atmosphere of the Cold War in the 1950s and 1960s, thousands of unionized miners crippled the English company with strike after strike in an era of rising inflation and eroding wages. In that age of economic nationalism from both the right and left, foreign control of Brazil's largest and most important gold mine became increasingly unviable. With the price of gold frozen at thirty-five dollars an ounce after 1945 and rapidly rising labor costs, making a profit became impossible. A group of US investors bought control of the St. John d'el Rey in 1960 to gain control of the company's vast landholdings, which contained large, unexploited iron ore deposits. The investors promptly sold the iron properties to Hanna Mining Company of Cleveland, Ohio, and Brazilian mining magnate Augusto Azevedo Antunes. Unwilling to take on the failing gold mine, Hanna handed it over to three Brazilian bankers for the symbolic price of one dollar. It was a wise decision for the bankers.[42]

In the 1970s the Anglo American Corporation of South Africa bought control of the Morro Velho mine as the company expanded its holdings into Brazil. At the same time, the price of gold took off, especially after the Iran-Iraq War in 1979, revitalizing the international gold mining industry—and the Morro Velho mine. Overnight the price of gold jumped from two hundred to eight hundred dollars per ounce. Anglo American reopened a number of much smaller old mines in Brazil, especially in Minas Gerais and Bahia. The costs of renovating the old Chalmers mine, however, remained astronomical, as the quality of the ore kept declining. In 2004 Anglo finally shut down the mine and began removing the aboveground industrial plant. For the first time in more than a century, the stamping mills in the enormous reduction plant shut down, and an unknown and eerie silence settled over the mine and the town.

As Richard and Isabel prepared to depart their weeks-long stay at Morro Velho, they could take notes on all the racial and social inequalities with a blithe disregard for the attitudes or views of the thousands of enslaved workers and lower-class Brazilians around them. They did not have to face any noticeable challenges to or questions about their worldview or their attitudes about race

FIGURE 5.7. Morro Velho mine works, looking west, 2022. Marshall C. Eakin.

and inequalities. For the next few weeks, Richard and Isabel would inspect a circuit of gold mines around central Minas Gerais, nearly all owned by English investors and operated by British managers. Seemingly, expatriate Brits were everywhere in this rugged, mountainous mining zone.

CHAPTER 6

ENGLISHMEN, GOLD, AND IRON

> Here all men, especially free men who are not black, are white; and often a man is officially white, but naturally almost negro. This is directly opposed to the system of the United States, where all men who are not unmixed white are black.
>
> —RICHARD BURTON

Never short on words, from the 1840s to the 1860s, Richard Burton regularly produced accounts of each of his expeditions in two or three volumes. *Explorations of the Highlands of the Brazil* appeared in 1869 in two stout tomes of around 450 pages each, including a map of Brazil with Burton's route traced in red (see page 2). The second volume begins with his departure from Sabará on the Rio das Velhas and ends with his arrival at the mouth of the São Francisco River three months later. The first volume runs 443 pages—about 100 pages on the trip from Rio de Janeiro into Minas Gerais and his arrival in the mining zone at São João del Rei, another 100 pages from his inspection of the mines from São João del Rei to Morro Velho, and then nearly 250 pages on his five weeks at Morro Velho and travels through the surrounding region. Burton carefully catalogs the mines as he closely inspects them, opining on the prospects for each.

The subtitle of his two volumes, *A Full Account of the Gold and Diamond Mines, Also, Canoeing down 1500 Miles of the Great River São Francisco, from Sabará to the Sea*, captures the principal focus of each volume. Although he eyes all he encounters through the lens of economic opportunity, the first volume takes him through a region that had been covered by many other foreign travelers—English, French, German—for more than five decades. This is not the terrain of the intrepid British explorer revealing lands and peoples previously unknown to fellow Europeans. Burton frames the second volume as more one of the adventurer or explorer moving downriver through territory not well known, and certainly not as well traveled as Minas Gerais. Tracing the length of the São Francisco River certainly does not compare to the search for the source of the Nile, but the region was still relatively new to the outside world—and to most Brazilians.

Brits, Business, and Empire

Burton's worldview, his role as consul, and his self-interest frame his detailed scrutiny of these mining properties. As with much of his large body of work and that of other nineteenth-century travelers and explorers, Burton sees himself as moving at the forefront of the rational, scientific, and progressive movement to uncover and reveal the vast diversity of the world and its peoples. To explore is to learn, and then to exploit. He embodied "the sheer gall of a small island nation that had never set out to rule the world, and yet did so with such flair."[1] Burton moved in a Victorian world of immense optimism about the ability of science and rationality to reveal and unlock the mysteries of the universe for the improvement of humanity. His belief in science, his antagonism for organized religion and religious beliefs, and a sense of moral superiority that the power and sweep of the British Empire seemed to confirm undergirded a Victorian worldview that he shared with so many of his compatriots. Yet his vast ethnographic experience, attraction to Islam, and almost clinical fascination with sexual practices set him apart from most of his contemporary upper-class Englishmen, even the more anthropologically oriented of them.[2]

As consul in Santos, part of Richard's job was to survey the economic potential of Brazil, always with possible British investment and expertise in mind. His most powerful arguments to persuade his superiors to allow him months of leave to travel into the interior were founded on the importance of reconnoitering the region for economic opportunities and checking on the state of British investments in the mining region, as well as the hundreds of British subjects residing in Minas Gerais. Edward Thornton's official request to Foreign Secretary Lord Stanley requesting the leave of absence for Burton pointed out that the "great undeveloped resources" in the region were poorly known and that "it would be decidedly advantageous to commercial interests that it should be visited and reported upon by an observant and intelligent traveller."[3] From the correspondence of Richard and Isabel we know that the personal opportunities for investment and profits also drove Richard's careful study of the gold mining zone and its many properties. During his years as consul in Trieste, Richard and Isabel purchased shares of a number of mining ventures in Africa and the Middle East.[4] His interest in gold and diamonds did not stem just from his desire to enlighten his readers and his superiors. Richard's tour of the gold mining properties in July 1867 was in many ways the high point of his professional—and personal—interest in the commercial and economic prospects of the Brazilian interior.

Richard accompanied Superintendent Gordon to the nearby mine at Cuiabá in early July, just a few days after his arrival at Morro Velho. In one of the quirks of his account, he places the visit at the very end of the first volume, after his description (in early August) of Sabará, and just before he begins his river voyage. This brief, two-day trip provided him with an introduction to the smaller mines in the region, the complicated connections among the various English mines and managers, and a link to Isabel's friend in São Paulo, the infamous Marquesa de Santos.[5]

Nearly all the significant gold deposits of Minas Gerais are scattered across the center of the state through what geologists have labeled the Iron Quadrangle (see fig. 4.3). The French founding director of the School of Mines in Ouro Preto, Claude-Henri Gorceix, in the 1870s described this geological formation as a "heart of gold in a chest of iron."[6] With the recent closure of the Morro Velho mine, a scattered group of gold deposits continue to produce in the region. Brazil, today, accounts for a tiny fraction of world gold production.[7] As gold mining declined over the last century, iron mining took off. Brazilian and multinational corporations moved into Minas Gerais and developed some of the largest iron ore mining operations in the world. The chest of iron now overshadows what little is left of the shrunken heart of gold.[8]

As Richard describes moving through these gold mines in 1867, the reader meets a strange assortment of characters struggling to make them profitable. Only after many decades of my own excavations in the incredibly dispersed sources on three continents have I come more fully to understand the seedy web of Brits engaged in financial schemes, fraud, and acrimony often woven together through kinship ties. Much like the euphoria that accompanied the opening of eastern Europe and Russia in the 1990s, the wars for independence opened Latin America to a flood of foreign investment in the 1820s and 1830s. In both cases, nearly two hundred years apart, the initial enthusiasm soon ran aground from a lack of infrastructure, local resistance to sudden change, greedy speculators, and cronyism. A wave of British investment flooded into Latin America, primarily through the London Stock Exchange, ostensibly to create companies to build roads, ports, utilities, and reopen old mines, especially in Mexico and Brazil. One historian estimated that nearly four hundred mining companies were floated on the London Exchange in the 1820s and 1830s, and less than a score ever yielded a profit for stockholders. The vast majority took investor funds (often for their own enrichment) and rarely moved very far beyond the enthusiastic initial company prospectus.[9]

In Brazil, the royal family's arrival in Rio de Janeiro in 1808 opened the country to foreign merchants, primarily the British, after three centuries of closed colonial rule.[10] John Mawe, a British mineralogist, wrote one of the very first travel accounts (published 1812) about his visit to Diamantina and other parts of Minas Gerais.[11] Among the many merchants moving into Rio was Edward Oxenford. In his early twenties, Oxenford and his younger brother, Ferdinand, spent a decade learning their way around commercial and political networks in Rio. Through the influence of powerful, aristocratic friends, he persuaded Emperor Pedro I to issue a decree in September 1824 permitting the formation of the Imperial Brazilian Mining Association to exploit the gold mine at Gongo Soco in central Minas Gerais. As in much of Latin America for centuries, the monarchy controlled all subsoil rights, and royal decrees granted concessions to investors to work underground claims in exchange for paying the royal "fifth" on production. After 1824 all prospective mining companies followed the same pattern of acquiring a decree from the Braganza monarchy to work mining concessions. Oxenford was seemingly everywhere in the mining zone for the next three decades, speculating, buying and selling properties, causing legal problems, and engaging in multiple fraudulent schemes.[12]

Oxenford obtained the royal decree, arranged to buy the Gongo Soco property from the Baron of Catas Altas, then sold his claim on the property to the newly formed Imperial Brazilian Company in London—at a profit. Initially, he served on the company board, but he quickly became a problem, demanding more compensation from the directors and arguing that the mine claim belonged exclusively to him. He and the company parted ways acrimoniously after a substantial payment and Oxenford immediately negotiated the purchase of the Cocais mine at São João do Morro Grande (Saint John of the Big Hill), just a few miles north of Gongo Soco, from the Baron of Cocais. The baron was the cousin of the Marquesa de Santos's husband, and he even wrote to her in the 1820s to try to persuade Pedro's mistress to lobby for him to concede a royal mining concession to Oxenford to exploit the mine. The marquesa apparently ignored the request, but other prominent Brazilian aristocrats intervened, and Oxenford got his second mining concession from the emperor.[13]

He then floated another company on the London Exchange, the National Brazilian Company, but subsequently refused to hold stockholder meetings or to hand over the accounts to the investors. As at Gongo Soco and Morro Velho, a crew of Cornish miners, a superintendent, and a Cornish mining captain, Thomas Treloar, arrived in 1834, at precisely the same moment that the St. John started up operations at Morro Velho. On the side, Oxenford purchased the Cuiabá mine between Sabará and São João do Morro Grande. For years he diverted funds and labor from the Cocais mine to work his own operations at Cuiabá. He eventually sold his properties to the National Brazilian Company, and facing legal action from investors in England, in the mid-1850s he fled to France, where he lived comfortably in Tours until his death in 1876. Before departing Brazil, he engaged in yet one more financial scam.[14]

Given the deeply intertwined English communities and mining companies, Gordon had, no doubt, fully informed Richard about Oxenford and his sordid affairs. As they left Sabará and took the road to Cuiabá, the group followed the "Lilliputian riverine valley" of a stream that has since disappeared from the landscape, plowed under with piping and paved over with a highway. By the 1860s, the East Del Rey Mining Company (another St. John copycat) had purchased the Cuiabá mine and surrounding properties from what Richard called the "grantor," "formerly of Minas Geraes, now of France," obviously referring to the fugitive Oxenford. They passed the old casa grande where Oxenford had, for a few years, installed his wife and infant daughter. The nearby village of Pompeu "often mentioned by travellers" consisted of "a wretched chapel and broken walls," all that remained "of its old magnificence." A few miles past Pompeu, they arrived at what remained of the Cuiabá mine and were "received with a true Scotch greeting by Mr. Brown."[15]

The Scottish-born James Pennycook Brown had served as Oxenford's secretary in London during the 1850s but eventually turned against him after Oxenford returned to London from Brazil, emptied the safe of the company's records, and fled to France. The investors who had been suing Oxenford in British courts ironically had sent Brown out to Brazil in 1859 to attempt to salvage company operations at Cocais. Brown remained in Brazil until his death in 1873, apparently developing a long and intimate relationship with one of his enslaved women. During those fourteen years, he deeply enmeshed himself in the network of British mining enterprises. Just before his final departure from Brazil in 1856, Oxenford had "rented" out three hundred enslaved workers to work for Mariano Procópio Ferreira Lage to help build and maintain the famed "Union and Industry" road between Petrópolis and Juiz de Fora, the highway the Burtons had recently traversed and admired. Oxenford pocketed half of the £23,000 ($115,000) payment, which must have made his "retirement" in Tours very comfortable.[16]

Short on funds, labor, and equipment, Brown could not salvage the Cocais operation although a variety of investors would continue to try to make a go of the property for decades afterward. He moved on to work for Gordon and the St. John as the manager of the "Blacks Department" in the 1860s, overseeing a thousand captives, many of them the Cocais slaves Oxenford had "rented" to the company. In the striking Riedel photograph of the "slave *revista*," Brown stands front and center between the two enslaved groups of men and women and planted firmly between James Newell Gordon and the Duke of Saxe-Coburg (see fig. 5.3). His flowing white beard reaches down to his arms folded across his chest and his white locks down his upper back. When Burton appeared in 1867, Brown was living on the Cuiabá estate with his niece Mary Dundas, trying to make a go of it there. Gordon would serve as the executor of Brown's estate in 1873. Apparently, some suspected poisoning when Brown was quickly interred at Cuiabá.[17] At Gordon's urging the St. John's board purchased the Cuiabá mine under dubious circumstances that led to more than a decade of legal wrangling with the investors Brown was supposedly representing back in England.[18] Although the Morro Velho mine finally closed down in 2004, AngloGold Ashanti reopened the Cuiabá mine in the 1990s. Incredibly enough, the small mine Richard visited in early July 1867 at Cuiabá has become the most important asset of the successors to the St. John d'el Rey. Worked on and off for two centuries with little success, Cuiabá today forms the most important part of AngloGold Ashanti's operations in Brazil.[19]

Just as the crude technology of the mid-nineteenth century made it difficult to turn a profit at Cuiabá, the highly sophisticated operation today reflects the early twenty-first century, highly industrialized Brazil. AngloGold Ashanti has turned the old Casa Grande into a museum that not only preserves the past but also introduces the public to current operations in the most positive light.[20] A virtual reality headset offers the visitor a stunning visit to the Cuiabá mine from the massive scarred and scraped mountaintop down three thousand feet via the main shaft. Underground operations are not only highly mechanized, but operators on the surface control much of the blasting, excavation, and crushing machinery with equipment that looks like sophisticated video game technology. Operators direct massive equipment deep beneath the earth reducing human presence, injuries, and fatalities. AngloGold Ashanti is one of a handful of global mining companies that have emerged out of a consolidation over the past few decades that has concentrated the extraction of the planet's mineral resources by multinationals operating on every continent. Just as the incipient English mining companies of Burton's time reflect the nature of industrial capitalism in the mid-nineteenth century, Anglo Gold reveals the face of postindustrial capitalism in the early twenty-first century. With its enormous iron resources, Brazil has become a key player in this arena.

A Circuit of Foreign Owned Mines

After their short foray to Cuiabá, Richard and Isabel returned to Morro Velho, and a week later they began their circuit of the other English mining companies. Over the next twelve July days, Richard and Isabel, along with Superintendent Gordon and the ever-present Mr. L'pool, circled the Caraça mountain range heading east to Cocais, then southward along the eastern edge of Caraça through several small mines and to the colonial city of Mariana (see fig. 4.3). They visited the Passagem Mine between Mariana and Ouro Preto, and then headed north, back to Morro Velho along the western slopes of the Caraça range. Averaging about twenty-five miles a day on mules and horses, on this expedition the Burtons passed through some of the oldest geological formations on the planet. The bedrock that underlies most the region dates back some 2.8 billion years. During the last billion years the geological structure has been alternately uplifted, heavily eroded, buried beneath the sea, covered with layers of sediment, and crumpled and crushed by movements of the earth's crust. About 500 million years ago, the intrusion of superheated magma from deep within the earth recrystallized minerals in the ancient bedrock, forming major deposits of iron, manganese, gold, and other valuable ores.[21]

The group set out at 9 a.m. on Wednesday, July 10, with five riders and ten mules—"allowing to each of us a change." The fifth rider was their guide. Two of the company's enslaved men accompanied them on foot: Miguel, who "was assisted by a sturdy and very black black, João Paraopéba, named like Lord Clyde from the nearest river." Gordon also brought along his "servant Antonio, gorgeous in the usual lively Minas livery, tall glazed hat and top-boots, turned up with gamboge-yellow; a large silver goblet, venerable article of luxury and ostentation, hung by a chain over his shoulder."²² It is unlikely that Antonio was enslaved, as he was not barefoot, a universal trait of the enslaved in Brazil. Although not mentioned or counted in the entourage in this section of the book, it is clear that the ever-present Chico also accompanied Isabel, most likely on foot.

The party descended the Casa Grande hill eastward into the basin of the Cardoso Stream, an area that served in the nineteenth century as the final refining stop for the most difficult (refractory) crushed ore. Extending several hundred yards along the stream and southward toward the town, this flat stretch was known for at least a century as the Praia (Beach). When George Chalmers rebuilt the mine at the end of the nineteenth century, he spread out most of the new mine plant—crushing mill, refining works, shops, and power plant—in this short, flat valley (see fig. 5.6). The Burton party crossed a small bridge on their left (over the Cardoso) and headed up a steep hill that separates the mine from the nearby town of Raposos (Foxes), a mere five miles from their starting point.²³ One of the earliest settlements in Minas, located on the east side of the Rio das Velhas, the local church, Nossa Senhora da Conceição (Our Lady of the Conception) lays claim to be the first built in Minas (1714). The St. John began mining gold on the west side of the river in the early twentieth century, transporting the ore via an aerial tramway in enormous metal buckets to the Morro Velho processing plant to the west.²⁴ When the Burtons passed through in July 1867, apparently no one was exploiting these deposits, and the entire parish contained about six thousand inhabitants, about 15 percent of them enslaved.²⁵

Moving quickly through Raposos, the group rode "up an ugly hill" and entered a pleasant plateau (*chapada*). They followed the northern slope of the ridge nearly due east, prompting Isabel to declare she was reminded of "crossing the Wiltshire Downs," her family homeland in southwestern England. "Gentle swells," Richard observed, "heave up the surface, backed by bolder elevations, confused and billowy ridges forming an irregular crescent on each side."²⁶ The enormous demand at Morro Velho for timber and charcoal had already begun to thin the old woods, a process that would strip the region over the next few decades. As Richard passed through, "Every hollow had its dense coppice hanging from the sides, and forming thick and thicketty jungle along the bottom."[27] The striking colors of the forest contrasted with the large silvery leaves of the cecropia trees, a favorite of three-toed sloths, and locals in search of wood for flutes or piping.

At midday, the dusty group rode into the small town of Morro Vermelho (Red Hill) that Richard describes as "a mere Arraial [village], a long, straggling 'encampment,' like a fair or market, with one street."[28] Continuing due east through the hills, the Burtons passed quickly through the Roça Grande (Large Clearing) mine and came upon "a tumbledown ranch" that Isabel described as "the wildest, most desolate, and most beautiful spot imaginable."[29] The Cornish mining captain, a Mr. Brockenshaw, offered the group a meal, which they declined in their desire to make it to their next stop before dark. As with so many of the properties Burton visited, this was yet another small operation, with just "fourteen very depressed white men, a few free Brazilians, and no slaves" in sight.[30] A Canadian company has reopened the mine in recent years, and it is a small, well-equipped, and profitable operation.[31]

An enormous, water filled, inactive, open-pit iron mine now blocks the path the Burtons followed from Roça Grande to Gongo Soco in 1867. This carved-out wound in the chest of iron looms on the ridge hundreds of feet above the ruins of the long-exhausted heart of gold that was the Gongo Soco mine. The Burtons approached the abandoned gold mine from the northwest along the west to east ridgeline, dropping down the southeastern slopes through dense vegetation, what Richard called "closed forest" (*floresta fechada*). Uncharacteristically, Richard waxes lyrical for several pages on the *mato dentro* ("inner woodland formation"), what many would translate loosely as the "bush." For Isabel, the "the immense avenues of leafage looked like mysterious labyrinths, with castles and arches of ferns forty feet high."[32] After a century and a half of despoliation at the hands of several hundred thousand Portuguese invaders, enslaved Africans, and their descendants amid efforts to farm, ranch, and extract minerals, the forests of the mining zone in the mid-nineteenth century bore visible environmental scars. Burton could see that much of the forest around him had long ago been cleared and had "been succeeded by tall second growth, stunted scrub, and the sterile fern. Here and there, however, vast tracts of the primitive timber remain."[33] Just as it had with so many foreign travelers, this dense old growth forest captivated the Burtons.

Richard marveled at "this pomp and portent of nature, this disorder of vegetation, through which the tropical sun shot rare shafts of golden light." The forest floor was "a layer of soft, spongy, chocolate-coloured humus, the earth of leaves, trunks, and root stools, in which the well-girt walker often sinks to the knee. After travelling through it, man learns to loathe the idea of a march amid the state of nature."[34] The description in these pages also reflects his nineteenth-century notions of climate and geography as key determinants of racial types. The "suffocating, damp heat" caused "a cold perspiration to follow the slightest exertion," and the "nights and mornings are chill and raw; and during storms the electricity is excessive." Fevers abounded, and the few human beings who lived in this environment were, for Richard, "a sickly race, sallow and emaciated, bent and etiolated," as if fresh from prison.[35]

Unimpressed with the human inhabitants, the "endless diversity" of the verdant forest awed the normally restrained Burton. Around him, "every shade of green, however, appears from the lightest leek to the deepest emerald." Epiphytes and parasitic vines enveloped the massive trees. "Every tall, gaunt, ghastly trunk, bleached with age and grimly mourning its departed glories, is ringed and feathered, tufted and crowned with an alien growth that sucks, vampire-like, its life-drops till it melts away in the hot moisture, and sinks to become vegetable mould." Each of the ancient trees was "converted into a conservatory, a botanical garden, 'un petite monde,' numbering a vast variety of genus and species, admirable in diversity of aspect, and clothed in a hundred colours—with truth, it is said that a single trunk here gives more forms than a forest in Europe."[36]

As they began slowly to move down the steep hillside directly into the decaying Gongo Soco mining complex, out of the forest emerged the irrepressible James Pennycook Brown "with a merry face and snow white hair and a beard like floss silk down to his waist," looking, to Isabel, like "a picture of God the Father."[37] Given his long history with Oxenford, Brown must have given the Burtons an earful on the Gongo Soco mine and the Imperial Brazilian Mining Company, "once gay and rich, now worked out, abandoned, and poor."[38] From the late 1820s until the mine collapsed in ruin in 1856, Gongo Soco had been the first and most

FIGURE 6.1. Sketch of the Gongo Soco mining complex, 1839. Image in the public domain. Ernest Hasenclaver.

lucrative in Brazil. Its success had, in fact, been used to promote the creation of another half a dozen gold mining companies on the London Exchange including the St. John d'el Rey, Brazilian Company (Cata Branca), and National Brazilian (Cocais).[39]

Employing hundreds of enslaved Blacks and dozens of Cornish miners, the Imperial Brazilian tunneled into the very hillside the Burtons now descended. The substantial mining complex—hauling shafts, stamp mills, refining houses, chapel, store, hospital, and casa grande—barely a decade earlier had bristled with activity but now sat empty and abandoned along the road that ran west to east along the base of the mountains. A few old and infirm Blacks emerged from the crumbling slave quarters (*senzalas*) to beg for alms. For Richard, it was "melancholy to see ruins in a young land, grey hairs upon a juvenile head."[40] The Imperial Brazilian Company had gone into debt to the powerful Francisco de Paula Santos in its final years, and he took control of the mine and its five hundred enslaved laborers, renting them out for the construction of the Union and Industry toll road, and then to Gordon and the Morro Velho mine.[41]

Each time I return to Gongo Soco, the fragility of memory and history weigh heavily on me as I sweat my way through the ruins in Brazil's sunny, tropical "winter." Much like Morro Velho, the longest enduring material culture are the crumbling walls of the superintendent's home and a small English cemetery. Even though iron mining multinationals have ripped away much of the mountainside above the old gold mine, the iron ore ran out before the company could descend farther down the slopes where the old English company once prospered. The Instituto Estadual do Patrimônio Histórico e Artístico, or IEPHA, the state institute for preserving historical sites in Minas Gerais, managed to demarcate the site and protect it, although entry is possible only through the company's guard post.[42] Blocked by the massive open-pit mine crater to the west, I approached the site on a winding dirt road from Barão de Cocais, some ten miles to the east. When I first came here in the 1990s, tropical forest had taken over most of the old buildings. Along with a team of researchers from the IEPHA, I struggled to make my way among the three-foot-thick walls of the company hospital, casa grande, and the remains of a few refining rooms. On a later trip in 2019, the area had been completely cleared of trees and bushes that had slowed me in my earlier visit. The crumbling ruins now rise up on cleared fields alongside the old road that the Burtons traversed coming from the opposite direction.

FIGURE 6.2. Gongo Soco ruins, 2019. Marshall C. Eakin.

A few hundred feet above the valley floor, a handful of English graves remain surprisingly intact on the crest of a small hill. Surrounded by a grove of trees and a stone wall surrounding a 40-by-40-foot square plot, impressive stone slabs cover the burial plots. Nearly two centuries after these interments, intact 3-by-6-foot stone slabs still cover the graves of the British who perished deep in the Brazilian interior thousands of miles from home. Carved by an

English stone mason, each plinth contains information about the deceased with a poem etched in the polished stone. Anne, the wife of mine Captain William Jeffrey of Gwennap, Cornwall, passed away in August 1841 at the age of thirty-eight. The carvings on her grave remain clean and easily visible. At the foot of her burial slab, the mason carved these words from the poet, George Gordon Lord Byron, "When sorrow weeps over virtue's sacred dust / our tears become us and our grief is just / such were the tears he shed who grateful pays / This last sad tribute of his love and praise." As with most of these old mining sites, we have no idea where the English managers buried the enslaved. They certainly left no enduring stone markers or poetry.

Iron and Steel

Each time I return to Gongo Soco, the power of iron mining companies and their impact on the local environment have increased. All across the Iron Quadrangle mountaintops have disappeared, replaced with reddish-brown terraced hillsides barren of any vegetation. In some locations, like Gongo Soco, Bento Rodrigues just to the south, or Brumadinho to the west, strip mining produced enormous craters now filled with wastewater from tailings. Dams across the quadrangle hold back billions of gallons of deadly liquefied toxic materials. Vale and other multinational mining companies claim these dams and reservoirs are safe and secure. Disastrous accidents in recent years have proven them wrong killing hundreds of Brazilians and wreaking a series of ecological catastrophes.[43]

Despite Richard's sharp appreciation for the forests of the mining zone and the impact the enterprises had already taken on the environment, it is unlikely he would have much sympathy for today's environmentalists. After riding all day through old growth and second growth forest around Gongo Soco, the Burtons finally reached their destination. At 6 p.m., "waxing tired after our long day of mist, drizzle, sunshine, and many emotions," the Burtons reached an iron foundry on the estate of a local fazendeiro. They were received "with the normal Brazilian hospitality," and their hosts "lost no time in supplying us with what our souls most lusted after, supper and sleeping gear."[44] Richard describes the fazenda as "the usual country abode" with a ground floor to house the animals and "negroes." Up a wooden staircase, the guest room took up the front of the main floor with a kitchen and "women's quarters" at the back. "The front room is furnished with a wooden table, always six inches too tall, a bench or two for the humbler sort, and a dozen chairs with cane backs and bottoms; these are famous for wearing out overalls, and are instruments of torture to those who remember the divan." The uncovered walls were adorned "with hunting trophies, weapons, horse-gear, prints of the Virgin, the saints," and sometimes a mirror or a "Yankee clock." In the "wild parts" one might find a "portable oratory" a couple of feet high covered with "patron saints, prints, flowers, and bouquets."[45] In the windowless guest room, the travelers found "one or two cots, bottomed with rattan, hide, or board, and mattresses stuffed with grass or maize leaves." A tablecloth always adorned the main dining table, along with a toothpick holder, something Richard found indispensable in the tropics. "Altogether," he declared, "the small fazenda lacks many things desirable to the comfortable traveler. But in its roughness there is a ready hospitality, and, if the master be a traveler or an educated man, a hearty good will and a solicitude about the comfort of his guest which I nowhere remember except in the Brazil."[46] High praise from the normally irascible world traveler.

The next morning, the party inspected the fazendeiro's iron factory, a small but effective adaptation of a Catalan forge, a rough masonry bench, some ten feet long and two feet high. A "negro"—undoubtedly an enslaved Black man—stoked the charcoal hearth, and worked the high-grade hematite, ultimately to produce both cast and wrought iron bars. As Richard observes, the hematite in Minas contains very high percentages of iron ore (60–85 percent), more than double that of hematite in England. An enterprising Frenchman, João (Jean-Antoine Felix Dissandes de) Monlevade set up an iron foundry around 1820 near the origins of the Rio Doce (Sweet River) some thirty miles to the east of Gongo Soco.[47] He pioneered the exploitation of iron ore and iron working for the next five decades—using enslaved labor. The town that gradually took shape around his foundry bears his name today, and local life revolves around the ArcelorMittal iron and steel works.[48] In the nineteenth century, the old Frenchman supplied the local mining establishments and textile mills with iron tools and bars. Although many locals and foreigners had already remarked on the enormous iron lands in the region, it would be more than fifty years before the transportation advances of steamships and railways would make it possible to mine the region's ore profitably.

With the exception of the Morro Velho and few other small gold mines, the heart of gold no longer attracted investment or economic activity to central Minas after the late eighteenth century. In the 1920s, the Belgian-Luxembourg consortium ARBED (Aciéries Réunies de Burbach-Eich-Dudelange) invested heavily in building iron and steel mills on the same spot as Monlevade's foundry, and in Sabará, effectively initiating the large-scale industrial exploitation of the massive iron deposits of the quadrilateral. In the 1950s, the recently created, state-run Companhia Vale do Rio Doce began to mine and export the ore on a scale that would eventually make it the largest iron mining company in the world. It would carve up the breast of iron on a massive scale. ARBED's Belgo Mineira steel company merged with the massive Indian Mittal Steel in 2006 forming ArcelorMittal, the world's largest steel company, whose mills are scattered across the region.[49]

After "an ample breakfast" on 11 July 1867, the Burtons headed east into the town of São João do Morro Grande, known today as Barão de Cocais, after the aristocrat who had worked so closely with Edward Oxenford. At the "decayed village" of Brumado to the south, they changed mules at the casa grande of Commander João Alves de Sousa Coutinho, who decades earlier had been a favorite of Pedro I. What was "once a gay house in great repute" was now "withered" and "fallen into decay." Richard noticed the red clay hillsides and streams scarred by decades of "hydraulicking."[50] Much like Cuiabá, the small mines in this region have experienced a resurgence in recent years, and the route from Barão de Cocais to Mariana bears the scars of decades of strip mining. Huge Scania and Mercedes trucks fill the two-lane highway, carrying loads of ore to the railway cars that flow in long trains to the coast in the state of Espirito Santo just north of Rio. The rust-colored soil produces dust that covers nearly everything—the roads, surrounding forests, and vehicles. The towns on Richard's route are still small, and many of the locals work for the mining companies.

Heading south-southeast, the Burtons came upon yet another small English mine in the adjoining parish of Santa Bárbara. The Pari mine has been worked on and off for at least two centuries, and today is one of several mines owned by the Canadian Jaguar Mining Company.[51] In 1861 British investors created the Santa Barbara Gold Mining Company Limited, and spent about £60,000 purchasing and equipping the operation. When the Burtons passed through in mid-1867, the works were nearly abandoned, "in the hands of an ex-mechanic, two English miners, and a very few free Brazilians."[52] After consuming some oranges and wine, the travelers bid adieu to their host and "the extremely '*entêté*' [ornery] Mr. Brown."[53] Rising up in front of them loomed the imposing Serra da Caraça, the road to Mariana, and the provincial capital, Ouro Preto.

CHAPTER 7

LIFE AND DEATH IN MARIANA

> My experience is that on matters of pure faith or belief—that is to say, taking statements on trust—all nations are as nearly equal as their development of imagination, of the marvelous, permits them to be. Amongst the most civilized peoples of Europe it is right easy to point out tenets which, submitted to the eyes of reason, appear identical with those held by the savages of the Bonny River [Nigeria].
>
> —RICHARD BURTON

The eleven-day tour of these gold mines effectively took the Burtons in a circle around the imposing Serra da Caraça, the "very pivot and centre of the mid-Minas gold mines" (see fig. 4.3).[1] On the morning of Thursday, 11 July, as they headed due south toward their next stop, Catas Altas (High Excavations), the Caraça range rose up thousands of feet directly in front of them. A series of craggy peaks, the range has the profile of a sleeping giant, "a grisly spectacle," according to Richard, "that Big Face, a huge mass of iron slate towering several thousand feet above the high downs." To his eye, the giant's face assumed "the appearance of a rhinoceros head."[2] In the mid-eighteenth century, at the height of the gold boom, a mysterious priest from Portugal built a hermitage high atop the range on a three-square-mile plateau. In the early nineteenth century, the royal family turned the buildings over to priests from the Mission Congregation, founded by Saint Vincent de Paul in the seventeenth century. These French priests created a private school (*colégio*) for boys alongside the hermitage. For the next 150 years, the school educated the sons of the Minas elite, producing a long line of prominent writers, administrators, and politicians, including two presidents of Brazil.

FIGURE 7.1. View of Caraça, 1872. Image in the public domain. Marianne North.

The experience of these young boys must have been chilly and austere despite their location in the tropics. Rising up to elevations as high as six thousand feet, cold nights and misty mornings would have been the pattern of their days. From November to March, rains turn the forests and steep slopes into a slightly warmer and much more humid environment. Built in the 1860s and 1870s, the cathedral shoots upward with a tall steeple, producing an eerie scene in the dense forest something like Mayan pyramids rising out of the Guatemalan rainforest. Decades ago, the Lazarist priests forged an agreement with the Brazilian government to turn their twenty-five thousand square acres into a nature preserve with the sanctuary and school at its center. The designation and the area's relative isolation have kept the mountaintop green and densely forested. The surrounding woodlands still contain significant wildlife including foxes, sloths, and monkeys.[3]

Today the narrow country road from Barão de Cocais to the Caraça Sanctuary winds through forest that is likely thicker and more robust than when the Burtons passed through in 1867. As July morning mists gradually dissipate, clear blue skies and blinding sunlight reveal the occasional open pasture amid a sea of green shades and dense vegetation. For most of the slow rise to the sanctuary, walls of trees turn the road into a virtual tunnel.

The cathedral-school complex has become a tourist attraction, off the beaten path of those visiting the "historical cities" of Congonhas, Mariana, and Ouro Preto. The crumbling wattle-and-daub walls of the original structure are surrounded by nineteenth-century dormitories and the imposing cathedral. Other than the local caretakers, the complex is largely empty. Flocks of the endangered Minas Gerais tyrannulet (*Phylloscartes roquettei*) eagerly swoop from the rooftops to devour the breadcrumbs tourists scatter on the patio of the visitors' entrance.

Excavations High and Low

According to Richard, the road from Cocais to Catas Altas was "the most important line of communication in the Province," connecting Diamantina in the north with Ouro Preto to the south. Indeed, since the discovery of gold and diamonds in the early eighteenth century, the path he followed had been officially recognized as the Royal Road, and regularly spaced stone markers along the route now commemorate this designation. The construction of Belo Horizonte in the late nineteenth century, and the construction of the highway from Belo to Rio in the early twentieth century, turned this ancient road into a backwater. Motoring along a two-lane asphalt highway in June 2022, I spent most of my time studiously avoiding the gigantic trucks servicing the many iron mines along the route. With most of the gold mines long exhausted, iron mining companies now carve away the mountaintops turning them into vast terraces of red dirt and rock.

Much to the Burtons' surprise, as they moved along this road, they spotted "a cavalcade of eleven Sisters of Charity in gull-wing caps, mounted on poor hack-mules, and travelling, like Canterbury Pilgrims, in single file under the escort" of the vice principal of the Caraça school, Father François Sipolis. On their way to establish a new convent in Diamantina, the sisters had begun the long trip inland from their nunnery in Rio de Janeiro. Isabel had met some of the sisters in Rio and was pleased to chance upon them again out in the wilds. Richard lamented that "the only pretty Sister, who, moreover, sat her horse well, and who wore a neat riding skirt, went forward, and would not join in" his chat with the French priest. The two agreed to meet up later in Diamantina, and the Burtons then made their way into the village of Catas Altas.[4]

FIGURE 7.2. Iron mining zone near Caraça. Marshall C. Eakin.

Dating back to the early years of the gold rush in the first decade of the eighteenth century, scattered along both sides of the main road on the eastern base of the serra, the tiny settlement's baroque churches dedicated to Our Lady of the Conception, Our Lady of the Rosary, Saint Quiteria, and Our Lord of the Good End bore large and silent testimony to a golden age long past. The Burtons did a quick tour of the churches before heading to dinner at the Hotel Fluminense, owned and operated by a João Emery, the "son of English parents, and thoroughly John Bull in burliness of look," but who spoke only Portuguese. Emery explained that his "face was British, but all the rest was Brazilian."[5] With only a handful of small mining deposits worked erratically, this once-prosperous village at the heart of the mining zone bore similarities to so many other of the once-prosperous but now decaying towns with little but their crumbling churches to indicate their earlier glories.

After a frigid night in Emery's hotel, they resumed their way toward Mariana, but first, Gordon took the Burtons from their tour of gold mines to show them what appeared to be a substantial coal seam nearby. In Morro d'Água Quente (Hot Water Hill) Gordon introduced them to Leandro Francisco Arantez, who took them to the nearby hamlet of Fonseca on the western banks of the Piracicaba River. The seam appeared to Burton to be an inferior form of lignite, what he called "brown coal." Nevertheless, shifting into his sales mode, he carefully described the possibilities of deeper anthracite deposits, "a veritable black diamond" hidden below the surface. Superintendent Gordon then headed back to Morro Velho retracing their route of the past few days. The rest of the party made its way back to the west to the Royal Road and to Inficionado (Infected), so named, as local lore has it, for the poor quality of the gold nuggets encountered in local streams.

Although Richard described a tiny, decaying village with a dry public fountain, two chapels, no priest, and a bevy of beggars and disabled people, the village also boasted "of one great birth."[6] José de Santa Rita Durão, the son of a Portuguese colonist, was born in this tiny village in 1722, during the early surge of the gold boom. Educated by Jesuits in Rio de Janeiro, he became an Augustinian priest and professor of theology at the University of Coimbra, the institution in Portugal that would long be the destination for nearly all elite Brazilian men in search of higher education. In his fifties, he wrote the epic poem *Caramurú* (Son of Thunder), about the life of Diogo Álvares Correia, a Portuguese sailor shipwrecked on the northern coast of Brazil in 1509. Correia assimilated into Tupinambá society, married an indigenous woman (Catarina Paraguçu), eventually heading to France in 1526. The wife of explorer Jacques Cartier assisted in Catarina's baptism, and in the mythmaking of early Brazilian history, the couple became the first "Christian" Brazilian family, the fusion of the two races. Correia returned to Brazil and helped establish the colonial capital of Salvador da Bahia in the 1550s. Richard, who was slowly translating the epic *Lusiads* of Camões, had high praise for the author of *Caramurú*, who died in Portugal in 1784. As so often happens in the history of literature, Santa Rita Durão is one more example that genius may come from even the smallest and most obscure corners of the globe. Today, the old hamlet of Inficionado bears the name Santa Rita Durão.[7]

The following day, the party left this village of people with "sallow brown" skin that "showed a mixture of races, with much intermarriage"—the racial undertones once again surfacing in Burton's account—heading for Mariana.[8] In the great spectrum of skin tones in Brazil, Minas Gerais historically straddles the middle ground. The expansion of sugar plantations in the regions around Salvador and Recife created the first substantial wave of the transatlantic slave trade, bringing millions of captive Africans to the Northeast. Today, the coastal areas of the Northeast are the most Africanized of Brazil and have by far the highest percentages of Black and racially mixed Brazilians. European immigration in the late nineteenth and early twentieth centuries transformed southern Brazil, from São Paulo to Rio Grande do Sul, into the phenotypically and culturally whitest region of the country. The discovery of gold and diamonds in the eighteenth century and the expansion of coffee cultivation in the nineteenth century shifted the bulk of the slave trade to southeastern Brazil. Rio and Minas became the racial melting pot between the "European" South and the "African" Northeast. Richard's passage through Minas in 1867 came less than two decades after the end of the Brazilian transatlantic slave trade, and probably the moment when the region's African influence peaked. The Brazilians in this region today remain a rainbow of shades of black to white, although census figures reveal a Minas Gerais that is whiter and culturally less black and African than 150 years ago.[9]

After passing through Bento Rodrigues and Camargos, the travelers ascended the Morro da Venda da Palha (Hill of the Straw Store), to enjoy "a noble view of enormous extent."[10] To the northwest rose the Itabira Peak, to the east the Rio Doce River Valley, and straight ahead to the south, the southern tip of the Caraça range blocked their view of Ouro Preto to the southwest. Today, they would have seen below them the ruins of the town of Bento Rodrigues buried in sludge. The many iron mines in the region have constructed earthen dams to contain poisonous tailings from the refining processes. In November 2015, the dam above Bento Rodrigues collapsed, spilling more than forty million cubic meters of toxic mud on the town and into surrounding rivers and streams. The massive wave of dirt and noxious waters then surged into the Rio Doce, one of the major waterways in southeastern Brazil. Over the next two weeks this enormous reddish slurry of toxic chemicals and metals made its way five hundred miles downriver to the Atlantic Ocean, killing millions of fish and wildlife along the way. Nineteen people died in Bento Rodrigues, buried beneath the tidal wave of mud. A few walls are all that remain of about a dozen structures, surrounded by the tons of dried sludge. For the past decade, the two largest iron mining companies in the world, BHP (Australia) and Vale, have faced multiple lawsuits for tens of billions of dollars in courts in Brazil, the United Kingdom, and Australia.[11] The river is no longer "sweet."

CORNISH KING OF THE MINES

Richard approached Mariana expecting to visit the Morro de Santa Anna (Saint Anne Hill) mine, but a dying woman changed his plans. The superintendent of the mine was Thomas Treloar, a mining captain with thirty years' experience in the region. Born in Helston, Cornwall, at the age of twenty Treloar married Allarina Symons (age nineteen) in early 1834, and the couple shipped out to Brazil to work at Edward Oxenford's Cocais mine. In the 1840s, Treloar served as the mine captain first at Gongo Soco and then (after 1845) at Morro Velho. He had a falling out with James Newell Gordon in 1862, believing Gordon rashly exploited the mine's lode to produce higher yields over the short term. Ironically, Treloar must have felt vindicated in his views when the Morro Velho mine collapsed in late 1867, but that was still a few months away when the Burtons appeared on his doorstep. Gordon most likely split off from the Burtons just before their arrival at Morro de Santa Anna to avoid meeting up with Treloar. The Cornishman's wife bore nine daughters and three sons in Brazil between 1834 and 1857 and regularly sent them back to England for their schooling. Not only did they all survive what must have been challenging frontier conditions for childbirth and infancy, but most lived into their sixties and seventies. Several married other Englishmen working in other mines, and their children and grandchildren spread out across the British empire in succeeding decades. In honor of their location, they named their first daughter, born nine months after their arrival in Brazil, Jane Cocais Treloar.[12]

After leaving Morro Velho, the highly experienced Treloar helped organize the Don Pedro North Del Rey Mining Company (once again playing on the St. John's success and name) on a mountainside along the Royal Road approaching Mariana from

FIGURE 7.3. Thomas & Allarina Treloar. W. G. Smith.

the east. While the Morro de Santa Anna soon proved nearly worthless, Treloar promptly purchased the Maquiné Mine on the eastern hillside just across the valley. For about a decade or so, the Don Pedro North Del Rey would be one of the rare English gold mining companies to produce some profits and returns for investors.[13] Perhaps because his knowledge of Treloar came primarily from Gordon, Richard painted a grim portrait as he moved along the road through the mine works. Rising up the ridge on the west side of the road, the site was "a bleak and treeless hill-side, front east" with "its tall, naked face burrowed for gold; an ugly contrast to the picturesque approach that characterizes Morro Velho." A chapel, "dull clay huts of the native workmen," a hospital, the officers' houses, "the white quarters of the English miners, the Casa Grande, large, neat, and well situated, and the 'blacks' kitchen,' a tall, white tenement, bald and bare," and a line of huts for the enslaved spread out across the "dwarf eminence rising from the valley" floor. Along the "bottom land are the shops, smith, carpentry, stamps, and other furniture."[14]

Richard's vivid description of the scarred landscape on the depleted Morro de Santa Anna mine could not have anticipated how much more abandoned and decrepit the site would be a century and a half later. The dense traffic on the road leading into Mariana today follows the same path Richard traversed on his sturdy mule. The old Maquiné Mine on the north side of the road, and the site of the Morro de Santa Anna on the south side mark the end of the countryside and the beginning of Mariana's urban perimeter. Although the former mine has been worked on and off for decades, it now sits abandoned, the hilltop carved away. The long, rising hillside of the Morro de Santa Anna on the right side of the road has been declared an archaeological park, but one that is dangerous to enter. Decades of drifting shafts in the steep hillside in the nineteenth century have left it pockmarked with deep pits now overgrown with bushes and vines. In many ways, walking through this rocky, brush covered terrain is like navigating a minefield, where the danger is falling into deep pits rather than being blown up. The foundations and a few walls are all that remain of the complex of buildings Richard so harshly described. Even the old British cemetery has vanished. At the top of the hillside, the modern traveler has an expansive view—to the north the old Maquiné Mine, to the south Mariana, and to the west the towers of the colonial cathedrals of Ouro Preto.[15]

Across the valley, the Maquiné Mine had saved the Don Pedro North Del Rey Company stockholders and in 1867 became the focus of all mining operations. The mine captain, a Mr. McRogers, and a Mr. Hosken took the Burtons through a section of the underground operations, the walls covered with timber and planking to shore up the rock. Over the next decades the mine would be productive, but under difficult geological conditions. Not long before the Burtons' visit, the mine had produced a gold nugget measuring eighteen by eight inches, but the lode was fragmented and not very deep. The mine employed 350 workers (mostly enslaved Blacks) and it was, in Richard's words, "one of the only two successes which can be claimed by English mining in Brazil."[16] Disactivated in recent years, a series of rock terraces with sparse grass and bushes, and a small tailings pond, are all that remain of the old mining operations. The twentieth-century successors to the old English company stripped away all the old machinery and works. To the eye of even the keen observer, there is almost no hint of the complex honeycomb of shafts and galleries buried beneath the hill.

As the Burtons approached the Morro de Santa Anna mine carrying letters of introduction, they expected to spend the night with the Treloars and then inspect the mining operations the following day. Sending the enslaved Miguel ahead, they were shocked when he returned to report that Captain Treloar could not receive them. The fifty-three-year-old Allarina lay dying in the casa grande, surrounded by her large family. After pausing at a local shop to write a note of sympathy to the Treloars, Richard and Isabel trudged another two miles into Mariana in search of housing for the night. Lamenting that the town had nine churches but only three inns, they "came upon the best of the three inns," the Hotel Mariannense, an establishment Richard thought typical of the "country inn of the old Brazil." The reception room "was in fact a barber shop" and the "long corridor to the back of the house . . . was so badly boarded that one risked falling through." Bare walls in the bedchambers, plank couches, and a dining room with a sparsely supplied armoire made for a "wretched inn." They had to wait two hours for dinner, and the "negroes and negresses prefer staring, whispering, and giggling, to work, however light." Time, he complained, "is not worth a thought here, and regularity is next to impossible." To add to the misery, "there is never less than one screaming child to make night horrid; and generally there are two fierce dogs that bay responsively at the shadow of an opportunity." Isabel complained that her "feet stuck out the end of my miserable, short, straw bed, and it was a bitterly cold night."[17] As if these inconveniences were not enough, the bill for their stay "would have done honour to the Hôtel des Ambassadeurs, St. Petersburg."[18]

There is no shortage today of hotels, inns, and wonderful places to stay in Mariana, and the nearby Ouro Preto. Both cities are major tourist attractions with their iconic baroque architecture, including the many churches Richard so disliked. Ouro Preto was the capital of Minas Gerais until the 1890s, and its economy today revolves around tourism. It is home to a federal university and Brazil's most famous mining school. Only a few miles to the east, Mariana is less visited but equally charming with its cobblestone streets and colonial buildings. As Richard approached Mariana, the town reminded him "of picturesque old Coimbra," but he quickly dismissed the architecture of the churches and commented on the dullness "of cathedral towns." "Evidently," he archly notes, "we are in a city which is clerical and not commercial," filled with "big black ants"—the seminary students in their black soutanes—strolling through town and lolling "listless about the shops." Shopkeepers stared vacantly into the streets, "Negro urchins" squatted on steps along with "vagrant pigs and dogs," and "old black women hobbled about picking up rags and compost."[19]

Mariana—along with São João del Rei, Ouro Preto, and Sabará—was one of the first officially recognized royal towns (*vilas*) in the first two decades of the eighteenth century. Seeking to quell the chaos and lawlessness as prospectors flooded into this mountainous terrain some 250 miles north of Rio de Janeiro, the Portuguese Crown singled out the most active mining camps and appointed government officials to settle in and establish control. Troops, judges, accountants, and artisans set up jails, courts, and royal mints in an effort to regulate the distribution of mining claims, tax gold production, and maintain order. Vila Rica de Ouro Preto became the capital of the new captaincy of Minas Gerais in the 1720s, and Mariana the ecclesiastical center. Throughout the eighteenth century, bequests and tithes from successful miners funded the construction of an extraordinary number of churches, convents, and seminaries in the mining zone, in the distinct baroque style that today draws millions of tourists to the *cidades históricas* (historical cities).[20]

Economic decline helped save the built historical record in these mountain towns. Even the influx of English capital in the nineteenth century failed to return the region to another golden age. With the major exception of the Morro Velho, and some of the smaller, short-lived successes at other mines, these eighteenth-century boom towns remained small and economically marginal well into the twentieth century. With the construction of Belo Horizonte in the 1890s, Ouro Preto even lost its key role as the state capital. In the 1920s and 1930s, as the modernist culture elites in Rio, São Paulo, and even the young Belo Horizonte rediscovered

Brazil, they were drawn to the baroque architecture of these out-of-the-way colonial towns. In succeeding decades, Belo Horizonte exploded as the industrial and economic center for the region—from 40,000 inhabitants in the 1910s, to 400,000 by the 1950s, and more than 4 million by the early twenty-first century. With the exception of the local history museum, not a single structure in Belo Horizonte predates 1890! Ouro Preto, Congonhas, São João del Rei, Tiradentes, and Mariana have successfully re-created themselves by renovating the baroque architecture in their old town centers. As so often happens in history, decline and neglect allowed the survival of historic buildings until locals realized the value of saving and revitalizing them.[21]

Both Richard's skepticism of Catholicism and his admiration for the "civilizing" influence of the church pervade his account of the brief stay in Mariana. He and Isabel spent their day visiting with Bishop Antonio Ferreira Viçoso and the Sisters of St. Vincent de Paul. Richard was clearly impressed with the "venerable ecclesiastic, now aged eighty," who had spent decades in Brazil and was "still in feature and pronunciation a Portuguese: his eye was bright and intelligent, and his face calm and intellectual."[22] Leaving the bishop, they toured the local seminary, home to nearly two hundred "pupils," and marveled at the remarkable "cleanliness and order; even the kitchen was neat."[23] The sisters, from the same French order they had recently passed on the road to Mariana, had been working in the town for more than a century. In an age when the role of the state was to tax, adjudicate, and maintain order, the Catholic church provided the social services that we take for granted today as a function of the modern welfare state. The sisters ran a school, an orphanage, and a hospital with little financial assistance from the government.

Again, impressed with the cleanliness, order, and efficiency of the nuns and their facilities, Richard also noted the "respect and affection" all showed for the mother superior.[24] After several pages of laudatory comments, Richard's anti-clericalism resurfaces at the end of his chapter on Mariana. Many Brazilians (meaning the wealthy), he observes, "send their daughters to these places of instruction because they can get no better," but they do not like the outmoded education, which "is fifty years behind the world." After six to eight years of this education, girls graduate with "a peculiar state of ignorance, and supplied with certain remarkable superstitions . . . and an *engoument* [infatuation] for penance and mortification which everywhere should be obsolete." The nuns, he believed, should step back from their role as teachers in the classroom and instead take their place "in the hospital, or by the sick bedside, where their heroism and devotion deserve the highest respect."[25]

Having shown his anti-clerical and misogynistic attitudes, Richard immediately adds a footnote that reveals the incipient cultural relativism that always struggles with his own elitist, Victorian, masculine worldview and marks his entire life work. He notes that he could name a convent school in London where "children learn that on Christmas Eve all animals kneel down and pray; and that thunder is the voice of the deity—the merest fetishism." In a remarkable statement he continues, "My experience is that on matters of pure faith or belief—that is to say, taking statements on trust—all nations are as nearly equal as their development of imagination, of the marvelous, permits them to be. Amongst the most civilized peoples of Europe it is right easy to point out tenets which, submitted to the eyes of reason, appear identical with those held by the savages of the Bonny River [Nigeria]."[26] For a moment, his anthropological relativism overcomes his racist, Eurocentric core, but only briefly.

Thomas Treloar's son-in-law Francis Stanfield Symons rescued the Burtons from their despised lodgings in Mariana, inviting them to stay at his home at the nearby Passagem Mine, just a few miles west on the road to Ouro Preto. The house was empty while the family gathered around his deathly ill mother-in-law at Morro de Santa Anna. Thomas Treloar, Symons, and another son-in-law, Thomas Tregellas, helped organize the Anglo-Brazilian Gold Mining Company, Limited in 1863 with £100,000 of initial capital investment and Symons as superintendent. Although this company would limp along for a little over a decade, the Passagem Mine would be worked with relative success by other owners and companies throughout much of the twentieth century. Happy to be with their countrymen in English surroundings, the Burtons stayed on for three days enjoying, in Isabel's words, "Bass's ale, sherry, and everything imaginable to eat and drink, a piano, and plenty of books."[27] As Richard remarked in his account, "we had every reason to be grateful for the proverbial hospitality of the Cornu-Briton."[28]

What Richard could not foresee is that the Passagem Mine would ultimately be the second most successful of the local gold mines in the nineteenth and twentieth centuries, although worked, at various times, by Brazilian, English, and French owners. The Baron von Eschwege mentions the property during his survey of the mining zone in the 1810s, but it was obviously still a small operation.[29] Despite an influx of serious investment and expertise, the mine limped along under a series of owners for decades. The ubiquitous Francisco de Paula Santos even owned the property before selling it to the Anglo-Brazilian Gold Mining Company in 1865. Richard did predict a "promising and brilliant future" for the mine, and he was partially right.[30]

A few miles to the southwest of the Morro de Santa Anna, the Passagem Mine sits on the east bank of the tiny Carmo River. After donning the "correct 'underground' costume," the Burton party, including Isabel's servant Chico, descended on foot several hundred feet down a "well timbered" incline to a vaulted cavern. It was "lit up with torches, and the miners—all slaves, directed by white overseers—streamed with perspiration, and merrily sang their wild song and chorus, keeping time with the strokes of hammer and drill." Richard noted "the heavy gloom, the fitful glare of the lights, the want of air, the peculiar sulphurous odor, and the savage chaunt" created a "Swedenborgian hell." The frightened Chico enthusiastically agreed, exclaiming, "It looks like Hell." To which Isabel responded, "I was rather struck by the justice of the observation."[31] Richard estimated the work force at about twenty Europeans and nearly four hundred enslaved men and women, about fifty working underground on each shift.[32]

Finally deactivated for good in the late 1970s, the Passagem mining complex remains relatively intact as a tourist destination. Most of the surviving buildings date from the early twentieth century. The ruins of the old superintendent's house, church, and cemetery on the hill above the main entrance to the complex is now densely forested, and off-limits to visitors. Once again, the English graves, including that of Allarina Symons, have been preserved thanks to their relative isolation from the urbanization of the last century. The modest museum contains a hodgepodge of old mining equipment and instruments. The main attraction is a tour of the old underground works. The old winding engine still lowers a tram—one that holds a dozen visitors in six rows of seats. Following the path of Richard, Isabel, and Chico, the tram descends several hundred feet down a forty-five-degree incline into the underground galleries. Modern visitors can move back and forth through a series of galleries, each ending at underground pools of water. The wide, brightly lit tunnels have little in common with Richard's Swedenborgian hell. The guides have little to say about the long history of the mine or the hundreds of enslaved miners who carved out most of the works.[33]

On Wednesday morning, 17 July, just as the Burtons had saddled up and prepared to depart, word reached them that Allarina Treloar had died. Symons asked Richard, as the British consul, to "read the burial service over his mother-in-law."[34] In her own account, Isabel remarks that "women do not attend funerals in Brazil," so she stayed at the casa grande during the service.[35] The ever-skeptical Richard read the official service of the Church of England and "was struck by the coldness and deadness of the rite, the absence of consolation to the living, and the want of comfort for the dead." One wonders how his reading came across to the bereaved. He goes on to criticize the specific biblical verses in the rite—the fifteenth chapter of Paul's First Epistle to the Corinthians, demonstrating his knowledge of both Christian and ancient and biblical history. "The Cornishmen," he writes, "seemed resolved to add a little life to the ceremony," and "they sang in a nasal tone a lengthy hymn, which gave them, I presume, some spiritual refreshment."[36] Richard was not the most empathetic critic.

Thomas Treloar would return to England in 1871, then die in London in 1880, the most experienced and knowledgeable expert on gold mining in nineteenth-century Brazil, having worked at Cocais, Gongo Soco, Morro Velho, Morro de Santa Ana, and Passagem. One of his obituaries in the British press called him the "King of the Brazilian Gold Mines." He is buried in a South London cemetery alongside his daughter Ellen and her husband, Thomas Tregellas, more than five thousand miles from Allarina.[37] The descendants of the Treloars have bridged time and distance in recent decades, along with many those of many of his fellow Cornishmen. They have constructed digital memorials on websites that provide capsule summaries of the great Cornish migrations out to mines across the globe in the nineteenth century. With the digitization of census, parish, and local records and the increasing popularity of genealogical research, the stories of these nineteenth-century Cornish miners have now become densely interconnected and visible across the globe.[38]

The digital revolution of the early twenty-first century has transformed life on the planet, and it has fundamentally reconfigured historical research and writing. When I began my work on the Morro Velho mine in 1979, I spent a year going through the unorganized records of the British company that (fortunately) had been stashed in a small room below the Casa Grande, and the surviving London office records that had made their way to the Latin American Collection at the University of Texas at Austin. Luckily for me, the South African management had installed the latest generation of photocopying machines in a room down the hall from the chaotic archive. In the 1990s, local historians working on a grant organized and stored these records in a state-of-the-art archival facility in the Casa Grande. More than forty years after my first research visit to Austin, the London office records are better organized and accessible, but in both locations, very little has been digitized. A historian still needs to spend time going through the papers and photographs in both locations, although the difference today is the ability to use a phone camera to snap thousands of photographs. The historian, as a result, does not have to spend as much time in the archive hand-copying or photocopying and reading as in the past. Vast numbers of documents can be read and analyzed much later in the comfort of one's own office.

The digital turn has had a more profound effect on access to all sort of other records in reconstructing the past in Richard Burton's Brazil. The creation of online genealogical sites such as Ancestry.com and the ability of nearly anyone to post their own records on the internet has revolutionized access to the histories of individuals and places. Most of the old gold mining sites in Minas Gerais now have their own web presence and, in some cases, archaeological reports and findings on websites. The descendants of Cornish miners around the globe have posted their own family information, and even an academic website for aggregating this material, The Cornish in Latin America. Many of the archival documents in Britain have been digitized, opening up the possibilities for recreating the networks of the British operators and investors working in Brazil in the nineteenth century. This digitization not only democratizes and opens up historical materials to a vast public; it has significantly speeded up the work of the professional historian. This digital transformation of access to information has made possible the recreation of Richard Burton's movements through nineteenth-century Brazil at a level of detail that simply was not possible forty years ago.

Delayed by the burial service for Allarina Treloar, the Burtons finally departed for Ouro Preto late in the afternoon. Located just a few miles to the west, even in the mid-nineteenth century, the "whole length" of the road was "more or less inhabited." As Richard made his way along the road, he once again reveals his notions of geographical determinism, observing that "Men who live too long in the Tropics often fall into a nervous, solitary habit of life." At Passagem, he notes that he had lived "within a stone's throw" of a "compatriot," "a labouring man" who "had become a capitalist" with a large house. This Englishman, Richard goes on, had too quickly and deeply learned patience (*paciência*), wait a wee bit (*espere um pouco*), and tomorrow (*amanhã*) from his Brazilian "teachers." In Burton's view, he had "gone native," completely corrupted by the tropics.[39] As he made his way into the provincial capital of Minas Gerais, his thoughts turned to the corrupting influences of the tropics, even on his fellow Brits. In Ouro Preto, he would take a break from his British compatriots to mingle with the local Brazilian elites.

CHAPTER 8

TOWN OF TARNISHED GOLD

They have a very decided sotaque or brogue, which at first is not easily understood. The Paulista speaks with his mouth unduly open; his is the Doric, the North-country dialect of Brazil. The Mineiro closes his lips and eats his words till they fail to catch the strangers' ears; it is Lancashire versus Northumberland.

—RICHARD BURTON

The five miles from the Passagem Mine westward to the heart of Ouro Preto did not impress Richard, nor did his first view of the town. He made note of hillsides honeycombed with "abandoned gold works, now used by the poor as pig-styes." Taken aback by the small size of the *mineiro* capital, he declared that it "is nothing but a great village" built along a single street resembling "a provincial town." As with any traveler arriving in Ouro Preto today, he immediately reacted to a town built on a series of steep hills with many ups and downs, houses scattered about on sharp slopes. Ouro Preto, he declared, lacked "all the grace and grandeur of a city." It was, he conceded, a singular place full of surprises and, as is still true today, "romantic and picturesque, thoroughly Mineiro." The Burtons entered the "Rich Town of Black Gold" (Vila Rica de

TOWN OF TARNISHED GOLD

FIGURE 8.1. Ouro Preto and Itacolomi Peak, circa 1870. Image in the public domain.

Ouro Preto) around six in the evening. Once again, they benefited from the exceptional hospitality of well-connected Brazilian hosts, on this occasion, their wealthy and powerful friend, Francisco de Paula Santos. In the absence of the commander, who was away in Rio de Janeiro, his brother Dr. José Marçal dos Santos "did the honors of the Golden City."[1]

Located at the convergence of two extensive mountain ridges, Mariana and Ouro Preto sit on the southeast corner of the "Iron Quadrangle" (see fig. 4.3). The first ridge line thrusts out in a southeasterly direction from the Caraça range, and the second runs from west to east on the southern rim of the quadrilateral. On a physical relief map, the converging ranges appear to form a boar's head with a large basin filling in most of the head expanding away from the nose in a northwesterly direction. At the convergence, the ranges are blunted, forming the silhouette of a snout, with Mariana at the nostrils and Ouro Preto at the mouth. Moving from Morro de Santa Anna to Mariana, then Passagem, and Ouro Preto, the Burtons rounded the snout. A short spur ridgeline splits off to the southeast just to the west of Ouro Preto, and the old city developed in the basin between the two ridges, in the open mouth of the boar. The city spontaneously took shape on a series of steep hills and deep gorges in this basin as thousands of fortune seekers poured into the area in search of gold in the early eighteenth century.[2] The challenge for the Burtons, and the modern traveler, is to traverse these sharp inclines and declines to take in the many striking baroque churches and colonial buildings.

Officially designated as a UNESCO World Heritage Site, most of the urban core of Ouro Preto today retains the styles of the eighteenth and nineteenth centuries. Buildings rarely reach more than three stories, and most sport red tile rooftops, whitewashed exterior walls, and bright pastel trim around windows and doors. Irregular and craggy paving stones line the streets, and on rainy days the traction on the steep streets presented a challenge to mule-drawn carts in the nineteenth century—and the motorist today. The pedestrian must be ready for hiking up and down, trying not to stumble on the rough stones, and dodging vehicles as they wind their way along narrow streets, often with parked cars on both sides.

Today, many of the buildings in Ouro Preto have plaques or historical markers heralding their earlier occupants. Much like the other "historical cities" in Minas, the influx of migrants from the countryside into the cities has dramatically expanded the town. Outside the old urban core with its carefully preserved colonial exteriors, tens of thousands of more recent residents reside in a sprawling city that spills over the surrounding mountainsides. Despite the expanding population over the past few decades, the roads into and out of Ouro Preto remain narrow and winding. The drive in from Mariana offers the prospects of narrow scrapes with passing and parked cars, street vendors, and stone walls. At times, the narrow lanes lead to a game of chicken with oncoming automobiles and trucks.

Colonialism and Conspiracy

The decadent "village" that the Burtons toured in 1867, created out of a gold mining camp in the 1710s, had experienced its greatest glories in the middle of the eighteenth century. The mountainous region, which had been home to nomadic and semisedentary Native people for centuries, if not millennia, produced 80 percent of the world's gold supply and most of its diamonds for about eight decades. Gold and diamonds gave birth to the richest families in Brazil, surpassing the fortunes of the wealthy sugar planters in the Northeast. As gold production began to decline steadily after 1770, these elite *mineiro* families found themselves overextended financially, with considerable mortgages and tax bills from the Crown that had accumulated for years. When José I became king of Portugal in 1750, he appointed a powerful noble, José Sebastião Carvalho e Melo (eventually the Marquis of Pombal), to reorganize and revitalize Portugal's declining empire. The gold rush had made Brazil Portugal's "milk cow" and the most important possession of the global empire. Once the greatest commercial network in the world, since the mid-seventeenth century, the Dutch, French, and English had gradually supplanted Portuguese traders across Asia, Africa, and the Atlantic world. Pombal, along with the Bourbons in Spain, sought to strengthen monarchy through the centralization of political power, the reorganization of the administrative apparatus of the empire, and the promotion of new forms of economic activity.[3]

The efforts to plant cotton, rice, and other crops achieved some small success, but it would not be until the 1820s when the Brazilians would finally find their next major export crop. Pombal did rationalize much of the administrative structure of the empire, including Brazil. He separated off the northern tier of the colony, Grão Pará and Maranhão (roughly today's states of Pará and Amazonas), from the Viceroyalty of Brazil, to have them report directly to Lisbon. He moved the colonial capital from Salvador to Rio de Janeiro, in part to locate it strategically between the rich northeastern captaincies and the weaker ones bordering on the Spanish empire in the Rio de la Plata. The gold and diamond rush had made the sleepy village of Rio de Janeiro the most important and richest port in the colony as hundreds of thousands of enslaved Africans poured into the mining zone through its stunning bay, and astonishing amounts of gold and diamonds flowed out to Portugal. The gold rush relocated the axis of economic and political power in Brazil from the Northeast to the Southeast, where it remains some 250 years later.[4]

For the *mineiro* elites, Pombal's reforms brought increased pressure to pay current and back taxes even as gold production and their revenues steadily declined. The increasingly unhappy colonials began to ponder a challenge to the Crown, with the successful revolt of the British colonials on the Eastern Seaboard of North America fresh in their minds. A conspiracy began quietly to take shape in Vila Rica (as it was called in the colonial period), a *conjuração* or *inconfidência* in Portuguese, a story Richard relates in great detail in his account.[5] More than two dozen of the powerful conjured up a plot to seize the governor and declare the independence of Minas Gerais, abolish the detested taxes and debts, and open up the Crown-controlled diamond mines. They had already designed a white flag, a triangle at the center, with the motto *Libertas quae sera tamen"*—a line from Virgil meaning "liberty even if delayed." (Today, this is the flag of the state of Minas Gerais.) They recruited key military officers to join them, most notably, José Joaquim Xavier da Costa, better known to history as Tiradentes (the Toothpuller).[6]

Unfortunately for the conspirators, one plotter got cold feet and betrayed them, possibly to gain help with his own large debts to the Crown. The powers of the state machinery went into action and rounded up anyone with any links to those involved in the plot. Months of brutal interrogations ensued, and high social status proved no protection from the wrath of the Crown. Royal officials rounded up more than thirty prominent figures for trial, among them Cláudio Manuel da Costa and Tomás Antônio Gonzaga, two of the leading literary figures of the era. After nearly two years of interrogations and hearings in Rio de Janeiro, seven prisoners charged with treason were condemned to be hanged, decapitated, and quartered. Four men were to be hanged on unusually high gallows, then beheaded. The court ordered five more to exile for life in Angola, often a sentence of death by disease in the most insalubrious climate a European could imagine. Given the powerful social and political status of so many of the conspirators, Queen Maria I commuted ten of the eleven death sentences to banishment. Only Tiradentes would die at the gallows.

This low-ranking officer who dared to challenge the monarchy would be enshrined as a martyr to the cause of Brazilian nationalism, but only after the overthrow of the Braganza monarchy a century later. In the iconography of Brazilian nationalism, Tiradentes generally appears with long flowing locks, an ample beard, and in a sackcloth, looking suspiciously Christlike. On 21 April 1792, in an execution witnessed by thousands, a Black executioner and his assistant hanged Tiradentes, decapitated him, then quartered his body. They salted the head and limbs. Royal officials nailed the four quarters of his body on posts along the roads leading into Vila Rica, then placed his head on a pike in the heart of the city, all as a warning to those who might contemplate challenging the Crown's authority. The gallows in Rio stood on the south side of what would eventually (in the 1810s) become the imperial palace. The building on this ground today housed the Brazilian legislature for much of the twentieth century. Although the inn where Tiradentes lodged in Vila Rica was slated for destruction, the order was never carried out, and a plaque on the two-story stucco building commemorates the martyr, less than a hundred yards down the street from the Casa dos Contos (treasury building) and Francisco da Paula Santos's nineteenth-century home.

After the overthrow of the Braganza monarchy in 1889, the new republican regime elevated Tiradentes to mythic status. April 21, the day of his execution, has long been a national holiday, and images of the Christlike figure—statues and paintings—have been built and hung prominently in cities across Brazil. Although clearly a response to the toppled monarchy when the republicans began the mythification in the 1890s, today, Tiradentes is one of those national symbols that all political parties and movements can, and do, claim. He forms part of the mythmaking process that builds a nation—a community of people who see themselves as sharing a common set of myths, symbols, and rituals, an "imagined community," in the words of the late Benedict Anderson.[7] As Richard Burton moved through Brazil describing regional differences in the 1860s, he glimpsed the early stages of this nation formation. The Brazilians had inherited a state apparatus—courts, military, and other institutions of control—from the Portuguese, but they had to create their own nation—to invent their own historical narrative. The canonization of Tiradentes played a role in this process of mythmaking, history, and nation-building.

Rich Town of Black Gold

Richard Burton was an experienced and truly cosmopolitan world traveler. A sensitive and nuanced architectural and art critic he was not. His strong anti-Catholic bias probably also helps account for his lack of appreciation for the rich baroque art and architecture of Minas Gerais. For the traveler today, so many of the restored structures in Brazil's historical cities are churches and sites deeply marked by religious traditions. Richard and Isabel dutifully visited the numerous churches of Ouro Preto, but, even more so than in other sections of the account, Richard seems to be checking off the sites for the reader, much as if he were preparing a guidebook. Yet again, he pauses to criticize the artistry of Aleijadinho, who he refers to as the "indefatigable 'Aleijado,'"[8] a figure who has been nearly universally elevated to mythic proportions by those who have carefully documented and explored the baroque era in Brazil.

Richard divided up the city into sections for his grand tour that takes up three days, three chapters, and some thirty pages near the end of the first volume of his account. This "second-rate town" that was "unworthy of the vast Province which it commands" he estimated to contain some 1,500 houses and only about 8,000 inhabitants (compared with 75,000 today).[9] Along with many other observers, Brazilian and foreign, he concluded that the "sooner another site for a capital is found the better." Some 150 years after its founding, *mineiro* elites debated possible sites for a new capital, but it would be another thirty years before intense negotiations led to the creation of Belo Horizonte some fifty miles northwest of Ouro Preto.[10] Although the transfer of the political capital effectively reduced Ouro Preto to a backwater, it proved fortunate for architectural historians. Belo Horizonte took shape as a modern, urban metropolis filled with concrete, steel, and glass, and now encompassing nearly five million inhabitants. Ouro Preto's classic colonial architecture remained largely intact due to neglect. By the 1920s and 1930s, the city had already begun to develop a tourist business and to make efforts to restore its many churches, old government buildings, and colonial residences. Today, the principal revenue source for Ouro Preto, Mariana, Tiradentes, Congonhas, and São João del Rei is tourism, as Brazilians and foreigners flock to the towns for their charming colonial architecture, numerous inns, and restaurants. Designated a World Historical Site in 1980, in some ways Ouro Preto is the equivalent of colonial Williamsburg, Virginia, except that the Brazilian town has been constantly renovated and restored rather than built from scratch in the twentieth century, as in Williamsburg, on the foundations of the colonial Virginia town.[11]

Towns like Williamsburg or Ouro Preto have been consciously constructed and reconstructed as living museums. For the historian, they satisfy a certain nostalgia for the past and the hope that not everything will be razed in the relentless pursuit of "progress" and "modernity." For the nation builders, these sites become monuments to past glories that educate their citizens in the national narrative. As with enclosed museums, historians' desire to recover the past as faithfully as possible often clashes with the state's need to craft a narrative for its own political purposes. Getúlio Vargas's support for the preservation of Ouro Preto in the 1930s and 1940s, and the monuments he created to enshrine the Inconfidência as central to his own version of the national narrative, enormously assisted the work of historians to preserve the Brazilian past, but on Vargas's terms.

Richard described the layout of Ouro Preto as a "huge serpent" with its "biggest girth" around the central plaza. Using my imagery of the boar's head, the serpent would be the boar's tongue. From the commander's home, the Burtons crossed a small bridge heading southeast. To their left rose the imposing Casa dos Contos (Counting House), originally the royal mint, and used as a prison that briefly housed the ill-fated Cláudio Manuel da Costa. Following Contos Street and steadily rising, after a block they turned left, heading east. Up the very steep Rua Direita (Straight Street) they rose to the main city plaza, today named after Tiradentes. To the right, at the south end of the plaza, sits the massive Museum of the Inconfidência Conspiracy, and to the left, at the north end, the equally massive original home of the School of Mines. In Richard's day, the building served as the palace housing the provincial president (essentially governor), and the museum served as the jail, holding nearly five hundred prisoners. At the palace, Richard met with the provincial vice president (in the absence of the president) and the secretary of government. They provided him with letters of introduction to facilitate his travels and with "the first detailed and correct account of" the Inconfidência "which has ever appeared in England," in Richard's words, of course.[12]

An imposing obelisk rises up out of the center of the main plaza today in honor of Tiradentes, on the spot where the royal governor supposedly placed his salted head on a pike for all to see. (There is some debate over where his decaying head was actually placed in the colonial capital.) In the 1930s, the government of Getúlio Vargas converted the old jail and town hall into a museum to honor the 1789 conspirators (*inconfidentes*). Vargas and rebel forces overthrew the government in October 1930, after a hotly disputed election and claims of fraud by the opposition (Vargas was the losing presidential candidate). Over the next fifteen years, he ruled as provisional president, then indirectly elected president, and then, from 1937 to 1945, as an authoritarian dictator. Forced from power at the end of World War II, he ran for president in 1950, winning nearly 50 percent of the vote, and then served a highly contentious four years before killing himself in 1954.[13]

Vargas brilliantly and ruthlessly centralized power in a nation that had been very decentralized from 1890 to 1930. The big states—São Paulo, Minas Gerais, Rio de Janeiro—dominated national politics and let the other states run themselves, as long as they did not buck the policies of the central government in Rio. Vargas understood the need to forge a stronger sense of national identity. From the 1930s to the 1960s, the most potent symbols and rituals of national identity emerged—football, carnival, samba, and the myth of racial mixture. This was not a top-down, imposed-from-above process but a subtle and unpredictable interplay between popular tastes and the efforts of Vargas and later governments to put their stamp on a singular national identity. All these symbols and the rituals associated with them (such as carnival and football championships) arose out of their popularity with the masses.[14]

Under Vargas, the creation of a national school curriculum, the glorification of the Minas Conspiracy, and the promotion of tourism that highlighted key regional sites and traits (such as the Africanized culture of Bahia or the cowboy culture of Vargas's own Rio Grande do Sul) helped consolidate a national narrative of Brazilian history and identity. Just like in the United States, battles over this narrative have marked recent elections and administrations in Brazil. After the 1930s, Minas became famous for its historical cities, and Ouro Preto served as the founding site of Brazilian republicanism and independence. National mythology enshrined Tiradentes and his co-conspirators as the progenitors of the modern Brazilian republic.

The museum contains a large, dimly lit room that takes on the dimensions of a chapel. Around the perimeter of the vault are square slabs that appear to serve as the burial markers for each of the *inconfidentes*. In fact, the remains of these men disappeared decades, if not centuries, ago, and the stones are really just monuments sitting on fictional graves. Along with the obelisk at the center of the plaza, they remind Brazilians of the centrality of Ouro Preto and Minas Gerais in the formation of Brazilian nationalism. Most of this is probably lost on the millions of tourists, Brazilian and foreign, who pass through this crowded space more interested in buying precious stones, carved soapstone, and tasting local *cachaça* than in the didactic symbols of a consciously constructed narrative of national identity.

As a great lover of literature, Richard recounts the tragic tale of the poet Tomás Antônio Gonzaga and his teenage love, Maria Dorotéia Joaquina de Seixas Brandão. Born in Portugal in 1744, Gonzaga was raised in Brazil, returned for his university education in Portugal, and then, in the early 1780s, arrived in Vila Rica to serve as a local judge. Deeply influenced by the French Enlightenment, he published the *Cartas Chilenas* (Chilean Letters) reputedly modeled on Montesquieu's *Persian Letters* (1721). The "letters" are a series of satirical poems mocking the royal governor of Minas Gerais that circulated as pamphlets around Vila Rica in the 1780s. As legend has it, the fifteen-year-old Maria Dorotéia was betrothed to the middle-aged Gonzaga, and he wrote her a series of love poems before he was imprisoned for his suspected role in the Minas Conspiracy and more while languishing in prison in Rio de Janeiro (on the Island of Snakes, Ilha das Cobras, just across from the wharf where Richard departed from Rio). The poems are addressed to Marília from Dirceu. Alas, the Crown shipped Gonzaga to Mozambique, where he would die around 1810, after marrying the daughter of a wealthy Portuguese merchant and raising two children. Maria Dorotéia also married and lived into the 1850s. Gonzaga's neoclassical verses have long been celebrated as some of the greatest poetry in Portuguese.[15]

Just two blocks southeast of the plaza, the Burtons visited the former residence of Gonzaga's close friend and fellow poet, Cláudio Manuel da Costa, reputedly the gathering point for many of the conspirators as they planned the 1789 uprising. Conveniently, it looked down across the street at the home of Marília. A poet of the first rank in his own right, born in Mariana, and educated in Portugal, Cláudio Manuel arrived in Vila Rica in the 1750s and made his living as a lawyer and goldsmith. His extensive volumes of poetry place him among the greats in Brazilian literature. While imprisoned in the Casa dos Contos in July 1789, he died under mysterious circumstances, either by suicide or at the hands of his captors.[16] A few blocks to the west rises the Morro da Forca (Gallows Hill) where colonial officials carried out frequent hangings. One of the highest hills in the city, Richard recommends to the reader that the spot be "visited for the sake of the view."[17] Landscaped, restored, and with a (steep) tile staircase, the location today remains impressive, with a 360-degree view of the entire city.

Before leaving Ouro Preto, Richard made one last side trip, to climb the Itacolomi Peak, a geological landmark that towers over the city. Rising nearly 6,000 feet above sea level and 2,500 feet above Ouro Preto, this solid quartzite ridge strikes up abruptly and, like many of the ridges in the region, has a sharp, jagged, and angular profile. At the highest point along the ridgeline, a massive shaft of weathered stone juts out several hundred feet with a slight lean to the west. The image is something of a Rorschach test. For some, it is a huge snout sticking out of the surface, for others something more sexual. The distinctive *serra* and the striking protuberance dominate Ouro Preto's southern horizon. On the Burtons' last day in Ouro Preto, one of the commander's employees guided them back east toward Mariana, then south to the peak. The gigantic rock rose up before them, "a spectre looming tall through the grey mist, then completely wrapped in cloud-swathe, then standing out with startling distinctness." For Richard, it was the "diamond edition" of the Serra do Caraça.[18] Near the top of the peak, looking slightly to the northwest, Richard could see the Serra do Caraça, and slightly to the northeast, the craggy Morro de Santa Anna and the scattered ruins of its mining operations. Far off to the southwest rose the "jagged walls" of São João del Rei he had visited a few weeks earlier.[19]

Ever the linguist, Richard reviews the various meanings of Itacolomi (spelled Itacolumi in the nineteenth century) and its indigenous roots. The name is generally translated as "child of stone," but Richard insists that it means "stone and child." The tall spire that rises out of the ridgeline, "black and polished like a metal casting," had side surfaces "striped by wind and weather."[20] The trail to the peak today remains much the same as in 1867. This area on the south side of Ouro Preto has been set aside as a state park with hiking trails, especially along the rocky ridges leading up to Itacolomi. Somewhat like Diamantina to the north, bizarre rock formations litter the mostly barren mountainside. The trails are mostly populated by mountain biking enthusiasts who alternate between riding and carrying their bicycles. Whether at a distance from the center of Ouro Preto, or up close on the mountaintop, the peak is striking, jutting upward at an angle resembling a fat finger—or something else, depending on one's imagination.

On the return home, the "descent was far more pleasant than the ascent, not always the case in Brazilian mule-traveling." The "afternoon was magnificent," and he was "delighted with our excursion, and grateful to our guide." The only flaw in the trip that ended "long before sunset" was Richard's annoyance with the two enslaved servants they had sent ahead with provisions early that morning. He and Isabel had left the two at the base of the mountain as they made the ascent. On their return from the peak, they found them as "drunk as drunk could be" and proceeded back into town on their own, leaving the two to their own devices to find their way home. The offenders, according to Richard, "paid the penalty by not reaching home before midnight." How they reached it at all, he declared, "is still a puzzle to me."[21] As always, Richard showed little sympathy or respect for the enslaved.

Richard the Anthropologist

After nearly four hundred pages filled largely with descriptions of his travels, Richard quite self-consciously pauses near the end of volume one of *Explorations of the Highlands of the Brazil* to assume his role as the anthropologist studying the Brazilians, focusing on the people of Minas Gerais. His "descriptive anthropology" ostensibly dissects the *mineiro*, "who, like his ancestor the Paulista, is still the typical man from Brazil."[22] His Victorian views on race and racial mixture frame the analysis. Racial mixing with Indians and Africans, "the servile mixture," is "at all times and in all places a dishonour amongst the white races." As he observed in the accounts of some of his other world travels, where whites are in short supply, especially white women, "mulattism became a necessary evil."[23] The racial "science" of the late nineteenth century considered the racially mixed doomed to degeneracy and backwardness, a widely accepted "scientific" claim that bedeviled Brazilian elites and intellectuals for the next half century.

Along with his notions of racial hierarchy, Richard shared the very common view of the time that climate also deeply shaped racial formation and a nation's destiny.[24] Just as Euclides da Cunha would do thirty-five years later in his powerful analysis of the Canudos rebellion, Richard ascribed much of Brazil's fate to a detrimental mix of both race and climate.[25] The Luso-Brazilian in South America and the Anglo-American in North America, he asserted, had "been modified morally as well as physically by climate" and had "assimilated in national character to the aborigine."[26] The mixing of races and the tropical climate had produced in Brazil a stunning array of skin tones, most of them non-white. Richard here, in a somewhat offhand manner, makes an observation that many other foreigners have made over the last two hundred years about Brazilian race relations: "Here all men, especially free men who are not black, are white; and often a man is officially white, but naturally almost negro. This is directly opposed to the system of the United States, where all men who are not unmixed white are black."[27] As with the Caribbean, whites from the North Atlantic world were both dazzled and dismayed at the results of centuries of racial mixing and the more fluid racial hierarchies in Brazil.

During Richard's lifetime and into the 1930s, Brazilian intellectuals grappled with the consequences of centuries of racial and cultural mixing, nearly all believing that this heritage handicapped "progress" and the advance of "civilization" in their country.[28] Only in the 1920s and 1930s did the powerful grip of racist social science begin to ease in the North Atlantic world and in Brazil.

Intellectuals like Gilberto Freyre turned the theory on its head proclaiming racial mixture as not only the key to Brazil's essential identity, but also that it made Brazilians superior to other peoples. First under Vargas, then succeeding administrations, Freyre's vision of the "myth of three races" became the official story of Brazil and Brazilians. Most of those governments also took the next big leap with Freyre and declared Brazil a racial democracy. Whether racism exists as a serious problem in Brazil or not offers one of the most potent and divisive issues in contemporary Brazil.[29]

In his travels across Brazil in 1867, Richard also assumed the role of the physical anthropologist, completely imbued with the racist social science of the times. As he moved through Minas Gerais, he summed up the *mineiros* by body types, skin tones, and skull shapes. As was so common in his day, he sought to catalog and rank "races" by drawing clear boundaries that could be measured and systematized. Centuries of living, intermixing, and reproducing in the Americas had created new types with "a more nervous temperament" than the European and "lighter in weight." The Brazilian man, he declared, was "rather wiry and agile than strong and sturdy" and weighed in, on average, at 128 pounds. The "nervous temperament" took shape in a "thin, arched, and decided" form of nose, "with the nostrils convoluted," and a "Roman profile, full at once of energy and finesse."[30] Women were "plump and rounded," and in later life became "pulpy"! "Not a few," he pauses to note, "possess that fragile, dainty, and delicate beauty which all strangers remark." "The sturdy German fraus who land at Rio de Janeiro," he asserts, "look like three American women rolled into one"!

Richard described the typical *mineiro*'s skin as "a warm dark brown," the same "tint of Portuguese Algarves, where the Moor so long had his home."[31] He then goes on to attribute some of the more yellowed skin tones to bile secretions, in line with the typical racial theory of the times. As did so many foreign travelers, he found in the Brazilians every "variety of hue . . . from the buff color of Southern Europe to the leathery tint of the mulatto."[32] Like many of his contemporaries, he was obsessed with skull shapes and sizes. He places the Brazilians in the "dolichocephalic" group, the "long heads," as opposed to "brachycephalic," the "short heads." Much of nineteenth-century racial science was built on these now-discredited skull measurements under the belief that cranial capacity was somehow a measure of intellectual capacity and the distribution of racial groups.[33] The Brazilians, Burton believed, had "cocoanut heads," and he provided the reader with detailed descriptions of types of hair, lips, eyes, and teeth. Burton judged the "Mineiro's countenance . . . more serious than that of the European," and his gait "the light springing step of the Tupy." He worked "hard upon a spare diet" but made up "manfully for an enforced fast." "Self-reliant and confident," the mineiro, he declared, "plunges into the forest, and disdains to hive with others."[34]

The childless Burton offered a surprisingly positive view of Brazilian parents and their childrearing. "In no country," he sweepingly declared, "do progenitors sacrifice themselves so much to their progeny." "As in all new countries," he continues, "the 'infantry' grow up almost wild, and infinitely prefer the fazenda to the town; so in the United States, the traveler first remarks the tameness of the horses and the wildness of the children."[35] Noting the early age of marriage (in the teens) and the long childbearing years of women, he pronounced Brazil just as fertile in its childbearing as in its natural endowments. As did so many foreign travelers, Burton notes the "semi-seclusion" of women, attributing the custom to the Portuguese and the strong influence of Islam in Iberian history. At one estate, the woman head of house made Richard and Isabel coffee and dinner and sat chatting with them all evening. Richard notes how rare this exposure to the woman of the house was in his Brazilian experience, likely because Dona Conrada "still in her teens, was the mother of three children and the widow of a tropeiro."[36] "In none but the most civilised families do the mistress and daughters of the house sit down to the table with the stranger." All men, he claims, protect their women in one of two ways, either through seclusion to keep them "out of temptation" (in the Orient) or "as we do, they expose them freely, but with the gaslight of publicity turned full upon them." "The girls are never prettier than between thirteen and sixteen," he says, "when they are little women."[37]

In one of his typically sweeping judgments, Richard asserts that "cities and large towns are mostly on a par as regards morality all the world over; a nation must be judged by its village and country life." He finds the conduct of Brazilian women "exemplary," although his evidence comes from Brazilian women who have married English husbands.[38] A "breach of virtue is almost impossible," in his view, because the "opportunity is almost wholly wanting" and the strong possibility of a bullet in the head or a knife in the heart dissuades the potential seducer. Surely another factor was the powerful patriarchal structures in Brazilian society. In a careful assessment of statistics on crime in Minas, Richard also observed that the "wife-beater" may "rest assured that nowhere in the wide world they will be treated so kindly and considerately" by the judicial system.[39]

After praising the honor and virtue of wives, he notes the "extreme prevalence of professional prostitution in the country towns of Brazil."[40] While discussing the need for the clergy to marry, Richard declares that the "climate is not favourable to chastity," and that "the race, especially where the blood is mixed, is of inflammable material." He adds that "the sayings and doings of slaves do not comport with early modesty." Long a supporter of polygamy (if not a practitioner himself), he criticizes virginity as "an idea revolting to reason and common sense, especially in a young country, where polygamy is morally justifiable, the evils being more than counterbalanced by the benefits."[41] He had made a similar argument in *The City of the Saints* after his visit with Brigham Young in Utah in 1860.[42]

As in the West of the United States, all men in Minas carried arms. After analyzing the official provincial statistics on crime, Richard concludes that the rich murder their countrymen for one of three reasons—land disputes, political conflict, or "affairs of the heart." The "poor kill one another after quarrels about land, gambling losses, love, and liquor: the cachaça or drunken fray ends in bloodshed."[43] In an odd footnote that betrays yet again his low opinion of Black people, he observes that many of the offenses listed in the statistics "are committed by the servile population ... under the excitement of the expected emancipation." He claims to have heard many a Black person "chattering at the fountain" that the "English are soon coming to set us free."[44] In the end, he concludes that the "ratio of crime to population is trifling," despite a very small police force. "Nowhere is travelling safer for foreigners who do not engage in politics, amours, or law suits."[45]

In a section that must have contributed to Isabel's motivation to insert her controversial preface to the account, Richard asserts that the *mineiro* as well as the *paulista* "is a religious man but a lax Catholic," more superstitious than fanatical in his beliefs, and with "a certain horror of any one non-Catholic."[46] The Brazilians, he believed, were "ripe for religious reform," in particular the need for greater tolerance of non-Catholic religions and beliefs. "Brazil," he goes on, "will do well to consider the example of the United States, which have risen to their present state of prosperity by thorough and unlimited toleration."[47] Brazil will not be a truly cosmopolitan country, he asserts, "until complete equality in civil as in religious matters shall level all obstacles in the path of progress."[48]

Despite his relativistic view of cultures and plea for religious toleration, Richard at times exhibited antisemitic attitudes, a topic long debated among his many biographers. Although he declares, at one point in his description of *mineiros*, "Had I a choice of race, there is none to which I would belong more willingly than the Jewish—of course the white family." After a later disastrous experience in Damascus with Jewish merchants, Burton wrote an antisemitic tract that would not be published until well after his death, and then with some of the more extreme sections edited out.[49] In describing the Brazilians, Burton compares them to the Hebrews, saying both races are "smart," producing "first-rate men of business, and many have colossal fortunes in a few years." There is, he goes on, "little of the grasping, tenacious covetousness vulgarly attributed . . . to the Hebrew." Commerce is well regarded, and "half the titled men in the land have been or are in trade, directly or indirectly."[50]

Assuming the role of fashion critic, Richard critiqued in detail the typical garb of both men and women. "The dress" of the upper class he characterized "as purely European." Having given up the old Iberian styles, a "gentleman never appears in the street, even at dawn, without chimney-pot tile (chapéo alto), black coat, waistcoat, and overalls black or white, cane or umbrella." Travelers like Richard had to follow "the semi-barbarous custom, and dress in broadcloth behind a bush before they enter a house."[51] The *mineiro* on the road wore a Panama hat and "huge loose-topped boots" and linens or cotton kept "scrupulously clean." The poor, in his view, "imitate the wealthy; but their garments are often home-woven and home-cut." Upper-class women, he believed, delighted "in flowers and perfumes" and had a "predilection for diamonds and rich toilettes." Among the well-to-do, bathing was frequent, a custom Richard attributed to the influence of the Indigenous peoples on Brazilian culture.[52]

Contradictory attitudes and ambivalence run throughout Burton's detailed two-volume account of his travels across Brazil. At times, he is the enthusiast and promoter extolling the virtues of the Brazilians, especially of the upper classes, and what he sees as a bright future for the country. His own sense of superiority as an Englishman, world traveler, and intellectual frequently lead him to disparage Brazilians of all social classes, although his strongest criticisms invariably are directed at the poor and the enslaved. His ambivalence and contradictions reflect his own internal conflicts and incongruities. Richard's anthropological outlook at times approaches the cultural relativism of the twentieth century, recognizing that all cultures and peoples have their own internal logics and traditions that make sense for them. His accounts of his travels through South Asia, the Middle East, Africa, the US West, and South America constantly reveal his understanding, and even at times (grudging) empathy, for the peoples he observes. Yet he never makes the final step to a full cultural relativism and its logic that all cultures are equally valid, and that none has a lock on "truth." Instead, his Victorian English classist prejudices reassert themselves as he turns to the racist social theory of the era, a worldview that condemned the racially mixed Brazilians and their enslaved Africans to backwardness and inferiority.

Drawing on his time in São Paulo, he found the *paulista* to be more "at home with strangers than his cousin" the *mineiro*. The former, he believed, was less reserved and more receptive to strangers met along the road. *Mineiro* travelers he met along the way sometimes "stared at me surlily and angrily" and the women "made faces." He speculated that the wariness may have been on account of the ongoing war in Paraguay and the fear of conscription agents seeking "recruits." The war "made the people of the interior consider every foreigner as an agent of government, or travelling for some dark purpose." The increasing number of foreigners in the region, he notes, had not taught the locals respect for foreigners "and no wonder." "Familiarity with such men—I hasten to say that there are many notable exceptions—can breed only contempt." Surely, Richard thought of himself as one of the exceptions.[53]

Richard's optimism appeared when discussing education in Minas Gerais, a province that had produced great poets and many distinguished figures in the arts. The minimal system of education, he believed, was very uneven: it produced exceptional men in the humanities, but modern science and the mechanical arts were "unknown" in the province. His view of the schooling system was exceptionally optimistic based on government statistics. It "may be safely said that every poor man's son, except in the remotest places, can obtain primary instruction, that the three R's are generally studied, and that those unable to read and write do not number as many as England and France." He then goes on to make the astonishing statement that "the total darkness still found among the lower orders in Europe, the utter absence of knowledge, is here confined to idiots."[54] The literacy rate in Brazil at the time he made this claim was likely around 10 percent, and the literate were primarily concentrated in urban areas.[55]

Books and magazines were "rare and expensive," and the newspaper served as the principal literary venue of the region. There was but one printing press in Minas, and two newspapers, one liberal and one conservative, both located in Ouro Preto. For Richard, "the newspaper is progression, it is the literature of the Future."[56] In Minas, "as elsewhere, the tone of the newspaper is the expression of society," and advertisements struck Richard as the "most characteristic part of a newspaper."[57] Patent medicines filled most of the two pages of advertisements in the local papers, along with items for sale, real estate, and runaway slave ads. In such ads "fugido" (fled) was printed in large letters, along with notice of a substantial reward and the image of "an anthropoid with a bundle over his shoulder and a switch in his hand."[58]

Before departing the "Imperial City," Richard reiterated the need for the province to build "postal and telegrammic communication, or roads, and railways." Minas had no railway lines in 1867 and no river navigation services. In a moment of Victorian optimism, he declared that "with these improved [Minas] may confidently look to a great and glorious future."[59] In Brazil he found "another symptom of strong and healthy national vitality," where men were not content to rest on their laurels. Richard declared that there "is everything to hope from a race with prepossessions for progress towards such a high ideal," that of the European nations.[60] To achieve its potential, the Brazilians would have to follow the path blazed by Europe, especially Great Britain. The many different peoples of the planet might each have their own cultural logic and traditions, but in the end, Richard's England stood at the top of the evolutionary chain of humanity.

CHAPTER 9

A RAFT, A RIVER, AND A LONELY RIDE

> At Sabará we concluded our 500 miles of land journey through the richest and the most popular part of Minas Geraes. Here, however, ends the excursionist portion . . . But what now comes is not yet exactly a pleasure trip down the Thames or up the Rhine: there are hot suns, drenching rains, and angry winds to be endured; there is before us a certain amount of hardship, privation, and fatigue, with just enough risk to enliven the passage; and, finally, there are nearly 1300 miles to be covered by the craziest of crafts, caulked with Sabará clay.
>
> —RICHARD BURTON

Richard and Isabel's days in Ouro Preto concluded their tour of the mining zone, and on Saturday, 20 July, they left the provincial capital for a two-day, fifty-mile ride north, back to Morro Velho. Shortly after leaving the western edge of Ouro Preto, they headed northwest into the Rio das Velhas River Valley, a tributary that would become the first leg of Richard's voyage down the São Francisco River. Thirty-six hours of rain soaked the ground under them on the route and turned the "clay greasy as tallow." About halfway to Morro Velho they came across yet another of the ill-fated English gold mines, Morro do São Vicente (Saint Vicente Hill).

One of Edward Oxenford's companies (East Del Rey) had purchased the estate in 1864 for more than $175,000, and some three years later all that remained were a few houses for miners and a casa grande "of notable size."[1] Thomas Treloar's brother ran the operation, but he was not in residence. "Failure," remarks Richard, "is its actual state."

Small iron mining operations and luxury condominium communities now spill across the western slopes of the river basin between Ouro Preto and Morro Velho that the Burtons traversed in July 1867. The Canadian company Jaguar Mining Inc. now owns the tiny Morro do São Vicente gold deposit and has stripped away the mountaintop.[2] A few miles to the west sits Itabirito (known as Itabira do Campo in 1867) and nearby the famous Itabira Peak, with the ruins of the Cata Branca Mine on its eastern slopes. Just north of Itabirito the old Royal Road narrows and turns rugged, making passage the rest of the way to Morro Velho possible only with the sturdiest off-road vehicle today. The only passable route for an automobile runs west through iron mining and gated communities built on the shores of lakes the St. John d'el Rey constructed to power its hydroelectric power plants in the early twentieth century. Returning to Morro Velho from Ouro Preto and the south now requires heading back to the west and the interstate highway BR-040.

Return to Morro Velho

In an age before highways and automobiles, the Burtons and their entourage rode on through driving rain into the small town of Rio das Pedras (River of Stones), where the churches were numerous "and far exceed in cubic contents the dwelling-houses—a pleasant aspect to the ecclesiastic, and an eye-sore to the economist"! At the "pigmy hostelry" they encountered a group of about a dozen Confederate expatriates from Mississippi and Georgia, led by an elderly fellow in a black swallowtail coat.[3] This was neither Burton's first nor last encounter with these "Confederados." Richard's view of them, like his view of the Brazilians, combined both condescension and optimism. In the immediate aftermath of the Civil War, several thousand Southerners emigrated to Brazil with promises of land in the largest remaining slave society in the Americas. As with most land colonization schemes, these promises proved illusory for most, but in the eastern Amazon (around Santarém) and in the state of São Paulo, clusters of the Confederados created lasting communities that today remain proud of their heritage, and Brazilians with American surnames (e.g., Jones, Vaughan, Riker) bear witness to this Southern exodus. The neighboring cities of Americana and Santa Bárbara d'Oeste about an hour northwest of the city of São Paulo host an annual festival that honors the food, clothing, and symbols of the antebellum US South.[4]

Richard notes that he had already met up with "several parties of these refugees," and this group would not be the last. Isabel's memory of this group was much more favorable than Richard's. She found them "amusing, clever, and intelligent."[5] Richard laments that "the first impression made by our Transatlantic cousins—speaking only of the farmer and little educated class—is peculiar and unpleasant." In them, "the bristly individuality of the Briton appears to have grown rank" and their ideas were "rigid and cast in iron." "They are," he complains, "untaught, but ready to teach everything." Richard describes them as narcissistic, lacking in geniality, suspicious of strangers—and complainers. Nevertheless, he believed they would be able to teach Brazilians "practical mechanical knowledge" and leaven Brazil's "population with rugged northern energy."[6] After explaining why the French, Portuguese, Irish, Scots, and even the English all fail to contribute productively to Brazil, he finds it "impossible not to admire the pluck and spirit of these pilgrims."[7] Imbued with the evolutionary thinking of the time, Richard believed that these immigrants represented "the young, the brave, and the adventurous" and that they would strengthen the Brazilian population, "improving the race." The result would be that Brazil could then "expect to play a conspicuous part in the great drama of Human Progress."[8]

As I was surprised to discover only a few years ago, some of my own ancestors formed part of this Southern migration. My maternal grandfather's grandmother, Elizabeth Hanna Pyles (1821–1891), left Anderson County, South Carolina, with her husband and children in the aftermath of the Civil War and settled in central Texas. Her brother Samuel Milton Pyles (1816–1898) and sister Mary Rochester Pyles Seawright (1824–1897) left for Brazil in 1867 with their spouses and many children, settling in what would become the city of Americana in the state of São Paulo.

Today, they rest among the more than five hundred well-tended graves in the Confederado cemetery in Santa Bárbara d'Oeste just outside Americana.[9] They arrived in Brazil at the very moment Richard came upon groups of their compatriots in Minas Gerais. It would be a delicious historical irony if they had crossed paths with the Burtons before the couple left Brazil!

On Sunday, 21 July, the Burtons set out (once again) through the wind and rain, covering the last 25 miles of their nearly two-week expedition through the heart of the mining zone. They had made a circuit of some 13 days, covering 130 miles, and spending more than 40 hours in the saddle. In the late afternoon, they arrived "home" at Morro Velho, where the two of them would spend another two weeks as guests of the Gordons in the *sobrado* alongside the Casa Grande. During this time, they made their descent into the mine, and Richard thoroughly explored the works. If we are to believe Isabel's account in her autobiography, Richard was still contemplating whether to allow her to accompany him down the 1,300 miles of the São Francisco when "the question for me was settled by an accident."[10] On 27 July he gave a lecture about his world travels to the English officers and their families, apparently meant as a farewell talk. Afterward, during a "concert," after joining in the singing, Isabel forgot "the drop behind the open-air theatre [and] when I backed off, I fell. I sprained my ankle so badly that my leg was all black, and I could not move." In her version of her failure to accompany Richard down the river, she says, "This was a dreadful bore for Richard, who could not take" her down the river, for "it was impossible to take a woman who could not walk," and he "did not like to leave me, so he good-naturedly put off his journey for ten days."[11]

But leaving Isabel behind was likely Richard's plan from the beginning. In a letter to a friend in England just days before the couple departed from Rio de Janeiro in June, he wrote, "I am off for a few months trip to the Gold Mines & the Great Interior. My wife accompanies me part of the way."[12] This discrepancy between the two firsthand accounts we have of Richard's expedition, however seemingly minor, points directly to the fundamental question of how we know what we know, in this case, for the veracity of the Burtons' observations in all their travels through Brazil. The historian has to read Richard's accounts understanding that his overtly hypermasculine, self-assured, and imperial gaze colors his perspective on all he sees—and does not see.[13] Although Isabel brings with her many of the same imperial Victorian prejudices, she also speaks from a much less cosmopolitan and much more deeply religious worldview than Richard, and one that is much more feminine. Her account appears in the "autobiography" completed by W. H. Wilkins in 1897. Although much of the book draws directly on letters and documents produced during her time in Brazil, all of her account is mediated by nearly thirty years of hindsight, memory, and things long forgotten. At times, the historian—certainly *this* historian—is reading nineteenth-century Brazil through the eyes of both Burtons, each of whom has their own strengths and weaknesses.

Ten days after her accident, Richard headed just over the Serra do Curral (Corral Range) to the city of Sabará, where he would begin three months navigating the São Francisco. Mr. L'pool (Arthur Earle) had decided to head back to his fiancée in Rio de Janeiro and accompanied the fortnightly Morro Velho "gold troop" southward on 28 July. They would marry in Rio in November. With his new wife, Earle would return to Liverpool for a long career running his father's seed oil export business, leaving behind a considerable fortune of more than £600,000 (roughly $100 million in 2025 dollars) on his death in 1919 at the age of eighty.[14] Richard "bade adieu to the Casa Grande" on Tuesday, 6 August, with "a peculiar cat-like feeling," looking forward to the next stage of his trip and "to being one of the pioneers of a great national movement."[15]

As they departed, the group headed north, crossed the Cardoso Stream, passed through the mine works, then headed uphill past the slave quarters on their left and with the Morro Velho rising on their right. Isabel accompanied Richard in a litter, a sort of "covered stretcher" carried between two mules, with a driver for each mule.[16] The entourage had to follow along the southern slopes of the Serra do Curral, which today serves as the dividing line between the municipalities of Nova Lima and Belo Horizonte. It was also the northern limit of the original Morro Velho estate. Running in a north-northeast direction, some sections of the range contain massive deposits of high-grade hematite. In the late twentieth century, these iron ore deposits would become more valuable than the exhausted gold mine. A Brazilian-US mining conglomerate dismantled the top of the range in a huge open-pit mine in the final decades of the century, leaving a stunning gap in the once-iconic mountain skyline between the two cities.[17]

Cresting the *serra*, the group had a magnificent view to the northeast of Sabará some eight miles away and, even closer, the tiny village of Curral d'el Rei to the west. Given the small village's scarce few hundred inhabitants and one prominent church, little could Richard know that thirty years later, the new capital for Minas Gerais would arise on the spot. He would never have been able to imagine that a century and a half later, it would comprise a metropolis of some five million. Rather than 120 square miles of concrete, glass, and densely packed urban sprawl, Richard and Isabel took in a 360-degree panorama of fields, forests, mountain ranges, and river valleys dotted with the occasional village and farm. Sabará, just a few miles away, was the largest and oldest town in the region.

The River Expedition Begins

For Richard, Sabará was a "picturesque city," "the usual long, narrow, mining settlement." In a day he scouted the usual churches (eight by his count) and plazas and checked out the local jail and school. He visited the old mint building and recounted the history of this colonial mining center. Founded along with São João del Rei, Mariana, and Ouro Preto in the second decade of the eighteenth century, Sabará served as the administrative and legal center for a large part of Minas until the creation in the 1890s of Belo Horizonte, a mere ten miles to the west.[18] By the 1860s the town had become economically dependent on the commerce generated by the Morro Velho mine, especially purchases of timber, foodstuffs, and cloth. Richard found "a mortal dullness about the place. . . . It seems to die every night, and to recover only half life in the morning," a fairly definitive observation from someone just passing through. Nevertheless, he believed that the opening of the Rio das Velhas and the São Francisco to regular navigation would transform the town, and "it must become, with time, another St. Louis, Mo." He was so sure of this that he thought "travellers of the next generation will read my description, long and somewhat tedious as it is, with interest."[19]

FIGURE 9.1. Sabará, 1868. Image in the public domain. Auguste Riedel.

A community of less than seven thousand inhabitants in the 1860s, the town contained fewer than three dozen foreigners. Today, with a population of more than 125,000, Sabará forms an integral part of Greater Belo Horizonte, a metropolitan area of more than thirty counties and five million people.[20] The old center of Sabará remains one of the principal stops among the historical cities of Minas Gerais. In the 1920s and 1930s, the Luxembourg iron and steel consortium ARBED established its headquarters and first plant in Sabará, attracting a substantial European community of employees for the Brazilian subsidiary Belgo Mineira. Attracted by the enormous iron deposits in Minas, the company forged iron and steel using charcoal fuel. This required the planting of hundreds of square miles of fast-growing eucalyptus trees to supply the blast furnaces. These eucalyptus farms cover hundreds of square miles of hillsides in the surrounding region today. The massive Indian conglomerate ArcelorMittal now controls Belgo

FIGURE 9.2. *Ajôjô* on the Rio das Velhas, 1868. Image in the public domain. Auguste Riedel.

Mineira's many industrial operations, and the company continues to fuel its furnaces with charcoal in a country with no significant coal deposits.[21]

Richard contracted a local merchant, Manoel Pereira de Mello Vianna, to construct his river boat and supply his provisions for the trip. Mello Vianna, a Portuguese immigrant, had become a very successful businessman and fazendeiro, and an important supplier for Morro Velho. His son, Fernando, born a decade after Richard's passage through Sabará, would serve as governor of Minas Gerais and vice president of Brazil in the 1920s. In one of those strange twists of history, this Portuguese immigrant's grandson, Fernando de Sousa Mello Vianna, trained as a mining engineer at the School of Mines in Ouro Preto in the 1920s, would become the president of Mineração Morro Velho, the Brazilian company that assumed control of the gold mine in 1960.[22] According to Richard, Mello Vianna "unfortunately" had "been in England; he spoke our language, and thus he could exploit all the hapless Anglo-Americans who fell into his hands." So disgusted was Richard with the bill from Mello Vianna that he translated it fully in a footnote with comments on the exorbitant charges for the "very old" canoes, poles, lumber, and carpentry work to build the boat. He also complained that "in addition to the extortionate charges," Mello Vianna sent him "down a river like the Mississippi in a raft whose starboard canoe had a 'racha,' or leak, hardly stopped with Sabará clay."[23]

A RAFT, A RIVER, AND A LONELY RIDE

The craft, one common to the São Francisco River Valley, known as an *ajôjô*, consisted of two thirty-three-foot-long canoes hollowed out of logs underneath a twenty-two-foot-long raft made of ten wooden planks. Iron bars connected the two canoes to each other, fore and aft, with each canoe some three feet wide. A tent-like cotton awning, supported by wooden stanchions, rose some seven feet over the deck with "wax-cloth from Morro Velho" over Richard's bunk. He had carpenters build a tall writing desk, and behind this was a boarded bunk, "for sofa and bed," raised on four uprights. "Amidships was the table, a locked box of provisions flanked by two stools." A small galley with a brick stove sat in the stern complete with pots, cups, a frying pan, and two large earthen jars for their water supply. On the advice of Mr. Gordon, the builders had included "a stout boat-hook, with an anchor in the bows."[24]

Burton's initial provisions included jerked meat, what Brazilians call *carne seca* or *carne do sol*, lard, beans and rice, and *cachaça* for the crew. In a separate locked box, he kept his personal stores of salt, sugar, pepper, tea, cognac, gin, and "a few tins of beef, sardines, and potted meats." One of the English officers at Morro Velho had given him "a few valuable boxes" of excellent Cuban cigars. Richard also brought along about $700 in Brazilian banknotes (ranging from about $0.50 to $5.00) and coins to pay his crew and for purchases. Three Black men (following Isabel's description) crewed the craft, "old Vieira and his sons." Mr. Gordon "lent" him "a Morro Velho boy, named 'Agostinho'" who knew "something of the river, of gold washing, of diamond digging, and rough cookery," to attend to Richard during the journey. "Despite occasional attacks of dipsomania [drunkenness], he proved very useful," according to Richard, and on his return to Rio de Janeiro in November, "he was returned to store with all the honours."[25] Like so many of those attending to the English and the Brazilian upper classes, Agostinho was just another piece of property to be returned to his owner.

At the beginning of the trip, Richard brought along some passengers. One was the "mastiff-pup" Dr. Lee had given Richard in São João del Rei in mid-June. He described Negra as "lank in body, with brindled coat, square head, broad shoulders, and huge hands and feet."[26] Wild-eyed as a leopard, she "becomes very savage when tied up, and barks as if under a waggon tilt. She is the terror of those who see her for the first time, and she will prove useful—in these parts all men travel with fierce dogs." Two men briefly accompanied him—a local Brazilian who departed quickly a short way down the river, and Mr. Hock, the old Confederado (of the swallowtail coat) he and Isabel had encountered in Rio das Pedras as they returned to Morro Velho from Ouro Preto. Apparently, "this old pilgrim father" had brought about twenty souls with him, and all had been "spirited away by the indefatigable" Mello Vianna. Hock now had grandiose plans to build a railroad. He disembarked after just two days.[27]

Richard launched his "old Noah's Ark" on Wednesday, 7 August (exactly eight weeks after leaving Rio), with a bit of fanfare. Miss Dundas (James Pennycook Brown's niece) broke a bottle of *cachaça* "with all possible grace upon the bows, and christened my craft the 'Brig Eliza'" (no doubt named after Isabel's mother). After many "vivas" honoring the Burtons, the Gordons, and the emperor, Isabel, Miss Dundas, and a dozen others stepped on board, nearly swamping the boat. Heading northwest down the river, after two miles, the launch party stepped off the craft at Santo Antônio da Roça Grande, where mules awaited the "non-voyagers" for the ride back to Morro Velho. As Richard and his crew continued downstream, Isabel stood "as the setting sun sank behind the mountains—and watched the raft turn the last corner and float off into the far mysterious unknown." Richard confessed "to having felt an unusual sense of loneliness as the kindly faces faced in the distance, and, by way of 'distraction,' I applied my brain to the careful examination of my conveyance."[28]

Isabel's "Lonely Ride to Rio"

Isabel and the entourage returned to Morro Velho that evening, and she stayed on for nearly another three weeks, allowing her ankle to heal. One day, while Isabel was sitting on the steps of the Blacks' Catholic church, mourners passed by on the way to the Blacks' cemetery, carrying "some hammocks with bodies lying in them. They were carried by others, all dripping in blood."[29] The kibble chain had broken, "the same one we had been down the mine in," killing these enslaved workers. In the evenings, she entertained herself by organizing "singing parties." After she tired of "catching butterflies, which really was my principal occupation at Morro Velho," she "begged Mr. Gordon" to lend her seven animals, a muleteer, and two enslaved workers to take her back to Rio de Janeiro.[30] After nearly two months with the Gordons in this English village in the tropics, Isabel departed Morro Velho on the afternoon of Sunday, 25 August, heading south toward Rio de Janeiro. Mr. Gordon rode with her for the first few miles as she passed through the mine works, the village of Congonhas de Sabará, and to the house of the entrepreneurial widow Dona Florisbella.

Isabel described her trip as "returning after a taste of bush life . . . to the cab shafts of semi-civilization in Rio de Janeiro."[31] Although she gives the impression in her own writing that she made this mule trip largely unaccompanied except for Chico, calling it "a lonely ride," she did have an entourage. In addition to her muleteer (Senhor Jorge) and the two enslaved men, the head of the Morro Velho gold troop, Mr. Fitzpatrick, commanded the group, and the ever "faithful Chico" filled out the group with their six mules for riders and baggage. (Once again, the two enslaved men, no doubt, made their way on foot.) The troop headed due south through towns they had passed through some weeks earlier. The scenery fascinated her more than it did Richard. "The gigantic earth-slips in this part of the world present a very remarkable appearance," she remarked. "They appear as yawning gulfs, as if some awful convulsion of Nature had just taken place." The centuries of erosion created the appearance of a vast "plain that had sunk, leaving gigantic walls, fanciful castles, and pyramids of earth standing alone in the middle," all of bright red clay that reflected the sun "like a kaleidoscope."[32]

Passing through Queluz (present-day Conselheiro Lafaiette), Isabel arrived in Barbacena, where she renewed acquaintances with the Frenchman Renault, and with her German coach driver, Godfrey. The Morro Velho mule team bid farewell and headed back north, while Isabel once again boarded a coach along with Chico. "The country," she lamented, "is very much the same during all this journey, perpetual mountain, valley, forest, and river, and the only great feature is the serra [da Mantiqueira]."[33] Godfrey, who was in a hurry to return to his new bride, made the normally twelve-hour trip back to Juiz de Fora in just over eight hours! Three of her companions in the coach were US Southerners. One of them was General Alexander Travis Hawthorn. Born in Alabama, he practiced law in Arkansas before rising through the ranks in the Confederate army and fighting at the Battle of Shiloh. Like so many of the Confederados, he returned to the United States within a few years. He eventually became a Baptist minister in east Texas.[34] While touring Commander Lage's gardens again the next day, Isabel reencountered the Southerners, who were "engaged in a violent political discussion."[35] She also ran into Captain Thomas Treloar, who was returning to Mariana.

From Juiz de Fora, Isabel took the twelve-hour coach ride back to Petrópolis. Not wasting time, the next morning she headed back to Rio at 6 a.m. When she embarked on the small steamer at the northern end of Guanabara Bay, she "hid in the ladies' cabin," ashamed of her looks. "My boots," she says, "were in shreds, my only dress had about forty slits in it, my hat was in ribbons, while my face was of a reddish mahogany hue and much swollen with exposure."[36] Although she had left her maid and her luggage at the Hotel dos Estrangeiros, she discovered that it was full. So embarrassed was she by her appearance, she waited until dusk and then attempted to check into the "next best hotel" in Rio. According to Isabel, the manager was so put off by her appearance that he suggested a lower-class hotel. She demanded a room, then sent for her maid and luggage. After cleaning up, the manager did not even recognize her, and when she explained that, yes, she was the same woman he had treated rudely, "he nearly tumbled down." She rested for a few days in Rio, "reading and answering a sackful of welcome letters from home that had accumulated during my three months' absence."[37] Then she headed back to São Paulo to await Richard, a wait he had told her could be anywhere from three to six months.

CHAPTER 10

RIVER OF OLD WOMEN

> I never saw such an old Noah's Ark, with its standing awning, a floating gypsy "pál," some seven feet high and twenty-two feet long, and pitched like a tent upon two hollowed logs. The river must indeed be safe, if this article can get down without accident.
>
> —RICHARD BURTON

On 7 August 1867, two months after departing from Rio de Janeiro, Richard began the second stage (volume 2) of his "explorations," a three-month-long river voyage. He would emerge on the Atlantic coast of northeastern Brazil in early November having navigated 1,300 miles—with a one-week overland detour to Diamantina. Making his way first along the winding Rio das Velhas, he would not reach the São Francisco until mid-September. For the following two months, he and his ever-changing crew made their way down this major waterway until he reached the stunning Paulo Afonso Falls. After quickly reconnoitering the impressive cascade, he quickly covered the last 150 miles by mule to Penedo, near the coast, and then caught a steamer back to Rio de Janeiro—and to the anxiously waiting Isabel.

Highway of Nations

Unlike so many of his explorations in Africa in the 1850s, Richard was not by any means the first European to traverse this lengthy waterway through the interior. For more than two centuries, the São Francisco had served as an important route into and out of the mining zone, and its farms and ranches had long supplied dried beef, corn, and manioc flour downstream to the Atlantic littoral and upriver to Minas Gerais. The Portuguese and the increasingly mixed-race population of the colony fought, pushed back, enslaved, and exterminated the Native peoples they encountered along the length of the river basin.[1] While the transatlantic slave trade produced a racially mixed population of Africans and Europeans on the coastal regions around Bahia, Pernambuco, and Rio de Janeiro, the clash of Indigenous peoples and Luso-Brazilians gave rise to other varieties of racial mixture in the interior of the Northeast. These tough frontier people, *sertanejos*, would become the iconic figures of the parched interior (*sertão*). By the mid-nineteenth century, the region had a long-established farming and ranching economy, a civilization, in the words of an eminent Brazilian historian, of cowboys (*vaqueiros*) and leather.[2]

The route had long been touted as one with the potential to channel commerce through the Brazilian interior just as the Mississippi River gradually had become a vital commercial corridor in North America. In 1852 Pedro II contracted Henrique Halfeld, the energetic German founder of Juiz de Fora, to survey the São Francisco from the falls at Pirapora in northern Minas Gerais to the Atlantic coast. His three-volume account was published in 1860 complete with a map drawn by a fellow German emigré, Frederico Wagner.[3] Richard, no doubt, had queried Halfeld thoroughly during their encounter in Juiz de Fora in June. In the early 1860s the emperor employed the French astronomer Emmanuel Liais to survey the Rio das Velhas from Sabará to its terminus in the São Francisco, and then to follow the São Francisco upriver (southwest) to its origins in central Minas.[4] The São Francisco and the Rio das Velhas originate nearly at the same latitude about 250 miles apart, the former flowing to the northeast, and the latter to the northwest, until they converge just north of Pirapora. On a map they form an inverted V at the southern end of the São Francisco.

RIVER OF OLD WOMEN

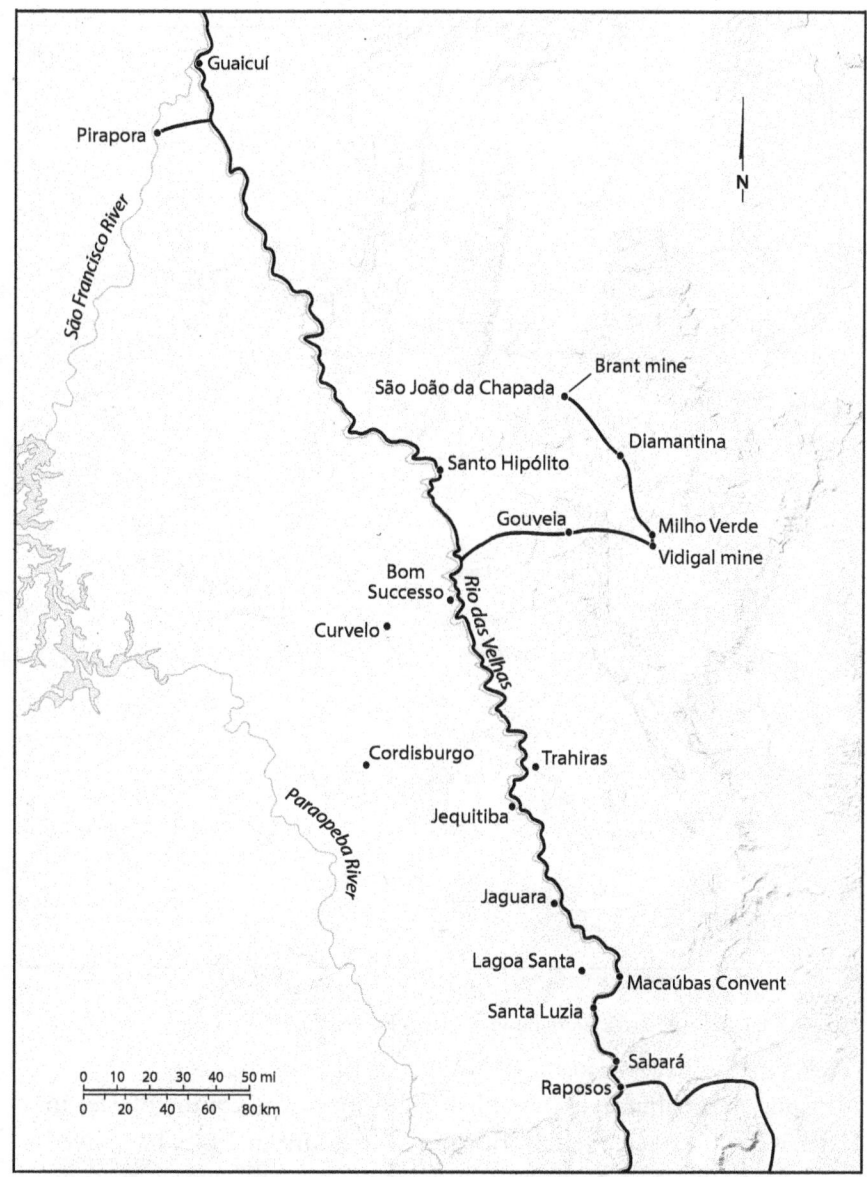

FIGURE 10.1. Richard's route down the Rio das Velhas.

The work of Liais on the southern sources of the São Francisco in mid-1862 complemented that of Halfeld from Pirapora to the sea.

Two Brazilian engineers accompanied Liais on his survey charting both rivers in great detail—every small island, set of

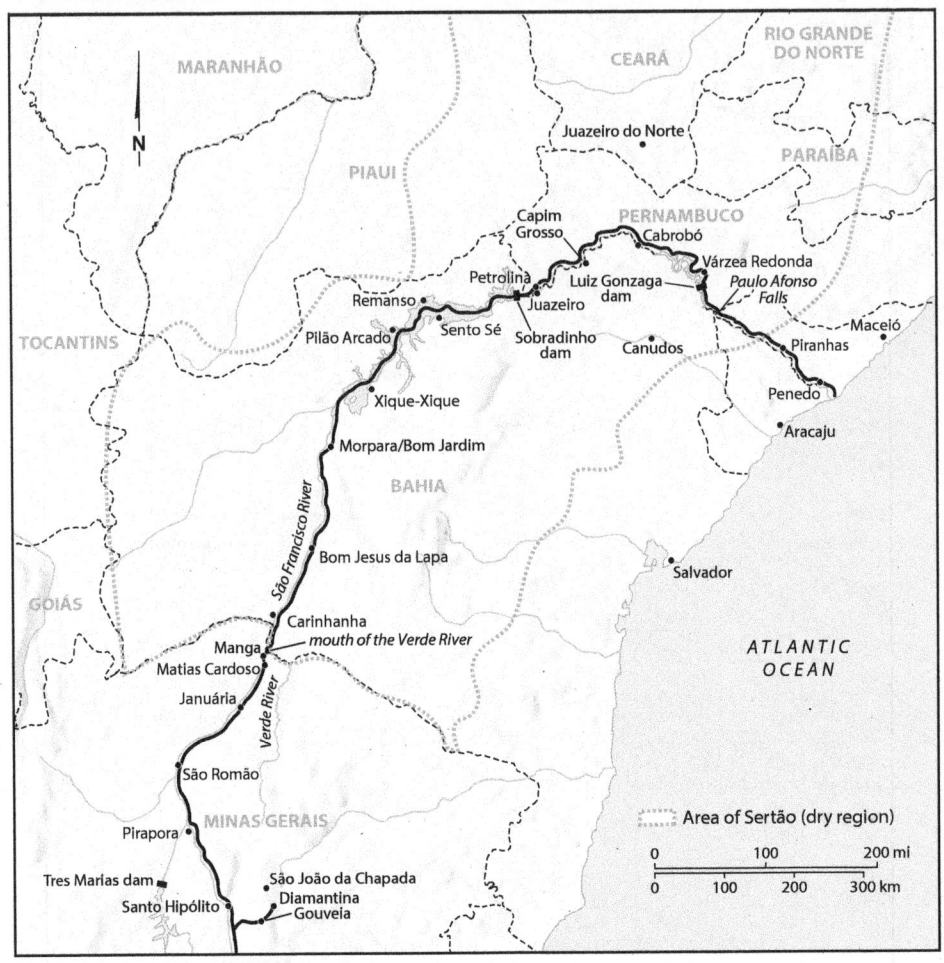

FIGURE 10.2. Richard's route down the São Francisco.

rapids, and tributary. He published his maps and commentaries in Paris in 1865—in French. Born in Cherbourg in 1826, he arrived in Brazil in 1858 to observe a solar eclipse and ended up staying for more than twenty years. During the 1870s he directed the Imperial Observatory in Rio. Richard carried copies of the works of both men with him and made a point of constantly correcting them in his footnotes.[5] Although other "explorers," most notably Halfeld and Liais, had covered large sections of the São Francisco or the Rio das Velhas, Richard asserted that he was "the only traveller who has yet passed down from Sabará to the Rapids of

Paulo Affonso."[6] Halfeld, in fact, had also began his exploration on the Rio das Velhas, and upon reaching the mouth of the São Francisco had headed upriver, retracing his path back to central Minas Gerais! Richard was clearly aware of the German Brazilian's earlier trips. This river expedition, although rugged, was certainly not anything like the Richard's arduous and death-defying explorations through uncharted East or West Africa in the 1850s and early 1860s.[7]

Burton's initial pilot, Manoel de Assumpção Vieira, and the pilot's two sons, guided the canoe-raft along a river that flows on nearly a north–south axis but wanders back and forth continually with dozens of horseshoe-shaped bends and loops. Although the distance from Sabará to where the Rio das Velhas empties into the São Francisco is about 250 miles, the mileage the river covers is nearly twice as long. Geographers today divide the Rio das Velhas River Basin into three zones.[8] The first stretches from the origin of the waterway, some 3,300 feet above sea level, on the northern fringe of Ouro Preto to Sabará. Even in the nineteenth century, this fifty-mile-long upper section of the river coursing the length of the Iron Quadrangle was too shallow and narrow for anything larger than a small canoe. Richard's voyage began at Sabará precisely because it was widely considered the southernmost reach of riverboats, even those as small and crude as his wooden *ajôjô*.

The middle region of the river stretches about 125 miles from Sabará to Santo Hipólito, a city about fifty miles west of Diamantina. Richard covered most of this stretch during his first three weeks on the water (with a detour overland to Diamantina). The emergence of the massive metropolitan area of Belo Horizonte over the last half century, and the intensification of iron mining have siphoned off enormous quantities of water and, in exchange, the urbanization and industrialization have dumped massive amounts of sewage and pollution into the river. Richard had been warned not to drink the river water, yet he did so. Drinking the dark reddish water tainted with iron tailings and many other minerals and chemicals today would be very, very unhealthy.[9]

The upper Rio das Velhas covers about another hundred miles until it empties into the São Francisco at Guaicuí, about fifteen miles north of Pirapora. While the upper section of the river crosses the Iron Quadrangle, as the river moves north from Sabará it flows into the heart of the Brazilian backlands (*sertão*), descending to an altitude just above 1,500 feet at Guaicuí. As Richard moved down the Rio das Velhas and then the São Francisco, he penetrated deeper into this almost mythical place in Brazilian culture. It would be a dramatically different environment from his experience along the Brazilian coast in Santos and Rio, and the mineral-rich mountains of Minas Gerais. For geographers, the *sertão* forms a zone stretching from northern Minas Gerais through most of the interior of the states of Bahia, Alagoas, Pernambuco, and Paraíba, all the way north to the Atlantic coast in the states of Piauí, Ceará, and Rio Grande do Norte. Known for its semiarid climate, extended droughts, scrubby vegetation, tough inhabitants, and extreme poverty, the region carries with it a vivid regional identity somewhat similar to Appalachia in the United States.[10]

João Guimarães Rosa, one of Brazil's greatest writers, wrote some of the most evocative and lyrical prose about the *sertão*.[11] Born at the beginning of the twentieth century, some fifty miles north of Sabará, Guimarães Rosa's hometown of Cordisburgo lies to the west of the river. Much like Burton, a self-taught linguist who mastered a dozen languages, Guimarães Rosa was raised in the *sertão* and the new state capital, Belo Horizonte, where he trained as a physician in the 1920s. He would produce one pathbreaking, brilliant novel, *Grande sertão: veredas* (translated into English as *Devil to Pay in the Backlands* [1963], but more literally meaning "Big Backlands: Pathways"), and many short stories and novellas.[12] Considered Brazil's greatest novel by many, *Grande sertão* is the long, complex story of Riobaldo, a *jagunço* (gunman or mercenary), written in a prose often compared to that of James Joyce's *Ulysses*. Filled with invented vocabulary, dialect, and wordplay and written in one long, almost stream-of-consciousness segment of five hundred pages with no chapter or section breaks, *Grande sertão* is a challenge to both the reader and the translator. Riobaldo, as an old man, tells his story to an anonymous listener, a tale of battles between clashing ranchers and their gunmen, of deep friendship and love, betrayals, and a pact with the devil. The São Francisco River and its environs play a large role as the setting for *Grande sertão*.

The first leg of Richard's voyage was a short, three days and forty miles from Sabará to the Jaguara estate where he would stay a week. He paid the crew of "old Vieira and his sons" about $2.50

per day and meals. The "working day" ran from seven in the morning until five in the evening and involved poling the craft down river, around the many bends, and through numerous rocky rapids, called *cachoeiras* (waterfalls) by the locals. While Vieira guided from the crude rudder in the stern, his two sons in the bow used 15 to 20-foot-long poles (*varas*), of a "supple Peroba" wood, about two inches in diameter to help move the craft forward and to push it way from rocks, trees, and riverbanks. Iron tips covered the ends of the poles for greater strength in combating the rocks and sandbars. Paddles, Richard discovered, were essentially useless. He complained that the crew had no system, and that when the water "is almost dead," the crew "lie upon their oars and lazily allow themselves to be floated down" the river. They did, however, heartily enjoy blowing a cow horn (*bozina de chifre*) to announce their arrival at villages and salute those on the passing shores![13]

In the early going, Richard lamented the narrow riverbed. The banks were "often perpendicular" and of "gravel, sand, or dark puggy clay." During the rainy season—from November to January—the water levels could rise as much as four to five feet. Moving down the river at the end of the dry season, the big problem was low water levels, at which the river would grow wider and shallower, and the boat would "ground with unpleasant regularity." The crew had to "tumble" into the water to move the craft through shallows and around tree trunks protruding from the riverbed. To make matters worse, the climate created even more obstacles—heavy "morning mists" that "enforce idleness" followed by a hot sun in the late August afternoons. In compensation, the surrounding forest teemed with the beauty of the purple glory tree (*flor de quaresma*) and tall palms.[14] The lack of humidity reminded Richard of the Persian Gulf, "where water-colours cannot be used because the moisture is absorbed from the brush."[15]

At the end of his first day afloat, Richard docked at Santa Luzia, a sizable town of some twenty thousand souls on the east bank of the river.[16] He quickly checked out the two main churches on the principal street, Rosário at the western end and the main cathedral (*matriz*) at the eastern end atop the highest point in the area. After his brief foray around town, he concluded that "prostitution is the most thriving trade" in this "church town" visited "by the planters on Sundays and holidays." Saint Lucy, he reminded the reader, is "the patroness of the blind, and generally holds in her hand an eye apparently gouged."[17] The cathedral still towers above the town and the surrounding countryside. The massive outward expansion of Belo Horizonte has drawn Santa Luzia into its northeastern perimeter. Saint Lucy has, apparently, turned a blind eye on the steady destruction of the few remaining colonial and nineteenth-century structures around the old town center.

The next "delicious" morning, the crew cast off headed for the Macaúbas Convent. The river deepened, and Richard wrote enthusiastically about the fishing potential of the region describing in detail the various nets, baskets, and lines used by the locals. He complained that he could not even get his crew to throw a line into the water. He noted that "little game appears on the banks" and that marshes and climate made walking in search of game "detestable."[18] Just about fifteen miles downriver, the convent sits on a hill on the east bank. Dating back to the first years of the eighteenth-century gold rush, the main building took shape in the 1740s, purportedly "the oldest religious house in Minas."[19]

Richard had met the first cousin of the local priest, Padre Lana, while visiting the Itacolomi Peak in Ouro Preto, and the cleric now gave him a full tour of the premises. Exhibiting his usual skepticism of Catholicism, Richard noted the influx of conservative (ultramontane) priests from Europe who were imposing an ascetic set of rules for the nunneries in Brazil, whose sisters previously had been more public and devotional. "The thirty-six reverend women," he observed, were "dressed in white veils, and petticoats with black scapulars in front, and over all a blue capa or cloak."[20] He found the reverend mother a "rather pretty person." She also accompanied him through the tour and then shepherded twenty-five giggling students to their classes. The enslaved housekeeper who met him as he initially entered the building "refused to give coffee before we declared our names," leading him to observe, "Such is the effect of a single party of highly Protestant emigrants visiting so highly Catholic a place."[21] Surely Richard did not include himself among the "highly Protestant"?

Mr. Hock had apparently had an unhappy encounter with a priest on an earlier occasion who had accused him of heresy. The Southerner asked Richard, "with Ay-merican gravity," if he really thought that the sisters "were chaste," leading Richard to observe that these Anglo-American men were "so jealous of their countrywomen's honour" that they found "libertinism" everywhere. Padre Lana, observing "the old man champing in melancholy silence, behind his thin drawn-down lips" a huge plug of tobacco, remarked, "What a sad (triste) race they seem to be."[22] The monastery continues to function, still isolated in the rural hinterland, with a small group of nuns who produce wines and sweets for local markets. Sheds and fields for mules and cattle, looking very much like they could take in the nineteenth-century traveler, greet the modern adventurer. The beautifully designed gardens and patio in the front of the monastery look out across the floodplain to the Rio das Velhas a few hundred yards to the west.

After a clear, cool night the moans of the dove and piping of cranes served as Richard's wakeup call, and the motley crew set out for the Jaguara estate. After an overnight stop on the river, on a clear morning they made their way to their destination in a couple of hours. The estate compound rose up on "the left bank a large and much decayed square of white-washed and red-tiled building, backed by a neat church."[23]

Jaguara and the Holy Lake

Richard spent "five pleasant days" at "this hospitable house" making final arrangements for his trip to Diamantina, finding another crew for his boat, and taking a side trip in search of a venerable Scandinavian naturalist in nearby Lagoa Santa (Holy Lake).[24] The vast Jaguara fazenda dated back to the early eighteenth century but had been recently purchased by the wealthy and ubiquitous Francisco de Paula Santos. His son-in-law Henrique Dumont administered the property. (Dumont's wife would give birth six years later to a son, Alberto, who would become Brazil's most famous aviator in the early years of the twentieth century.) Dumont built an iron-hulled, flat-bottom steamship that carried massive loads of enormous timbers to Sabará to supply the Morro Velho mine. More than one hundred feet long and twenty-four feet wide, this shallow-draft flat boat, when fully loaded with lumber, took twelve days on the trip upriver and, once empty, two to three days to return. The German photographer Auguste Riedel captured a wonderful image of the main buildings of the estate not long after Richard's visit (see fig. 10.3).[25]

FIGURE 10.3. Jaguara estate, 1868. Image in the public domain. Auguste Riedel.

Dumont was not the first to build a steamboat on the river. As early as 1833, William Kopke, a German who had come out initially with the British mining company at Cocais, began building a steamboat at Sabará. This early attempt at navigating the Rio das Velhas and the São Francisco was short-lived. On its maiden voyage, Kopke's craft struck a submerged tree trunk only a few miles downstream from Sabará and sank on the spot. The first attempt at steam navigation on the Rio das Velhas lasted less than an hour![26] More than thirty years later, Richard passed the partially submerged ruins of the ill-fated vessel shortly before reaching Jaguara. Kopke and Dumont were two of the first entrepreneurs attempting to install the infrastructure to integrate regional markets and the empire.

In August 1867 a cluster of about a dozen buildings formed the fazenda complex atop a hill on the west side of the Rio das Velhas. With its back to the river, the casa grande faced to the west, with a substantial chapel just out the front entrance to the right, and a large quadrangle complex for the slave quarters (*senzala*) in the rear. On the hill that sloped down to the river from the *senzala*, Dumont had constructed a crude set of wooden rails for sliding timbers down the banks and onto the flatboat. In the early twentieth century, the powerful superintendent at Morro Velho, George Chalmers, purchased the estate from the Paula Santos family and established a sort of model farm. As he gradually groomed his eldest son to take over management of the gold mine, Chalmers spent more and more time on the estate hunting and fishing. He donated the large and ornate wooden *retablo* from the chapel to the cathedral (*matriz*) in Nova Lima. Some believe it was carved by Aleijadinho. He also removed the decaying old *senzala* and added on to the casa grande. The Chalmers family eventually sold off their final interest in the property in the 1960s.[27]

Much like so many of the structures along this route, isolation has been an ally. The residence as reworked by the Chalmers family remains fairly intact as a sometimes country inn, resort, or wedding venue. Two hours' drive along a dirt road north of the old center of Santa Luzia, most of the old estate has been broken up. While isolation may have preserved many of the buildings from destruction, neglect and the elements have gradually degraded others. Steel bracing holds up the walls (all that remain) of the once-stately chapel.[28] As with so many of the old chapels of Minas Gerais, the altars, statues, and artwork were stolen or removed to other locations. The old hillside leading down from the compound to the Rio das Velhas—a pathway for tons and tons of timber moved by the enslaved—is now covered with trees and undergrowth. The estate's once vital connection to the river has long been severed and forgotten, except by historians.

While at Jaguara, Richard made a side trip to nearby Lagoa Santa to pay a visit to the eminent Danish scientist Peter Wilhelm Lund.[29] Born into a wealthy family in Copenhagen in 1801, as a youth Lund often socialized with his close relative, the future philosopher Søren Kierkegaard, who was then just a youngster. Lund first arrived in Brazil in the late 1820s to collect specimens of tropical flora and fauna, primarily around Rio de Janeiro. He returned to Europe, completed a doctorate in comparative anatomy, came under the influence of the famous French zoologist Georges Cuvier, and then in 1832 returned to Brazil, where he would spend the rest of his long life. In the 1830s, in the expanses north of Sabará, he came across a series of caves that became his life work and made him the father of Brazilian paleontology and archaeology. His scientific publications and the collection of fossils he sent to European museums gave him an international reputation. Charles Darwin enthusiastically cited his work in *The Origin of Species* (1859) and *The Descent of Man* (1871).[30] A stop in Lagoa Santa to visit the "fossil man" became obligatory for all the European travelers through Minas Gerais in the mid-nineteenth century. Lund worked with many young (mainly Scandinavian) acolytes who went on to prestigious scientific positions in Europe, and he carried on a voluminous correspondence for decades with scientists around the Atlantic world.

Over millennia, water filtering through underground layers of limestone and dolomite (known as karst to geologists) in this area of Minas Gerais has carved out hundreds of caves, some of them extending for miles underground.[31] Lund discovered ancient paintings on cavern walls, and a mixture of human remains with the prehistoric bones of extinct mastodons, giant anteaters, armadillos, and sloths. By his crude calculations, the human remains in the caves dated back ten thousand years. The antiquity of the remains, and the fossils of extinct species, contributed to the disruption of the traditional creationist worldview when his publications appeared in the 1830s and 1840s. The extinct species seemed to bolster Cuvier's theory that a series of global catastrophes had eradicated many species over centuries, but the presence of humans alongside them appeared to be clear evidence that the human species was at least twice as old as traditional religious estimates based on a very literal reading of the Bible. By 1850 Lund had chosen to stop his paleontological work. Suffering from tuberculosis, rheumatism, and hypochondria, Lund remained in Brazil rather than returning to Europe.[32]

Accompanied by José Rodriguez Duarte, whose family he had met in Ouro Preto, Richard rode south-southeast, passing the Sumidouro (Sinkhole), a lake adjacent to a series of underground caves connected to the Rio das Velhas just to the east. During several dry seasons, Lund and a Norwegian artist, assistant, and collaborator, Peter Andreas Brandt, had worked in these caverns, drawing and collecting an astonishing array of fossils and artifacts. After three and a half hours and twelve miles, Richard and his companion reached the tiny village on the north shore of the

"Holy Lake." They stopped for breakfast at a "French hotel" run by a veteran of Napoleon's Russian campaign. Upon arriving, they sent their "cards" to Dr. Lund only to be put off by his faithful German secretary Friedrich Wilhelm Behrens, who "came over with many excuses and prayers that we would wait until the next morning." Alas, Richard left disappointed the next morning without having secured an audience with Lund and suspecting that his "failure was caused by the nervous fear of strangers, which often affects even strong men after a long residence in Brazil, and indeed in the Tropics generally."[33]

FIGURE 10.4. Brandt's tomb, Lagoa Santa, 1868. Image in the public domain. Auguste Riedel.

Once again, we have the German photographer Auguste Riedel to thank for the wonderful images he took as he accompanied Pedro II's son-in-law across nearly the same route as Burton only months later, in 1868.[34] Riedel has left us with a striking portrait of Lund, a photograph of him sitting on the porch of his home staring out into the lake, and another of the grave of Lund's dear friend Brandt, who died in 1862 (see fig. 10.4). The thin, angular Dane, in wire-rimmed glasses, a felt hat, high starched collar, and elegant jacket, was sixty-seven when he sat for the photograph. When he died twelve years later in 1880, he was buried alongside Brandt. In Riedel's photograph, Brandt's grave is surrounded by a neat, four-foot-tall white picket fence with a white wooden cross rising another four feet above the head of the grave. Although thick vegetation forms the background, the grave site is a patch of dirt with some dried flowers on the burial mound. An elderly Black man with white hair kneels on the left side of the grave praying, while another man in dark pants, dark jacket, and white shirt stands at the left corner, just outside the fence. His bare feet tell us he is enslaved. Diagonally from him at the top right, outside corner of the fence, stands a member of Prince Ludwig Auguste's entourage in white pants, long dark coat, and knee-high leather boots, gripping his hat and the fence with his right hand. The image captures the convergence of Europe, Africa, and Brazil and, though no doubt not the photographer's intention, the extremes of social class structures.

Lund lived in a relatively modest home on a rise at the northern end of the Holy Lake. Today, the building serves as a municipal school named in his honor. It sits on a busy confluence of streets surrounded by shops and businesses. About one mile to the northwest, the once-isolated plot Lund purchased for the grave of his friend Brandt, and for his own burial, has been enclosed by a substantial wall and a heavy wrought iron gate. Inside the cemetery, over decades, Lund's admirers have constructed a beautiful garden with several sculptures, plaques, and monuments to honor the Danish naturalist. As with his old home near the lake, the cemetery has been surrounded by urban development, especially residential buildings. Alongside the small park sits a major hospital. The massive urban expansion of Belo Horizonte and the construction of its international airport just a few miles to the west have threatened the destruction of the hundreds of caves that fascinated Lund and drew him to the area for most of his adult life. While his bones appear to be safe within this garden alcove, the prehistoric fossils he uncovered in the karst caves will likely face increased destruction in the coming decades.

Navigating the Rapids

On his return to Jaguara, Richard hired on a new three-man crew, the second of six he would employ during his expedition. He describes his new pilot, Chico (Francisco) Diniz de Amorim, a local farmer, as "skilful and prudent." In contrast, his second crewman, Joaquim, was a "shockhead, unable to work." The third, João Pereira, "was the hardest worker of my five crews, but as fierce and full of fight as a thorough-bred mastiff." The former enslaved of a local priest, Pereira got along well with Burton, but Richard did not take him down the São Francisco, fearing that he was a bit too quick to use his firearm and might get them into trouble.[35] Their biggest challenges were the daunting rapids down the Rio das Velhas, ten of them by Richard's calculation. Although the locals called them *cachoeiras* (falls) they were really "broken waters" (*quebradas*), "tide-rips" (*maretas*), and "runs" (*correntezas, corradeiras, pontas d'agua*). He purchased a small "tender-canoe," about two feet wide and twenty-five feet long, for Joaquim to reconnoiter the many upcoming rapids.

On Friday, 16 August, Burton "packed up [his] chattels by an effort of the will" and departed Jaguara.[36] About ten miles downriver the craft anchored at the fazenda of Manoel Francisco de Abreu Guimarães, "a fine, handsome, middle-aged man, Portuguese by birth," who had inherited the estate from an uncle some eighteen years earlier. Richard, and so many other foreign travelers, took in the range and scale of operations and concluded that the fazendas in the interior were "isolated villages on a small scale." These thousands of large estates scattered throughout the eastern edge of the continent may have seemed isolated, yet they formed a vast network of powerful landowners stretching from the mouth of the Amazon to the Rio de la Plata. Three centuries of conquest, colonization, and destruction had created a zone that extended inland two to three hundred miles dominated by the rural oligarchs that Richard periodically encountered as he moved through the interior. The most important of these oligarchs controlled multiple estates mostly worked by enslaved workers. By the 1860s, three centuries of enslaved labor, several million Africans and their descendants had powered the Brazilian economy, and the thousands of fazendeiros who had purchased and extracted their labor ran Brazil from the rural villages to the national parliament.

In his description of the Guimarães estate could have easily come from the classic work of Gilberto Freyre, *Casa-grande e senzala* (translated into English as *The Masters and the Slaves*). Freyre's 1933 book is widely viewed as one of the two most important and influential books ever written and published in Brazil (along with Euclides da Cunha's *Os sertões*).[37] Freyre's description of plantation society in colonial Pernambuco reflected his own childhood on his grandparents' fazenda in the early twentieth century. As many critics have pointed out, his intimate and detailed description of life and relations on the estate strikingly resembles the novelistic and cinematic portrayals of *Gone with the Wind*.[38]

Both Burton and Freyre admirably sketch the impressive infrastructure of the plantation complex while blinded by their own racial assumptions about the nature of relationships between the fazendeiros and the enslaved. At the center of the Guimarães estate, known as Casa Branca (White House), stood the "big house," "fronted by a deep verandah, from which the owner can prospect the distillery, the mill, whose wheel informs that sugar is the staple growth; and the other offices." To one side of the manor was the Chapel of Our Lady of Carmel "with her three gilt stars upon a wooden shield painted blue." The slave quarters (*senzala*) "are, as usual, ground-floor lodgings within the square" around "a raised wooden stage for drying sugar and maize." The "tenements are locked at night" with the "married blacks" separated from the unmarried.[39]

Much like the vast haciendas in Mexico and Peru, and the plantations in the Caribbean, these Brazilian estates sometimes achieved an impressive self-sufficiency, producing "dry beef, pork and lard, flour of maize and manioc, sugar and spirits, tobacco and oil; coarse cloth and cotton thread; coffee, and various teas." They had to bring in the iron for tools and horseshoes, along with salt, porcelain, and wine.[40] The substantial fazendas employed iron smiths, masons, carpenters, shoemakers, butchers, and many other skilled artisans. In Brazil slaveholders generally employed the enslaved in these artisanal and craft trades, even the most sophisticated such as the mechanics and distillers in the sugar mills (*engenhos*). Richard toured the mill and carefully described the refining processes, lamenting the "utter absence of European chemical science and of modern machinery."[41]

His description of "the life of the planter" is not flattering. Rising at dawn, the fazendeiro's "slave-valet" brings him coffee and a silver washbasin. He then strolls through the mill and over the estate to make sure that "the hands are not idling." From 9 to 11 a.m. he breakfasts with his family, then takes a siesta during the "sunny hours," reads the newspapers, and receives visitors. Dinner takes place from 3 to 4 p.m., followed by coffee and tobacco. A visit to neighbors or to town at times breaks the "monotony" of this "Friar's life." In Richard's eye, almost all the planters "are excellent sportsmen, good riders, and very fond of shooting and fishing." When taken ill or when assisting others, he claimed, they turned to homeopathic medicines rather than modern methods.[42]

Once again, here Richard encountered another group of Confederados. The "American" party "consisted of nine souls, including a wife and three young children, white-headed, blue-eyed, red-cheeked rogues, always blessed with health, restlessness, and accidents." He contrasted these children with the local youth, "the slow, dull, whity-browns of the land." The group had spent a month in the area and had yet to set down permanent roots. Among the group was a Mr. Davidson from Tennessee, who "volunteered to accompany me as adjutant-general." Richard "liked the man," and this Southern expatriate would tag along all the way to the Paulo Afonso Falls.[43]

Freshly supplied with a strong liquor derived from sugar cane (*restilo*) and bricks of brown cane sugar (*rapadura*), Richard set off down the river on Monday, 19 August, after a weekend on the fazenda. He embraced the fazendeiro and "parted from him with regret." The rich vegetation along this section of the river included wild fig trees (*gameleira*), oranges, bananas, hibiscus, and acacias. He was especially struck by the fan-shaped arrow cane (*ubá*), rising up to fifteen feet tall and exhibiting multiple shades of green that contrasted with the broad, silvery leaves of the cecropia trees.[44] That evening, the group slept on the board the "Coffin" before proceeding on the next morning to Jequitibá, where Brazilian hospitality, once again, delayed the trip. At the sugar plantation of Captain Domingos Diniz Couto, "it was impossible to pass," and "the visit led to the expected result; a room was shown, breakfast was ordered, and with difficulty I extracted a promise for dismissal on the next day—after the early meal." Burton did not complain about these delays, for he always found "sufficient intelligence, especially on local matters, to make up for lost time."[45] The captain's estate was so large that they would travel alongside it for the next three days downriver.

Over the next few days, the Rio das Velhas constantly threatened to destroy Burton's canoe-raft. Rounding one horseshoe bend, an overhang nearly tore off the tent-like awning. Closely following the detailed maps of Liais, Richard could see trouble ahead. Chico Diniz filled the small tender they had taken on at Jaguara with all their "damageable goods" just in case the larger craft went down. After navigating a difficult section, the crew bivouacked for the night on a sandbank. When lucky enough to catch some fish, they were grilled over a campfire. Inevitably, two of the staple dishes of the Brazilian interior provided the typical evening fare. *Angú*, "that almost universal dish," is a porridge or mush consisting of boiled maize meal (*fubá*). "The favorite national dish," beans, "floating in lard, is kept upon the fire all night so as to be ready for dawn-breakfast."[46] At times, *mingau*, a mush made with manioc flour, took the place of the corn porridge.

Richard prepared for a series of rapids by loading some of his personal belongings onto the tender. It turned out to be a mistake. While the *ajôjô* managed to lumber through the rough spots, Richard was whirled up against some trees, saw some of his precious books disappear into the water, and nearly lost his personal journals. The Onça (jaguar) Rapids left him with "a more unpleasant impression than all the other combined difficulties of the Rio das Velhas."[47] For the entire length of the river, sandbars, rapids, small islands, and rocky patches constantly challenged Richard and his crew. He goes into great detail as he navigates each and every one of them, regularly referring to Liais's maps. The detail provides today's historian with precious information—but does not make for compelling reading.

Unsure of the terrain and the river's obstacles, Richard and the crew regularly attempted to recruit locals to aid them on this stretch. Most refused. A "ragged youth punting a dugout" assisted them for a short stretch until they reached the pack train crossroads of Trahiras (known today as Jequitibá). After a brief visit, and failing to recruit any local help, they headed back down the river into "a succession of sand-bars and rapids" and rocks. Unable to recruit a pilot from locals along the shore, they were able to persuade four men to help them around a difficult stretch using ropes to "cordel" through yet another set of rapids. For Richard, "Rapids resemble in one point earthquakes—the more you see of them the less you like them."[48]

Approaching one of the larger rapids (Cachoeira Grande), they came upon a tough looking group with "pistols and daggers under their open jackets."[49] Richard suspected they would not be recruited, but Chico Diniz managed to persuade some to come on board to help navigate. These heavily armed men proved very capable through the rapids, and after several rounds of moonshine, they parted "with abundant tripping and stumbling" with a small monetary reward and a bottle of the "much prized restilo." "I had every reason," Richard notes, "to be grateful to them, for they had most civilly saved me an immense amount of trouble." Not long after, he received "reports" of some "little deaths" in which his armed companions had been involved, showing "that they were not exactly lambs." Mr. Davidson, apparently happy with the day's work on the river, "was in ecstasies, and began to talk of the Yazoo and to sing."[50]

Despite the constant obstacles along the Rio das Velhas, Richard remained exceedingly optimistic about its future, declaring that "this desert stream will presently become a highway of nations, an artery supplying the life-blood of commerce to the world."[51] He was convinced that engineers, explosives, and dredging equipment would "silence" the rapids and sandbars, freeing up the river to Progress. As with so many of his predictions, Richard once again exhibited the overly optimistic vision of the booster. The Rio das Velhas is even less navigable in the twenty-first century than it was in 1867, with its waters diverted for the mass urbanization and polluted by industrial growth around Belo Horizonte. The long transition after World War II to highways and trucking stymied the construction of railways. Even the minimal shipping on the river has almost entirely disappeared. As Richard headed toward his next objective—the diamond mining zone—he moved deeper into the backlands, far from population clusters in nineteenth-century Brazil. More than a century and a half later, this region remains on the fringes of Brazil's demographic and economic heartland.

CHAPTER 11

CITY OF DIAMONDS

> My old longing for the pleasures of life in the backwoods—for solitude—was strong upon me. . . . I sighed unamiably to be again out of the reach of my kind, so to speak—once more to meet Nature face to face.
>
> —RICHARD BURTON

Two hundred and fifty years ago, deep in the backlands of Minas Gerais, thousands of enslaved miners—most of them born in Africa—clawed the bulk of the world's supply of diamonds out of the rocky, arid, ancient mountains of the Serra do Espinhaço. After finding gold in the rivers and streams of central Minas in the first two decades of the eighteenth century, prospectors had gradually worked their way up from Sabará and Ouro Preto, searching for more gold deposits, only to discover diamonds some two hundred miles to the north. While the widely dispersed gold workings made royal control of production impossible, the concentrated diamond deposits allowed the Portuguese monarchy to seal off the region and monopolize the extraction and distribution of these precious gemstones. The Crown eventually extended the Estrada Real from Rio de Janeiro to Vila Rica de Ouro Preto due north to Tejuco (present-day Diamantina) in the heart of the diamond zone (see fig. 10.2).[1]

Diamonds and gold from Minas Gerais in the eighteenth century made the Portuguese monarchy the wealthiest in the world. These great riches allowed King José I (1706–1750) to rule as an absolute monarch, never bothering to convene the Parliament during his near half century in power.[2] Parliament, after all, consisted primarily of wealthy landed lords who ultimately held the power to raise taxes and potentially challenge the king's authority. Why bother to raise domestic taxes on the peasantry, merchants, and nobility, and anger them in the process, when the monarch could finance the kingdom and the empire with the wealth extracted from the rich geological formations of Minas Gerais? Brazilian diamonds flowed into Lisbon, then out to Antwerp and Amsterdam for cutting. Unlike gold, for which there never seems to be enough, diamonds in the eighteenth century, and today, owe their value and price to producers who control and limit supply. In the decades after 1720, the Portuguese monarchy piled up large diamond reserves in its vaults.[3] It was the allure of diamonds drew Richard into the heart of the eastern Brazilian Highlands.

A Three-Part Story

Just three weeks into his river expedition, Richard paused for ten days in late August and early September to head overland to inspect the diamond zone. Since the early eighteenth century, these mines had produced about 80 percent of the world's diamonds. Richard's visit came at the very moment that white colonists, quite literally, stumbled on the first diamond strikes in southern Africa.[4] Within a decade, Brazil would be producing just 3 percent of the world's diamonds, and South Africa would dominate world production well into the twentieth century. As with the gold mines he reconnoitered in central Minas, Richard's interest in diamond mining was not simply to provide intelligence to the British government or public. He and Isabel also held out hope for their own possible investment in profitable mining enterprises.[5] As he moved eastward from the Rio das Velhas, he entered an almost otherworldly, mountainous landscape of fantastic rock formations with sparse vegetation—a geological zone formed hundreds of millions of years ago when the South American land mass broke away from the ancient supercontinent Gondwana.

The Rio das Velhas and São Francisco rivers bisect eastern

FIGURE II.I. Landscape near Diamantina. Marshall C. Eakin.

Brazil, running north-northeast and slicing the highlands into two substantial mountain chains. To the west of the São Francisco River, beginning near the river's origins some two hundred miles west of Belo Horizonte, the Canastra Range eventually ends near the meeting of the two rivers. Another, much larger chain rises up at that point, between the São Francisco to the east and the Tocantins River Basin to the west. The Tocantins flows northward out of central Brazil, coursing about 1,500 miles into the Atlantic just below the mouth of the Amazon River. The Serra Geral do Goiás (General Range of Goiás) extends about five hundred miles to the north along the western boundary of the state of Bahia with the states of Goiás and Tocantins, and to the north with Piauí and Maranhão.

To the east of the São Francisco looms the Serra do Espinhaço, which extends from central Minas northward through western Bahia, spanning about six hundred miles. As the first Europeans and Brazilians moved down the São Francisco from Minas, and up the river from the Atlantic coast, they encountered hostile Natives, some extraordinary flora and fauna, and fantastical rock formations. Thousands of immigrants poured into the mountains with the discovery of diamonds and two principal towns eventually emerged around the most important diamond washings. Initially, Vila do Príncipe (Princeville) arose on the southeastern slopes of the Serra do Espinhaço, only to be gradually replaced in its importance by Tejuco some fifty miles to the north in the heart of the mountains. After independence in the early nineteenth century, imperial officials renamed the towns Serro and Diamantina. As with nearly all Brazil, the Crown closed off the gold and diamond zones to nearly everyone except Brazilian and Portuguese subjects. Royal troops monitored the main roads and toll booths (*registros*) throughout the last century of Portuguese rule to deter smuggling.[6]

One of the first "outsiders" to visit the region was the Englishman John Mawe.[7] Born at Derby in the English Midlands in 1764, Mawe shipped out to sea as a young man before returning home in the 1790s to apprentice with a local mason—and marry the mason's daughter. With his father-in-law he ran a retail shop in London that sold marble goods from Derbyshire. His interest in marble apparently led him into geological and mineralogical work in the region. Around 1800 he toured the mines of Scotland and England, collecting minerals for the Spanish Crown. In 1805 he made his way to the Rio de la Plata and Buenos Aires, where he became entangled in the early efforts at Argentine independence. Seeking calmer waters, he sailed north to Rio de Janeiro, where he gained the patronage of the newly arrived royal family. With the king's soldiers as his escort, Mawe moved through the mining zone in 1809–1810, becoming the first in a wave of non-Portuguese Europeans to survey the diamond lands. Mawe's *Travels in the Interior of Brazil* (1812) became the first of many accounts by European travelers through Brazil in the nineteenth century.[8] His account became the reference point for nearly all who followed him through Minas Gerais in the succeeding decades. Mawe published at least a half dozen works on mineralogy, and even a couple of books on shells in later life. He died in London in 1825. His wife, Sarah, carried on his work and became the "Mineralogist to Her Majesty" Queen Victoria in the late 1830s.

John Mawe's precise and detailed descriptions of the processes of diamond mining became an indispensable manual for all subsequent visitors including Richard. The watercolor illustrations for the work were widely reproduced and became a well-known part of popular iconography in nineteenth-century Britain. Given the incredible paucity of firsthand descriptions of diamond mining from this jealously guarded region in the eighteenth century, Mawe's early nineteenth-century images and accounts became the basis for later historians writing about the eighteenth century. Too often, later historians, right up to the present, cite Mawe's descriptions of diamond mining techniques when writing about processes throughout the previous century, as if nothing had changed over many decades. The incredible scarcity of earlier accounts has made this early nineteenth-century traveler the standard authority on decades of mining he never witnessed. It is clear from his account that he had the full cooperation of the monarchy, and that their support opened the doors and archives of the powerful miners and government bureaucrats. Later visitors, including Richard, verified his descriptions of the geology and the mining processes, many of which probably had not changed for more than a century. Given the lack of documentation on diamond mining in the eighteenth century, however, we cannot know if this assumption of continuity is really true.

While at Jaguara in mid-August, Richard had made the preparations for the side trip to Diamantina, hiring a guide, Francisco Ferreira, to precede him to Bom Successo, along with a muleteer, Manuel, and four mules James Newell Gordon had sent for his use. The ever-present young enslaved Agostinho, acting as "page-cuisinier," filled out the traveling quartet. Mr. Davidson, it seems, had taken ill and would wait with the river crew and craft for Richard's return. Although not exactly in the state of "solitude" Richard had hoped for (his "old longing for the pleasures of life in the backwoods"), the size of his crew had shrunk—a bit. Quoting the English poet William Cowper, Richard laments, "O Solitude, where are thy charms?" He then criticizes a noted French traveler and naturalist who preceded him through Minas in the 1810s and 1820s, declaring, "How unhappy is the traveller who, like St. Hilaire, is ever bemoaning the want of 'society,' of conversation, and who 'reduced to the society of plants,' consoles himself only by hoping to see the end of his journey!"[9]

A Wild and Illiterate Land

Today, a state highway follows much of the same path that Burton and his entourage traveled on muleback some 150 years ago. The route through the mountains has not changed much except for recent urbanization. Ever the meticulous traveler, Richard carefully calculated the times and distances from his anchorage on the Rio das Velhas to Diamantina. Over three days and seventy-five miles, averaging eight hours per day, he clambered up and into the heart of the Serra do Espinhaço. By car, the trip takes less than three hours today. The stark, deeply eroded rocky landscapes in this range seem almost a fantasy, alien world. Had the Portuguese not found diamonds amid these craggy cliffs, I doubt they would have bothered even to pause here in their movements into the Brazilian interior. Richard described a landscape "whose surface is sandy, gravelly, or pebbly, with scatters of loose stones, bearing stunted vegetation."[10] He complained of the smoky air along the route. As they had done for centuries, peasants and *fazendeiros* alike burned the stubble in their fields in August and September, hoping to clear the land and fertilize it with the ash from the burnings (*queimadas*) as warmer weather and the rainy season approached. The practice continues today, especially among small landowners, and still fills the skies with ash and smoke for weeks before planting begins.

As the group moved into the mountains, the remarkable landscape moved Richard to one of the lyrical moments in his account. The view, he observes, "strikes at once. It is a complete change of scenery." The landscape "is a fracas of Nature," crisp mountains "stripped to the bones, prickly and bristling with peaky hills and fragments of pure rock separated by deep gashes and gorges; some rising overhead black and threatening, others distant with broken top lines, with torn blue sides, striped with darker or lighter lines." Scattered around "the stern peaks, lie patches of snow-white sand or a narrow bit of green plain, confused and orderless, a fibre in the core of rock-mountain." Unable to find any fossils—"those medals of the creation"—he described the land as "illiterate" and "wild."[11]

Despite the urban expansion of Diamantina and the smaller cities along the route, stretches of the road remain vast panoramas of craggy mountains with very few built structures. Occasionally, scarred terrain bears witness to the efforts of diamond miners from previous centuries. Jutting up out of the undulating mountains, bizarre rock columns and boulders strewn across fields probably do not look very different than they did in the 1860s. Blackened fields and plumes of smoke mark preparations for the approaching wet, summer season. Gradually along the road toward Diamantina under a brilliant sun and cloudless sky, the temperatures moderate with rising elevation. In the forties at night and the low seventies during the day, the air is crisp and bracing.

To guarantee a "sober start" to his own trip, Richard sent his "Calibans" ahead, "beyond the reach of liquor," and followed them the next morning, Tuesday, 27 August. From Bom Successo, the four men passed through a tiny village, a "single straggling street of some seven mud hovels" on the west bank of the Paraúna River, today known as the Cipó.[12] After crossing the river by ferry, they bivouacked for the night just short of the serra. Under starry skies and facing gale-force winds, the crew decamped at 6 a.m. and headed into the mountains along the old colonial toll road. The rock formations reminded Richard of "antediluvian" beasts, with fragments of enormous rocks "pitched about as if in the play of giants."[13]

At the end of the second day of hard riding, Richard's crew arrived in Gouveia with its 120 or so houses and three churches. He describes in detail the flaws of the main cathedral, Santo Antônio, facing southwest, "unpolitely presenting to Jerusalem its dorsal region." He found the building "crooked from cross to door, apparently the people's eyes cannot see a straight line."[14] The locals got under his skin by staring at him, even while he shaved and brushed his teeth. Despite his disdain for the architecture and irritation with the stares, he was moved by the hospitality of Dona Chiquina, the wife of a Diamantina merchant. During his overnight stay in her home "began the civility of which I afterwards experienced so much in the part of the Province" of Minas Gerais. On his departure the next morning, Dona Chiquina "refused everything, even a gift," and "declared that her sons also were wandering over the world abroad."[15]

Along the road to Diamantina the winds had eroded the sandstone into "fantastic forms," looking like "watch-towers and pyramids" with walls of stone that "no Cyclops could have raised." With a population of around fifty thousand today, Diamantina's residents probably numbered around ten thousand in the mid-nineteenth century. "The site of Diamantina is peculiar," Richard notes. "It is almost precipitous to the east and southwest, whilst the northern part is a continuation of the broken

CITY OF DIAMONDS

FIGURE II.2. Diamantina, 1868. Image in the public domain. Auguste Riedel.

prairie-land." "The 'Cidadesinha' [little city] runs down the western face of a strongly inclined hill to meet on the sole of the deep valley the Rio São Francisco, or Rio Grande." The waters running through the town disappeared long ago, diverted or rechanneled away from the city center. Richard entered the city from the same route and direction as most travelers do today. Located near the center of a valley running from northwest to southeast, steep and barren mountains rise up in all directions. The old road traversed by Burton in 1867, and by others today, drops down off the escarpment on the city's western edge. "Viewed from the 'Alto da Cruz,'" Richard observed, "the city has a well-to-do and important look." "Below us lies a sheet of houses dressed in many colours, pink, white, and yellow, with large green gardens facing broad streets and wide squares, whilst public buildings of superior size, and a confusion of single and double church-steeples, testify to the piety of the place."[16]

As with gold, diamonds had attracted a colorful cast of foreign characters who settled into life in Diamantina. Two Cornishmen, John Rose and Thomas Piddington, had originally come out to work at Morro Velho, and both had moved up in the world, forging successful careers over decades. Rose had transformed himself from miner to mason to architect. He apparently worked on a number of the most iconic structures in Diamantina including two hospitals and the Bishop's Palace. A close associate of the bishop, Rose married a Black woman and produced a large family with hundreds of descendants in the region today.[17] Piddington had left a wife and children back in Cornwall three decades earlier and had not been home for "upwards of a generation" but, "to do him justice," Richard tells the reader, "he always talks of returning 'home,' and perhaps he might do so." Piddington was a mechanic who could work on all types of machinery and consulted for mine owners all over the region. "A fine-looking man, with straight features and jovial countenance," Richard declares, "he is still the model of a Britisher, and he would hardly be persuaded that I was not an American; in fact he probably still preserves his opinion."[18]

One of the most fascinating characters Richard encountered spawned a family whose achievements would continue long after his death. Born in Barbados in 1808 to a slave-owning plantation family, John Dayrell went off to London for medical school.[19] On his graduation in 1830, he married Alice Rice Callender, also born in Barbados, to a family with connections to Liverpool. The couple immediately shipped out to Brazil, where John would serve as the company physician for one of the early British mining companies at Cocais—probably Edward Oxenford's National Brazilian Mining Association. Within a few years, the Dayrells had relocated to Diamantina, moving from time to time to some of the surrounding towns and villages. Alice would give birth to at least fifteen children, and the family eventually settled in Diamantina. John bought up several mining properties and worked them with his sons while serving as one of the physicians at the local Catholic hospital (Santa Casa). He is buried beneath the front steps of the hospital, and a metal plaque above his grave honoring the "Doutor Inglês" has tripped up many a pedestrian on the steep street, still composed of smooth paving stones.

John and two of his sons, Felisberto and Carlos, showed Richard around two properties they worked, one which descended 180 feet underground, as well as other small workings as they circled back toward Diamantina. By the 1860s, the rocky terrain continued to offer up diamonds, but the costs of production increasingly made operations barely profitable. The rise of South African production over the next few decades would gradually put nearly all diamond mining in the area out of business by the early twentieth century. As he surveyed the works around Diamantina, Richard "found in the most civilized diamond-diggings of Minas Geraes no trace of kibble, crane and pulley, or rail, no knowledge of that simplest contrivance a tackle." The "negro" (likely meaning the enslaved) "was the only implement, and he carried as much as a schoolboy would stuff in his pockets." Dayrell's mine at Barra da Lomba "was unwatered by a pump which John Mawe sketched in 1801"![20]

The route to the Dayrell mines followed along the old Royal Road to Serro or Vila do Príncipe. A local notable, Francisco Vidigal, served as Burton's guide on the first part of this foray. As the group departed Diamantina in a southeasterly direction, the Itambé Peak rose up more than 6,500 feet directly in front of them some twenty-five miles off in the distance. Again, through this rocky terrain Richard marveled at the bizarre shapes of the massive stones looking like "a man in a liberty cap, a sphinx, a frog-like labyrinthodont, and old mutilated lion, gravestones with inscriptions, stones with hands, gaps, arches, circular holes, and every variety of outlandish shape." The road, he despaired, "proved to be especially vile."[21] Near Vidigal's mine, about four miles southeast of Diamantina, they passed through the village of Milho Verde (Green Corn), one of the first settlements that took shape in the early eighteenth century, and birthplace of the most famous enslaved woman in colonial Brazil. At the mine, as with many of the diamond washings, an earthen dam blocked and diverted the river waters during the dry season. The "moveable plant" came down at the end of each dry season, for when the rains came each year around November, the waters rose thirty or forty feet, washing away the dam.

Sr. Vidigal employed some three hundred enslaved miners he had purchased for $600–$750 each, a clear sign of his personal wealth. As they had since the early eighteenth century, the enslaved handled the backbreaking work of shoveling the rough gravel out of the earth and then sifting it through multiple sluice boxes, hunched over for hours in the early morning mist and cold, then blazing sunshine at midday. John Mawe had immortalized

FIGURE 11.3. Slaves mining diamonds. Image in the public domain. John Mawe, *Travels in the Interior of Brazil.*

these workers, bent over the sluice boxes embedded in the earth, surrounded by their overseers, seated in tall chairs, carefully watching to make sure none of the enslaved concealed a rough diamond in his clothing, hair, or body cavities. In the covered shed at Dayrell's washings, Richard "at once recognized the drawing familiar to my childhood, and copied from John Mawe into every popular book of travels."[22]

Ever the optimist about the region's potential, Richard portrayed the mines as profitable, if investors would modernize mining techniques. Far "from the diamonds being exhausted," he believed "that the true exploitation" of the region "has still to begin, and that it will extend 800 miles along the Serra do Espinhaço." Exuding his most optimistic and boosterish tendencies, he declared that, "when the rail shall have reached Sabará, and the paddle-wheel shall connect the Rio das Velhas with the great São Francisco, the immigrant may be expected, and the Diamantine country will attain its full development"![23] Clearly, another overly optimistic prediction.

The Legendary Slave Mistress

After traveling south-southeast with Vidigal and the Dayrells to inspect their diamond washings, Richard made another foray to survey what must have been the largest operation in the region—at São João da Chapada (Saint John of the Tableland) to the north-northwest of Diamantina. The Caldeira Brant family worked the Duro (Hard) Mine just on the northwestern outskirts of the town of the same name. Superintendent Gordon had given letters of introduction to "the brothers Lieutenant-Colonel Felisberto Ferreira Brant, and Major José Ferreira Brant."[24] The history of the Brant family has long been intimately linked to the diamond riches, opulence, and the complex race relations of colonial Brazil, and the present. The patriarch of the Brant family had arrived from Portugal at the dawn of the eighteenth century as a royal official and moved into Minas Gerais as the gold and diamond mining boom took shape.[25] His son, Felisberto Caldeira Brant, was born in São João del Rei. In the 1730s and 1740s, when the monarchy demarcated the diamond zone and moved to a contract system to administer it, Brant secured the contract and eventually partnered with João Fernandes de Oliveira, a Portuguese man who had also built up a small fortune mining diamonds in Goiás to the west. Oliveira's son, with the same name, would become enamored with an enslaved woman who has been written about, mythologized, and even celebrated in Brazilian cinema. In the words of her best biographer, how do we describe this extraordinary woman—was she a "witch, seductress, heroine, queen, or slave: who, after all, was Chica da Silva?"[26]

The mother of the most famous enslaved woman in Brazilian history, Maria da Costa, was an African who probably took her last name from her owner, Domingues da Costa. Shipped to Brazil from the coast of West Africa, Portuguese records labeled Maria and others from the region as "Minas." Maria gave birth to Francisca (Chica or Xica, for short) most likely in the early 1730s in Milho Verde. Chica's father was a free white official named Antônio Caetano de Sá. Following Roman law, the child of an enslaved person was born enslaved. Baptized in a small church, Our Lady of the Pleasures (Nossa Senhora dos Prazeres), Chica faced a daunting childhood in a time and place that saw probably fewer than half of all enslaved children survive their first year. She spent her youth as the domestic servant of a physician in Tejuco, Manuel Pires Sardinha. As many slaveholders did, Sardinha made his young female servants his sexual partners. In the 1750s Chica gave birth to two sons fathered by Sardinha, who also produced (at least) another two sons with two more of his enslaved servants.[27]

Chica's fortunes veered in a radical new direction with the arrival of João Fernandes de Oliveira to Tejuco in 1753. Oliveira's father, the Portuguese diamond contractor, had come to Minas Gerais in the early 1700s in search of fortune—and he found it. Generating his initial fortune from diamond mining, João's father became one of the most important figures in the captaincy. Born in Mariana in 1720, the younger Oliveira went off to Portugal for his education and training, and he married into an elite family while taking a law degree at Coimbra, the most prestigious Portuguese university. Oliveira Sr. secured the diamond contract for most of the period from 1740 to 1760, at first working with Caldeira Brant. By the 1750s he was back in Portugal and decided to send his son out to Brazil to handle the royal contract.[28]

Soon after arriving in late 1753, Oliveira (in his early thirties) quickly fell under the charms of Chica (probably around twenty years old at the time). In the great mythology of Brazilian history, Chica's beauty and sexual allure bewitched Oliveira. Probably the most powerful purveyor of the legend is Carlos Diegues's 1976 film *Xica*, a highly romanticized retelling that reached tens of millions through cinemas and a television series.[29] In the film, Chica seduces the diamond contractor with her sexual charms, and he provides her with a lavish home and servants and even builds her a boat to sail on an artificially constructed lake. He eventually frees her but is forced to leave Chica when called back to Portugal to answer for "irregularities" in the diamond contract, leaving her abandoned and destitute. Chica most certainly charmed Oliveira, lived an opulent life, gained her freedom, and had to watch her lover leave her in 1770. Unlike in the film, in real life, Chica gave birth to thirteen children with Oliveira over a fifteen-year period. When he returned to Portugal, he took four of his sons, and Chica's two sons with Sardinha, to Portugal, where they received an elite upbringing and education. Their daughters entered the convent Richard had visited at Macaúbas. Chica died in 1796, likely in her early sixties, and was buried in the Church of São Francisco de Assis in Tejuco, a privilege normally reserved only for elite whites. She most certainly did not die destitute and abandoned. Several of her children married well and gained titles.[30]

Part of the appeal of the story of Chica da Silva is that it mixes many of the most sensitive issues at the heart of Brazilian society and culture—sex, race, and power. Historians have shown in recent years that Minas Gerais in the eighteenth century became a crucible of racial mixture—largely of Portuguese, Africans, and their racially mixed descendants—sometimes through the power of white men exploiting enslaved Black women, and sometimes through consensual relationships. Racial categories, as we think of them today, were incredibly fluid and shifting on this colonial frontier. Of the tens of thousands of inhabitants of the mining zone during Chica's lifetime, the majority consisted of enslaved Africans and Afro-Brazilians, as well as the racially mixed free population. Most of the time, slaveowners either refused to recognize the paternity of their enslaved children or granted them a sort of subordinate status as members of the family network. Other slaveowners sometimes granted freedom to their enslaved children and mistresses, at times on the death of the patriarch. The result of all this rape and cohabitation was the densest population in Brazil by the beginning of the nineteenth century, and one with an astonishingly diverse racial complexion.[31]

Intermixing and familiarity clearly did not produce toleration. The Portuguese and Brazilians created a colony marked by entrenched hierarchies, patriarchy, inequalities, and racial prejudice. The enslaved regularly fought back against their constraints, at times through uprisings, and sometimes through flight. All over Brazil, those who succeeded in fleeing created communities of former enslaved known in Portuguese as *quilombos*. Richard asserts that "nowhere, as far as I know the Brazil, are negroes so troublesome as those in and around Diamantina. Many of them take to the bush and become 'Quilombeiros,' black banditti, ready for any atrocity which their cowardice judges safe." He notes that those who resist and fail pay a high price. One slaveowner he met was poised to "make a terrible example" of an enslaved person who had poisoned one of the masters.[32]

The Most Sympathetic Spot in Brazil

Heading north-northwest on mules (once again), the group reached the small village of São João around five in afternoon and presented their letters of introduction to the "mistress of the house," who cordially fed them before they headed off to the diamond washings. Once again, we have Auguste Riedel to thank for another striking panoramic photograph, this time of the Brant family's main diamond washing (see fig. 11.4). Riedel captured the image facing to the southwest looking into "a large hollow" some ninety feet deep, "the breadth 300 yards, and the length about double," according to Burton. To the left is a dammed river and to the right the ravine slices away as the two form a large V with a vast open pit

FIGURE II.4. Felisberto D'Andrade diamond mine, 1868. Image in the public domain. Auguste Riedel.

in the foreground at the base of the V. On the high ground between the river and ravine a deep road cuts through to a depth of some twenty to thirty feet. Above the road to the left sits a small white stucco building housing a steam engine of a few horsepower for hauling the loads of extracted gravel and mud. Rails run down the length of the road, "traces of Messrs. Rose and Piddington," to the dam below.[33] Sluices lead out of the dam down into the bottom of the valley carrying the clay and gravel the enslaved have shoveled out of the valley floor. These sluices terminate in the foreground of the photograph in a series of trenches where enslaved miners could sift through the detritus in search of tiny, raw diamond crystals under the watchful eyes of overseers. To the right, a line of some seventeen miners, no doubt all enslaved, form a line along the bottom of the cut, each with his shovel working the clay-like soil, which is lightly softened with the runoff from the diamond washing trenches on the left. The rough diamonds that came out of this backbreaking labor generally weighed less than an eighth of an ounce! The Brant working had once employed more than "one hundred negroes, a number now reduced to half," and if the picture is an accurate rendering of daily operations, probably less than the half that number were working during Richard's visit.[34]

Richard apparently very much enjoyed his brief visit to the diamond fields, and he left the region "with regret." He found the social life appealing, saying that "it is the most 'sympathetic' spot in the Brazil, according to the light of my experience."[35] His three days at Diamantina "left upon [him] the most agreeable impressions of its society. The men are the 'frankest,' the women are the prettiest and the most amiable" that he had met in Brazil.[36] Despite the ill will caused by decades of British pressure on the Brazilians to end the slave trade, and the close encounter with war during the Christie Affair, Burton believed that the Brazilian "Empire respects us, and even likes us as much as, if not more than, her other visitors."[37] Richard's "last appearance in 'Society'" was a ball thrown by a wealthy widow for the baptism of a grandson, an affair that lit up the entire town.[38] Everyone dressed fashionably in black, and every "neck sparkled with diamonds," and "dancing was chiefly quadrilles"—involving four couples and plenty of experience on the dance floor. Richard excused himself "on the plea that my last performance had been with Gelele, king of Dahome"![39]

Before he left town, Richard reunited with the Reverend Michel Sipolis, the French priest he had encountered on the road to Ouro Preto in mid-July. They toured his school, where the students spoke in French during the midday meal, and afterward, they visited the bishop, "a man about forty, with a gentle, feminine voice and manners," and they discussed spiritualism and the possibilities of communicating with the dead. As an aside, Richard notes that "if after this life my psyche or pneuma, or whatever it may be, is to find itself at the mercy of every booby who pays a half-a-crown to his or her medium, evidently the future state of this person will be much worse than the present."[40] Ah, Richard, always the cynical skeptic.

We cannot leave Diamantina, however, without pausing to remember one of the town's most famous inhabitants, Alice Dayrell Caldeira Brant, better known by her pen name, Helena Morley. Born in 1880, Alice was the daughter of Felisberto Dayrell, who, along with his father John, had shepherded Richard through their diamond washings exactly thirteen years before Alice's birth. As a young girl, she kept a diary of her life spent among the Brazilian and British sides of her family. At the age of twenty, she married Augusto Mario Caldeira Brant, whose relatives had shown Richard around the São João da Chapada mine. Eventually, they moved to Rio de Janeiro, and Augusto Mario played a very prominent role in national politics well into the 1950s, including time as president of the Brazilian central bank. Alice became one of the grand dames of Brazilian society. In the 1940s, Alice published her diary from the 1890s as *Minha vida de meninice* (My life as a young girl), under the pseudonym Helena Morley. In the 1950s, the great US poet Elizabeth Bishop read the diary while living in

Brazil with her partner (another woman of Rio high society) and translated it for publication in English.[41]

Alice's book became an enormous success, evoking life in a small town in the interior at the end of the nineteenth century and the coming of age of a young woman. A rare example of the diary of a Brazilian woman, the account has long been lauded by literary critics in Brazil and abroad. Through the marriages of her aunts and uncles, her children, and theirs, the enormous Caldeira Brant and Dayrell clans merged and proliferated and count among their kin a significant number of politicians, intellectuals, writers, and artists in Brazil over the last century. The roots put down by the most successful early diamond miners and contractors continue to flower nearly three centuries later. This daughter of one of Richard's guides, from deep in the Brazilian hinterland, would die at the age of eighty-nine in 1970 in Rio de Janeiro as a celebrated member of the highest levels of Brazil's political and social elites.[42]

After his quick survey of diamond mining and an enjoyable few days of social life in Diamantina, Richard headed back to the Rio das Velhas to resume his river expedition. After a two-day march over the serra on "jaded beasts" that "now fell twice every twenty-four hours," he returned to Bom Successo on Thursday, 5 September. His pilots from Jaguara seemed unsure of the nature of the river ahead, so Richard hired "a third paddle," Antonio Marques, a "peculiarly tall, broad, and raw-boned" fellow who "was grim and angry-looking as a Kurdish 'irregular cavalryman.'" Antonio had picked up "bad habits" working at an English mine that included "drinking and brawling." Fortunately for Richard, Antonio had traveled "half-way down the São Francisco." Unfortunately, Antonio "greatly preferred conversationalizing to rowing, and drink to both." Richard's patience with him would not last long as he began his two-month-long descent of the São Francisco.[43]

CHAPTER 12

RIVER OF SAINT FRANCIS

The Pirapóra had been on the São Francisco my terminus *ad quem* [to which], and now it was *a quo* [from which]—the rest of the voyage lying down stream. The weather was still surly from the effects of the last night's cold, but the air was transparent, cleaned of atoms, spores, and molecules, whilst increased humidity, as in England, rendered it still clearer.

—RICHARD BURTON

The rusted railway bridge spanning the falls at Pirapora today offers a cautionary tale about both the dreams and the disappointments of those, like Richard Burton, who envisioned for nearly two centuries a dynamic transportation corridor through the eastern Brazilian Highlands. As Richard predicted, railways did eventually reach the São Francisco River Basin at key points, but the integration of rail and river traffic Richard prophesied never materialized. Rather than blasting and digging out the rapids and shallows, technocrats over the last century have chopped up this enormous river into discrete bodies of water enclosed with massive hydroelectric dams. The Mississippi-like visions that tantalized Richard have quite literally evaporated via dams and, more recently, a mammoth and misguided project to redirect the waters

FIGURE 12.1. Railway bridge at Pirapora. Marshall C. Eakin.

from the river into the drought-stricken backlands of the Northeast.[1] Thanks to Richard's detailed descriptions of the people and conditions along his route, we can glimpse both the promise and challenges of those living and working along this long stretch of the backlands more than 150 years ago. He also provides us with a window into the elite dreams of transforming the backlands into a vibrant pathway that would open up the Brazilian interior. As with so much of his work, Richard's ethnography, not his predictions, remain his most important legacy.

Leaving the River of Old Women

When he returned to the Rio das Velhas after his overland detour to the "diamond district," Richard had been on the move for nearly three months since his mid-June departure from São Paulo. He walked, rode mules, and canoed nearly a thousand miles into the Brazilian interior, yet he faced another week on the Rio das Velhas before he would finally reach the principal objective of his expedition—the São Francisco River. For nearly two more months he would navigate his way north and east down the river before emerging—some 1,300 miles later—on the Atlantic coast of northeastern Brazil. With the provinces of São Paulo, Rio de Janeiro, and Minas Gerais behind him, in September, October, and early November he moved through the sparsely populated backlands of northern Minas Gerais, Bahia, Pernambuco, Alagoas, and Sergipe. Compared with the cities of the three southeastern provinces, the towns of the interior would be fewer, smaller, and farther apart. Nearly the entirety of the travel that remained took him through the arid *sertão* and much of the enormous drought zone of the Northeast. From the rich, agricultural heartland of southeastern Brazil he moved into the rugged, arid savanna of the northeastern interior.

For his first leg on the São Francisco, Richard covered about two hundred miles to Januária in the far north of Minas Gerais (see fig. 10.2). Over the following two weeks, he traveled nearly four hundred miles, passing through the religious center of Bom Jesus da Lapa (Good Jesus of the Grotto) to Xique-Xique (a type of cactus, pronounced *shee-kee shee-kee*) and Pilão Arcado (Curved Mortar). Today these cities are still accessible by small boats on the relatively navigable yet winding upper river filled with islands and shoals. Pilão Arcado now sits on the southern shore of a massive, 150-mile-long reservoir created by dams near the twin cities of Petrolina and Juazeiro at the north end of the artificial lake. Richard arrived at Juazeiro on October 23. Two weeks and four hundred miles later, he finally reached the Paulo Afonso Falls, one of the most important sites on his list since the beginning of the expedition. Effectively, this was the end of the journey for him. After viewing the spectacular falls, he seemed to lose interest in addressing the reader, and he quickly concluded his story with very little said about the last leg of his trip, a stretch where the river leaves Bahia and for some 150 additional miles serves as the boundary between Alagoas (to the south) and Sergipe (to the north). (Richard did something similar in his *City of the Saints*

FIGURE 12.2. Xique-xique cactus near Belém de São Francisco. Marshall C. Eakin.

volume, filling most of the account with his three weeks by stagecoach to Salt Lake City, and his time with the Mormons. He says very little about the trip from Utah to San Francisco, and only a few lines about the thousands of miles by ship and rail back to England via Acapulco, Panama, and Saint Thomas.)[2]

Before he began his 1,300 miles on the São Francisco, however, Richard had a few more days on the Rio das Velhas as he made his way nearly due north toward Guaicuí, a distance of about 120 miles. On Saturday, 7 September—the forty-fifth anniversary of Brazilian independence—he began the last leg of his journey down the River of Old Women. After writing and dispatching some letters, he dismissed his muleteer from Morro Velho, Miguel, embraced his "kind host, Dr. Alexandre," and pushed off once again down the river. By the next morning, he passed what he called the "Porto do Curvello," a crossing point on the river on "the high road to Diamantina," what today is BR-259, the main highway between Curvelo to the west and Diamantina, seventy-five miles to the northeast.

The city of Curvelo sits about fifteen miles west of the river today. In the 1860s, Richard's "Porto" must have been nothing more than a docking point for traffic passing through the town. Founded during the early years of the gold rush, Curvelo was one of the notable towns of Minas Gerais well into the late nineteenth century.[3] With some eighty thousand inhabitants today, and at the junction of two state highways, it remains a hub for transportation moving north–south and east–west in northern Minas Gerais. At the point where the highway from Curvelo to Diamantina crosses the Rio das Velhas, the waters are shallow, and there is less boat traffic on the river than there was in 1867.

Along this last stretch of the river, Richard once again waxes about the potential of the land and the water route. "Here," he observes, "we enter the land best fitted for emigrants," no doubt thinking of all those Confederados he had run into along his trip. "The views," he goes on, "are beautiful, the climate is fine and dry, mild and genial, there is no need for the quinine bottle on the breakfast-table, as in parts of the Mississippi." The air was dry, and the temperature mild, ranging from 55 to 85 degrees. The weather, in fact, reminded his Confederado companion, Mr. Davidson, of a "fall day" in Tennessee.[4] Here Richard spots "fine sugar, castor plants 15 feet high, and magnificent cotton." Wildlife was abundant, especially ducks and birds. Richard falls into another of his more lyrical passages here: "The shadow of the vegetation . . . was nearly as well painted upon the mirror waters as in the soft blue air. The river seemed to sleep, and over its depths brooded unbroken silence. . . . The stars and the planets rose with no glimmering indistinct beams, as they appear upon the horizon in northern lands; the rays strike the eye at once in the full blaze of their beauty."[5]

He envisioned regular traffic on the river extending along the length of the São Francisco all the way up the Rio das Velhas to Sabará and the Morro Velho mine, and a "great central station" in this area to connect the São Francisco with Rio de Janeiro by rail.[6] Despite his optimism about the land and the waterways, Richard and his crew faced a series of rapids along this stretch that tested his watercraft, the *Eliza*, as it moved "like a vicious mare down" the shallow, rocky shoals.[7] On the night of the 13th, anchored alongside what today is the town of Várzea da Palma, "the boys fished successfully," with seemingly everything taking their bait. Richard's good humor and lyricism persisted as "clouds high in air flitted over the moon's full disk, which threw across the water a pillar of tremulous fire." In addition to the "charms" of the "mobile physiognomy" of the river, the crew was graced with a lunar eclipse. Despite his enthusiastic description for the reader, "the human beings there present hardly noticed the phenomenon." A "comet would not have roused their attention," Richard snidely adds. With the show over, by "way of anti-climax we 'turned in.'"[8]

Richard's last day on the Rio das Velhas was 14 September. As the crew set out at 6 a.m., "the hoarse roar of the Guariba monkey" (*Mycetes ursinus*, brown howler), a species John Mawe claimed snored so loud that it astonished travelers. Richard's pilot believed that the roar of the howler was a sure sign of the onset of the rainy season. He had hoped "to be far down the São Francisco River before the beginning of the wet summer," but "we had deceived ourselves." Along this stretch and along the rest of the route, alligators (*jacarés*) appeared on a regular basis, "protruding its snout from the water, basking in the mud, or lurking amongst the drift wood."[9] Richard found the meat "musky" and inedible, commenting that the Brazilians "ignore the alligator-skin boots which Texas invented."[10] At this point, he meticulously lists the deadly snakes in the region, including the rattlesnake (*cascavel*), pit viper (*jararaca*), and coral.

As he approached "the meeting of the two mighty waters," Richard described the "River of the Old Squaws" sweeping "gracefully" from its northeasterly direction to "nearly due west" to merge into the São Francisco just as the great river takes a sharp turn to the west.[11] The crew came ashore at the tiny village of Guaicuí, today the site where BR-365 crosses this final stretch of the Rio das Velhas. With the help of the local police chief, they found lodging in a rustic house owned by Major Cypriano Medeiro Lima, who had also assisted Richard in Diamantina. From 15 to 17 September, the unoccupied wattle-and-daub structure would serve as Burton's base of operations and the site of an unpleasant encounter with the sand flea (jigger) known in Brazil as the *bicho de pé* (literally, "foot bug"). Much like the infamous chiggers in the US South, these microscopic parasites burrow into the skin, in this case, usually on the soles of feet, often under toenails. As Richard painfully discovered, the bites are not fatal, but they do cause terrible itching, pepper-like dark spots on the skin, and, if untreated, open sores. Standard treatment in the mid-nineteenth century was to remove the intruder with a sharp pin or needle, usually in the able hands of "a negro, always the best practitioner."[12]

Richard's description of the confluence of the two rivers, and the potential of the site, reveal both his boosterish optimism for the country and his dark portrayals of local society in the interior. "If any place bear the stamp of greatness affixed by Nature's hand," he declares, "it is this Junction." Once the riverine and terrestrial transportation networks took shape, he believed that the Rio das Velhas would "become the garden of the land." In retrospect, he clearly grasped the favorable geographical location of the "junction" with the two rivers reaching southward deep into the interior of Minas Gerais and north and east into the future states of Bahia, Pernambuco, Sergipe, and Alagoas. These rivers connected the cattle ranches of the backlands, mines and farms of Minas Gerais, and the ports of the northeastern Atlantic coast. The São Francisco and the Rio das Velhas, in theory, formed a river network linking the two most populated (and adjacent) provinces of Brazil—Minas Gerais and Bahia. He had visions of the Brazilians dredging out the rough spots in the rivers and connecting the meeting of the waters with railway lines to the coast—creating a veritable inland hub of economic and commercial dynamism. So optimistic was he of his prophecy that he staked a claim on the future. Thus, "when my forecast of their future greatness shall have been justified, the traveller may compare his Present with my Past, and therein find another standard for measuring the march of Progress as it advances, and must advance with great strides, in the Land of the Southern Cross."[13]

Nevertheless, as soon as he concludes this almost euphoric forecast, he turns to a depressing description of Guaicuí as "a decaying village, doomed to destruction." The thirty or so structures along the river, "unwhitewashed cages of wattle and dab, roofed with half-baked tiles," could not compare with those he had seen just a few years earlier in West Africa.[14] Although he calls the climate "tolerably healthy," he then describes the decimation of the local inhabitants from "agues, typhus, and malignant marsh-fevers," leaving many "chronic invalids, paralytic" or suffering

FIGURE 12.3. Bom Jesus Chapel at Guaicuí. Marshall C. Eakin.

from goiters and eye trouble. "The houses," he goes on, "are impure to the last degree," with pigs in the parlors. His condescending British eye sees a people of "listless languor" and men who on Sunday evening do nothing but drink and smoke themselves into a stupor. "Having little else to do," he observes, "their libertinism is extreme." Idlers abounded and "churlishness increases with the deepening tint of the skin," and "when very dark, it indulges in the peculiar negro swagger which speaks of a not unintentional rudeness." Like many a Victorian British traveler, Richard simply cannot understand why the poor and darker skinned cannot behave properly for their superiors! Worse yet, the locals "stare like the gods of Greece and Rome, with eyes that never wink. They care not whether the man in the den is eating, shaving, or bathing"![15]

At the old cattle crossing on the north bank of the Rio das Velhas, and just a few hundred yards from where it emptied into the São Francisco, Richard found "painful climbing" up a muddy bank to inspect the "only conspicuous building" in this tiny settlement. Even in 1867, this relic of the eighteenth-century gold rush was already in ruins. The church of Bom Jesus de Matosinhos (Good Jesus of the Bush), "upon whose tall, gaunt, sloping roof of tiles the traveler's eye first lights," revealed "that in Colonial times the place knew better days; as usual it is half-finished." The impressive structure facing the river has a footprint of some 250 by 50 feet, and its walls rise up 50 feet, lacking any roof. In the front half the walls rose up only twenty-five feet, and scattered, unfinished stone pieces lay strewn around, where they had probably been left for more than a century. Richard found "the body of the temple . . . foul with weeds."[16]

Over the centuries, a Ficus tree has crept up both the inside and outside of the north wall, its roots covering most of the exterior side and all the inner surface. The dark green canopy spreads out like an enormous balloon, reaching upward another fifty feet above the church walls. Given how remote this tiny settlement remains from the economic and population centers of the state, this extraordinary colonial ruin has survived, untouched by historical renovations and engulfed by nature. Its fate sits in the middle of a continuum between the constantly renovated and refurbished colonial churches of the historical cities and the many other colonial buildings razed over the past two centuries. Richard's dreams of

FIGURE 12.4. Falls at Pirapora. Marshall C. Eakin.

development would have surely laid waste to this fascinating but non-utilitarian relic of another era.

Before heading down the lengthy São Francisco, Richard first headed some twenty miles "upriver," southwest from Guaicuí, to survey the town of Pirapora (an indigenous word apparently meaning "fish jump").[17] Although the São Francisco originates some three hundred miles to the south in the Canastra Mountains, for those traveling upriver from the northeast, the falls at Pirapora marked the end of the continuously navigable waterway. The short trip to Pirapora reminded Richard of his time in Africa on the Congo River, the water a shimmering "transparent green." Although, he asserted, this is "a true fall" split into two sections, Richard felt he had "come a long way to see a small sight, and we tremble to think what Paulo Affonso may really be."[18] Despite a height of only thirteen to fourteen feet, the falls presented the traveler with "a serious obstacle," and Richard speculated on the best way to excavate through the rock to open up the river to commercial traffic.[19]

With the coming of the railway in the 1920s, a 2,300-foot bridge finally spanned the falls, but the line was shut down in the

1970s. It serves today as a bike and pedestrian bridge. The heavily rusted iron plaque honoring the inauguration of the bridge in 1922 remains, a monument to the dreams of men like Richard, dreams now deferred, perhaps for good. Just slightly south, BR-365 passes over the São Francisco, moving cars and trucks through the backlands. The postwar shift to autos and trucks, accelerated by the military regime in the sixties and seventies, has left the few rail lines of the interior rusting in the wake of a massive expansion of paved roads and truck transport.

The "Old Frank"

At just over 1,800 miles in length, the São Francisco is the longest river that is entirely within Brazil's national borders.[20] Although touted for centuries as the "highway of national integration," dreams of dredging the river to make it navigable from central Minas Gerais to the Paulo Afonso Falls in Bahia died long ago. Since the 1940s, engineers and government officials have constructed a string of hydroelectric dams, chopping up the river into a series of large reservoirs. Over the last twenty years, an even more ambitious plan to divert water into the drought zone of the northeast has further disfigured the once-mighty river. Not only do the multiple dams make the river impossible to navigate at many points today, but many of the dams do not even have fish ladders, effectively splitting the waterway into separate ecological habitats. Rather than create a highway of national integration, technocrats and politicians have made commercial navigation over long stretches of the river physically impossible, even for the smallest of watercraft.[21]

From its source at nearly seven thousand feet in the Canastra Mountains of southwest Minas, the first section of the São Francisco River loops in a long arc to the west, then south, and finally to the east and then northeast as it winds through the mountains of central Minas Gerais (see fig. 10.2). One hundred and fifty miles west of Diamantina, the Três Marias (Three Marys) hydroelectric dam, built in the 1950s and 1960s, has turned the last miles of the upper São Francisco into a vast 400-square-mile reservoir. Pirapora, the dividing point between the upper and middle portions of the São Francisco, sits another 60 miles (north) downriver. The middle section of the river flows nearly 800 miles in a northeasterly direction to Petrolina and Juazeiro, twin cities that straddle the river. In the early 1980s, the Brazilian government's electric company built another gigantic earthfill dam about 25 miles to the west of Petrolina and Juazeiro, creating a 150-mile-long reservoir and another huge hydroelectric generating station. Between the late 1940s and the early 1980s, the same public utility (Chesf, Companhia Hidroelétrica do São Francisco) built a series of dams some 200 miles farther downriver, a few miles above the Paulo Afonso Falls. In effect, the dam diverted and shut off the water to the falls, causing them to disappear, except in period of high rains or periodic releases from the dam. The final, lower section of the São Francisco, about another 150 miles, flows from this hydroelectric complex southeast into the Atlantic Ocean. Much like the Columbia River in the Pacific Northwest of the United States, the complex of hydroelectric dams has refashioned the São Francisco into an "organic machine," to use the memorable term of historian of the US West Richard White.[22]

Much like the Nile River in Africa, the São Francisco flows through one of the driest regions on the planet. From roughly Pirapora to the northern coast of Brazil—nearly a thousand miles—the "polygon of drought" spreads across the interior of the Northeast.[23] A long, narrow coastal strip, the Forest Zone (Zona da Mata) of eastern Brazil, captures most of the tropical rainfall that comes off the south Atlantic. Spanning about two hundred miles from east to west, the semiarid interior has suffered for centuries from periodic droughts, some lasting for years. While sections of the Amazon can get 120 inches of rainfall per year, the average in the drought polygon is 15 to 30 inches, with nearly all of that falling from November to May. Just a decade after Richard passed through this region, a catastrophic drought lasting from 1877 to 1879 killed probably half the humans and livestock in the region. More than a hundred thousand refugees (*flagelados*, "the afflicted") descended on the capital of Ceará, Fortaleza, a city of less than thirty thousand.[24] In these parched and arid backlands, the waters of the São Francisco seem to offer a powerful solution to scarcity, especially during droughts.

In his first days on the waters of the mighty river, Richard saw his first large boats, and he speculated about people beginning to make their way up and down the "Old Frank" (Velho Chico) by steamship, navigation that was "upon the point of commencing."²⁵ Henrique Dumont, the wealthy planter who owned the Jaguara estate, struck a deal with the provincial government of Minas Gerais shortly before Richard's visit in 1867 to share the costs of bringing two steamships to the Rio das Velhas. In exchange for this financial help, Dumont agreed to use the ships for commercial shipping at specified rates, and systematically to clear the river of the sandbars and rocky shoals between Sabará and Guaicuí. Dumont purchased the ships in Bordeaux, France, and then transported them in pieces to Minas Gerais, where they were reassembled. Within a few years, Dumont gave up on the dredging project, and handed the ships back over to the provincial government. One of them, the *Saldanha Marinho*, began regular steam traffic on the São Francisco between Pirapora and Juazeiro in 1871 and remained in use until the late twentieth century. Today it sits on the banks of the river at Juazeiro and serves as a restaurant.²⁶

When Richard made his way down the river in 1867, his best estimate of the population of the basin ranged from one to two million inhabitants. The first national census of Brazil did not take place until 1872, shortly after Richard left Brazil. The population figures he employs throughout his account generally come from local officials providing rough tallies of surveys of their towns and counties. The Brazilian Institute for Geography and Statistics today serves as the most important government agency for statistical data, and it executes the national census about every ten years. The population of the river basin today hovers around seven million, much more densely populated than 150 years ago, despite the frequent and devastating droughts in the region, including one from 2010 to 2015.²⁷ The movement of people and goods along the river has accelerated of the last century and a half, but not in ways that Richard had imagined.

Richard envisioned a great "strategic circle" with a maritime arc connecting Santos, São Paulo, and Rio de Janeiro to Salvador and Recife on the Atlantic coast to the vast interior down the São Francisco and Rio das Velhas and then by rail back down to Rio and São Paulo. The opening of the upper São Francisco was "a gigantic work for which the country is not yet prepared" and, as time has shown, likely never will be.²⁸ Richard here is clearly drawing on his Brazilian elite informants, who were in the midst of a vibrant debate about consolidating the nation around the physical integration of a vast territory as well as the creation of a sense of national identity. Brazil's first great national historian Francisco Adolfo de Varnhagen (1816–1878) wrote one of his earliest essays on the importance of the São Francisco as a key axis to national integration. As the late scholar Betsy Kiddy observed, Varnhagen "postulated that the territory of the empire must be better organized, with a more rational division of the provinces, the opening of roads and communication networks, and means for moving the capital of the country to the interior." Varnhagen even proposed the creation of a new national capital on the river in northern Minas Gerais, a location relatively equidistant from the country's major coastal cities.[29] This was a widespread elite sentiment and the matter of regular debate in the Brazilian parliament.

As he embarked on his journey down the São Francisco, Richard once again took on a new crew for the *Eliza*, dispensing with the men who had shepherded him down most of the length of the Rio das Velhas. He "dismissed with the highest recommendations to future travellers my good old pilot, Chico Diniz and his stout-hearted companion João Pereira." Although "Joaquim volunteered to accompany" him on the São Francisco, Richard judged him "short-sighted and soft-bodied." He hired on two cousins at Guaicuí, both "very dark" and one over six feet tall, reminding him of one of his old Somali companions from his earlier travels in East Africa. The crew was "well acquainted with the water, civil and obliging, but they lacked the pluck and bottom" of the men they replaced. The best boatmen along the great river, he observed, were "quiet, intelligent, tolerably hardy, and perfectly respectful" to their boss. Unfortunately, Richard's new crew were desperately "addicted to strong waters and women" and dancing. They were "headstrong" and did "not like to be directed or contradicted," and "ate with the voracity of jaguars."[30] These boatmen were also filled with "superstitions," including a belief that a siren or mermaid, "clothed only in hair glittering like threads of gold," lurked in the waters of the river, seeking to seduce "beautiful boatmen."[31]

On his way back from Pirapora to Guaicuí, lightning flashed around him, and "grumblings of thunder" announced the onset of heavy rain and stiff winds. The first wet weather since late July, this rainstorm presaged the early onset of the rainy season.[32] Much like the Amazon basin, the São Francisco River Valley has two seasons—dry and relatively free of rain from June to November, then rainy from November to June. Richard had started his journey in mid-June precisely to complete it before the onset of the expected rains in November. Near Pirapora, the crew also got their first glimpse of the larger boats (*barcas*) that plied the river. Averaging 45 feet in length and 14 feet wide, they were always flat-bottomed to avoid the many shoals, and had both the bow and stern raised. Without sails, a crew of ten or so with long poles (20 to 24 feet long) pushed and pulled the craft forward down river. In the late 1860s, perhaps a few dozen of these boats worked up and down the Old Frank.

The new crew, along with Richard, Mr. Davidson, and the enslaved Agostinho, set out for the final, major stage of the expedition on Wednesday, 18 September. This was, as Richard pointed out, Ember Day, a quarterly time in the Roman and Christian calendars dedicated to fasting, abstinence, and prayer—an odd reference for the religiously skeptical explorer.[33] At noon, the crew poled off from the banks of Guaicuí, and the "Brig Eliza" headed "downwards" into the "Great Stream." Richard deemed this portion of the river, "indeed, we may say the whole course" of the river, "more civilized, tamer, and less picturesque than the Lower Rio das Velhas." Huts and other structures appeared at regular intervals. The river averaged more than a thousand feet across often widening to as much as four times that breadth. He found the vegetation "uninteresting" after "the magnificent avenues of the Rio das Velhas," with its thick woods.[34] Alligators and otters entertained the crew. They also began to encounter other *ajôjôs* amid a slow and steady rain.

On 20 September, the crew reached São Romão, a town Richard deemed a "God-forgotten place." Most of the many travelers who had passed through "left with the worst impressions." Despite his own dim view of "St. Roman," he once again exudes great optimism about it potential and future. As he came ashore, a "fine barca" moored on the shoreline carried a load of more than twenty thousand pounds of brown sugar (*rapadura*). At the top of the steep riverbank, Richard passed through a grove of enormous fig trees (*gameleiras*) as he entered a "village of the dead." His harsh words may be a reaction to the cold reception he faced from the local officials, who were unimpressed with his personal card, letters of introduction, and his imperial passport complete with the signatures of the powerful in Rio de Janeiro.[35] The old Rosário Church in town was "definitely broken down" and Our Lady of the Abbadia "wore a mutilated, noseless look."[36]

As he surveys the locals, Richard's Victorian views on race and culture surface, and "the São Romanenses did not affect [him] pleasantly." All around him were the results of more than three centuries of racial and cultural mixing in the Brazilian interior. "I did not see a single white skin amongst them," he notes, as he expresses his disdain for the racially mixed. After listing some of the local terms for different types of mixtures (*cabras, mulatos, caboclos*), he takes issue with those who had argued that the way of "saving" the "Red Man" was to mix him with Blacks. "This is," he declares, "unanthropological. There is no need to preserve a savage and inferior race, when its lands are wanted by a higher development," and the racially mixed result "would be worse than either of the natural races."[37] In the evening, while moored on the river, a "Babel of sounds," music, "seemed to rage in concert" with the "drifting rain and cold shifting winds." For Richard, "the twanging of the instruments and the harsh voices screaming a truly African chaunt, suggested" an orgy like those from his experiences in East Africa. "Evidently," he concludes, "much reform is here wanted, and it comes in the form of a steamer."[38] European technology would bring order and progress to the wild and backward interior.

For two days, a "ceaseless drenching rain reduced" Richard's crew to a "torpid hibernating state." They passed around a series of small islands in the middle of the river they called "Steamboat Islands" as they rose up out of the water with the shape and size of "a river steamer in the United States."[39] Despite the mild temperature (seventy degrees), a north wind and the rain left them trembling with cold. Soon, however, the air became muggy, "damp and tropical, like Western India, and, for the first time after leaving Rio de Janeiro, we began to disuse the blanket." Here, momentarily, Richard "recalled to mind with regret" his time on the Rio das Velhas, "the clear limpid air . . . the splendid forest scenery of the wild banks, the music of birds and beasts, even the song of the rapid and the fall, and the cheerfulness of nature in general."[40] This was a rare moment of nostalgia for Richard after his harsh comments about the challenges of the route along the Rio das Velhas.

BLACK AND BROWN IN THE BRAZILIAN INTERIOR

On the evening of 23 September, the crew reached Januária, "the most important place on the Upper Rio de São Francisco" with the next major town, Juazeiro, another three hundred miles downstream. This strategically located town was named in honor of Pedro II's sister, who was in turn named in honor of the city of Rio de Janeiro.[41] As he came ashore, the setting reminded Richard of an "African market" with the "monotonous chaunt of the negroes." Women washed clothes on the riverbank, "more than half-nude" boys squatted on tree trunks, "dark boatmen, clad in the sleeveless waistcoat" of the Guinea coast, and "splendid and majestic" macaws (*araras*) with their plumes glittering in the sunshine presented a scene reminiscent "of distant Zanzibar."[42] The town "showed her civilization by crowding to inspect us with extreme avidity." A "very drunken youth" angered the young Agostinho by calling him a "moleque" (roughly "little brat"), "very offensive," says Richard, "to a big slave boy." In the ensuing "row" another drunken youth lifted an "Engineer's Pocket-book," which the local authorities immediately recovered and returned. They "consoled us with the intelligence that we might expect to be extensively plundered down-stream." Fortunately for Richard, Januária "was the only place where anything of the kind was attempted."[43]

Despite the initial "row," Richard was impressed with Januária, no doubt partly due to the hospitality he received from local notables. His host was a distinguished politician who placed his house at the crew's disposal, and the town officials gave him a full tour of the urban center and the surrounding region over the next three days. Local farmers produced cotton, tobacco, rice, and manioc and shipped it up and down the river. The once-vibrant river traffic in Januária has long been replaced by overland truck transport. BR-135 crosses the river just south of town, nearly 150 miles north of the last crossing at Pirapora, and some sixty miles from the next bridge to the north.

Centuries of miscegenation had created a rainbow of phenotypes in Januária. Perhaps about a thousand enslaved workers made up about a fifth of the local population. The imprint of

Africa on this town deep in the Brazilian interior clearly struck Richard more so than in many of the other places along his path. Observing a group of (apparently) Black women engaged in making lace, he disparagingly notes that they "were hardly clad with decency, and on the bank" of the river stood "a yellow girl with unveiled bosom, as if she had been in the Bight of Biafra."[44] Richard detected a pattern of selling the enslaved "down country" to the more economically dynamic region around Rio de Janeiro. With the end of the slave trade into Brazil in 1850 and the growing demand for labor on the coffee plantations of Rio de Janeiro and São Paulo, prices for the enslaved gradually rose, and planters in the Northeast sold their captive labor to planters in the more economically dynamic Southeast.[45]

Richard did not spare many groups from his ethnic and religious biases. A large number of the locals descended from one of the earliest families to settle in the region, the scion of an early Portuguese *bandeirante* and his Indigenous partner. The hundreds of mid-nineteenth-century descendants still bore "traces of this Brazilian Pocahantas" with their "coal-black hair, brown skins," and more prevalent epicanthic fold ("sub-oblique" eyes).[46] A Spaniard who had recently passed through distributing Bibles and two Jewish merchants also drew barbed commentary. The two merchants—one from Poland, the other from Germany—paid Richard a visit. Samuel Warner, the German Jew, "called himself a New Yorker; unfortunately he could not speak English; twenty years ago he settled in these parts, made money, and spent it."[47] Richard would later write an essay on Jews, no doubt deeply shaped by his clashes with Jewish merchants during his disastrous, and brief, period as consul in Damascus (1869–1871). He apparently delayed publishing the essay knowing it might cause him problems. Part of the essay was eventually published after his death, and the clear antisemitism in the tract has long dismayed many of Burton's biographers, a number of whom choose to ignore the issue.[48] Like so much of his work, Richard's writing on Jews displayed both a deep and extensive reading, erudition, and the ever-present and contradictory tendency to both grasp the cultural logic of this group while simultaneously disparaging them and their beliefs.

At Januária, the crew he had assembled only days earlier at Guaicuí refused to go any farther downriver. They were, Richard comments, "doubtless, anxious to look after their wives." After much negotiation, he hired "a pilot and a paddle-man."[49] His "excellent friends" helped stock up plenty of tobacco, sugar, rice, flour, beans, lard, meat—and more *restilo*—for the next stage of the journey. Careful to acknowledge their help, Richard listed each one of the local notables "who took so much interest in the passing strangers," noting that he would "miss the frank and ready hospitality of Januária." As they prepared to shove off, there "was an ugly frown upon the forehead of the western sky, thunder growled, and lightning flashed in all directions."[50] The rainy season threatened an early arrival as he moved deeper into the arid backlands.

CHAPTER 13

MYSTICISM AND VIOLENCE IN THE BACKLANDS

> I was astonished at the absence of all progress in these western ostentations of the great Bahian province, whose chief city [Salvador] was once the metropolis of the country, and whose seaboard is now one of the most prosperous and populous portions of the Empire. Everything we see denotes poverty, meanness, and neglect.
>
> —RICHARD BURTON

As Richard navigated his way down the São Francisco River, he penetrated deep into the backlands of the eastern Brazilian Highlands, into a region rarely experienced by the vast majority of Brazilians in the mid-nineteenth century, or even today. (The region is a rough equivalent of rugged interior of the US Southwest in the nineteenth century, with the Colorado River serving as the parallel to the São Francisco.) For the Brazilian elites of the nineteenth century, the Atlantic coastal cities represented "civilization," and the interior—the *sertão*—embodied "barbarism." Brazilian intellectuals (nearly all of them from the coastal zone) constructed a powerful and influential portrait of the backlands as populated with tough, racially mixed peasants scratching out a bare subsistence in a harsh, hot, and arid environment. The backlands and its people (*sertanejos*) serve as the setting for what many Brazilians consider the most important and influential book ever written by a Brazilian about Brazil: Euclides da Cunha's *Os sertões* (*Rebellion in the Backlands* in the English translation).[1]

CIVILIZATION AND BARBARISM

Trained as a military engineer, da Cunha (1866–1909) worked as a journalist in the 1890s and witnessed the systematic and bloody suppression of one of the great social upheavals in late nineteenth-century Brazil at Canudos deep in the backlands of the state of Bahia. Led by a religious mystic, Antônio the Counselor, the thousands of inhabitants of Canudos clashed with local authorities in a series of skirmishes that eventually escalated into a major uprising. The determination and tenacity of these backlanders who wanted to be left alone proved too much for local police and then the state militia. These tough *sertanejos* also proved a formidable challenge for the Brazilian army, which had played the key role in toppling the monarchy just eight years earlier. The federal army eventually mobilized and surrounded Canudos in 1897. A six-month siege and thousands of dead and wounded civilians was the price to crush the rebellion and its charismatic leader. Antônio died during the siege, probably from dysentery. The army dug up his corpse, photographed it, and then severed his head and sent it to the medical school in Salvador. After being placed on display in the school's museum, his remains were consumed by a fire in 1905.[2]

Da Cunha wrote an epic account of the conflict that combines journalism with social commentary and ruminations on the nature of Brazilian identity. Published in 1902, *Os sertões* offers a window into the psyche of the Brazilian intelligentsia at the turn of the century as they grappled with how to reconcile their fixation with European culture as their ideal with the profound impact of Native and African heritage on the formation of Brazilian culture and society. Da Cunha had a grudging admiration for the racially mixed people of the interior, especially their grit and tenacity, and he recognized that they were the true Brazilians, forged out of a long and evolving adaptation to their hostile environment. They were not European, nor Indigenous, nor African, but something novel—a mix of races and cultures—and it was that mixing and adaptation that made life in the backlands possible. Yet he desperately wanted Brazil to be modern, to be European, and that required, in his view, the gradual elimination of the racially mixed inhabitants of the backlands and their replacement with white European immigrants. Imbued with the positivist social thought of the times, he emphatically declared, "We are condemned to civilization." "Either we shall progress or we shall perish. So much is certain, and our choice is clear." Da Cunha and other intellectuals were trapped in what seemed to be an inescapable dilemma: to be "progressive" and "modern" meant to turn their backs on their own heritage—on this racial mixing that had produced the *sertanejos*, indeed, most Brazilians—and to stop being what had defined them for centuries.[3]

Da Cunha's experience in the *sertão* impressed him with the need to reshape the nation and the state. The key to national integration would be the completion of infrastructure—roads, railways, telecommunications—to achieve the dream of so many of the nineteenth-century elites. Instead of an archipelago of regions, islands across the vast expanses of the South American continent, Brazil would become a country of continental dimensions unhindered by geographical obstacles. Modern technology would bridge the troublesome rivers, arid savannas, and broken highlands to weave together these isolated islands into a single, uninterrupted land mass. The state would then coincide with the national territory.

The experience at Canudos also convinced da Cunha that the construction of the nation—of the imagined community of Brazilians—also required a sustained campaign to create new Brazilians. By the mid-nineteenth century, Brazil had relatively stable state and a dominant class, but not a nation. Anti-British or anti-Portuguese sentiments, or anger directed at Paraguay during the War of the Triple Alliance in the 1860s, are a taste of the type of xenophobia that often accompanies nationalism. Nevertheless, regional differences, social and racial divides, little economic integration, lack of connecting infrastructure hampered the creation of a sense of belonging to a national community. For intellectuals like da Cunha, the rough-and-tumble inhabitants of the interior, whether in the backlands of the Northeast, the vast river systems of Amazonia, or the already developed coastal cities, had to be "civilized." For most intellectuals and elites in nineteenth-century Brazil, this meant the creation of their own Brazilian version of European culture. The forging of a modern Brazil, of a true nation-state, required the expansion of the state into the vast interior and the forging of a uniquely Brazilian national identity. Da Cunha's pessimistic appraisal of the racially mixed backlanders reflected the widespread sentiment among Brazilian (coastal) elites, and held by Richard Burton as well, that only through the elimination of the non-European influences (Africa and Native America) could Brazilians truly forge their own unique identity. Da Cunha's book vividly laid out this Eurocentric vision that has persisted among many elite Brazilians to the present. Not until Gilberto Freyre's landmark *Casa-grande e senzala* (1933) would another elite intellectual offer an equally powerful, alternative vision of Brazilian national identity.[4]

Although the rainy season had not yet fully begun in the arid backlands, Richard and his crew now faced difficult weather on a regular basis on a much wider and deeper river. The evening of 25 September "was an abominable night." A storm with powerful winds battered the *Eliza*, nearly beating down her canvas awning. Early in the morning of 26 September, "rain and thunder" forced the crew to seek shelter for their fragile *ajôjô* in a narrow inlet. Fortunately, the new crew "proved themselves real watermen; they talked much, but they worked more, and better still, neither of them drank." The new pilot, José Joaquim de Santa Anna, was "silent and dignified" and dressed for work in "a black coat." In contrast, Manuel Felipe Barboza sang, roared, recited verse, and went by the nickname Poison Beard.[5]

Over the next two days, Richard would float northward, out of the province of Minas Gerais and into the province of Bahia. Passing the villages of Nossa Senhora da Conceição dos Morrinhos (Our Lady of the Conception of the Little Hills, present-day Matias Cardoso) and Manga do Amador (Cattle Crossing, today just Manga), at the mouth of the Green River (Rio Verde), the craft passed into a twenty-mile section of the São Francisco, with Bahia on the right bank and Minas Gerais on the left. Just before reaching the town of Carinhanha, the boat crossed the western boundary between the two provinces, and for the next six hundred miles the river passes through the western backlands of Bahia. Just as when Richard had passed overland from Rio de Janeiro into the province of Minas Gerais, here at Malhada ("a shady place where cattle gather during the hot hours"), on the eastern bank, a customs house levied duties on goods crossing from one province into the other.[6]

Just as when Richard and Isabel had passed from Rio de Janeiro into Minas Gerais at Paraibuna, a "registry" charged passing traffic tolls and tariffs. Brazil was not a single national market but rather a series of provinces that, despite the centralized political system, consisted of regional markets separated by official, internal customs houses. Ironically, this provincial separation would, in some ways, worsen under the First Republic (1889–1930) as the powerful states of São Paulo and Minas Gerais helped create a system with even greater autonomy for state politicians and less federal control over their economies. Not until the authoritarian regime of Getúlio Vargas (1937–1945) and the military dictatorship (1964–1985) would a truly national integration of regions and states fully take shape.[7]

Richard came prepared for the border crossing with a letter of introduction to the officer in charge of collecting tolls. Lieutenant Loureiro hailed from Ouro Preto and had "spent twelve months in this vile hole," where only one of the five men who had accompanied him to the post remained. While with the lieutenant, they were surprised by the entrance of a "white man" who walked in and "astonished" them "by his civilised aspect, amongst all" these people of color (*gente de cor*). A physician trained in Rio de Janeiro, João Lopes Rodrigues, had "inexplicably" settled in this "wild country." He quickly "accepted a passage in the raft to his home, about two miles down stream" at São José de (Saint Joseph of) Carinhanha.[8] The good doctor invited them to his house on the square and "offered us the luxuries of sofa and rocking chair, wax candles," and he gave Richard his photograph. On returning to spend the night aboard the *Eliza*, the crew had "to prepare for a night of devilry" as a "cold wind from the north rushed through the hot air, and precipitated a deluge." The wind howled and screamed and "thunder roared and the lightning flashed from all directions."[9] "Worn out and cross," they headed off on Sunday, 29 September, for Bom Jesus da Lapa, some eighty miles downriver.[10]

For this long stretch, the São Francisco flows northward with only a slight easterly bent. Richard acknowledges that this inland region was once the home of numerous Indigenous peoples who were eradicated or pushed deeper into the interior in the eighteenth century. In the mid-nineteenth century, the once ferocious Xavantes, along with Chacriabas and the Botocudos had roamed over western Bahia and northern Minas Gerais until forced into villages in the Tocantins River Basin hundreds of miles to the west. As they were forced even farther into central Brazil, disease and starvation decimated these tribes. In recent decades, the Xavantes relocated to a reservation in northern Mato Grosso near the Amazonian state of Pará.[11] The warriors and hunters have been reduced to a life of poverty on a massive reservation that has been deforested and illegally carved up by hundreds of ranchers, farmers, and investors from southeastern Brazil.

It was not Native people, however, but the dark-skinned racially mixed peoples of the backlands who preoccupied Richard as he floated downriver. Many of them, he believed, had "a fever-stricken look,"[12] and the clusters of huts along stretches of the river reminded him of "villages on the Old Calabar and the Gaboon Rivers" in West Africa. While stopping to caulk a leak in one of the two canoes that supported the raft deck, they chanced upon "a dark carpenter, who told us five lies in three minutes."[13] In another encounter, a bit farther downriver, despite receiving excellent hospitality from one of the local miners, Richard tartly remarks, "as the leopard cannot change his spots, so the negro skin, even in a freed man, remains negro." Fraternization with the Black man ("Hamite"), he goes on, "does not prepossess one in his favor."[14]

God and the Devil in the Land of the Sun

On Tuesday, 1 October 1867, Richard came ashore at Bom Jesus da Lapa (Good Jesus of the Grotto), which was by then already a shrine. He thought the "settlement" of about a thousand inhabitants "detestably situated." In the late seventeenth century, a wealthy Portuguese immigrant living in Bahia, Francisco Mendonça Mar, marched deep into the *sertão* carrying an image of Jesus in an act of profound penitence. Some five hundred miles inland, he stumbled upon a cluster of caves at the base of an enormous solid rock hill projecting straight upward several hundred

FIGURE 13.1. Bom Jesus da Lapa, 1868. Image in the public domain. Auguste Riedel.

feet from the banks of the river. At the far end of the largest cave, Mendonça Mar installed the image and lived like a hermit. Word gradually spread of the "holy man," attracting the devout and the curious. Over centuries, the grotto has become one of the major pilgrimage sites in Brazil.[15] Richard, always the religious skeptic, found the cavern "very vulgar" and "with an odour of death." He rankled a local priest when he suggested the crucifix in the sanctuary was not as ancient as the padre claimed. "His red face became redder" at the suggestion, and Richard believed the priest's "devotion to Bacchus had dislodged part of his intellect"![16]

The "village, with its three small streets branching from their nucleus, the square," has grown substantially over the last century and a half to around seventy thousand inhabitants. The faithful eventually erected a replica of Jesus's crucifixion on the rocky summit above the shrine complete with the three figures on their crosses and a Roman soldier, Mary, and Mary Magdalene. Pilgrims today make their way up through a series of caverns and crevasses to a vista of the São Francisco River, winding through the arid, scrub covered savanna stretching far off into the distance. Richard would surely be appalled by the sprawling complex that has taken shape in and around the grotto. An expansive plaza spreads out from the grotto with massive stone archways, a series of statues, and hundreds of small shops and vendors. Hundreds of thousands of pilgrims (*romeiros*) pass through Bom Jesus every year.

Brazilians have long commented on the relationship between popular religion, miracles, and the backlands of the Northeast. At nearly the same time that Antônio the Counselor began assembling his followers in the western Bahian interior at Canudos, about one hundred miles south of the São Francisco River, another charismatic religious figure, an ordained Catholic priest, had begun to rally the faithful around a miracle in the dusty town of Juazeiro do Norte (Juazeiro of the North), two hundred miles to the north in Ceará, on the border with Pernambuco. Born in Crato, just a few miles to the west of Juazeiro, Cícero Romão Batista (Cicero Roman Baptist) was ordained at the seminary in the provincial capital of Fortaleza in 1870, at the age of twenty-six. On a brief visit to Juazeiro in December 1871, Jesus appeared to him in a dream, surrounded by his disciples at the Last Supper. The room filled with poor *nordestinos*, and Jesus instructed Padre Cícero to take care of them. Rather than returning to teach in the seminary on the coast at Fortaleza, he remained the rest of his life in Juazeiro, until his death at the age of ninety in 1934.[17]

According to the faithful, at a mass on 1 March 1889, in the chapel at Juazeiro, as the young Maria de Araújo received the white Eucharist wafer from Padre Cícero, her mouth filled with blood. Over the next two months, during Lent, Maria experienced the same extraordinary event repeatedly. For Padre Cícero and the devout parishioners, this was miraculous—the real-life transformation of the communion bread (Jesus's body) into the blood of Christ. For the more skeptical, including the higher authorities of the Catholic church, no miracle had occurred. Eventually, the Holy Office in Rome—the Congregation for the Doctrine of the Faith formed in the sixteenth century in the heat of the Counter-Reformation—charged Padre Cícero with heresy. The Vatican suspended his authority to say Mass. After he visited Rome, spoke with the Holy Office, and met with Pope Leo XII, he was once again allowed to perform his priestly functions. Despite the official position of the Vatican and the Brazilian church hierarchy, word of the miracle spread, and Juazeiro has become the destination of millions of pilgrims over the last century and a half. Padre

Cícero spent the last four decades of his long life promoting the miracle, raising funds, building a new church, and even serving for decades as mayor of the town.[18] Along with the Canudos tragedy, the charismatic Padre Cícero and the "miracle at Juazeiro" have fueled the long-standing association of violence and mysticism with the backlands of the Northeast.

As we have seen, Richard's skepticism of organized religion, especially Roman Catholicism, pervade his regular commentaries on the priests, nuns, and churches he encounters in the Brazilian interior. He has a sort of anthropological interest in popular religion, but his dismissive attitude toward the faithful exhibiting their popular religiosity is clear. No wonder that Isabel, the devout Catholic, felt compelled to comment on Richard's portrayal of Catholicism in her infamous preface to *Explorations in the Highlands of the Brazil*. Richard's clear antipathy to Roman Catholicism prevented him from truly anthropological empathy with and any attempt to comprehend the worldview of Brazilians. Yet these cultural and religious blinders affect everyone looking back into the past, especially at peoples that are so different from the culture that nurtures and shapes each of us. It has taken decades of self-conscious education and experiences to try to overcome my own upbringing in the hellfire and brimstone of East Texas Southern Baptist culture and to approach the Catholic heritage and culture of Latin America with the sensitivity and empathy it deserves.

As he floated through the Brazilian *sertão*, Richard's optimistic assessment of the region's resources and economic potential contrasted sharply with his consistently negative portrayal of most of the *nordestinos* he encountered. Whether writing on carnauba wax palms, castor beans, cotton, or diamonds, he continually boosted the opportunities and potential of the land. So many of his commentaries, as always, reflected his pessimistic views of people of color in the tropics and the backwardness of the environment. Soon after leaving Bom Jesus da Lapa, in a small riverside settlement, he spied the village stocks "in excellent repair," a form of punishment that had "disappeared from rural England."[19] The next day, in a more substantial village, he harshly criticized the locals, who lived and died "in the greatest ignorance" and were unwilling "to put shoulder to the wheel" to improve their lives. "Everything we see" in this region, Richard declared, "denotes poverty, meanness, and neglect."[20] In one of his more pessimistic moments he opined that "in the Brazil, men" were as "untameable as flies." The "minds must grow, like those of infants or 'Indians,' by example rather than by precept."[21] His kindest words nearly always went to local officials who invited him into their homes, fed him, and "exposed" themselves "to a well-furnished fire of questions."[22]

Bad weather and bugs perhaps intensified Richard's ill temper. On the evening of October 2, "a roaring gale compelled us to anchor," and he and his crew "passed a night of scanty comfort." A guinea hen clucked loudly all night, and their anchorage proved "a rich breeding-ground for a small and almost minute mosquito, whose sting was like a needle-prick."[23] Food began to run low, and the crew had nothing to eat but salted cod. Richard gave "a bit of meat" to the ever-present but rarely mentioned Agostinho, who "in a few minutes" had hooked "enough for a day's food."[24] A bit farther down the river, on the right bank, at the settlement of Bom Jardim (Good Garden), Richard found one of those rare spots that he liked—for its location, however, not necessarily its inhabitants. After "the wretched pallid faces" of the previous stops, the "people appeared comparatively healthy," and "even the horses seemed better bred." He thought the village's name a "good augury," and he touted the place as a potential location for the capital of "the long-expected province or territory" of the São Francisco.[25] Today, the city of Morpará does provide a key transportation hub at the crossing point of three major highways. For once, Richard's analysis was at least partly correct.

Travel on this section of the river proved relatively uneventful, and Richard's commentary often becomes a very detailed assessment of the river, ways to remove its obstacles, and pointed corrections of the maps of both Liais and Halfeld. On 6 October, he came ashore at the town of Barra, and he did not like what he saw. The town had "a mean look" and the landing spot—the "port"—was "the common sewer."[26] Richard and his crew made their way into town amid a crowd of the faithful celebrating the feast day of Barra's patron saint, Saint Francis of Assisi, also known in the Northeast as Saint Francis of the Wounds (*chagas*). The women filled the church and the men clustered "at the door like a swarm of bees." The "usual grotesque old negro" wore a "caped cloak of the thickest blue broadcloth," despite the nearly hundred-degree temperature. The ever-skeptical but always curious Richard paid a visit to the chapel later in the evening and observed the locals kneeling "to kiss the Saint's very diminutive feet" and "deposit a few coppers" in the offering plate.[27]

Richard estimated that some ten thousand souls lived in the area. He spent most of his "time wandering about the town, and trying to detect its latent merits." The "silty and sandy thoroughfares" all boasted names, but none had pavements. At the center of the community, construction had begun on a cathedral, and the town council building stood nearby, on a spot prone to river flooding. The local militia consisted of a "sergeant and ten men, whose duties seem principally to sound the bugle."[28] The town, he pointedly noted, had "a high and unmerited reputation" largely because a native son, João Maurício Wanderley, had become one of the most powerful politicians in mid-nineteenth-century Brazil.

Born into a powerful landholding clan in 1815, João Maurício's family traced back to a cavalry officer who participated in the Dutch occupation of Recife in the mid-sixteenth century (hence the very un-Portuguese Van Der Ley—Wanderley—last name). He served as president of the Province of Bahia in the 1850s, senator, and foreign minister in the 1860s and 1870s. Emperor Pedro II ennobled Wanderley as the Baron of Cotegipe. An ardent opponent of abolition, he headed up the imperial cabinet in the mid-1880s and was one of only a handful of senators to vote against the final abolition of slavery (the "Golden Law") in May 1888. On several occasions he advocated for the creation of a province of the São Francisco River with its own capital at Barra. Richard considered the town "one of the worst sites I have yet seen" and not fit to be more than a commercial outpost for Bom Jardim or Xique-Xique, the next stop on his way downriver.[29]

So many of Richard's observations on land and people reflected, no doubt, what he had heard from his elite interlocutors back in Rio and São Paulo. Much like Euclides da Cunha some three decades later, coastal elites understood that the vast majority of their national territory sprawled across the millions of square miles to the north and west, beyond the reach of state apparatus, outside the "national" economy and markets. The physical integration of these immense and very diverse ecological and geographical zones would require the construction of infrastructure—roads, railways, shipping, telegraph lines—to bring the aspirational boundaries on nineteenth-century maps into the reality of a state and economy stretching from the Atlantic across the expanses of the Amazon to the official borders with Venezuela, Colombia, Ecuador, Peru, and Bolivia.

Equally daunting for these elites was the creation of a nation and a national identity—how to forge a truly national community sharing a common set of myths, symbols, and rituals. In practical terms, this meant the integration of regional identities and communities into a single, interconnected imagined community. As da Cunha's epic work so vividly reflected, elites faced the challenge of repopulating the interior, of sweeping away those they envisioned as inferior and problematic—Indigenous peoples and the racially mixed *sertanejos*. In the late nineteenth century, the Brazilian elites would witness this process take shape in Argentina and Uruguay as millions of European immigrants from Italy and Spain transformed these countries into the whitest nations in Latin America.[30] By the early decades of the twentieth century, Brazilian intellectuals would anguish over the rise of Argentina, in particular, as "modern," "civilized," and economically vibrant as they bemoaned the backwardness of Brazil and its "tainted" people.

The legacy of slavery and the slave trade was a population of some fifteen million at the moment of abolition in May 1888, a majority with some African ancestry. The dilemma for many Brazilian intellectuals in the aftermath of abolition would be how to eliminate this ancestry, a heritage that even national census officials would do their best to obscure.[31] In the 1860s, however, enslaved labor remained the heart of the economy, especially sugar in the Northeast and coffee in the Southeast. As *paulista* planters had already grasped in the 1860s, their preferred option was European immigration to replaced enslaved Afro-Brazilians. As Richard moved through Brazil in 1867, he also preferred this strategy, and it would accelerate in the 1880s and 1890s.[32]

A Violent Land

Named after a type of tall cactus, Xique-Xique does not sit on the banks of the São Francisco but can only be reached via a winding, mile-long channel that stretches directly south from the river to the local docks. Even today, no bridge or highway connects the town with the river or the opposite bank. As Richard approached the shoreline, "lads in naturalibus were preparing to bathe, and washerwomen and carpenters plied their trades." Facing to the northwest Richard came upon "a poor, mean pile of brick and lime" on a stone foundation, with "the usual preposterous front" of four windows and no belfry towers.[33] Today, the church of Our Lord of the Good End (Bomfim) towers above the main square with city hall off its southwest side. During my own stay, several young men (not "in naturalibus") were washing their horses in the waters near the shoreline.

At Xique-Xique Richard decided to give his crew a bit of a rest and "indulge [him]self in a short visit to the nearest diamond washings."[34] He hired a recently freed Black as his guide, and he provided the reader with a two-paragraph diatribe on the man's flaws. Once again, he shows his dim view of Africans and their descendants. A "tall, thin, old black man, with a preposterous masticatory apparatus, and a scanty, scowling brow," Cyriaco Ferreira "had been a good man and true as a slave; a false idea of charity had emancipated him, and with freedom appeared all the evils of his race." He "was surly as a mastiff" and "recalcitrant as a mule."[35]

The motley crew, apparently including Mr. Davidson and Agostinho, headed straight south from town to the tiny village of Santo Inácio some twenty miles away. Richard marveled at the rugged geology, with its bare rock molded into fantastic shapes "of strange beasts, colossal heads and masques." Over millennia, wind and rain had sculpted "huge portals, towers, and cyclopean walls."[36] Consisting of a handful of houses in 1867, even today Santo Inácio remains essentially just several blocks of a few dozen houses and shops. Stopping to drink some coffee and eat some biscuits, Richard and his entourage were observed by "the eyes of brown-faced men, whose principal office in life seemed to be expectoration." The habit, he noted, "is general, as in the United States: perhaps the climate of the New World has tended to preserve it from abolition." The Brazilians told him that the spitting kept them from getting fat![37]

Despite his usual optimism about the land, the small diamond wash Richard visited produced very little, and at a loss for the proprietor, who sat in an armchair "with book and snuff-box" carefully watching his few workers, who included children (likely enslaved).

According to the owner, should he leave the workers unattended, they would "lie down to sleep" if they could "find nothing to thieve." After returning to Xique-Xique "with all possible speed," Richard optimistically concluded that his "short excursion had proved that 'Cactus-town' has around it lands of immense fertility, salubrious mountains, which as yet have only been scratched and played for diamonds and gold."[38] (The copy of *Explorations* I have used for my own close reading was once owned by the eminent geographer of Latin America Preston James, who made many comments in the margins. At this point in the text, he scribbled, "more false prophecy"!)

While enroute to Santo Inácio, Richard had observed that he encountered few people along the road but that "all were armed, and most were talking about a late murder in three acts—a drinking bout, a stab, and a shot."[39] The *sertão* has long had a reputation for violence and deadly feuds between rival clans, much like the stories of the Hatfields and McCoys in the United States. Along this section of the São Francisco, "the rival houses were those of the Guerreiro and Militão families," whose names translate, quite appropriately, as Warrior and Militant. This long-running feud in the mid-nineteenth century involving the families of some of the most powerful politicians in the empire (including the Baron of Cotegipe) contributed to the region's reputation for violence and backwardness.[40]

As in much of the Brazilian interior, for centuries powerful landowners and their families de facto dominated local society in the absence of any real presence of Brazilian government officials. Much of the story of Brazilian history from the mid-nineteenth to the early twenty-first century is the gradual spread of the institutions and authority of the central government into the backlands, and the clashes and collaboration with the *poderosos do sertão* (the powerful of the backlands). In the centralized, imperial political system, the emperor and his immediate subordinates appointed the provincial presidents (governors), who then appointed local officials—judges, police officials, and national guard officers. Even intellectuals and artists depended on state patronage for their survival and success. This enormous and sprawling system of patronage created a network of office holders all beholden to those above them for their positions.[41] The system fostered both loyalty and resentment, for those who did not receive the rewards they expected. In effect, the inland edges of this web of patronage marked the fringes of "civilization" of any serious claim by the state to exercise power over "national" territory. Ultimately, the ability to establish order and peace depended on the powerful local landowners, who owed their appointments and authority to the provincial president. Although Richard occasionally brushed up against armed men in the backlands, he never witnessed any serious violence.

The *sertão* is also notorious in Brazilian popular culture and memory for its bandits, and the most celebrated of those is Virgulino Ferreira da Silva, better known as Lampião (meaning lantern or lamp). Ranging over a vast area including Ceará, Pernambuco, Bahia, Sergipe, and Alagoas, in the 1920s and 1930s, Lampião and his band of *cangaçeiros* (loosely translated as bandits) bedeviled the Brazilian authorities. Well-armed and dressed in leather garb, including distinctive leather hats with the wide brim raised up in the front and back, these bandits became notorious across all of Brazil for their crimes and exploits. They are often compared to the legendary Bonnie and Clyde in the United States. Ruthless and cold-blooded, they would take over small towns, throw a party for the inhabitants, and then execute the local police before heading back into the backlands. For some they were modern-day Robin Hoods, and for others, simply ruthless criminals. Lampião was also a fervent follower of the (then elderly) Padre Cícero. Lampião's partner, Maria Déia—better known as Maria Bonita (Pretty Mary)—was always at his side. Betrayed by one of his comrades, Lampião and his lieutenants were ambushed by police in 1938, killed, and decapitated. Their heads were posted in public, photographed, and stored in a museum in Salvador—for the next thirty years—finally receiving a burial in a local cemetery in 1969![42]

On Friday, 11 October, the *Eliza* headed off again on the "Old Frank," still heading northeast. On 13 October, about thirty-five miles downstream, the crew came upon Pilão Arcado on the left bank of the river. Today, this small settlement in many ways marks the beginning of a new stage of the great river, one forged by technocrats, politicians, and engineers. Rather than blasting and clearing the path of the river, as Richard had dreamed, engineers eventually constructed hydroelectric dams that flooded and widened the São Francisco. From Pilão Arcado to Sobradinho—about 120 miles—the river is now an immense reservoir. In the 1970s, the rise of the river reservoir forced inhabitants to move Pilão Arcado about five miles north to higher ground.[43] In the mid-nineteenth century, the town had suffered from the long feud between the Guerreiro and Militão families. Over the years, some of the locals had fled the violence and resettled downriver at Remanso (Backwater). The town of some three hundred houses that Richard visited is now drowned at the bottom of the great river, and an entirely new city of Remanso sits some five miles away on the northern banks of the waters. The "snags, shoals," and large rocks that worried Richard along this stretch of the river now lie far below the surface.[44] Engineers effectively washed away the blood feud towns.

Over the next week, now heading due east, the wind and rain constantly slowed down the *Eliza*, often forcing the crew to seek protected anchorage. From Richard's comments, his Southern shipmate, Mr. Davidson, was experiencing chills and a fever, likely the aftereffects of an earlier bout with malaria. During these moorings, they scouted the arid lands around them, surrounded by many species of cacti, palms, iguanas, and lizards. Richard took time here to do some reading, having brought along "a few pocket-classics, the woe of my youth, the neglect of his manhood, and the delight of my old age."[45] At one stop, the rarely mentioned Negra barked constantly at the "village drunkard," and Richard described another village as swarming "with negrolings and poultry."[46] The local military officer on this encounter refused to speak with the crew in the absence of an "introductory letter," leading Richard to remark that "had he been a Paulista or a Mineiro"—and not a Bahiano—the official would have invited them into his home for a visit rather than leaving them out in the yard.

On Saturday, 19 October, the *Eliza* reached the tiny town of Sento Sé (a Portuguese corruption of an indigenous name). The "port" consisting of a few "fishermen's huts in a row, separated by a tall wooden cross," and the walls of the thatched-roof structures "showed a water-mark three feet high."[47] The village proper sat back about a mile from the shoreline on a "poor dry plain" of "coarse yellow sand" sprinkled with carnauba palms that bore the signs of recent flooding. Once again, Richard's voiced his disdain for the *nordestinos*. "The people say of the country" that it is very backward (*muito atrasado*), "and they show in their proper

FIGURE 13.2. Boats on the São Francisco near Xique-Xique. Marshall C. Eakin.

persons all the reasons for the atraso [backwardness]." "It is," he goes on, "every man's object to do as little as he can." According to Richard, they all wanted the government to "do everything for them," but "they will do nothing for themselves." They "cannot persuade themselves to undertake anything, and all exertion seems absolutely impossible to them." Places like these in the *sertão*, he concluded, were "hot-beds of indolence." For Richard, the locals spent the hot hours of the day "in the hammock, swinging, dozing, smoking, and eating melons." At night, "the song and drum, the dance and dram are prolonged till near daybreak."[48]

The racial angle on his dismissal of the backlanders emerges when he pauses at the riverbank to question an "intelligent old Moradora (habitantess)." The "washerwomen" around them, "officially called white," he snidely remarks, "worked nude to the waist." Richard then goes on to mock the hair of these Black women (and some children), comparing their look to Nubians, Somalis, and "a Papuan negro." His only favorable comment was to note "the twanging of a Jango, or African music-bow, which, in the hands of a boy, produced a murmur which was not unpleasant."[49] The instrument was most likely a *berimbau*, a wooden bow with a gourd attached to the bottom and a metal wire running from the gourd up to the top of the bow. The instrument, with its origins in Africa, is one of the iconic instruments in Afro-Brazilian music and dance.[50]

As with Pilão Arcado and Remanso, Sento Sé now sits at the bottom of the massive river reservoir created in the 1970s. Its reincarnation took shape in the 1970s some forty miles back downriver on the south bank, not far from the new version of Remanso. Richard's objective, as he left Sento Sé, was to hire a pilot to guide his *ajôjô* through the rapids a few miles farther downstream, at Sobradinho. Several boats had followed the *Eliza* into the dock at Sento Sé. While "the barcas were all asleep," the crew headed out at 3 a.m. on Sunday, 20 October, to get a head start. At this point, the São Francisco widened to nearly a mile across, and Richard passed a prosperous and well-designed fazenda on the right bank. In a rare moment of praise, he observed that the "countryman is evidently more industrious than the townsman, and I was surprised to see so many evidences of civilization, where all is supposed by Rio de Janeiro to be a barren barbarism." Given his surprise, evidently, he brought to the region the same biases. On this October day, the sun waxed so hot "it stung," and at sunset the river "was a grand spectacle, of immense breadth, smooth as oil, and reflecting, like a steel mirror, heaven and earth."[51] Buoyant with having covered more than thirty miles in nine hours, the *Eliza* moored near the left bank, just as the weather shifted, along with Richard's mood.

The strong winds that swept across the craft's decks overnight continued into the next morning, and making headway now became difficult. Once again, Richard railed about the locals, declaring that "the people should be well off," but "they are in tatters." Despite his complaints, he managed to engage a pilot to guide them through the rapids at Sobradinho. "During the last 720 miles," Richard observed, "we have seen nothing but a wind-ripple; this is the portal of a new region, and the river will offer ever-increasing difficulties, culminating in an impossibility."[52] After receiving "solemn warnings," the *Eliza* and its new pilot, Jacinto José de Souza, set out in the early afternoon to take on the imposing Sobradinho Falls.

CHAPTER 14

DROUGHTS, DAMS, AND FALLS

> Here then is the great terminus of navigation on the mighty Rio de São Francisco, down which we have floated some 309 leagues, nearly thrice the length of England. I felt the calm which accompanies the successful end of a dubious undertaking, whilst the beauty of the site and the most splendid future which awaits it, supplied the most pleasing material for thought.
>
> —RICHARD BURTON

For centuries, the São Francisco River has been a precarious and much-abused lifeline through the perilous, drought-stricken northeastern backlands. As Richard Burton approached the Paulo Afonso Falls, he steered into what would become some of the most manipulated and troubled waters of Brazil in the twentieth century. Engineers, economists, and government planners—technocrats—have studied, proposed, and executed dozens of projects over the last century to harness and reroute the vital waters of the Velho Chico. Richard would no doubt be pleased with the reengineering of nature, even though it was not the plan he had for the great transportation corridor through the Brazilian interior. In the late twentieth and early twenty-first century, these projects have become ever grander and even more controversial. While ostensibly designed to alleviate the scourge of drought that has killed hundreds of thousands of *sertanejos* and scarred millions more over centuries, grinding poverty and profound inequalities continue across vast stretches of the arid *sertão*—and the disastrous droughts continue. These works of infrastructure in many ways have carried out the state-building dreams of the mandarins of the empire. They have also helped bring together a national community, albeit one fractured by deep regional inequalities and identities.

Completed in the 1980s, the enormous Sobradinho Dam buried Richard's "last patch" of rapids deep beneath a massive reservoir, elevating water levels in the river for nearly one hundred miles back to the west of Juazeiro and Petrolina (see fig. 10.2). As with Pilão Arcado, Sente Sé, and Remanso, many of Richard's final stops now lie far beneath the calm waters of one of the largest artificial lakes in the world.[1]

AN ORGANIC MACHINE?

With a new pilot, Jacinto José de Souza, the *Eliza* set out at 2 p.m. on Tuesday, 22 October, on a course filled with small islands, jagged rocks jutting up out of the water, and frequent boat wrecks. With ropes, poles, and paddles, the battered vessel negotiated a series of substantial rapids over the next three hours. Richard praised local pilot Jacinto José as "a good man, careful and dexterous, and, wonderful to relate, he works without noise"! The crew bid him adieu with his payment and a parting shot of cachaça.[2] The much-anticipated Paulo Afonso Falls were still another two weeks down river.

As he neared the end of his three months on the rough wooden *ajôjô* he called the *Eliza*, Richard paused in his account to reflect on his daily routine. The crew would rise each day before dawn and then, from 7 to 8 a.m., snack on coffee and "biscuits," Richard's English way of describing Brazilian *rosca*—a very light, donut-shaped fried bread. He would often wait to eat his own share until 11 a.m., "when the neck of the day's work ha[d] been broken." On hot days, the "bow of one of the canoes [was] a good place for a cold bath." In the afternoon, "the labour became lighter," and the crew would sometimes turn to making handicrafts or rolling cigars while Richard read or wrote in his journal. Near sunset, all would "feed in the humblest way, upon rice when there is any, and upon meat or fish," if they were available.[3]

During his months on the river, "with alternations of storm and rain, cold wind and hot wind, mists and burning suns," he boasted that he "had not an hour of sickness." In contrast to his expeditions in Africa in the 1850s, his trek across the Brazilian interior had barely tested his physical endurance. While in search of the Nile, Richard had suffered from a host of punishing maladies, including spells of blindness and delirium, nearly dying on more than one occasion. In his Brazilian travels he certainly never faced hostile warriors like the ones in East Africa who had speared him through both cheeks, leaving him with striking facial scarring. Mr. Davidson did experience what must have been malarial chills, but even this ailment, Richard explained, came from an earlier bout of "bad health," and "he improved in condition as we went" down the river.

Richard adopted few precautions and followed his long-standing rule "to alter diet as little as possible." He was convinced—based on a certainly long and varied experience on five continents—that "the sojourner in foreign lands . . . *must not attempt to conform to the 'manners and customs of the people'*" (emphasis added). He carefully scrutinized the water he consumed, drank coffee to keep up "the vital heat," and—much like sailors on the high seas—drank lime juice to fend off scurvy. On cold mornings, "and every night," he had a glass of wine or cognac, when available, and cachaça when they were not. Curiously, he took a couple of grains of quinine each day to avoid what he called "nervous depression."[4] After "two months' diet of manioc, rice and fish" he felt physically weakened. While climbing a steep hill near the end of his trip he "complained of shaky knees and short breath," a foreshadowing perhaps of the devastating illness that awaited him a few months down the road.[5]

On 24 October, Richard reached Juazeiro, just a few miles downriver from today's Sobradinho Dam. He was unimpressed with the town of some two thousand inhabitants, a city some one hundred times larger today. Richard opens his description of Juazeiro saying that he "had long heard of this place as the future terminus where the great lines of rail were to meet" to integrate water and land routes across the vast interior of northeastern Brazil. He goes on to reveal that "it had been spoken of as a centre of civilization, a little Paris." "So much for the imagination," he sighs. "Now for the reality." The town had but one significant house, with fourteen different owners, "and even this has not a sign of glass windows." One could not find a carriage within three hundred miles, the post office—"that civilization-gauge"—was also a dry goods store, and the town had no physician.[6] Still, he believed the location a "central site" as the convergence and crossroads for traffic that would eventually bloom on a dredged and deepened São Francisco moving east and west, and the rail lines moving from the northern coast south to Salvador. He was partially right in yet another of his misguided predictions. Major highways today do connect to Fortaleza, Ceará to the north, Recife to the east, and Salvador to the south, crossing and intersecting at Juazeiro. The railway would eventually make its way to Juazeiro not long after Richard's brief visit.

When Richard passed through Petrolina on the north bank of the river, the Pernambuco side, it consisted of a small chapel "and half a dozen tiled houses fronting the stream, backed by a few huts."[7] A ferry connected the Bahian and Pernambucan banks of the river. Much has changed in the last 150 years. The twin cities of Petrolina (north bank) and Juazeiro (south bank) have grown by leaps and bound with the construction of the Sobradinho Dam some fifteen miles away, and as the major transportation of hub of the *sertão*. This economically vibrant urban center is one of the few places in the interior that has experienced in-migration over the past half century. With more than five hundred thousand inhabitants straddling the river, and sophisticated irrigation for cultivating grapes, Petrolina and Juazeiro would, no doubt, both please and surprise Richard were he to pass through today.[8]

After the local military commander ignored his letter of introduction, Richard sought out and dined with another officer and visited with several local notables. From them, he heard the story of another attempt to commence steam navigation on the river. The president of the province of Bahia had commissioned the building of a vessel for the task, but his successor had stymied the project. A merchant in Juazeiro bought the vessel for eight thousand dollars, dismantled it on the coast near the mouth of the São Francisco, and began to transport the pieces via mules to a point on the river above the falls. In October 1867 the many pieces of the steamship were scattered along the roads and banks of the river over hundreds of miles. By late 1869 the ship had been successfully reassembled and made its inaugural voyage in 1872 to Pirapora and back, taking about ten days round trip. The *Presidente Dantas* (named after the governor) would ply the waters of the São Francisco well into the twentieth century.[9]

The proposal to make Juazeiro a pivotal railway terminus was not simple speculation on Richard's part. For some time, English railway companies in Recife and Salvador had proposed to build lines inland to this river crossing point. The initial stock offerings and investments had been squandered leaving the Brazilian government, the key loan guarantor for the companies, in greater debt. Even though Richard had witnessed the completion of the English-built railway from Santos into the interior of São Paulo over the previous two years, he believed that at "this moment railway enterprise in the Brazil may be said to stand still." He laid the principal blame on foreigners (his fellow countrymen) who planned and administered the finances poorly.[10] He was cheered by the news that weekly steamer navigation had begun between Penedo (near the mouth of the São Francisco) and Porto das Piranhas, just below the Paulo Afonso Falls.

A British-owned railway had already begun construction from Bahia inland in the early 1860s but would not reach Juazeiro until the mid-1890s. The Bahia and São Francisco Railway "proved an unrelieved financial failure," according to one of the most distinguished US historians of nineteenth-century Brazil.[11] By the time Richard departed Brazil, the country had less than 500 miles of rail lines, expanding to nearly 5,000 by the end of the empire, with another 9,000 under construction.[12]

As he prepared to depart Juazeiro, Richard surveyed his crew and the locals with his usual biting condescension. José Joaquim and Barboza, who had come aboard at Januária, "had always won [his] gratitude by keeping themselves" sober and able. The young man (*menino*) he had added to the crew had "at night returned to the Eliza on all-fours, like one of the lower animals." The young enslaved Agostinho "was successively drooping with 'sea-sickness,' and unpleasantly surly." He then turned his attention to the washerwomen on the shore, "who were grotesque objects" (no doubt because of their gender and color), and the "excessive display of shoulder" they dared to reveal.[13] For Richard, their baring of skin "was truly remarkable," even exceeding that of the Black women in the markets in Salvador and Minas Gerais.

The *Eliza* faced "wind night and day, cold and furious by night, hot and furious by day," over this last stretch of water.[14] Mornings broke cold and cloudy, and the afternoon sun burned off the morning chill to bake the crew. Richard gave a "young fellow" passage from Juazeiro, and when dropped off the next day, the three women who came down to meet him "were wild-looking beings, their very small faces were set in a frame of hair, and their beady eyes peeped out from the profusion of unkempt, witch-like looks."[15] A few miles farther down river, at the village of Capim Grosso (Thick Grass, known today as Curaçá), which he described as "the wildest place that we have yet seen; it did not show a trace of hospitality or even civility." Disdainful of the locals, he highlighted their racial mixture and remarked that only "one man approached whiteness," and he "squatted Hindu-like, upon a stone." Before departing he summed up his visit by saying, "I hope that the next travellers may be justified in giving a better account of" the place.[16]

Many of the wild and untamed locals he encountered here were on horseback sporting the classic dress of the arid backlands. The land of cattle and cowboys (*vaqueiros*), in the words of one the great Brazilian historians of the nineteenth century, had emerged during the colonial period in an "age of leather."[17] Their saddles were made "country fashion," raised up in the front and back to handle the uphill and downhill riding. The *caipiras*—hicks or hayseeds—wore "ugly 'Sombreiros'" with the front brim pushed up and attached to the crown to form a sort of "three-corner hat."[18] The leggings, boots, and outer garments were also crafted from leather—from cattle, goats, sheep, and deer. Developed over centuries to protect the *sertanejos* from the sun, heat, dust, thorns, and snakes, the leather-clad *vaqueiro* remains today one of the iconic figures of the northeastern backlands.

The Works of Pharaohs?

Since the nineteenth century, engineers and technocrats have dreamed of dredging, channeling, damming, and redirecting the waters of the São Francisco. After measuring their way down the river in the mid-1800s, both Henrique Halfeld and Emmanuel

Liais proposed ways to blast through the various rapids and falls to open up the river to traffic from Pirapora to the Paulo Afonso Falls. Halfeld even argued for digging a channel to divert waters into Ceará, foreshadowing by a century and a half the largest engineering project in Brazilian history.[19] The transposition of the waters of the São Francisco initiated by the leftist government of President Luiz Inácio Lula da Silva has reminded many of the so-called pharaonic works of the military dictatorship in the 1960s and 1970s. Similar to the construction of the Itaipú Dam or the Trans-Amazonian Highway, this project involved digging more than five hundred miles of aqueducts, tunnels, and pumping stations along two main axes. One axis (splitting into three channels) flows north into Ceará, Paraíba, and Rio Grande do Norte. The other, flows east through Pernambuco and then Paraíba.[20]

Once again, Richard changed his boat crew. At Capim Grosso, the "Januaria men here found relatives," and a short way down the river—at Boa Vista (Good View)—the local military commander helped him find a new pilot. The departing José Joaquim de Santa and Manoel Felipe Barboza (a.k.a. Poison Beard) headed home, and according to Richard, "we separated well satisfied, I hope, with one another." Richard was duly impressed with his new helmsman, Manoel Cypriano, saying, "he is the only real pilot that I saw upon the river." He was dark-skinned and fifty years old, but looked "at least sixty-five." He was "certainly no beauty," but "he was stout-hearted and true," and Richard "soon learned to confide in his nerve, force and precision." Manoel declared that "his premature age ha[d] been brought on by a fast life." With a "queer dry humour," he delighted in twanging a guitar, taking snuff, and sipping from "a private bottle of country rum wrapped up carefully as if it were a baby."[21]

Richard gave Manoel Cypriano "carte blanche to choose his oarsmen, and this was a prime mistake." The new pilot took on José Alves Marianno, although "he knew the man to be a noted skulk," someone no one else would engage. The man's "immense curly head-mop of jetty colour, proves an African maternity." He was, Richard lamented, "hopeless, he drinks like a whirlpool, and eats like an ogre." Despite all this, Richard could not get "seriously angry with the rascal; he is abominably good-tempered, and he seems to look back on himself as the greatest fun in the world." At the end of his tour of duty, Richard was more than relieved to see "his back."[22]

From Boa Vista to the Paulo Afonso Falls, the São Francisco River turns from its northward path in a four-hundred-mile-long arc, moving first to the northeast and then curving downward toward the southeast for the rest of its path to the Atlantic Ocean. For the first half of this great arc, Richard and his crew faced constant rapids, multiple islands, and rough waters. When approaching these difficult stretches, the crew lashed down everything on board with ropes to avoid losing stores and equipment when surges of water swept across the low-lying deck. Here they would learn to value Manoel Cypriano's steady hand at the helm. Along this stretch of river, the earth began "to show her skeleton bare." The riverbed, Richard observed, "broadens in many places to a league, and is worn down to its granitic floor; it is a mass of islands and islets, all bearing names, of reefs and rocks sand-scoured, cut and channelled by the waters, which glaze them to a grisly black." At one point, six days out from Boa Vista, the *Eliza* confronted "nine rapids, two whirlpools, and two shallows, during the space of five leagues, obstructions as serious as the whole course of the Rio das Velhas."[23]

Today, this section of the river remains a complicated series of channels and islands at the top of the great arc in the waterway. In the seventeenth and eighteenth centuries the Jesuits penetrated this region seeking to evangelize the Indigenous peoples, as they did in many parts of Latin America, by concentrating the seminomadic peoples into villages (*aldeias*). After a long power struggle, the Spanish and Portuguese monarchies expelled the Jesuits from the Americas in the 1750s and 1760s.[24] Their work lay in ruins in the 1860s, and Richard believed that the descendants of the "villaged Indians" were "fast relapsing into savagery." The missionaries who eventually replaced "the old Fathers," in his eyes, had done a poor job and were "thinly scattered" among the old settlements.[25] At one set of ruins, the monastery, church, and chapel "were all a mere shell," and an inscription dated 1734 marked the remains of a collapsed church, by then inhabited by pigeons and lizards with cactus growing on the walls. The scene left Richard sad, and he remarked that "there is something unpleasantly impressive about these transitory labours, upon which the lives of men have been wasted."²⁶ The "whole scene" reminded him of ruins he had encountered in Benin.

The *Eliza*'s new oarsmen continued to disappoint Richard. On the morning of Wednesday, 30 October, the "old Menino" was drunk, and his new hire, José Alves Marianno, "began to droop in all save the matter of singing." They could not set out until 11 a.m., and José (who Richard referred to as "Captain Soft") decided he had worked enough by 3 p.m. He "neatly let slip" his new paddle, which quickly disappeared downstream. When they tied up and came ashore to cut a replacement, who should appear but his old oarsman Poison Beard! His brothers had apparently brought him back to the family fazenda "to receive his mamma's blessing." Richard and the crew joined the family for a raucous evening. The "fatted calf was killed, men and women complimented the truant [Poison Beard] in extempore verse," and "the drum was not silent till sunrise."²⁷ As they headed back down the river, strong winds lashed "the now crazy Eliza, manned by a crew that would not work."²⁸

On 1 November, the *Eliza* reached the northernmost point of the São Francisco, and the river began its long and steady two-hundred-mile arc to the southeast, and eventually, the Atlantic Ocean. Near Cabrobó, on Pernambuco's northern side of the river, the locals "collected to see us." They came armed with knives, bows, and arrows. Once again, Richard the ethnologist emerges as he describes in detail the mix of races comparing Brazilian bodies with those he had encountered in Asia and Africa. "The old savages," he observed, had "all died off," and these *sertanejos* were "mostly a mixed breed, whose curly hair comes from Africa." From his perspective, these mixed people had "Mongol faces" and "oblique Chinese eyes." Their hair "was that of the Hindú, jetty and coarser than in the pure Caucasian." He judged them "well-made men, except that the trunk appeared somewhat too long and large for the legs, and the shoulders seemed to project horizontally just below the ears." Their "skin was brown-yellow and ruddy only when exposed to the light and air."²⁹

The next few days were Richard's last navigating the river. Monday, 4 November, provided the last great challenge, what he called "the critical day—the acme of our rapid-troubles." Over some thirty miles and "nine bad places," the repeatedly tested *ajôjô* faced her last major hurdle to complete the three-month voyage. Islands, rocks, reefs, sandbars, and shoals littered the course of the river. Richard found "something majestic" in this section of the São Francisco, "whose turbid waters, here building up, there lieing low, now flowing in silent grandeur, fanned by a gentle breeze, and reflecting the gold and azure of the sky, assume an angry, sullen, and relentless aspect when some obstacle of exceptional important would bar its mighty path."[30]

As the *Eliza* shot through the rapids, Richard had to "confess to having felt cold hands at the sight" of the jagged rocks and furious whirlpools. "It was," he wrote, "a wild scene; the Eliza swayed and surged to and fro, as she coursed down the roaring, rushing waters that washed the platform; the surge dazzled the eyes when it caught the sun, and on the smooth depths the beams were reflected as by a mirror."[31] As the craft passed through this stretch, Richard noted that it was "said to be the worst upon the river."[32] At the end of the day, after passing through the last rapid, having covered some twenty-seven miles, Richard writes, "Thus satisfactorily ended all my troubles with cachoeiras [rapids] upon the Rio de São Francisco, and the sensation was certainly one of great relief."[33]

Over his last three days on the river, the waters of the São Francisco turned calm and easy, and the scenery reminded Richard of the "valleys of the Nile and the Indus when they reach the dry country."[34] Late in the evening on Thursday, 7 November 1867, the *Eliza* and her crew came to their final stop at São Pedro Dias da Várzea Redonda (Saint Peter Days of the Round Floodplain). Here, Richard declared, "is the great terminus of navigation on the mighty Rio de São Francisco."[35] He "dismantled the 'Brig Eliza,' which had now been 'home' for the last three months." He gave the floor planking away, arranged to send the anchor back to Morro Velho and Mr. Gordon, and sold the two canoes that had provided the base of his sturdy craft.

A local judge generously offered his home to Richard, who declined the offer, "wishing to make some last arrangements before paying off the crew and dismantling" the *Eliza*. He soon regretted his decision to sleep one last night on board. A furious wind and waves "nearly beat the old raft to pieces," and the crew, "having reached the end of their work, had the usual boatman's 'spree,' hard drinking, extensive boasting, trials of strength, and quarreling intermixed with singing, shouting, extemporizing verses, and ending in the snores and snorts of Bacchic sleep." The following morning, the Menino and Captain Soft "shed tears of contrition, and cane-rum." The latter took not only two months' pay for "work-shirking" but also Richard's dog, Negra, who "combined the unpleasant qualities of cowardice and savageness" and "could not be trusted near children and small animals." (Having acquired Negra more than four months earlier in Minas Gerais, Richard had barely mentioned the dog in his account.) Richard remained impressed with his departing pilot, but a "sensation of deep rest followed the last glimpse" of the two oarsmen.[36]

Sixty years after Richard passed through Várzea Redonda, a raggedy band of hundreds of soldiers crossed the river, at that very spot, from Pernambuco into Bahia, at the halfway point on one of the most famous military expeditions in modern Brazilian history. From July 1924 to March 1927, the Prestes Column marched some fifteen thousand miles through the interior of Brazil from Rio Grande do Sul in the far South to the backlands of the Northeast, and then back across central Brazil to Bolivia.[37] Young military officers deeply discontented with the coffee barons who had dominated national politics since the 1890s took up arms against the government in 1922, and again in 1924. These nationalistic officers, trained in the technocratic, engineering worldview of Brazil's military academies, desperately desired to make their country into a modern, industrial, and technologically sophisticated nation. They felt that the powerful coffee oligarchy (mainly from the powerful states of São Paulo and Minas Gerais) was holding Brazil back, burdening it with a dependence on agriculture and coffee exports.

In 1922 the centennial of national independence, many young officers (known as *tenentes* or lieutenants) rose up in revolt against the republic and their more conservative commanding officers. The revolt failed, but many of the mutineers were only lightly punished. Two years later, a second, more widespread revolt broke out in Rio de Janeiro, São Paulo, and Rio Grande do Sul. When confronted by the loyalists in the army, the rebel officers and their followers in São Paulo and Rio Grande do Sul retreated into the interior rather than surrender. After regrouping in western Brazil, some 1,500 men under the leadership of Luís Carlos Prestes (a *gaúcho* from southern Brazil) and Antônio Siqueira Campos (from São Paulo) marched through the Brazilian interior in hopes of attracting more of their countrymen to the rebellion. They also hoped to weaken the regime steadily through regular attacks from the heartland.

Over the next two years, these men came to know a Brazil that most of them, and certainly most Brazilians, had only read about—one of grinding poverty, economic underdevelopment, and social inequities in the interior. Ultimately, the Prestes Column skirmished repeatedly with both the Brazilian army and large bands of gunmen (*jagunços*) amassed by powerful landowners, yet they survived and kept moving. As they marched through the backlands around the São Francisco River in 1925–1926, the local populations became more hostile, the bands of *jagunços* more threatening, and the rebels ultimately chose to retreat to western Brazil and, eventually, across the border to exile in Bolivia. A number of the rebel officers eventually became prominent in Brazilian politics and have become lionized in popular history. Siqueira Campos died in a plane crash in 1930. Eduardo Gomes, another of the *tenentes*, would be a candidate for president in the 1940s and 1950s, for a major right-wing political party. Luís Carlos Prestes would spend his exile in Argentina reading Karl Marx. From the 1930s to the 1980s, he headed the Communist Party of Brazil. After a failed attempt to stage a Communist coup in 1937, Prestes would spend years in prison, then even more time in exile in Moscow.[38] In its own way, the northeastern *sertão* put its stamp on key political figures and on national politics. As with so many Brazilians in the nineteenth century, these twentieth-century urbanites from the coastal zone, no doubt, had almost no direct experience with the interior before their epic march. In the aftermath, they grappled with how to continue the state-building dreams of the empire under a republican and technocratic Brazilian leadership with dreams of integrated national development.

Much like the recovery and recasting of Tiradentes after 1889—from traitorous soldier to republican visionary and martyr—the history of the rebels in the Prestes Column has been recast over the decades. The traitors of the 1920s and 1930s gradually became in the second half of the century noble visionaries who recognized the flaws of the old regime, even if they failed to defeat it. They came to be seen as the harbingers of a modern, industrial, socially aware Brazil, one that would address the profound regional, cultural, and political divides that have plagued the nation. In both cases, new political regimes recast their roles in a new narrative of the nation's history. The victors not only write history; they also rewrite it from generation to generation.

To the Disappearing Falls

Richard's host in Várzea Redonda helped arrange a guide and mules to take him to the Paulo Afonso Falls. He had to wait for three days until the muleteers, Ignacio and João, were ready, and "the party consisted of the worst men, the worst beasts, and the worst equipments" that he had seen in all Brazil. The two *tropeiros*, he asserted, were "not worth one Paulista, or Mineiro." Both were "extra lazy." He longed for the mules and muleteers from Morro Velho. In addition to the two much maligned muleteers, a small boy who looked "twelve" but claimed to be fourteen also joined the expedition. Joaquim Gomes Lima had a gruff voice, rolled his own tobacco, offered drinks "to women thrice his age," and pursued "every adult vice."[39] As he had so notoriously done in Zanzibar at the end of his brutal expedition with Speke, Richard may have refused to pay them, or paid them much less than originally promised. Richard implies that he dealt with the men harshly at the end of the trip so they would not take advantage of other travelers who would come later.[40]

Despite his unhappiness with the crew, an excitement gripped Richard as he finally approached the long-awaited visit to the Paulo Afonso Falls, "the cream of the expedition" that "was now to be tasted."[41] The heat had by now became scorching, reaching as high as 120 degrees in the shade. As the group made their way along the riverbank, they could hear and sometimes see a series of rapids, small cataracts, and rocky terrain that made boat travel impossible on this stretch of the river. In the dry season, the water receded, the jutting rocks emerged, and "a man with a leaping-pole might cross dry-footed" the entire width of the São Francisco at this point.[42] Water churned and crashed through giant holes and crevasses in the rocky riverbed. As he moved past this terrain, the river became "generally repulsive" and narrowed drastically, and a ferry crossing connected the two provinces.[43]

FIGURE 14.1. Paulo Afonso Falls, 1868. Image in the public domain. Auguste Riedel.

That night, on the eve of finally seeing the falls, the crew "slept in the bush," and Richard "felt all that depression with which one approaches a long looked-for object, whose fruition appears so fair from afar."[44] He began to fear that the falls would not live up to their reputation, and that he "was doomed to a bitter disappointment." As they neared the falls the next morning, "the nakedness of the land" and the absence of houses heightened Richard's fears. Unsure of the path, he asked directions of a local, "liked his manner, and engaged him as a guide."[45] Very quickly, Richard's fears and anxieties evaporated as the "rumbling of a distant storm" grew in volume. He "heard a deep hollow sound" that "seemed to come from below the earth," and the "ground appeared to tremble at the eternal thunder" at their feet.[46]

He immediately headed for the largest of the falls, the so-called Mother of the Rapids, "where all the waters that come scouring down with their mighty rush are finally gathered." He advised his reader that to see cataracts truly "aright" is to "begin with the greatest enjoyment, the liveliest emotion, and not to fritter away one's powers, mental and physical, by working up to the grandest feature."⁴⁷ For the next ten pages, Richard describes in great detail the "magic" in the atmosphere at the falls. For him, the visual effect of "all great cataracts—is the 'realized' idea of power, of power tremendous, inexorable, irresistible. The eye is spellbound by the contrast of this impetuous motion, this wrathful, maddened haste to escape, with the frail stedfastness of the bits of rainbow, hovering above."⁴⁸

With a drop of some three hundred feet, and broken up into a series of falls, Richard judged the Paulo Afonso to lack "the sublime and glorious natural beauty of Niagara." Continuing the comparison, he writes, "If Niagara be the monarch of cataracts, Paulo Affonso is assuredly a king of rapids" that are "so wondrous and so awful."⁴⁹ In a commentary on the commercialization and tourism of Niagara Falls, Richard observes that Paulo Afonso had not yet been discovered and overrun by tourists. He "could hardly look forward to the time when it will have wooden temples and obelisks, vested interests, 25 cents to pay, and monster-hotels."⁵⁰ That day did come, but it has been stunted by the technology of hydroelectricity and efforts to control and redistribute water.

Hydroelectric dams stand as monuments to state-building in Brazil. As Richard made his way down more than a thousand miles of river, his account reveals the minimal presence of the state in this vast interior region. The occasional soldiers, tariff collectors, and local officials provided the expansive *sertão* with the few visible reminders of state presence, and they were concentrated in towns. The low level of economic activity could not produce the tax revenue to justify a larger state presence, and the region stood in stark contrast to the booming coffee region of the Southeast. As the surge in production took off in the 1870s, coffee exports generated taxes that built infrastructure, especially in the nation's capital and the city of São Paulo. As municipalities in the coffee zone would gradually discover, however, most of that tax revenue flowed to the national and state capital, and very little came back to the locales that produced the coffee. Then, as today, a highly centralized tax system left municipalities constantly short of revenue for even the most basic necessities—roads, bridges, and public buildings.⁵¹

The sprawling complex of three dams and five hydroelectric power plants is impressive testimony to the developmentalist vision of the postwar decades, especially the projects of the authoritarian

FIGURE 14.2. Paulo Afonso Falls, 2022. Marshall C. Eakin.

military regime. Engineering, however, has overwhelmed nature, as the dam has effectively shut down the Paulo Afonso Falls that Richard so coveted. The power company, Chesf, allows highly controlled tourism to enter the dam complex and walk out onto a multistory concrete pavilion to gaze into the empty rock canyons that once channeled the powerful waters of the São Francisco at a rate of 500,000 cubic feet per second through a series of gorges with a maximum drop of more than 275 feet into the river below. Today, the falls only occasionally reappear when water levels become excessive in the enormous reservoir and officials have to divert the excess water over the normally dry falls. As local officials like to say, they have the only massive falls in the world that turn on and off at will![52]

After experiencing the long-awaited and exhilarating visit to the Paulo Afonso Falls, Richard considered his expedition completed. "My task," he declared, "was done. I won its reward, and the strength passed away from me."[53] Having written some nine hundred pages in two volumes, including details on everything from food prices to temperature tables, his account ends abruptly.

One final paragraph covers the two-day mule ride to the port of Piranhas, a leisurely descent of the lower São Francisco by steamer, a trip up the coast to Maceió, the capital of Alagoas, then passage back to São Paulo via Bahia and Rio de Janeiro—some 1,200 miles, nearly the length of his trip down the São Francisco. Apparently, five months on mule and boat had sapped Richard's strength—or maybe his will—to continue writing. Weeks behind his original schedule, he now headed south to reunite with the anxious Isabel awaiting him in Rio, and then back to a near-death experience in São Paulo.

EPILOGUE

BURTON, BRAZIL, AND THE SHATTERED MIRROR

> I know I probably don't know what I think I do,
> but there's something to some of it.
>
> —BOBBY PINSON, ERIC CHURCH,
> CLINT DANIELS, AND JEFF HYDE, "SOME OF IT"

The Brazilian empire collapsed in ruins in November 1889, and eleven months later, Richard Francis Burton died of heart failure in the free port of Trieste. The imperial monarchy that the Braganzas had constructed with the support of the Catholic church, the military, and a landed aristocracy on the wealth generated by a coffee economy and a slave society crumbled virtually overnight. The dramatic abolition of slavery in 1888, conflicts with the Vatican, and deep unrest within the ranks of the army weakened and then fatally fragmented the three powerful pillars that had sustained the Americas' only true experience with a resident monarchy.[1] The republic (1889–1930) that emerged spasmodically out of the coup d'etat that sent the royal family into exile in Europe would continue the process of nation-building that had begun nearly seventy-five years earlier, even before Pedro I's declaration of independence.

EPILOGUE

In many ways, the foundational pillars of the modern Brazilian nation-state had emerged by the end of so-called Old or First Republic in 1930. The series of republics that followed over the next few decades would complete the process that was already emerging in Richard Burton's Brazil. Under the populist Getúlio Vargas (1930–1945, 1950–1954), and the developmentalist postwar state—especially the administration of Juscelino Kubitschek (1956–1961) and the military dictatorship (1964–1985)—Brazilians gradually and fitfully gathered up and assembled the "myriad bits" of the shattered mirror scattered across the vast regional, racial, and cultural zones of Brazilian territory in the nineteenth century.[2] The state-building process had been consolidated by the end of the twentieth century across more than three million square miles. The aspirational map that imperial elites had envisioned in the early nineteenth century finally became a reality. The nation—the imagined national community—had fully emerged by the late twentieth century, but in ways that would no doubt surprise and even appall Victorian Britain's most notorious and cosmopolitan explorer.

RICHARD BURTON AFTER BRAZIL

Throughout his five months by coach, mule, and riverboat through the Brazilian interior Richard stayed healthy and strong. This was not the dangerous environment he had faced in Africa. A few months after returning to São Paulo, however, he fell deathly ill. A frightened Isabel feared that Richard was dying. Suffering from an intense pain in the side of his broad chest, he screamed and cursed incessantly. In East Africa a decade earlier he had come close to succumbing to various tropical parasites and diseases on his expeditions in search of the source of the Nile. After those punishing brushes with temporary blindness, delirium, and death, his expedition through Brazil had seemed almost tame in comparison—until now. Isabel gave him hot baths and then covered him with mercury chloride (calomel), a mineral widely considered a cure for nearly all ills in the nineteenth century. When he failed to improve, Richard instructed her to give him large doses of chlorodyne, a patent medicine that combined traces of opium, cannabis, and chloroform.[3]

The pain and paralysis persisted. Isabel concluded that he had contracted a "Brazilian disease" and sent for a doctor. The physician came down by steamer from Rio and moved into the couple's São Paulo home. Over ten days he bled Richard with leeches and cuts to dozens of parts of his ravaged body. He hemorrhaged huge amounts of "black, clotted blood." Nothing worked. So much for the cutting edge of modern medicine in the 1860s. Eventually, Richard couldn't move, speak, or even swallow without excruciating pain that prompted him to cry out. After nearly three weeks of constant agony and all these treatments, Richard appeared to be even nearer to death. Isabel turned to her last hope—prayer and bathing his head in holy water—a strange cure for a man who adamantly rejected all religions. Within days he began very slowly to recover.

At this point, he decided to resign his position, request a medical leave, and seek a position in the Middle East. He recommended his assistant, Mr. Glennie, as his replacement, headed off to visit the battlefields of Paraguay, and instructed Isabel to pack, pay, and he would follow. The unfortunate Mr. Glennie died suddenly, just as the Foreign Office prepared to name him consul![4] In July 1868 Richard and Isabel "descended for the last time the tremendous inclined planes of the Santos Jundiahy railway, and still shuddering, bade farewell to a three years home." They left Santos for the last time, "that Weston-super-mud of the Far West, peculiarly fatal to the European, species Consul," Richard heading south, and Isabel north to England.[5] In Argentina he met with both the outgoing president Bartolomé Mitre, and the recently elected president, the cosmopolitan intellectual Domingo Faustino Sarmiento (to whom he dedicated his 1870 book on Paraguay).[6] Isabel headed off with the manuscript of *Explorations in the Highlands of the Brazil*, and Richard spent the next year in Paraguay, Argentina, Chile, and Peru, where he would abruptly learn of his appointment in Damascus.[7]

When Isabel (July 1868), and then Richard (April 1869), finally departed Brazil, they seemed to have finally achieved their dream—a consular post in the Middle East, Damascus, no less. Unfortunately, Richard's short tour of duty was a fiasco, leading to his recall after less than two years.[8] The Foreign Office relegated him to the consulate in Trieste at the northern end of the Adriatic Sea, the home (and only) port of the Austro-Hungarian imperial fleet. Jules Verne called Trieste "a colossal emporium and a prodigious trading centre."[9] Despite a great deal of lobbying over many years for another post in North Africa or the Middle East, Richard would spend the last seventeen years of his life in Trieste. The days of the intrepid explorer had ended.

These would be prolific years for Richard the author, editor, and translator, who produced more than two dozen books in more than forty volumes, including those works that most contributed to his reputation as an "obscene" Victorian rebel—the *Kama Sutra*, the *Ananga Ranga*, *The Perfumed Garden*, and the (eventually) sixteen volumes of the *Arabian Nights*.[10] (Richard described the *Arabian Nights*: "during my long years of official banishment to the dull and dreary half-clearings of South America, it proved itself a charm, a talisman against ennui and despondency.")[11] On his death on 20 October 1890, Isabel enraged most of Richard's closest and oldest friends by giving him a Catholic funeral in Trieste, and then another in London. Although Isabel claimed that Richard was amenable to conversion to Catholicism, none of his friends believed her. They knew better that the man who had recently written, "The more I study religions the more I am convinced that man never worshipped anything but himself," was not a believer.[12]

Most infamously, Isabel burned many of Richard's papers before leaving Trieste, most notably his translation of *The Scented Garden*. Although she claimed this was Richard's wish, the claim is preposterous considering he had spent his final years laboriously completing the translation. Isabel then wrote a two-volume biography of Richard and started her own autobiography, which she left to a collaborator to complete when she died of ovarian cancer in March 1895.[13] She left behind very detailed instructions for her carefully selected executors to burn the remaining private diaries and manuscripts. Historians have long mourned the loss of what must have been an incredibly rich and revealing trove of sources produced by one of the most fascinating figures of the nineteenth century.[14] Although Richard Burton was one of the most documented figures of the era, historians are left to speculate on something as fundamental to understanding him as his sexuality. In the case of a man who pioneered ethnography and studies of comparative sexuality, the destruction of Richard's personal papers becomes even more frustrating.

EPILOGUE

In a region notorious for its complexity and volatility, Richard seemed to alienate just about everyone in Syria—Ottoman officials, Christian missionaries, some of his Foreign Office colleagues, and local Jewish merchants. A diplomat he was not. As Mary Lovell has noted, he "had a blind spot in his social skills. While adept at spinning yarns to entertain and amuse, he could not dissemble in his personal relationships. He either lacked the patience, or he could not be bothered to pretend to like, or work with, people he did not like or respect, no matter what their station or influence."[15] Richard's later antisemitic writings were, no doubt, shaped in part by his troubled experience in Damascus. While in Damascus, Isabel became a confidante of the extraordinary Jane Digby, the aristocratic Englishwoman famed for her beauty and notorious for her affairs with kings and generals. Digby ultimately married a Bedouin leader, residing half the year in Damascus and the other half in the desert with her husband's people. Isabel published her own book, *The Inner Life of Syria* (1876), that included a staunch defense of Richard's actions and criticism of his antagonists.[16]

Richard's predecessor in Trieste had supposedly been told by Lord Derby on his appointment, "Here is six hundred a year for doing nothing and you are just the man to do it."[17] Trieste was certainly more cosmopolitan a city than Santos or São Paulo, and the Burtons eventually settled into a villa overlooking the port, a home packed with the accumulated art, photographs, and curiosities of three decades of travels on five continents. Richard apparently had only about five months' work out of the year, a state of affairs well known to and grudgingly tolerated by the highest officials in the Foreign Office.[18] When not occupied with official duties, Richard the linguist spent the last years of his life translating and editing a series of erotic works that had the potential to run afoul of Victorian Obscene Publications Act (1857). He and his longtime collaborator F. F. Arbuthnot engaged some Indian scholars to translate an ancient sex manual from Sanskrit, the *Kama Sutra of Vatsyayana*, which they then edited and revised (1883). With its archaic and sometimes idiosyncratic English, the translation remains in print in various forms to the present.[19] They also refined the translation of the *Ananga Ranga* (1885), a sixteenth-century work that aimed "to promote sexual ecstasy in marriage." Both books appeared without attributed authors or translators and were privately published by a fictional invention of Richard, the Kama Shastra Society of London and the Benares! A third volume, *The Perfumed Garden*, was a sex manual originally written in Arabic in North Africa, then translated into French. Richard translated (from the French version) and published this work, and then spent the next years assiduously pursuing an original version in Arabic.[20] He had just completed the translation from Arabic as *The Scented Garden*, when he died. After so many years working on this project, it is highly unlikely that Richard would have wanted Isabel to burn the only copy.

His greatest accomplishment in these years was the translation and publication of the *Thousand and One Nights* (often referred to as the *Arabian Nights*). A collection of hundreds of ancient Middle Eastern folktales (many of them originally from South Asia) including the stories of Aladdin, Ali Baba, and Sinbad, these stories had entered into European culture with a French translation in the early eighteenth century, one that eliminated any bawdy language or sex. In the wisest financial move of his career, Richard offered the sixteen volumes by subscription for £1 each and secured a thousand subscribers. The £16,000 (more than twenty times his annual consular salary) from this venture in the late 1880s gave Richard and Isabel a financial security that had escaped them for a quarter century. Richard's "Terminal Essay" in the tenth volume created quite a stir as he graphically described customs across what he termed the "Sotadic Zone," the regions of the globe where he believed homosexuality was most prevalent. Along with the writings of Havelock Ellis (1859–1939), the essay (despite its many flaws) was one of the first truly scholarly efforts to study homosexuality. Isabel apparently spent her last years worrying that the British Society for the Suppression of Vice was pursuing her and Richard.[21]

Richard continued to travel—to West Africa, Saudia Arabia, Egypt, and Iceland—mostly on "consulting" trips, and usually as a mining expert studying supposedly promising finds for proposed business ventures.[22] He adeptly parlayed his time in the Brazilian mining zone as a claim to expertise. Despite his usual enthusiasm and boosterism, none of the ventures panned out. In the mid-1880s, he took Isabel to India, where they revisited his old haunts. At

EPILOGUE

every opportunity, the two of them lobbied for a consular post in North Africa, one that at several times they thought was coming, but never did. Isabel and friends were successful in lobbying the prime minister and Queen Victoria, and in 1886 the queen knighted Richard. After twenty-five years of marriage, they became Sir Richard and Lady Isabel Burton. For a man so openly contemptuous of Victorian society and morals, Richard nonetheless reveled in the knighthood, while resenting that the queen had taken so long to bestow it.[23]

FIGURE 15.1. Richard and Isabel Burton, a few weeks before his death in 1890. Image in the public domain. Dr. Grenfell Baker.

A series of photographs taken in Trieste shortly before his death reveal a fragile and grayed Richard with Isabel in flowing robes and head covering inspired by Catholic women's orders. As they approached the end of life, Isabel became even more devoutly Catholic and committed to converting Richard. On his deathbed, she badgered the local priest to give Richard last rites, most likely after he had expired. Despite the income from the *Arabian Nights*, she was short on funds and had to borrow and beg to pack up and ship two hundred boxes, and Richard's body, back to London. (She paid and packed, but certainly did not follow this last time.) Many of Richard's closest friends denounced her plans for a second Catholic funeral and burial at Mortlake Cemetery near Kew Gardens in the west of London. She mounted a national campaign to raise funds for their marble mausoleum designed as an Arab tent. Isabel then purchased a townhouse across the street from the mausoleum.[24] In her paranoia, and afraid of desecration, she also purchased plots alongside the structure with detailed instructions to her executors to bury the two of them should there ever be a revolution in England![25]

Continuing her lifelong role as Richard's publicist, Isabel produced a detailed and chatty two-volume biography that brought in much-needed income. Suffering from ovarian cancer, she hired an editor to help her with her own autobiography, which he completed and published after her death.[26] She also worked with publishers to reissue a number of Richard's works, including a condensed (and sanitized) version of the *Arabian Nights*. Isabel's very detailed instructions for her executors about her funeral, burial, and papers demonstrate her deep religiosity and efforts to shape Richard's legacy.[27] She instructed that their private diaries be burned along with correspondence and some unfinished manuscripts. Many of the great mysteries of Richard Burton's life stem from the zeal of Isabel, and her most puritanical executor, in destroying so many of his most personal papers.

Richard Burton's life coincided with the era of Britain's greatest imperial expansion. In the aftermath of the Napoleonic Wars, Great Britain would dominate world politics and the global economy until the catastrophic World War I. The British constructed a "world-system," as one prominent historian describes it, that connected formal colonies like India and Canada as well as informal power over many other regions of the globe, including Brazil.[28] In many ways, Richard was riding this wave of imperial expansion and power—in his military career in India, his explorations in the Middle East and Africa, and his time as consul in Brazil. As Britain went into decline in the decades after 1914, US power rose, and the so-called American Century followed Britain's global power in the nineteenth century. By the end of the twentieth century, it would be US scholars exploring Brazil on the wave of their own country's imperial reach.

Britain's power and influence in Brazil paralleled the larger global pattern. From the arrival of the royal family in 1808, until World War I, British commerce, technology, finance, and political pressure shaped Brazil and its development. In the first three decades of the twentieth century, that power declined drastically as US influence overtook and replaced it. In the nineteenth century, Richard Burton witnessed Brazil's emergence as a coffee-exporting behemoth, and the beginnings of Brazil's transformation from an archipelago of regions into a nation—an imagined community of Brazilians. As boosterish as he sometimes was about Brazil in his account, he would probably be astonished at the country's rise as a middle power with an economy that will soon likely overtake that of the United Kingdom. Brazil today, like all countries, bears the burdens of its past, especially of the nineteenth century, but it is a nation that is a world apart from Richard Burton's Brazil of the 1860s.

Brazil After Burton

Successful state-building requires the creation of infrastructure to link up the national territory—to weave together the disparate and far-flung regions of the more than three million square miles within Brazil's official borders. In Richard Burton's time, this meant good roads, shipping along the coastal and inland waterways, and railways (the cutting-edge transportation technology of the day). By the 1870s telegraph lines finally connected Rio de Janeiro to Europe and the United States, and the major cities of Brazil. Abolition in May 1888 became the first major national event to be transmitted simultaneously across the county via telegraphy.[29] In the early twentieth century, telephony would replace telegraphy. Not until the beginning of the twenty-first century, as a consequence of technocratic military rule in the 1960s and 1970s, would radar and microwave telecommunications finally cover the Amazon (some 40 percent of Brazilian territory) and fully integrate the vast Brazilian archipelago.[30]

In the 1860s, railways had just begun to appear in Brazil. Mauá's showpiece line from Guanabara Bay to the edge of the Serra dos Órgãos in the 1850s showed the possibilities for rail, but it was primarily a vanity project—for both Pedro II and Mauá. Richard and Isabel witnessed the construction of the first sections of what would become the Pedro II Railway, eventually penetrating deep into Minas Gerais by the 1890s. They also arrived in time to see the completion of the San Paulo Railway, which became a vital transportation corridor from the heartland of the coffee fields to Santos, turning Richard's relatively quiet consular city into the most dynamic port in Brazil and, eventually, in Latin America. Railways expanded across the eastern coastal zone of Brazil in the late nineteenth century but never became the engine of integration that they were in the United States, Mexico, or Argentina.[31]

The institutions of the state sometimes preceded, and sometimes followed, the paths of national integration. As Richard saw in his travels across Brazil, even in the smallest and most out-of-the-way towns, judges, police delegates, and soldiers marked the presence of the state in the interior, if in places a minimal one. The challenge of the empire, and then the Old Republic, was to install and support officials to carry out the most basic functions—security, legal adjudication, tax collection, and elections. The weaker the state, the more powerful the local landowners, and the greater their ability to ignore or contravene orders and laws emanating from Rio de Janeiro. Debates have gone on for decades about the power and weaknesses of the state in the Brazilian interior. The numerous regional revolts of the early empire show both a weak state, and its ability, ultimately, to mobilize and assert its will across regions as dispersed as the eastern Amazon or Rio Grande do Sul. The Canudos uprising in the 1890s and the Contestado Revolt (1912–1916) in southern Brazil signal the continuing weakness of the state into the early twentieth century.[32]

The centralizing thrust of the Vargas years consolidated state power across most of Brazil. Hundreds of thousands of prospectors, illegal loggers, land invasions, and thousands of murdered peasants at the end of the twentieth century and the beginning of the twenty-first point to the continuing weakness, and sometimes complicity, of state power in much of the vast Amazon basin.[33] Although this enormous region, and much of Center-West Brazil, experienced minimal state presence in the nineteenth century, state institutions (however meager) had effectively spread across the coastal zone from the mouth of the Amazon down to Rio Grande do Sul. The last few months of Richard's expedition through the interior skirted the western fringes of this zone that stretched 200 to 250 miles inland from the Atlantic.

Until the 1840s, the survival of Brazil as the vast territory shown on most maps was continually in doubt.[34] With the defeat of the last substantive regional revolts in the 1840s, Brazil became a confederation of islands of powerful landowners who were in effect the state incarnate in the countryside. As Vitor Nunes Leal, Raymundo Faoro, and others have shown, Brazil was a sprawling patrimonial system where powerful landowners (*coronéis*) dominated local life.[35] For Faoro, an aristocratic elite of lawyers and military officers provided the personnel who both administered the state and derived their status and power from it. They used the patrimony of the state to strengthen central government, reward allies, and resolve conflict.[36] Personal and political patronage served as the lubricant for the limited and often balky machinery

EPILOGUE

of the empire. Richard's visit to the Jaguara estate at the beginning of his voyage down the Rio das Velhas provides us with a glimpse of these powerful landowners. Francisco de Paula Santos and his son-in-law, Henrique Dumont, wielded their power locally, both through their economic resources and their participation in politics. The central government of Brazil, quite simply, did not have the means or the resources even to attempt to assert its control over this enormous area. In exchange for their obedience to provincial (later state) authorities, the landowners were left largely alone to run local affairs. When disputes among these landowners or from the poor masses threatened the peace, the provincial or state government would step in with its resources to restore stability. At the national level, provincial authorities remained obedient to the central government in exchange for their own relative autonomy. And when disputes at the level of the province or state became too pronounced, the central government would step in to restore order (as in the cases of Canudos or the Contestado).[37] In the words of one historian, "benevolent care gloved outright force."[38]

This system became even more highly developed after the overthrow of Pedro II in 1889 and the creation of the First (or Old) Republic. The decentralized United States of Brazil, in effect, was a federation of states dominated by powerful landowners (*os poderosos da terra*) who exercised impressive autonomy while maintaining loyalty to the central government. In the face of frequent uprisings and rebellions from the 1890s to the 1920s, the central government intervened in nearly every Brazilian state, often multiple times, to ensure the integrity of a system sometimes called the "politics of the governors."[39] The Brazilian state repeatedly acted to guarantee stability, enforce order, and impose unity on contentious local and regional elites. The need to act frequently offers impressive testimony to the continuing weakness of the Brazilian state in the early twentieth century.[40]

On the surface, Brazil was a constitutional monarchy from 1824 to 1889 with parliamentary politics self-consciously modeled on the English political system. Elections at the municipal and provincial levels took place regularly, and (especially under Pedro II) the two major political parties—Liberals and Conservatives—alternated in power for decades.[41] Despite the facade of electoral representation, the empire was built on the politics of exclusion:

EPILOGUE

The rights of citizenship were extended to very few. During Richard's time in Brazil, only about 10 percent of the population could vote and, especially at the local level, powerful landowners determined the outcome of elections through coercion, force, and alliances.[42] In the 1880s, electoral legislation further restricted the vote—to about 1 percent of the population, from more than 1 million registered voters to less than 150,000.[43] The Constitution of 1891, although modeled on that of the United States, severely restricted voting with requirements of wealth and literacy (even more so than in the United States). More important, those who controlled local politics determined who voted, whatever the official legal requirements. In the 1930 election, the last of the Old Republic (1889–1930), less than 3 percent of the population voted.[44] From the perspective of Brazilian elites, the system functioned fairly well. From the 1840s to 1930, this elite political consensus provided Brazil with an impressive stability compared with the other countries of the Americas—including the United States. Local revolts threatened the elite consensus but were contained. The most serious challenge to the system, the overthrow of the monarchy in 1889, ushered in five years of serious political turmoil, but by 1894 the powerful elites had once again reestablished a political system that balanced local and regional autonomy with national unity—as a federative republic rather than a (nominally) centralized monarchy. As Aspásia Camargo has observed of this period, "national identity ... appeared to be more virtual and symbolic than real."[45]

Already by Richard's time in Brazil, coffee had emerged as the most important factor in national economic development. Coffee would continue as the prime or one of the prime drivers for another century. Enslaved labor had powered the Brazilian economy since the late sixteenth century with the rise of sugar cane cultivation. The gold boom of the eighteenth century made slavery even more important for the colonial economy, and coffee accelerated demand again in the nineteenth century. As Richard moved through Brazil in the 1860s, he was witnessing a moment of transition. In the two decades after his departure, the immigration of European labor took off, the abolition movement intensified, and slavery finally ended in 1888, just two years before Richard's death in Trieste.

EPILOGUE

Gold (and diamonds) had shifted the axis of economic and political power from the Northeast to the Southeast in the eighteenth century, and coffee definitively established the triangle of Rio de Janeiro, Minas Gerais, and São Paulo as the heartland of a postcolonial Brazil. Sugar had produced an increasingly integrated market on the northeastern coast, mining gave rise to expanding markets in Minas Gerais and Rio de Janeiro, and coffee brought São Paulo into the southeastern market with a vengeance. The provinces or states south of São Paulo gradually developed into a third major market, and then the Amazon rubber boom added another dynamic economic zone, for a few decades. Yet Brazil once again functioned as a series of markets along the Atlantic coast from Rio Grande do Sul to Pernambuco, and to a lesser extent to the mouth of Amazon. The vast interior that Richard had barely skirted as he moved down the São Francisco would remain largely outside the nation's markets until the end of the twentieth century. The military regime's push into the Amazon, and the spectacular development of the agro-export economy of the Center-West finally consolidated a truly national market on the vast map of Brazil.[46]

Perhaps the most enduring legacy of the colonial period was the construction of a society with profoundly entrenched socioeconomic inequities. For three centuries, slavery and the slave trade created both national wealth and extreme inequality. The abolition of slavery in the late nineteenth century finally eliminated the deeply rooted legal chasm between the enslaved and the free but barely touched the socioeconomic divisions that continue to plague Brazilian society to the present. Richard Burton moved through Brazil just after his own empire had forcibly halted the traffic in enslaved Africans at its peak. By the late 1860s, the size of the enslaved population in Brazil had grown—from around 1 million in 1800 (one-third of the population of the colony)—to 1.5 million in the 1860s (less than 20 percent). By 1888 the absolute number of enslaved had declined to just over 700,000—less than 10 percent of Brazil's inhabitants.[47]

Brazil remained in the late nineteenth and earlier twentieth century an overwhelmingly rural society. Richard's Brazil was dominated by Rio de Janeiro, with its more than 250,000 inhabitants. Salvador had about half that population, and Recife (at

115,000) was the only other city with more than 60,000 inhabitants. Nearly half of the urban population resided in Rio de Janeiro, Salvador, and Recife. São Paulo was still a small town, but one on the verge of decades of explosive growth. The massive rural to urban migration of the post-1940 decades would finally fully urbanize Brazil and complete the process of integrating cities and the vast rural interior.[48]

The profound class differences that Richard described in the 1860s have persisted but have become much more complex in an urban, industrial, service economy with more than twenty times the population of the late empire. While those socioeconomic inequities may have slowed down national integration and nation formation in the nineteenth century, they clearly did not stop it in the twentieth century. These clearly shattered fragments in Richard's time divided the Brazilian archipelago and made the task of nation-building more complicated but did not keep Brazilians from assembling them into a national community. While the symbols of the empire, especially the monarchy, may have provided the weak bonds of individuals to the state in the 1860s, a shared mass culture of images, symbols, and rituals would provide the glue for an imagined community a century later.

Creating the nation proved even more challenging than forging the state. Like most Latin American elites in the nineteenth century, the Brazilians strove to create the symbols (flag, monarchy), rituals (holidays, national anthem), and beliefs (sovereignty, belonging) needed to forge an imagined community. The lack of national infrastructure (especially schools and literacy) hindered the dissemination and reinforcement of a national identity. A more serious obstacle was a lack of agreement on a national mythology shared across regions and races. Whites and the more Europeanized encompassed less than half of the ten million inhabitants in Richard's Brazil. Most of the Indigenous peoples of the interior resided beyond the authority of the state, and many were indeed unaware that it even existed.[49] The enslaved comprised some 15 percent of the population of roughly ten million in the 1860s. As Euclides da Cunha's classic account of Canudos shows, most elite Brazilians viewed the racially mixed (probably about five million people) as inferior and dispensable. The racist, scientific, and eugenic theories of the late nineteenth and early twentieth century led most Brazilian intellectuals to conclude that the only possibility for a coherent imagined community was the replacement of most Brazilians with European immigrants.[50]

With the rise of modernism in the 1920s and 1930s, Gilberto Freyre's *Casa-grande e senzala* (1933), and the Vargas regimes of the 1930s and 1940s, the Brazilian state gradually played a critical role in adapting a wide range of cultural traits across regions to assist in the formation of a national identity built on the so-called fable of three races, that the mixture of the genes and cultures of Native Americans, Africans, and Europeans defined Brazil and Brazilians. Despite the vastness of national territory, marked regional differences, multiple races, and profound class inequalities, the myth of *mestiçagem* became the glue that held together (however tenuously) the thousands of pieces of the shattered mirror. The racist, Eurocentric, and elitist intellectuals and political leaders of the empire would no doubt be shocked that this multiracial, multicultural ethos defined the Brazilian imagined community a century later.

The greatest challenge in the 1860s was how to forge a sense of community out of the immensely diverse peoples, languages, and traditions that spanned millions of square miles, most of them beyond the reach of the central government. This nation-building project succeeded by the late twentieth century, producing a powerful sense of national identity. The great challenge today is to hold together a people that now share a common language, symbols, rituals, and myths but are profoundly divided by income, cultural, and ideological differences. Today, each Brazilian needs to see their own "little bit" while remembering "the whole to own." Just as in the United States today, if a critical mass of Brazilians cannot see the commonalities that bind them together as more important than the differences that divide them, like Burton's mirror, the shattered pieces will produce a shattered nation.

THE SHATTERED MIRROR

For most of Latin America, the process of nation formation and the creation of an imagined community begins in the early nineteenth century and does not come to fruition until the mid- to late-twentieth century. A Eurocentric vision shaped the dreams of the elite nation builders in the first century after independence.

Although Brazilian elites were acutely aware that European-descended Brazilians of lighter skin had long been a minority, they still envisioned European nations as their model, especially France and England.[51] Their impossible task, one they refused to grasp, was how to pull together the diverse fragments—racial groups, classes, regions—that spanned their aspirational map of Brazil to create a European-style nation. The primary obstacle to the consolidation of the nation was centuries of trafficking millions of Africans to provide the muscle for the production of sugar, gold, diamonds, and coffee. Africans and their descendants in Brazil both made the creation of a Eurocentric nation plausible and ultimately made its completion impossible. By the 1860s many Brazilians grappled with this paradox. The most common solution they offered in the last decades of the century was the gradual elimination of the Black presence in Brazil, usually through European immigration.

Richard Burton, with his imperial, Eurocentric, racist worldview, shared this appraisal with Brazilian elites. In his constant and exhaustive travels across Brazil—both north and south—he saw the potential of this vast empire. He understood the need to pull the myriad shards into a cohesive whole, but his model was his own "homeland." Richard would without a doubt be shocked to see a Brazilian nation constructed around a multiracial identity, whatever its complexities, contradictions, and complications. He shared an elite bias toward highly controlled politics. He could neither have foreseen nor desired the massive democratization of his own country in the decades after the Reform Act of 1867, passed and enacted as he was making his way down the upper São Francisco River.[52] In a monarchical empire where fewer than 10 percent participated directly in electoral politics in 1867, he certainly could not have imagined Brazil would one day be the third-largest democracy on the planet.

Despite his inability, his incapacity, to envision a multiracial and more egalitarian Brazilian nation, Richard's reflections on Brazil provide us with invaluable and detailed firsthand reporting on the early stages of the nation taking shape in the 1860s. The dozens of foreign travelers who published accounts of imperial Brazil in the nineteenth century have long provided historians with priceless glimpses of daily life, customs, traditions, economic

EPILOGUE

activity, and environmental conditions, especially in those areas far from the urban centers of the coastal zone. With his unmatched experience exploring South Asia, the Middle East, Africa, and the United States, Richard brought with him to Brazil a much wider range of experience and comparison than any other travel writer in nineteenth-century Brazil. His ability to speak Portuguese and his insatiable appetite for information also gave him a much deeper and even scholarly knowledge of Brazil than most of his fellow travelers. In short, it is hard to imagine anyone in the nineteenth century better informed, both through books and "fieldwork," to traverse and analyze Brazil. Yet, like all of us, Richard brought to his travels and writing his own set of biases and cultural blinders. To complicate matters, although we see Richard and Brazil in the 1860s through Richard's eyes, especially through his two-volume travel account, our view of both Richard and the Brazil he experienced has also been shaped through Isabel's letters, her biography of Richard, her own autobiography, and her role in editing his works. The deeply hypermasculine imperial gaze was consciously reframed and refined by Isabel's eyes and hands.

As a historian of Brazil born and reared in East Texas, educated in the Midwest and California, and having spent more than forty years teaching in the rapidly changing US South, more than fifty years traveling across nearly every country in Latin America, and long periods living and researching in Brazil, I also bring to Richard's account of Brazil my own insights and limitations, my own extensive research and fieldwork. I do have the enormous advantage of the knowledge of the long arc of Brazilian history since 1867 that Richard Burton could only speculate on and imagine—I have 160 years of hindsight. Yet, just as Richard's imperfect analysis was inflected with the prejudices and values of his own time, the historian of the early twenty-first century offers his own inherently flawed interpretation—of Brazil in the 1860s and of Richard Burton himself.

These biases and imperfections have been magnified by the very process of our efforts to recover the past. In recent years, it has become something of a truism to speak of the "silence of the archive" to refer to the gaps in the surviving historical records. We are lucky to have any records of the past, yet most of what we have first began to be collected in the eighteenth and nineteenth centuries by governments and elites, primarily to document their own stories of the rise and triumph of nation-states and their leaders. The silences of the masses, however, are even vaster than those in the archives. The great majority of individuals who have lived and died on this planet have left little or no trace of their existence. What the archives have assembled is but a very small fraction of the past that we can partly supplement with archaeological, biological, and geological materials.

Part of what draws me back over decades to the graves of the English, Irish, Scots, Brazilians, and Africans on that hilltop at Morro Velho is how powerfully the place evokes the crux of the dilemma of the historian in search of the past. With its long history, the St. John d'el Rey Mining Company, and its successors, accumulated an enormous trove of documents, providing us with the rare opportunity to peer into the lives of thousands of people. Thanks to the persistence of local historians, especially at the Federal University of Minas Gerais in Belo Horizonte, what has survived of this gold mine of records has been professionally organized and stored in the old Casa Grande that once served as the superintendent's home. As has so often happened, the documentation of the lives of the English community and company operations is far richer than the material on ordinary Brazilians and the hundreds of enslaved workers whose ancestors now lie unmarked atop the hill across from the Casa Grande. Even with this extraordinary archive, the historian's efforts to understand people from such different times, places, and cultures—enslaved people from many parts of the African continent, men and women from the British Isles, Brazilian peasants, merchants, and wealthy landowners—is, admittedly, flawed and always imperfect. I can hope to try to comprehend them and the worlds they once inhabited, but always knowing my limitations.

This dilemma is built into the very nature of human understanding, and will not be resolved in the future, even with the trillions of bits of data about the billions of people who inhabit the planet today. Just as the record for the past is limited and unequally produced and stored, the insurmountable problems of storing and eventually retrieving digital information will bedevil the historians of the present and the future. It may be difficult to truly make sense of our contemporaries in the early twenty-first century, but it

EPILOGUE

will likely be even more so in coming decades and centuries when we are figures in a distant past for historians in future.

The fundamental dilemma and challenge of the historian is that all the knowledge that has survived of the past is partial and imbued with the biases of those who produced it, and that our understanding of this imperfect record of the past is inevitably tainted by the biases and values of the historian assembling the historical materials and offering the interpretation. We strive to assemble as much as possible from the shattered mirrors scattered across the globe, but most of the shards have been ground down, buried, or lost. Our account of the past is shaped by the pieces that have somehow been produced, managed to survive, and embody the perspectives of their producers. Imperfect historical records interpreted by imperfect historians: these are the essence of history and this history of Richard Burton in nineteenth-century Brazil.

NOTES

INTRODUCTION: KNOWLEDGE, PLACE, PERSPECTIVE

Epigraph: Lopez, *Horizon*, 60.
1. Eakin, *British Enterprise in Brazil*.
2. Hartley, *Go-Between*, 9.
3. Anderson, *Imagined Communities*.
4. Pettitt, "One-Man Multidisciplinarian," 319.
5. See, for example, Weaver, *Exploration*, 9–10.
6. Some of the best biographies of Burton are Lovell, *Rage to Live*; Rice, *Captain Sir Richard Francis Burton*; Brodie, *Devil Drives*; Farwell, *Burton*; and the much-debated one by his widow, I. Burton, *Life of Captain Sir Richard Burton*. Throughout this book I refer to the Burtons as Richard and Isabel rather than by their last name. His friends called him Dick, and Isabel, oddly, sometimes called him Jemmy. His critics sometimes referred to him as "Ruffian Dick"! Rice, 354.
7. Lovell, *Rage to Live*, 486 and 488.
8. See Cordiviola, *Richard Burton*; and McLynn, *From the Sierras to the Pampas*.
9. In one of his quirky, and literalist, habits as a translator, Burton insisted on translating *o Brasil* in Portuguese as "the Brazil" in English.
10. Falwell, *Burton*, 263; Brodie, *Devil Drives*, 245; Lovell, *Rage to Live*, 488; Burton, *Letters from the Battle-Fields*.
11. Falwell, *Burton*, 251; quote is from Cordiviola, *Richard Burton*, 45. One of Burton's earliest biographers wrote about Richard's nine books on West Africa, "Burton's prolixity is his reader's despair. He was devoid of the faintest idea of proportion." Wright, *Life of Sir Richard Burton*, 194.
12. Theodore Roosevelt, who would nearly perish on his own expedition through the Brazilian interior, said that Burton's "writings on the interior of Brazil offer an excellent instance of the value of a sojourn or trip of this type,

even without an especial scientific object." Roosevelt, *Through the Brazilian Wilderness*, 344.

13. McLynn, *From the Sierras to the Pampas*, 108. McLynn draws on Alan Moorhead's observations about Burton.

14. The correspondence can be found at *Letters and Memoirs of Sir Richard Burton*, in Tredoux, *Book of Burtoniana*. For an excellent survey of the Burton archives see Lovell, *Rage to Live*, Appendix 1, 800–802.

15. There is no single work that looks at foreign travelers in nineteenth-century Brazil. The tendency in the numerous works is to look at individual travelers, or a cluster of them, or to examine their works on a specific region or theme. See, for example, Sallas, "Narrativas e Imagens," 415–35. Gravatá, "Viajantes Estrangeiros em Minas Gerais," 11–12, lists more than two dozen traveler accounts (French, English, German) for nineteenth-century Minas Gerais. Other works often incorporate the accounts of travelers critically, but as a supplemental source. See, for example, Sadlier, *Brazil Imagined*.

16. See, for example, Pratt, *Imperial Eyes*; and Said, *Orientalism*.

17. See, for example, the classic Spivak, "Can the Subaltern Speak?" 21–78.

18. The classic statement on this complicated subject is Trouillot, *Silencing the Past*. See also Pratt, *Imperial Eyes* 5–6.

19. Eakin, *A History of Latin America*, 177–217; Barman, *Brazil*.

20. Barman, *Citizen Emperor*; Schwarcz, *As barbas do imperador*.

21. Darwin, *Empire Project*; Bayly, *Imperial Meridian*; and Bayly, *Birth of the Modern World*.

22. Elliott, *Old World and the New*; Elliott, *Empires of the Atlantic World*; Daly, *Rise of Western Power*.

23. Maltby, *Rise and Fall of the Spanish Empire*.

24. Disney, *History of Portugal*.

25. Schwartz, *Sugar Plantations*, esp. 1–70; Klein, *Atlantic Slave Trade*.

26. Onnekink and Rommelse, *Dutch in the Early Modern World*; Aldrich, *Greater France*.

27. Russell-Wood, "Gold Cycle," in Bethell, *Colonial Brazil*, 190–243.

28. Klein, *Atlantic Slave Trade*; Thomas, *Slave Trade*; Bethell, *Abolition of the Brazilian Slave Trade*.

29. Bayly, *Birth of the Modern World*, chapters 4 and 6; Pratt, *Imperial Eyes*, 11.

30. Osterhammel, *Transformation of the World*, 77–86; Weaver, *Exploration*, chapter 6, "Exploration and Empire," 83–99; Kennedy, *Mungo Park's Ghost*.

31. Thomas, *Cook*.

32. Desmond and Moore, *Darwin*, 101–94.

33. Lovell, *Rage to Live*, chapters 9–10, 12–14.

34. See, for example, Williams, "Decolonising Knowledge," 82–103; and the preface of Comaroff and Comaroff, *Of Revelation and Revolution*, xi–xv.

35. Edward Thornton to Lord Russell, 23 July 1866, and Lord Russell to Edward Thornton, 17 November 1866, Foreign Office Correspondence, National Archives, UK (hereafter FO), 13/438.

36. See Said, *Orientalism*, esp. 190–97, on Burton as a Middle Eastern traveler; and Kennedy, *Highly Civilized Man*.
37. Lovell, *Rage to Live*, 479–97.
38. Lovell, 654–56.
39. Faulkner, *Requiem for a Nun*, 85.

CHAPTER 1. A WILD LAWLESS CREATURE IN THE BRAZILIAN EMPIRE

Epigraph: Quoted in Brodie, *Devil Drives*, 139.
1. Lovell, *Rage to Live*, 358–71.
2. Lovell, *Scandalous Life*, 297.
3. Lovell, *Rage to Live*, 379–80.
4. Lovell, 382–84.
5. Lord John Russell, 7 January 1865, in Tredoux, *Book of Burtoniana*, vol. 2, no. 4.
6. Wills, *Envoys of Abolition*; and Burton and Wilkins, *Romance*, 171–243.
7. Burton, *Abeokuta and the Cameroons Mountains*; Burton, *Wanderings in West Africa*, vol. 2, *From Liverpool to Fernando Po*; Burton, *A Mission to Gelele*.
8. Pratt, *Imperial Eyes*, 204.
9. Lovell, *Rage to Live*, 419–23.
10. Brodie, *Devil Drives*, 213.
11. Herskovits, *Dahomey*.
12. Richard Burton to Monckton Milnes, 23 October 1865, in Tredoux, *Book of Burtoniana*, vol. 2, no. 38.
13. For a classic work on Rio in the nineteenth century, see Needell, *A Tropical Belle Epoque*.
14. See Said, *Orientalism*, esp. 190–97 on Burton.
15. The infamous essay is in the final volume of Burton's ten-volume *Book of the Thousand Nights and a Night*, 205–54.
16. Lovell, *Rage to Live*, 180, cites the original of the treating physician's account. This document is in the Burton papers at the Huntington Library, San Marino, California.
17. Quoted in Lovell, *Rage to Live*, 159.
18. Lovell offers the most detailed discussion of Isabel's purported burning of her husband's private papers, *Rage to Live*, 787–99.
19. Burton and Wilkins, *Romance*, 233.
20. Farwell, *Burton*, 249.
21. James Murray to Roderick Murchison, 25 November 1864, FO 13/426.
22. Richard F. Burton to Lord Russell, 13 July 1865, FO 13/432.
23. Richard F. Burton to Lord Russell, 8 September 1865, FO 13/432.
24. Wiltshire County Records Office, Papers of Sir Richard Burton, Explorer, Author, Diplomat and Husband of Isabel Arundell, Wiltshire and Swindon History Centre, Chippenham, UK (hereafter WR) contains a fifteen-page publication of the Royal Mail Steam Packet Company with all the details of the transatlantic shipping. Item 2667/26/4/1, "Memorandum book of Richard Burton about his term as consul in Santos, Brazil."

25. Richard F. Burton to Lord Russell, 8 September 1865, FO 13/432; Britton, *Cables, Crises, and the Press*, 29 and 42.

26. I. Burton, *Life of Captain Sir Richard F. Burton*, 1:418.

27. Although Canada gained its de facto independence in 1867, the British monarch remained the head of state, even after Canada adopted its own constitution in 1982. Unlike Brazil, or for brief periods Mexico and Haiti, Canada has never had a resident monarch. "History of Canada Day," Government of Canada, https://www.canada.ca/en/canadian-heritage/services/canada-day-history.html.

28. For an overview, see Eakin, *History of Latin America*, 200–265. A classic overview of the politics of the Brazilian empire is Graham, *Patronage and Politics*.

29. For a detailed and wide-ranging discussion of Brazilian geography, see Santos e Silveira, *O Brasil*.

30. An excellent introduction to the dimensions of Brazil and its regions is Théry, *Le Brésil*, especially the first two chapters. Latrubesse et al., "Late Miocene Paleogeography."

31. Sawyer, "Physical Setting," 90–103.

32. Kennedy, *Highly Civilized Man*.

33. Isabel Burton to Monckton Milnes, 1 January and 5 August 1865, in Tredoux, *Book of Burtoniana*, vol. 2, nos. 2 and 12.

34. Lovell, *Rage to Live*, 467–68; Burton and Wilkins, *Romance*, 247–48.

35. Lovell, *Rage to Live*, 468; Burton and Wilkins, *Romance*, 248–49.

36. Lovell, *Rage to Live*, 469–72; Burton and Wilkins, *Romance*, 251–52.

37. Burton and Wilkins, *Romance*, 257.

38. Frederick James Stevenson, 30 October 1867, in Tredoux, *Book of Burtoniana*, vol. 2, no. 38.

39. The brother apparently dined at the Burton home in the "second shift." Isabel describes serving the first meal to her and Richard, then to Kier and her brother, followed by German servants who would not eat with the Black people. The "emancipated blacks" then dined, followed by the enslaved. I. Burton, *Life of Captain Sir Richard F. Burton*, 1:267.

40. I. Burton, *Life of Captain Sir Richard F. Burton*, 1:422.

41. Burton and Wilkins, *Romance*, 252.

42. The photographs of Chico and Kier are located on reel 11 in the microfilmed archives of Isabel's papers at the Huntington Library. The originals are located in Isabel's papers at WR. Strachey, *Eminent Victorians*.

43. "Transcript of IB's Memoranda Book Trowbridge 2267/26," Mary Lovell notes, Sir Richard Francis Burton Collection, Local Studies Library, Borough of Richmond, Surrey, UK.

44. Burton and Wilkins, *Romance*, 266–67.

45. Lovell, *Rage to Live*, 472.

46. Luna and Klein, *Economic and Demographic History*, esp. chapters 1 and 4.

47. Bethell and Carvalho, "1822–1850," in Bethell, *Brazil*, 84–85 and 165.

48. Russell-Wood, "Gold Cycle," 190–243.

49. Holloway, *Immigrants on the Land*; Nozoe, *São Paulo*.
50. Klein, *Atlantic Slave Trade*; Bethell, *Abolition of the Brazilian Slave Trade*.
51. Luna and Klein, *Social Change, Industrialization*.
52. Schultz, *Tropical Versailles*; Malerba, *A Corte no exílio*; Barman, *Brazil*.
53. Barman, *Citizen Emperor*; Schwarcz, *As barbas do imperador*.
54. Pang, *In Pursuit of Honor and Power*.
55. Macaulay, *Dom Pedro*; Rangel and Araújo, *Cartas de D. Pedro I à Marquesa de Santos*.
56. Richard Graham, "1850–1870," in Bethell, *Brazil*, 138–45.
57. Alonso, *Last Abolition*.
58. Graham, *Patronage and Politics*; Carvalho, *Teatro de sombras*; Rodrigues, *Conciliação e reforma no Brasil*.
59. "It is likely that approximately 10% of the total population, 12% of the free population, and 24% of the adult population were registered to vote in 1872. In other words, about 1.06 million Brazilian citizens were active (*votantes* and *eleitores*) and the remaining 7.4 million were passive, disqualified from voting for one reason or another. Of the active citizens, approximately twenty thousand were electors, amounting to 0.2% of the total population and 0.5% of the adult." Holston, *Insurgent Citizenship*, 91.
60. Emília Viotti da Costa, "1870–1889," Bethell, *Brazil*, 161–213.
61. Graham, "1850–1870," 132.
62. Lanna, *Uma cidade na transição*; Gonçalves, *O grande porto*.
63. Manchester, *British Preeminence in Brazil*; Graham, *Britain and the Onset of Modernization*. The twenty largest import firms in Rio were all foreign owned, and handled 80 percent of coffee exports. Graham, "1850–1870," 130.
64. Barman, *Citizen Emperor*.
65. Bethell, *Abolition of the Brazilian Slave Trade*.
66. Graham, *Britain and the Onset of Modernization*, 168–70.

CHAPTER 2. RIO DE JANEIRO, SÃO PAULO, SANTOS

Epigraph: Burton and Wilkins, *Romance*, 250.
1. Isabel Burton to Monckton Milnes, 23 November 1867, in Tredoux, *Book of Burtoniana*, vol. 2, no. 40.
2. Isabel Burton to Monckton Milnes, 23 November 1867, in Tredoux, *Book of Burtoniana*, vol. 2, no. 40.
3. Richard Burton to Monckton Milnes, 23 October 1865, in Tredoux, *Book of Burtoniana*, vol. 2, no. 13.
4. Lanna, *Uma cidade na transição*; Gonçalves, *O grande porto*.
5. Saes, *As ferrovias de São Paulo*.
6. Weather Atlas, "Santos, Brazil," https://www.weather-atlas.com/en/brazil/santos.
7. Burton and Wilkins, *Romance*, 266.
8. Staden, *Captivity of Hans Stade*; Staden, *Hans Staden's True History*.
9. Cyrino, *Café, ferro e argila*, esp. 67–120.

10. "Santos & São Paulo Railway," University of New Brunswick, Canada, https://web.lib.unb.ca/archives/finding/ketchum/santos_sp_railway.html; Weather Atlas, "Santos, Brazil."

11. I. Burton, *Life of Captain Sir Richard F. Burton*, 1:420.

12. See Sargen, *Our Men in Brazil*, esp. chapter 7, "The Consul's Daily Life." At Richard's suggestion, in the early 1870s the Foreign Office made James Newell Gordon the British vice consul at Morro Velho, the only inland consular post in Brazil.

13. Anderson, *Rise of Modern Diplomacy*; Jones, *British Diplomatic Service*; Platt, *Cinderella Service*.

14. Anderson, *Rise of Modern Diplomacy*, 111–12.

15. For a view of the life in the British consular corps in Brazil in the first half of the nineteenth century, especially in northern Brazil and Rio de Janeiro, see Sargen, *Our Men in Brazil*.

16. Mattoso, *Bahia, século XIX*; Romo, *Selling Black Brazil*.

17. Bell, *Campanha Gaúcha*, esp. 176–79.

18. Kemper and Royce, "Mexican Urbanization since 1821," 267–89; "Liverpool: Trade, Population, and Geographical Growth," in *A History of the County of Lancaster*, vol. 4, ed. William Farrer and J. Brownbill (London, 1911), available at British History Online, https://www.british-history.ac.uk/vch/lancs/vol4/pp37-38; "Ville de Paris: Population and Density from 1600," Demographia, http://demographia.com/dm-par90.htm; "New York Urbanized Area: Population & Density from 1800 (Provisional)," Demographia, http://demographia.com/db-nyuza1800.htm; Boston University, "Population History of Philadelphia, 1790–1990," http://physics.bu.edu/~redner/projects/population/cities/philadelphia.html; Digital Panopticon, "London, 1780–1900," https://www.digitalpanopticon.org/London,_1780-1900.

19. Klein and Vinson, *African Slavery in Latin America*, 126–27; Bethell, "Appendix: Estimates of Slaves Imported into Brazil, 1838–1855," in *Abolition of the Brazilian Slave Trade*, 388–95.

20. Slave Voyages, https://www.slavevoyages.org/voyage/database.

21. Karasch, *Slave Life in Rio de Janeiro*, xxi, for urban enslaved population comparison. Bethell and Carvalho, "1822–1850," 108.

22. Jones, *British Diplomatic Service*, 180–84.

23. I. Burton, *Life of Captain Sir Richard F. Burton*, 1:439.

24. Burton, 1:438–39.

25. Burton and Wilkins, *Romance*, 245.

26. Bethell, *Abolition of the Brazilian Slave Trade*, 382–83.

27. Manchester, *British Preeminence in Brazil*, 274.

28. Manchester; Graham, *Britain and the Onset of Modernization*.

29. Lesser, *Immigration, Ethnicity, and National Identity*.

30. Lesser.

31. The historiography on the Confederados is substantial. See, for example, Marcus, *Confederate Exodus*; Dawsey and Dawsey, *Confederados*; Saba, "Seeking Refuge," 30–42.

32. See Platt, *Cinderella Service*, chapter 2, "The General Consular Service in the Nineteenth Century," 16–67.

33. Graham, *Britain and the Onset of Modernization*, 1–50; Manchester, *British Preeminence in Brazil*, 1–25.

34. See, for example, Guenther, *British Merchants in Nineteenth-Century Brazil*.

35. See, for example, 30 August 1866, FO 13/437, on Burton's efforts to assist two British men who had enlisted in the Brazilian army.

36. Burton and Wilkins, *Romance*, 246.

37. Isabel Burton to Monckton Milnes, 23 November 1867, in Tredoux, *Book of Burtoniana*, vol. 2, no. 40; Burton and Wilkins, *Romance*, 265; McLynn, *From the Sierras to the Pampas*, 111.

38. Thornton to Stanley, 4 October and 17 November 1866, FO 13/438; I. Burton, *Life of Captain Sir Richard F. Burton*, 1:425 (for Isabel's version).

39. Lovell, *Rage to Live*, 467.

40. Bergad, *Slavery and the Demographic*, esp. 81–95.

41. Marchant, *Viscount Mauá*, 63–75.

42. See, for example, Théry, *Le Brésil*, esp. chapter 4, "Combien des Brésils?"; "Mapas," Instituto Brasileiro de Geografia e Estatística, https://portaldemapas.ibge.gov.br/portal.php#mapa780.

43. See, for example, Weinstein, *Color of Modernity*.

44. Burton and Wilkins, *Romance*, chapter 5, 244–70.

45. Burton, 271–72; Stanley to Thornton, 23 July 1866, no. 14; Stanley to Thornton, 10 November 1866, no. 22; and Thornton to Stanley, 3 September 1866, n. 109, FO 13/438.

46. Richard Burton to Albert Tootal, 22 October 1866, in Tredoux, *Book of Burtoniana*, vol. 2, no. 27; and Richard Burton to Algernon Swinburne, 5 April 1867, in Tredoux, *Book of Burtoniana*, vol. 2, no. 34.

47. Burton, *Explorations*, 1:19.

48. Burton, 1:3–4.

49. Stanley to Thornton, 23 July 1866, n. 14; Stanley to Thornton, 10 November 1866, n. 22; and Thornton to Stanley, 3 September 1866, n. 109, FO 13/438.

50. Richard Burton to William Hepworth Dixon, 12 June 1867, in Tredoux, *Book of Burtoniana*, vol. 2, no. 37.

CHAPTER 3. THE EXPEDITION BEGINS

1. Burton and Wilkins, *Romance*, 272.

2. Boxer, *Golden Age of Brazil*; Furtado, *Chica da Silva*; Russell-Wood, "Gold Cycle."

3. Eschwege, *Pluto brasiliensis*.

4. Libby, *Transformação e trabalho*; Martins, *Crescendo em silêncio*; Bergad, *Slavery and the Demographic*; Fogel, *Without Consent or Contract*, 33.

5. Marchant, *Viscount Mauá*; Elizabeth Agassiz described the drive up the mountain to Petrópolis as "delightful, in an open diligence drawn by four mules

on the full gallop over a road as smooth as a floor." Agassiz and Agassiz, *Journey in Brazil*, 67.

6. Marchant, *Viscount Mauá*; Barman, "Business and Government in Imperial Brazil," 239–64.

7. Eakin, *Tropical Capitalism*, esp. 1–58.

8. On Brazilian economy in the nineteenth century, see Hanley, *Native Capital*, esp. chapter 2, "Native Capital Under the Empire"; and Villela, "Nineteenth and Early Twentieth Centuries," 40–62.

9. "Valongo Wharf Archaeological Site," UNESCO World Heritage Convention, https://whc.unesco.org/en/list/1548

10. Burton, *Explorations*, 1:99.

11. Burton, 1:19.

12. Burton, 1:22.

13. See, for example, Agassiz and Agassiz, *Journey in Brazil*, 28; Gardner, *Travels in the Interior*, 3–4; and the discussion of travelers in Rio in Karasch, *Slave Life in Rio de Janeiro*, "Introduction," xv–xxv.

14. For an example of the legal questions and efforts to grapple with control of captive labor, see Chalhoub, "Politics of Ambiguity," 161–91.

15. Needell, *Sacred Cause*; Alonso, *Last Abolition*; and Castilho, *Slave Emancipation and Transformations*.

16. Burton, *Explorations*, 1:24.

17. Burton, 1:27.

18. Burton, 1:27.

19. "Viagem do Imperador D. Pedro I," 305–84; Macaulay, *Dom Pedro*, 245–46.

20. Barman, *Citizen Emperor*, 114–6.

21. Burton, *Explorations*, 1:34.

22. The identity of the mysterious Mr. L'pool and his family only becomes apparent after reading the correspondence of Isabel with Monckton Milnes on 23 November 1867 and 18 April 1868, in Tredoux, *Book of Burtoniana*, vol. 2, no. 40 and no. 46.

23. Burton, *Explorations*, 1:34.

24. Burton and Wilkins, *Romance*, 273; Agassiz and Agassiz, *Journey in Brazil*, 70–71.

25. Flory, *Judge and Jury in Imperial Brazil*, 33.

26. Birchal, *Entrepreneurship in Nineteenth-Century Brazil*; Libby, *Transformação e trabalho*; Giroletti, *A industrialização de Juiz de Fora*.

27. Burton, *Explorations*, 1:50.

28. Burton, 1:35.

29. Burton and Wilkins, *Romance*, 274.

30. Dean, *With Broadax and Firebrand*.

31. Holloway, *Immigrants on the Land*; Luna and Klein, *Economic and Demographic History*; Lanna, *A transformação do trabalho*; Blasenheim, "Regional History of the Zona da Mata."

32. Graham, "1850–1870," 116.

33. See, for example, Agassiz and Agassiz, *Journey in Brazil*, 76–77.
34. Klumb, *Doze horas em diligencia*.
35. Burton and Wilkins, *Romance*, 286–87.
36. Percy Bysshe Shelley, "Ozymandias," Poetry Foundation, https://www.poetryfoundation.org/poems/46565/ozymandias.
37. See, for example, Instituto Estadual do Patrimônio Histórico, *Guia dos bens tombados*.
38. The extraordinary work of Marianne North can be seen today at a special gallery she financed at the Royal Botanical Garden (Kew), Marianne North Gallery.
39. Burton, *Explorations*, 1:41–42.
40. Burton, 1:43.
41. Boxer, *Golden Age of Brazil*; Russell-Wood, "Gold Cycle."
42. Burton, *Explorations*, 1:45.
43. Burton, 1:50.
44. Burton, 1:51.
45. Agassiz and Agassiz, *Journey in Brazil*, 74–78.
46. Burton, *Explorations*, 1:53.
47. Halfeld, *Henrique Fernando Guilherme Halfeld*.
48. Halfeld, *Atlas e relatorio*.
49. Halfeld, *Henrique Fernando Guilherme Halfeld*.

CHAPTER 4. INTO THE MINING ZONE

Epigraph: Burton, *Explorations*, 1:115.
1. Assunção and Zeuske, "'Race,' Ethnicity and Social Structure," 375–443.
2. Bergad, *Slavery and the Demographic*, 72; Klein and Vinson, *African Slavery in Latin America*, 57 and 89.
3. Bergad, *Slavery and the Demographic*, 210–11.
4. Eriksen and Nielsen, *History of Anthropology*, esp. chapter 2; King, *Gods of the Upper Air*, 79–86.
5. King.
6. Freyre, *Casa-grande e senzala*. *Casa-grande* was translated into English in 1946, as *Masters and the Slaves*.
7. Eakin, *Becoming Brazilians*, esp. 1–78.
8. Darwin, *Empire Project*, esp. part 1.
9. Osterhammel, *Transformation of the World*, chapter 17, "Civilization and Exclusion," 826–72. "The nineteenth century stands out from the sequences of ages by the fact that never before, and never again after the First World War, were the political and educational elites of Europe so sure of marching at the head of progress and embodying a global standard of civilization." Osterhammel, 836. See also Kennedy, *Mungo Park's Ghost*, 89–90 and 136.
10. The free rural population of Brazil remains one of the most understudied groups in the historiography. For a pioneering work, see Franco, *Homens livres na ordem escravocrata*.
11. Burton, *Explorations*, 1:6.

12. Burton, 1:54–55.
13. Lewis, *Public Policy and Private Initiative*; Saes, *As ferrovias de São Paulo*; Mattoon, *Companhia Paulista de Estradas de Ferro*.
14. Duncan, *Public and Private Operation of Railways*.
15. Burton, *Explorations*, 1:59.
16. Burton, 1:65.
17. Maraux, *Pierre Victor Renault*.
18. Burton, *Explorations*, 1:99.
19. Burton, 1:95–96; Ricketts to Marquis of Salisbury, 18 May 1879, 95–97, FO 13/501.
20. Burton, *Explorations*, 1:95.
21. Burton, 1:99.
22. Burton, 1:99.
23. Burton, 1:187.
24. Meneses, *Nossa comida tem história*.
25. Burton and Wilkins, *Romance*, 282.
26. "LafargeHolcim Opens High-Efficiency Cement Plant in Brazil," Holcim, https://www.holcim.com/media/media-releases/lafargeholcim-opens-high-efficiency-cement-plant-brazil; "Barroso, Cidades e Estados do Brasil," Instituto Brasileiro de Geografia e Estatística, https://cidades.ibge.gov.br/brasil/mg/barroso/panorama.
27. Burton, *Explorations*, 1:139.
28. Burton, 1:111.
29. James Newell Gordon to the Marquis of Salisbury, 18 May 1874, FO 13/501.
30. Burton, *Explorations*, 1:113.
31. Burton, 1:121.
32. Burton, 1:129.
33. Burton, 1:131.
34. Eakin, *British Enterprise in Brazil*, esp. chapter 1.
35. Burton, *Explorations*, 1:136–37.
36. The language of the translation is "characteristically Burtonian—by turns robust, pedantic, quaint, argumentative, ironic, but always original and personal." Gama, *Uruguay*, 25.
37. Burton, *Explorations*, 1:143.
38. iPatrimônio, "Tiradentes—Casa do Inconfidente Padre Toledo," https://www.ipatrimonio.org/tiradentes-casa-do-inconfidente-padre-toledo/#!/map=38329&loc=-21.110948999999984,-44.176467,17.
39. Barbosa, *Dicionário histórico-geográfico*, 510–11; "Cidades e Estados do Brasil," Instituto Brasileiro de Geografia e Estatística, https://cidades.ibge.gov.br/brasil/mg/tiradentes/historico.
40. Burton and Wilkins, *Romance*, 285.
41. Barroso, "A produçao do gênero na/da cultura popular," 9–27.
42. Burton, *Explorations*, 1:154.
43. Burton, 1:155.
44. Burton, 1:156.

45. Burton, 1:161.
46. Burton, 1:165.
47. Burton and Wilkins, *Romance*, 292.
48. Burton, *Explorations*, 1:163.
49. Bazin, *Aleijadinho*; Barbosa, *O Aleijadinho de Vila Rica*; Mello, *Barroco mineiro*.
50. Instituto do Patrimônio Histórico e Artístico Nacional, "Santuário do Bom Jesus de Matozinhos."
51. Burton, *Explorations*, 1:165.
52. Burton, 1:176.
53. Gair, *Geology and Ore Deposits*; Dorr, *Physiographic, Stratigraphic and Structural Development*; Baltazar and Lobato, "Structural Evolution."
54. Burton, *Explorations*, 1:179.
55. For data on iron mining in Brazil today, see "Brazil Iron Ore Mining Market by Reserves, Production, Assets, Projects, Fiscal Regime with Taxes, Royalties and Forecast to 2030," Global Data, https://www.globaldata.com/store/report/brazil-iron-ore-mining-market-analysis/.
56. Duval worked for several of the British gold mining companies beginning in the 1820s. He was the superintendent at Gongo Soco. Silva, *Barões do ouro*, 94–96. Richard mentions him having two other family members working in Brazil. Burton, *Explorations*, 1:118.
57. Eakin, *British Enterprise in Brazil*, 34–36; Evans, "Brazilian Gold, Cuban Copper," 118–34; Campbell, "Making Abolition Brazilian," 521–43.
58. Burton, *Explorations*, 1:189.

CHAPTER 5. AN ENGLISH VILLAGE IN BRAZIL

Epigraph: Burton, *Explorations*, 1:194.
1. The information in this chapter on the St. John d'el Rey Mining Company comes from Eakin, *British Enterprise*.
2. Instituto Brasileiro de Geografia e Estatística, *Estatísticas históricas do Brasil*, 29.
3. Eakin, *British Enterprise*, 157–58.
4. "Nova Lima, Cidades e Estados do Brasil," Instituto Brasileiro de Geografia e Estatística, https://www.ibge.gov.br/cidades-e-estados/mg/nova-lima.html.
5. Burton and Wilkins, *Romance*, 323.
6. Burton, *Explorations*, 1:193.
7. Burton, 1:195.
8. Congonhas de Sabará was on the route from Rio to Sabará and Diamantina, so many of the European travelers moving through Minas Gerais in the nineteenth century passed through, leaving at least brief comments on the mine and the community. Saint-Hilaire, *Viagens pelo distrito dos diamantes*; Gardner, *Travels in the Interior*; Castelnau, *Expedições às regiões centrais* are among the most notable.
9. Eschwege, *Pluto brasiliensis*, 1:46–47.
10. Eakin, *British Enterprise*, 13.

11. One of Lyon's descendants has self-published a wonderful and very well researched account of his extraordinary life. Lyon, *Like a Rolling Stone*.

12. Burton, *Explorations*, 1:220.

13. North, *Recollections of a Happy Life*, vol. 1, chapters 4–5.

14. "As far as I could see, the people [the enslaved] looked quite as contented as the free negroes did in Jamaica." North, *Recollections of a Happy Life*, 1:147.

15. Royal Botanic Gardens (Kew), "Marianne North Gallery," https://www.kew.org/kew-gardens/whats-in-the-gardens/marianne-north-gallery.

16. See, for example, Avery, *Not on Queen Victoria's Birthday*; Randall, *Real del Monte*; Hoong, *Development of the Tin Mining Industry*.

17. J. D. Powles, St. John del Rey Mining Company to Foreign Office and responses, May and June 1867, FO 13/451; and James Newell Gordon to the Marquis of Salisbury, 18 May 1874, FO 13/501.

18. Porter, *Thames Embankment*, 176. See also Bowley, *Wages in the United Kingdom*.

19. See, for example, Schwartz, *Cornish in Latin America*.

20. Eakin, *British Enterprise*, 33–34.

21. Eakin, 84.

22. Campbell, "Making Abolition Brazilian"; Evans, "Brazilian Gold, Cuban Copper."

23. Riedel, *Viagem de S.S.A.A. Real Duque de Saxe*.

24. Burton, *Explorations*, 1:236.

25. Burton, 1:238–39.

26. Kiddy, *Blacks of the Rosary*, esp. 160–65.

27. Thoreau, *Walden*.

28. Burton, *Explorations*, 1:423.

29. Burton, 1:242.

30. Burton, 1:227.

31. Burton, 1:228–29.

32. Eakin, *British Enterprise*, 60–61.

33. Burton and Wilkins, *Romance*, 308.

34. Burton, *Explorations*, 1:248.

35. *Passagem de Dom Pedro II em Nova Lima, 1881*, Wikimedia Commons, https://commons.wikimedia.org/wiki/File:Passagem_de_Dom_Pedro_II_em_Nova_Lima,_1881.jpg.

36. Burton, *Explorations*, 1:245–52.

37. Eakin, *British Enterprise*, 37.

38. "The Gordon Family Tree," https://sites.rootsweb.com/~gordon/gordonfam/pafg1759.htm#55488.

39. I. Burton, *Life of Captain Sir Richard F. Burton*, 2:294.

40. Eakin, *British Enterprise*, 41–42.

41. One of Chalmers's descendants has written a fascinating history of the man from a personal perspective. Chalmers, *Chalmers Miscellany*, chapter 6, "George Chalmers (1857–1928)," 98–144.

42. Eakin, *British Enterprise*, 64–65.

CHAPTER 6. ENGLISHMEN, GOLD, AND IRON

Epigraph: Burton, *Explorations*, 1:393.
1. Davis, *Into the Silence*, 42.
2. Kennedy, *Highly Civilized Man*; Stocking, *Victorian Anthropology*.
3. Edward Thornton to Lord Stanley, 3 September 1866, 109, FO 13/437.
4. Burton and Wilkins, *Romance*, 266; "Last Wishes of Isabel Burton," WR.
5. Burton, *Life of Sir Richard Burton*, 1:432–33.
6. Silva, "Claude Henri Gorceix," 319–40.
7. "200 Years of Global Gold Production by Country," Mining.com, https://www.mining.com/web/chart-200-years-of-global-gold-production-by-country/.
8. "Iron Ore Production in Brazil and Major Projects," Mining Technology, https://www.mining-technology.com/data-insights/iron-ore-in-brazil/; "Visualizing the World's Largest Iron Ore Producers," Mining.com, https://www.mining.com/web/visualizing-the-worlds-largest-iron-ore-producers/.
9. Rippy, *British Investments in Latin America*; and Rippy, "Most Profitable British Mining Investments."
10. Schultz, *Tropical Versailles*; Malerba, *A Corte no exílio*.
11. Mawe, *Travels in the Interior of Brazil*.
12. For an account of all the sordid exploits of Oxenford in Brazil, see Silva, *Barões do ouro*.
13. Silva, 91.
14. Silva, 91.
15. Burton, *Explorations*, 1:435–39.
16. Silva, *Barões do ouro*, 129–60.
17. Marianne North was resident at Morro Velho when this occurred and describes in detail the exhumation and reburial of Brown at the English cemetery. His name does not appear anywhere in the surviving English company records of the hundreds of individuals buried there. North, *Recollections of a Happy Life*, 1:154–55.
18. Silva, *Barões do ouro*, 129–60.
19. "Aga Mineração, Brazil," AngloGold Ashanti, https://www.anglogoldashanti.com/portfolio/americas/aga-mineracao/.
20. "Centro de Memória," AngloGold Ashanti, https://www.anglogoldashanti.com.br/sobre/centro-de-memoria/.
21. Alkmim and Marshak, "Transamazonian Orogeny," 29–58.
22. Burton, *Explorations*, 1:279–80.
23. Burton, 1:279–80.
24. Eakin, *British Enterprise in Brazil*, 147–48.
25. "Parochia de N. S. da Conceição de Raposos," in Brazil Directoria Geral de Estatística, *Recenseamento do Brazil em 1872*, part 1, *Minas Geraes*, https://dataspace.princeton.edu/handle/88435/dsp01h989r5980.
26. Burton, *Explorations*, 1:283.
27. Burton, 1:283.

28. Burton, 1:285.
29. Burton and Wilkins, *Romance*, 297.
30. Burton and Wilkins, 298.
31. "Assets: Caeté Complex," Jaguar Mining, https://www.jaguarmining.com/assets/caete-complex.
32. Burton and Wilkins, *Romance*, 297.
33. Burton, *Explorations*, 1:291.
34. Burton, 1:292.
35. Burton, 1:293.
36. Burton, 1:295.
37. Burton and Wilkins, *Romance*, 297.
38. Burton, 298.
39. Eakin, *British Enterprise in Brazil*, 14–20.
40. Burton, *Explorations*, 1:299.
41. Silva, *Barões do ouro*, 144.
42. *Slavery at Gongo Soco*.
43. Salvador et al., "Mining Activity in Brazil," 137–42.
44. Burton, *Explorations*, 1:301.
45. Burton, 1:303.
46. Burton, 1:304.
47. "João Monlevade," Cidades e Estados, Instituto Brasileiro de Geografia e Estatística, https://cidades.ibge.gov.br/brasil/mg/joao-monlevade/historico.
48. "Belval and João Monlevade: A Bond of Steel," ArcelorMittal, https://luxembourg.arcelormittal.com/en/news-and-media/news/belval-and-joao-monlevade-a-bond-of-steel.
49. Moyen, *A história da Companhia Siderúrgica Belgo-Mineira*; Ribeiro, "Learning from Minas Gerais," 91–104.
50. Burton, *Explorations*, 1:306; Burton and Wilkins, *Romance*, 298.
51. Jaguar Mining Company, "Assets, Paciência Complex," https://www.jaguarmining.com/assets/paciencia-gold-mine.
52. Burton, *Explorations*, 1:308.
53. Burton, 1:308.

CHAPTER 7. LIFE AND DEATH IN MARIANA

Epigraph: Burton, *Explorations*, 1:332.
1. Burton, 1:310.
2. Burton, 1:309.
3. Santuário do Caraça, https://www.santuariodocaraca.com.br/
4. Burton, *Explorations*, 1:311.
5. Burton, 1:312.
6. Burton, 1:319.
7. Voigt, "Writing Home," 208–54.
8. Burton, *Explorations*, 1:318.
9. Telles, *Race in Another America*, 19–21.
10. Burton, *Explorations*, 1:321.

11. Salvador et al., "Mining Activity in Brazil," 137–42.
12. "Thomas Treloar Captain," Ancestry.com, https://www.ancestry.com/family-tree/person/tree/32456697/person/18262460431/gallery.
13. *Maquine Mine*.
14. Burton, *Explorations*, 1:321–22.
15. Araujo, "Plano de Preservação das Ruínas."
16. Burton, *Explorations*, 1:337.
17. Burton and Wilkins, *Romance*, 302.
18. Burton, *Explorations*, 1:324.
19. Burton, 1:323–24.
20. The classic account of the emergence of these cities in the early eighteenth century is Boxer, *Golden Age of Brazil*, especially 61–83; Eakin, "Creating a Growth Pole," 390.
21. See, for example, *Culture Wars in Brazil*, 90–134.
22. Burton, *Explorations*, 1:328.
23. Burton, 1:330.
24. Burton, 1:331.
25. Burton, 1:332.
26. Burton, 1:332.
27. Burton and Wilkins, *Romance*, 303.
28. Burton, *Explorations*, 1:334.
29. Eschwege, *Pluto brasiliensis*, 2:24.
30. Burton, *Explorations*, 1:338.
31. Burton and Wilkins, *Romance*, 303.
32. Burton, *Explorations*, 1:340.
33. Pincus Tourismo Ltd., "Mina de Passagem," https://mariana.minasdapassagem.com.br/.
34. Burton, *Explorations*, 1:341.
35. Burton and Wilkins, *Romance*, 304.
36. Burton, *Explorations*, 1:341.
37. "Thomas Treloar," MyHeritage, https://www.myheritage.com/research/record-1-226111291-3-9539/thomas-treloar-in-myheritage-family-trees; "Thomas Treloar, in the London, England, Church of England Deaths and Burials, 1813–2003," Ancestry.com, https://www.ancestry.com/discoveryui-content/view/10351454:1559?tid=&pid=&queryId=5554341852a6c7432070e5c5d04a3719&_phsrc=acj61&_phstart=successSource.
38. Schwartz, *Cornish in Latin America*, 209–301.
39. Burton, *Explorations*, 1:342.

CHAPTER 8. TOWN OF TARNISHED GOLD

Epigraph: Burton, *Explorations*, 1:412.
1. Burton, 1:342–43.
2. Boxer, *Golden Age of Brazil*, 30–83 and 162–203; Russell-Wood, "Gold Cycle."
3. Maxwell, *Conflicts and Conspiracies*; and Maxwell, *Pombal*.

4. Maxwell, *Pombal*, 118–26.
5. Burton, *Explorations*, 1:346–53.
6. The best account in English is Maxwell, *Conflicts and Conspiracies*.
7. Anderson, *Imagined Communities*.
8. Burton, *Explorations*, 1:371.
9. Burton, 1:357–58.
10. Eakin, *Tropical Capitalism*, esp. 33–58.
11. Lengel, *Colonial Williamsburg*.
12. Burton, *Explorations*, 1:361–62. Richard must have read the Romantic poet Robert Southey's *History of Brazil* (1810–1819), certainly an earlier account in English of the Minas Conspiracy!
13. Levine, *Father of the Poor?*; Williams, *Culture Wars in Brazil*, 90–134.
14. Eakin, *Becoming Brazilians*, esp. 1–78.
15. Bosi, *História concisa da literatura brasileira*, 71–76.
16. Bosi, 61–64.
17. Burton, *Explorations*, 1:371–72.
18. Burton, 1:377–78.
19. Burton, 1:381.
20. Burton, 1:380.
21. Burton, 1:381.
22. Burton, 1:383.
23. Burton, 1:384.
24. Stocking, *Victorian Anthropology*, 110–85.
25. Burton, *Explorations*, 1:390; Cunha, *Backlands*, esp. 58–116.
26. Burton, *Explorations*, 1:391.
27. Burton, 1:393.
28. Eakin, *Becoming Brazilians*, esp. 1–78.
29. Silva and Paixão, "Mixed and Unequal," 172–217; Bernardino-Costa, "Opening Pandora's Box."
30. Burton, *Explorations*, 1:389.
31. Burton, 1:392.
32. Burton, 1:393.
33. Schwarcz, *Spectacle of the Races*, esp. 49–57.
34. Burton, *Explorations*, 1:394.
35. Burton, 1:398.
36. Burton, 2:21.
37. Burton, 1:408.
38. Burton, 1:409.
39. Burton, 1:401.
40. Burton, 1:410.
41. Burton, 1:406.
42. Burton, *City of the Saints*, 246–28.
43. Burton, *Explorations*, 1:402.
44. Burton, 1:399.
45. Burton, 1:403.
46. Burton, 1:406.

47. Burton, 1:407.
48. Burton, 1:408.
49. Burton, 1:403.
50. Burton, 1:410.
51. Burton, 1:398.
52. Burton, 1:399.
53. Burton, 1:411.
54. Burton, 1:412.

55. "Quadro da população livre considerada em relação aos sexos, estados civis, raça, religião, nacionalidades e grão de instrucção com indicação das casas e fogos," and "Recapitulação," first page, in Brazil Directoria Geral de Estatística, *Recenseamento do Brazil em 1872*, https://dataspace.princeton.edu/handle/88435/dsp01h989r5980.

56. Burton, *Explorations*, 1:413.
57. Burton, 1:414.
58. Burton, 1:415.
59. Burton, 1:388–89.
60. Burton, 1:374.

CHAPTER 9. A RAFT, A RIVER, AND A LONELY RIDE

Epigraph: Burton, *Explorations*, 1:442–43.

1. Burton, 1:417.
2. "Overview of Assets," Jaguar Mining, https://jaguarmining.com/assets/overview-of-assets.
3. Burton, *Explorations*, 1:418.
4. See, for example, Marcus, *Confederate Exodus*; and Dawsey, *Confederados*.
5. Burton and Wilkins, *Romance*, 306.
6. Burton, *Explorations*, 1:419.
7. Burton, 1:420.
8. Burton, 1:421.
9. "Elizabeth Hannah Pyles," Ancestry.com, https://www.ancestry.com/family-tree/person/tree/32987955/person/28450500232/story; "Campo Cemetery," FindAGrave, https://www.findagrave.com/cemetery/2246489/campo-cemetery.
10. Burton and Wilkins, *Romance*, 314.
11. I. Burton, *Life of Captain Sir Richard Burton*, 446; Burton and Wilkins, *Romance*, 315.
12. Letter to Hepworth Dixon, 12 June 1867, in Tredoux, *Book of Burtoniana*, vol. 2.
13. Dane Kennedy refers to this trait in nineteenth-century explorers as "mythic masculinity." Kennedy, *Mungo Park's Ghost*, 6.
14. *England & Wales, National Probate Calendar (Index of Wills and Administrations), 1858–1995*, Ancestry.com; Principal Probate Registry, *Calendar of the Grants of Probate and Letters of Administration made in the Probate Registries of the High Court of Justice in England* (London, England); "Arthur Earle," Ancestry.com, https://www.ancestry.com/discoveryui-con

tent/view/1682579:1904?tid=&pid=&queryId=add288a7229366fcfc01249bfe4c3e1b&_phsrc=HiM11&_phstart=successSource.

15. Burton, *Explorations*, 1:423.
16. Burton and Wilkins, *Romance*, 315.
17. Cavalcanti et al., "Geoconservation of Geological and Mining Heritage," 118–48.
18. Barbosa, *Dicionário histórico-geográfico*, 419–21.
19. Burton, *Explorations*, 1:433.
20. "Parochia de N. S. da Conceição do Sabará," in Brazil Directoria Geral de Estatística, *Recenseamento do Brazil em 1872*, part 1, *Minas Geraes*, https://dataspace.princeton.edu/handle/88435/dsp01h989r5980; "Sabará, Cidades e Estado," Instituto Brasileiro de Geografia e Estatística, https://cidades.ibge.gov.br/brasil/mg/sabara/panorama; "Belo Horizonte, Cidades e Estados," Instituto Brasileiro de Geografia e Estatística, https://cidades.ibge.gov.br/brasil/mg/belo-horizonte/panorama.
21. "A Colônia Luxemburguesa," https://colonia.lu/sabara sources on Belgo-Mineira.
22. "Fernando de Melo Viana" and "Fernando de Sousa Melo Viana," in Monteiro, *Dicionário biográfico de Minas Gerais*, 2:712–13; Mineração Morro Velho Ltda., *Morro Velho*, 195.
23. Burton, *Explorations*, 1:433–34.
24. Burton, 2:1–4.
25. Burton, 2:2–5.
26. Burton, 1:137.
27. Burton, 2:5–6.
28. Burton, 2:2.
29. Burton and Wilkins, *Romance*, 320.
30. Burton and Wilkins, 318.
31. Burton and Wilkins, 324.
32. Burton and Wilkins, 331.
33. Burton and Wilkins, 337.
34. David Sesser, "Alexander Travis Hawthorn (1825–1899)," Encyclopedia of Arkansas, https://encyclopediaofarkansas.net/entries/alexander-travis-hawthorn-7979/.
35. Burton and Wilkins, *Romance*, 338.
36. Burton and Wilkins, 340.
37. Burton and Wilkins, 341.

CHAPTER 10. RIVER OF OLD WOMEN

Epigraph: Burton, *Explorations*, 2:1.

1. The classic synthesis of historical, social science, and scientific literature on the São Francisco River Valley is Pierson, *O homem no Vale do São Francisco*. For a more recent, brief, introduction to the geography and history of the region, see Camelo Filho, "A dinâmica política," 83–93. See also Langfur, *Adrift on an Inland Sea*; and Langfur, *Forbidden Lands*.

2. For a classic account of the Northeast and (in part) of the intellectual creation of the backlands and the sertão, see Albuquerque, *Invention of the Brazilian Northeast*. The notion of a civilization of leather comes from Abreu, *Chapters of Brazilian Colonial History*.

3. Halfeld, *Atlas e relatorio*.

4. Liais, *Hydrographie du haute San-Francisco*.

5. Oliveira e Videira, "As polêmicas entre Manoel Pereira Reis," 42–52.

6. Burton, *Explorations*, 2:2.

7. Burton, *First Footsteps in East Africa*; Burton, *Lake Regions of Central Africa*; Burton, *Abeokuta and the Cameroons Mountains*; Burton, *Mission to Gelele*.

8. Lisboa et al., *Projeto Manuelzão*.

9. Trindade et al., "Tendências temporais e espaciais," 13–24.

10. For a classic work on the meaning and symbolism of the sertão, see Lima, *Um sertão chamado Brasil*.

11. Krause et al., "Boom Novel That Never Was," 603–20; Rodríguez Monegal, *Borzoi Anthology of Latin American Literature*, 677–79.

12. Rosa, *Grande sertão*. One of the most prominent Latin American literary critics of the twentieth century called Guimarães Rosa "beyond dispute Latin America's greatest novelist." Rodríguez Monegal, *Borzoi Anthology of Latin American Literature*, 679.

13. Burton, *Explorations*, 2:4–5.

14. Burton, 2:6–7.

15. Burton, 2:8.

16. Barbosa, *Dicionário histórico-geográfico*, 425–26; "Santa Luzia, Cidades e Estados," Instituto Brasileiro de Geografia e Estatística, https://cidades.ibge.gov.br/brasil/mg/santa-luzia/historico.

17. Burton, *Explorations*, 2:9–10.

18. Burton, 2:13–14.

19. Burton, 2:16–17.

20. Burton, 2:15–17.

21. Burton, 2:15.

22. Burton, 2:18.

23. Burton, 2:21.

24. Burton, 2:23.

25. Burton, 2:8.

26. Machado, *Navegação do Rio São Francisco*, 80.

27. Chalmers, *Chalmers Miscellany*, 143.

28. Instituto Estadual do Patrimônio Histórico, "Conjunto Arquitetônico."

29. Holten and Sterll, *Peter Lund*.

30. Darwin, *"The Origin of Species" and "The Descent of Man."* Lund is cited in *The Origin* on page 273, and in *The Descent* on page 531.

31. Auler and Pessoa, *Lagoa Santa Karst*.

32. Holten and Sterll, *Peter Lund*, chapters 7, 11, and 15.

33. Burton, *Explorations*, 2:32.

34. Riedel, *Viagem*.

35. Burton, *Explorations*, 2:35.
36. Burton, 2:38.
37. Cunha, *Backlands*. In a poll in the mid-1990s, Brazil's most important weekly news magazine asked fifteen major Brazilian intellectuals (all men!) to list the twenty most representative books of Brazilian culture. All fifteen listed *Os sertões* and fourteen listed *Casa-grande e senzala*. The next highest on the list was João Guimarães Rosa's *Grande sertão* with thirteen votes. Gama, "Biblioteca Nacional."
38. Mitchell, *Gone with the Wind*.
39. Burton, *Explorations*, 2:39.
40. Burton, 2:39.
41. Burton, 2:41.
42. Burton, 2:40.
43. Burton, 2:42.
44. Burton, 2:43–44.
45. Burton, 2:47.
46. Burton, 2:50.
47. Burton, 2:53.
48. Burton, 2:67.
49. Burton, 2:64.
50. Burton, 2:66.
51. Burton, 2:54.

CHAPTER 11. CITY OF DIAMONDS

Epigraph: Burton, *Explorations*, 2:70.
1. Chaves et al., "Diamonds from the Espinhaço Range," 277–89. For an excellent, succinct summary of the discovery and Crown efforts to control diamonds, see Klein and Luna, *Brazil*, 78–80.
2. Frédéric Mauro, "Political and Economic Structures of Empire," in Bethell, *Colonial Brazil*, 39–66; Marques, *History of Portugal*, 392–3.
3. Ferreira, *O descaminho de diamantes*; Bernstein, *Brazilian Diamond*, 9–40.
4. Worger, *South Africa's City of Diamonds*, esp. chapter 1, "The Industrialization of Diamond Digging, 1867–85," 9–63; Turrell, *Capital and Labour*.
5. Richard Burton to Albert Tootal, 22 October 1866, in Tredoux, *Book of Burtoniana*, vol. 2, no. 27; Richard Burton to Algernon Swinburne, 5 April 1867, in Tredoux, *Book of Burtoniana*, vol. 2, no. 34.
6. Boxer, *Golden Age*, 204–25; Furtado, *O livro da capa verde*.
7. Torrens, "Early Life and Geological Life," 267–71.
8. Mawe, *Travels in the Interior of Brazil*.
9. Burton, *Explorations*, 2:70–71.
10. Burton, 2:73.
11. Burton, 2:81.
12. Burton, 2:75.
13. Burton, 2:79.
14. Burton, 2:88.
15. Burton, 2:87–89.

16. Burton, 2:94–95.
17. Tibães, *John Rose, um inglês em Diamantina*.
18. Burton, *Explorations*, 2:119.
19. "John Lucy Smith Dayrell," Genea Minas, https://www.geneaminas.com.br/genealogia-mineira/restrita/enlace.asp?codenlace=1369521; Márcio Dayrell Batitucci, "Família Dayrell em Barão de Cocais," https://josep58.blogspot.com/2010/05/familia-dayrell-em-barao-de-cocais.html.
20. Burton, *Explorations*, 2:122.
21. Burton, 2:110.
22. Burton, 2:116.
23. Burton, 2:104.
24. Burton, 2:125.
25. Furtado, *Chica da Silva*, 73–102.
26. Furtado, 19.
27. Furtado, 47–72.
28. Furtado, 73–102.
29. *Xica*; *Xica da Silva*.
30. Furtado, *Chica da Silva*, 102–284.
31. Klein and Luna, *Brazil*, 71–77; Russell-Wood, *Black Man in Slavery and Freedom*, esp. 27–49 and 161–97.
32. Burton, *Explorations*, 2:97.
33. Burton, 2:129–31.
34. Burton, 2:131.
35. Burton, 2:133.
36. Burton, 2:98.
37. Burton, 2:100.
38. Burton, 2:102.
39. Burton, 2:103.
40. Burton, 2:101.
41. Brant, *Diary of "Helena Morley."*
42. Dilva Frazão, "Alice Dayrell Caldeira Brant, Escritora Brasileira," Ebiografia, https://www.ebiografia.com/alice_dayrell_caldeira_brant/. In 2003 the Brazilian director Helena Solberg turned the book into a feature-length film, *Vida de Menina* (on IMDB at https://www.imdb.com/title/tt0371586/).
43. Burton, *Explorations*, 2:133–4.

CHAPTER 12. RIVER OF SAINT FRANCIS

Epigraph: Burton, *Explorations*, 2:237.

1. Camelo Filho, "A Dinâmica Política," 83–93; Roman, "São Francisco Interbasin Water Transfer," 395–419; Lucas et al., "Significant Baseflow Reduction," 1–17.
2. Burton, *City of the Saints*.
3. "Curvelo, Cidades e Estados," Instituto Brasileiro de Geografia e Estatística, https://cidades.ibge.gov.br/brasil/mg/curvelo/historico.
4. Burton, *Explorations*, 2:164.

5. Burton, 2:172–3.
6. Burton, 2:159–61.
7. Burton, 2:170.
8. Burton, 2:175–6.
9. Burton, 2:176–7.
10. Burton, 2:178.
11. Burton, 2:186.
12. Burton, 2:188.
13. Burton, 2:188–89 and 202.
14. Burton, 2:190.
15. Burton, 2:190–92.
16. Burton, 2:190.
17. Almeida Barbosa, *Dicionário Histórico-Geográfico*, 364.
18. Burton, *Explorations*, 2:202–3.
19. Burton, 2:204.
20. See Pierson, *O homen no vale*; and Camelo Filho, "A Dinâmica Política."
21. Andrade, "'Third Bank' of the Lower São Francisco"; Nascimento and Becker, "Hydro-businesses," 203–33.
22. White, *Organic Machine*.
23. Nascimento, "Long Journey," esp. 25–29.
24. Buckley, *Technocrats and the Politics of Drought*, 19–21.
25. Burton, *Explorations*, 2:233.
26. Machado, *Navegação do Rio São Francisco*, 79–140.
27. Cunha et al., "Extreme Drought Events over Brazil," 1–20.
28. Burton, *Explorations*, 2:225–27.
29. Kiddy, "Militão and the Guerreiros," 9–32.
30. Burton, *Explorations*, 2:209–10.
31. Burton, 2:212.
32. Burton, 2:205.
33. Hardon, *Catholic Dictionary*, 171.
34. Burton, *Explorations*, 2:237–9.
35. Burtón, 2:244–47.
36. Burton, 2:247.
37. Burton, 2:249.
38. Burton, 2:250.
39. Burton, 2:251.
40. Burton, 2:254.
41. "Januária, Cidades e Estados," Instituto Brasileiro de Geografia e Estatística, https://cidades.ibge.gov.br/brasil/mg/januaria/historico.
42. Burton, *Explorations*, 2:258.
43. Burton, 2:259.
44. Burton, 2:256.
45. Klein and Luna, *Slavery in Brazil*, 173–77.
46. Burton, *Explorations*, 2:267.
47. Burton, 2:266.
48. Burton, *The Jew, the Gypsy and El Islam*. Fawn Brodie is the most direct

of Burton's biographers on this issue. Brodie, *Devil Drives*, 265–66. See also Kennedy, *Highly Civilized Man*, 185–93.

49. Burton, *Explorations*, 2:267.
50. Burton, 2:268.

CHAPTER 13. MYSTICISM AND VIOLENCE IN THE BACKLANDS

Epigraph: Burton, *Explorations*, 2:300.

1. Gama, "Biblioteca Nacional."
2. The classic translation is by Putnam, *Rebellion in the Backlands*. Elizabeth Lowe published a newer translation as *Backlands: The Canudos Campaign*. Chandler, *Bandit King*, 239.
3. Cunha, *Rebellion*, 54. Two classic histories of social thought and thinkers during the late nineteenth and early twentieth centuries are Skidmore, *Black into White*; and Schwarcz, *Spectacle of the Races*.
4. For a discussion of the view from the coast, see Blanc, *Prestes Column*, 3–14; Levine, *Vale of Tears*, chapter 1, "Canudos and the *Visão do Litoral*," 11–66; Eakin, *Becoming Brazilians*, chapter 1, "From the 'Spectacle of Races' to 'Luso-Tropical Civilization,'" 43–78.
5. Burton, *Explorations*, 2:269–70.
6. Burton, 2:276.
7. Leão, "Double-Edged Sword," 157–76; Skidmore, *Politics in Brazil*; Skidmore, *Politics of Military Rule in Brazil*.
8. Burton, *Explorations*, 2:278–79.
9. Burton, 2:281.
10. Burton, 2:282.
11. Garfield, *Indigenous Struggle*; "Xavante," Povos Indígenas no Brasil, https://pib.socioambiental.org/pt/Povo:Xavante.
12. Burton, *Explorations*, 2:279.
13. Burton, 2:284.
14. Burton, 2:335.
15. "Bom Jesus da Lapa, Cidades e Estados," Instituto Brasileiro de Geografia e Estatística, https://cidades.ibge.gov.br/brasil/ba/bom-jesus-da-lapa/historico.
16. Burton, *Explorations*, 2:288–92.
17. Della Cava, *Miracle at Joaseiro*, is the classic study.
18. Della Cava, *Miracle at Joaseiro*, describes the miracle on page 31 and treats the dispute with Rome on 32–51 and 78–79.
19. Burton, *Explorations*, 2:296.
20. Burton, 2:300.
21. Burton, 2:302.
22. Burton, 2:299.
23. Burton, 2:297.
24. Burton, 2:303.
25. Burton, 2:306.
26. Burton, 2:317.
27. Burton, 2:318.

28. Burton, 2:319–21.
29. Kiddy, "Militão and the Guerreiros"; Needell, *Sacred Cause*, 164–65; Wanderley Pinho, *Cotegipe e seu tempo*.
30. Moya, *Cousins and Strangers*.
31. Loveman, "Race to Progress," 435–70.
32. Holloway, *Immigrants on the Land*.
33. Burton, *Explorations*, 2:328.
34. Burton, 2:327.
35. Burton, 2:330.
36. Burton, 2:335.
37. Burton, 2:337.
38. Burton, 2:338.
39. Burton, 2:331.
40. Burton, 2:343; Kiddy, "Militão and the Guerreiros," 17–22.
41. Graham, *Patronage and Politics*.
42. Chandler, *Bandit King*, 239.
43. Chilcote, *Power and the Ruling Classes*, 296–99.
44. Burton, *Explorations*, 2:345.
45. Burton, 2:347.
46. Burton, 2:352.
47. Burton, 2:355; "Sento Sé, Cidades e Estados," Instituto Brasileiro de Geografia e Estatística, https://cidades.ibge.gov.br/brasil/ba/sento-se/historico.
48. Burton, *Explorations*, 2:357.
49. Burton, 2:358.
50. Assunção, *Capoeira*, 7, 40, 66, 113.
51. Burton, *Explorations*, 2:359.
52. Burton, 2:361.

CHAPTER 14. DROUGHTS, DAMS, AND FALLS

Epigraph: Burton, *Explorations*, 2:425.
1. Nascimento and Becker, "Hydro-businesses."
2. Burton, *Explorations*, 2:364.
3. Burton, 2:365–66.
4. Burton, 2:367.
5. Burton, 2:420.
6. Burton, 2:369–70.
7. Burton, 2:373.
8. "Petrolina, Cidades e Estados," Instituto Brasileiro de Geografia e Estatística, https://cidades.ibge.gov.br/brasil/pe/petrolina/panorama; "Juazeiro, Cidades e Estados," Instituto Brasileiro de Geografia e Estatística, https://cidades.ibge.gov.br/brasil/ba/juazeiro/panorama.
9. Machado, *Navegação do Rio São Francisco*, 163–67.
10. Burton, *Explorations*, 2:378.
11. Graham, *Britain and the Onset of Modernization*, 70. See also Duncan, *Public and Private Operation of Railways*, 33–34.

12. Costa, "1870–1889," 167.
13. Burton, *Explorations*, 2:376.
14. Burton, 2:381.
15. Burton, 2:383.
16. Burton, 2:384–5.
17. Abreu, *Chapters of Brazil's Colonial History*, 117.
18. Burton, *Explorations*, 2:385.
19. Burton, 2:386–7.
20. Stolf et al., "Water Transfer from São Francisco River," 998–1010.
21. Burton, *Explorations*, 2:390.
22. Burton, 2:391.
23. Burton, 2:393–94.
24. Alden, "Gang of Four," 707–24.
25. Burton, *Explorations*, 2:395.
26. Burton, 2:399–400.
27. Burton, 2:395–97.
28. Burton, 2:401.
29. Burton, 2:403.
30. Burton, 2:410.
31. Burton, 2:413.
32. Burton, 2:414.
33. Burton, 2:415.
34. Burton, 2:416.
35. Burton, 2:425.
36. Burton, 2:433.
37. Blanc, *Prestes Column*, is the most recent and complete account of this group.
38. Blanc, *Prestes Column*, chapter 9, "Visions of the Future: Culture and Commemoration," 185–215.
39. Burton, *Explorations*, 2:436.
40. Burton, 2:437.
41. Burton, 2:437.
42. Burton, 2:439.
43. Burton, 2:440.
44. Burton, 2:441.
45. Burton, 2:442.
46. Burton, 2:443.
47. Burton, 2:443.
48. Burton, 2:445.
49. Burton, 2:448.
50. Burton, 2:452.
51. Hanley, *Public Good and the Brazilian State*.
52. "Paulo Afonso I," Eletrobras, https://www.chesf.com.br/SistemaChesf/Pages/SistemaGeracao/PauloAfonsoI.aspx.
53. Burton, *Explorations*, 2:457.

EPILOGUE: BURTON, BRAZIL, AND THE SHATTERED MIRROR

1. Schwarcz, *As barbas do imperador,* esp. 455–64.
2. Ioris, *Transforming Brazil.*
3. "He had six cuppings, with thirty-six glasses and twelve leeches, tartar emetic, and all sorts of other things, and there was something to be given or rubbed every half-hour, of which a very large ingredient was orange tea." I. Burton, *Life of Captain Sir Richard Burton,* 450.
4. McLynn, *From the Sierras to the Pampas,* 111–12.
5. Burton, *Letters from the Battle-Fields,* 81.
6. Burton, 165–70.
7. Lovell, *Rage to Live,* 497.
8. Lovell, 490–589.
9. Morris, *Trieste and the Meaning of Nowhere,* 174.
10. For a full list of Burton's publications see Tredoux, *Book of Burtoniana*; for a take on his version of the *Arabian Nights,* see Al-Musawi, *Arabian Nights in Contemporary World Cultures,* 136–37, 152, 268.
11. Quoted in McLynn, *Burton,* 245.
12. Burton, "Terminal Essay," in *Thousand Nights and a Night,* 10:212n2.
13. The best accounting of these years is Lovell, *Rage to Live,* 590–799.
14. Mary Lovell makes the strongest case for easing some of the blame from Isabel for the burning of Richard's papers, laying more emphasis on the additional burning done by her executors. Given the very detailed instructions for destroying materials she left to her executors, I am not persuaded that Isabel should be given any slack for the wholesale destruction of nearly all of Richard (and her own) private papers, either by her own hand or at her instructions. Lovell, *Rage to Live,* 788–99. For another sympathetic view of Isabel's actions, see Kennedy and Casari, "Burnt Offerings."
15. Lovell, *Rage to Live,* 561.
16. I. Burton, *Inner Life of Syria.*
17. Lovell, *Rage to Live,* 584.
18. Lovell, 700.
19. See, for example, Burton, *Kama Sutra of Vatsyayana.*
20. Lovell, *Rage to Live,* 609–11 and 697–98.
21. Lovell, 687–89; Dixon, "Havelock Ellis and John Addington Symonds," 72–77.
22. See, for example, *Minutes of the Proceedings,* in West Africa Item 2667/26/2/x, WR; and Lovell, *Rage to Live,* 806–7.
23. Lovell, 693.
24. Lovell, 730–60.
25. "Letter from Isabel Burton to Mr. Courroux, 26 September 1893," in Papers Concerning Isabel Burton's Last Wishes, Item 2667/26/2/xii, B/Beth, page 13, WR.
26. I. Burton, *Life of Captain Sir Richard F. Burton*; Burton and Wilkins, *Romance.*

27. Papers Concerning Isabel Burton's Last Wishes, Item 2667/26/2/xii, WR.
28. Darwin, *Empire Project*.
29. Silva, "Integração, Globalização e Festa," 107–18.
30. Jensen, "Sivam Communication, Navigation and Surveillance."
31. Summerhill, *Order Against Progress*.
32. Diacon, *Millenarian Vision, Capitalist Reality*.
33. Brown, "Organized Crime Drives Violence."
34. Barman, *Brazil*; Needell, *Party of Order*; Costa, *Brazilian Empire*; Carvalho, *Teatro de sombras*.
35. Leal, *Coronelismo*; Faoro, *Os donos do poder*. For a more recent, and synthetic, overview of the evolution of State power across the twentieth century, see Pereira, "From the Patrimonial State," 141–73.
36. Holanda, *Raízes do Brasil*, is a brilliant precursor to the works of Faoro and Leal.
37. Under the empire (1822–1889) the captaincies of the colonial period became provinces. After 1889 the provinces became states. For an excellent analysis of efforts to forge a sense of national identity through civic festivities, see Kraay, *Days of National Festivity*.
38. Graham, "1850–1870," 160.
39. The most famous and serious of these revolts, in the backlands of the Northeast, was immortalized by Cunha, *Os sertões*.
40. "Without a doubt, the 'original sin' of Brazilian federalism was oligarchic regionalism, which ended up weakening through successive cycles of central government interventionism." Camargo, "Federalism and National Identity," 218.
41. Graham, *Patronage and Politics*; Carvalho, *Teatro de sombras*; Rodrigues, *Conciliação e reforma no Brasil*.
42. Holston, *Insurgent Citizenship*, 91.
43. Costa, "1870–1889," 195.
44. Bethell, "Politics in Brazil under Vargas," 3–86; and Graham, *Patronage and Politics*.
45. Camargo, "Federalism and National Identity," 226.
46. Klein and Luna, *Feeding the World*.
47. Klein and Luna, 72, 186–87.
48. Bethell and Carvalho, "1822–1850," 135.
49. For some striking examples of the lack of state presence in western Brazil and Indigenous lack of awareness of the existence of the Brazilian nation-state, see Diacon, *Stringing Together a Nation*.
50. Eakin, *Becoming Brazilians*, 43–78.
51. "In 1822 less than a third of Brazil's population was white," roughly the same proportion as the enslaved population. Bethell and Carvalho, "1822–1850," 45.
52. Saunders, *Democracy and the Vote*.

BIBLIOGRAPHY

ARCHIVES

Foreign Office Correspondence, National Archives, UK
Huntington Library, San Marino, California
Local Studies Library, Borough of Richmond, Surrey, UK
National Archives, UK
Wiltshire County Records Office, Papers of Sir Richard Burton, Explorer, Author, Diplomat and Husband of Isabel Arundell, Wiltshire and Swindon History Centre, Chippenham, UK

PUBLISHED SOURCES

Abreu, João Capistrano de. *Chapters of Brazilian Colonial History*. Translated by Arthur A. Brakel. Oxford University Press, 1998. Originally published as *Capítulos de história colonial*, 1907.

Agassiz, Louis, and Elizabeth Agassiz. *A Journey in Brazil*. Ticknor and Fields, 1869.

Albuquerque, Durval Muniz de, Jr. *The Invention of the Brazilian Northeast*. Translated by Jerry Dennis Metz. Duke University Press, 2014.

Alden, Dauril. "The Gang of Four and the Campaign Against the Jesuits in Eighteenth-Century Brazil." In *The Jesuits II: Culture, Sciences, and the Arts, 1540–1773*, edited by John W. O'Malley, S.J., Gauvin Alexander Bailey, Steven J. Harris, and T. Frank Kennedy, S.J., 707–24. University of Toronto Press, 2006.

Aldrich, Robert. *Greater France: A History of French Overseas Expansion*. St. Martin's, 1996.

Alkmim, Fernando, and Stephen Marshak. "Transamazonian Orogeny in the Southern São Francisco Craton Region, Minas Gerais, Brazil: Evidence for Paleoproterozoic Collision and Collapse in the Quadrilátero Ferrífero." *Precambrian Research* 90 (1998): 29–58.

BIBLIOGRAPHY

Al-Musawi, Muhsin J. *The Arabian Nights in Contemporary World Cultures: Global Commodification, Translation, and the Culture Industry.* Cambridge University Press, 2021.

Alonso, Angela. *The Last Abolition: The Brazilian Antislavery Movement, 1868–1888.* Cambridge University Press, 2021.

Anderson, Benedict. *Imagined Communities: Reflections on the Origins and Spread of Nationalism.* Rev. ed. Verso, 2006.

Anderson, M. S. *The Rise of Modern Diplomacy, 1450–1919.* Longman, 1993.

Andrade, Renata Marson Teixeira de. "The 'Third Bank' of the Lower São Francisco River: Culture, Nature and Power in the Northeast Brazil, 1853–2003." PhD dissertation, University of California, Berkeley, 2006.

Araujo, Wagner Muniz de. "Plano de Preservação das Ruínas de Edificações Existentes no Parque Arqueológico do Morro Santana Mariana/MG." Instituto Federal de Minas Gerais, Ouro Preto (2010).

Assunção, Matthias Rohrig. *Capoeira: The History of an Afro-Brazilian Martial Art.* Routledge, 2005.

Assunção, Matthias Rohrig, and Michael Zeuske. "'Race,' Ethnicity and Social Structure in 19th Century Brazil and Cuba." *Ibero-amerikanisches Archiv*, Neue Folge, 24, no. 3/4 (1998): 375–443.

Auler, Augusto S., and Paulo Pessoa, eds. *Lagoa Santa Karst: Brazil's Iconic Karst Region.* Springer Nature, 2020.

Avery, David. *Not on Queen Victoria's Birthday: The Story of the Rio Tinto Mines.* Collins, 1974.

Baltazar, Orivaldo Ferreira, and Lydia Maria Lobato. "Structural Evolution of the Rio das Velhas Greenstone Belt, Quadrilátero Ferrífero, Brazil: Influence of Proterozoic Orogenies on Its Western Archean Gold Deposits." *Minerals* 10, no. 983 (2020).

Barbosa, Waldermar de Almeida. *O Aleijadinho de Vila Rica.* Editora Itatiaia, 1985.

Barbosa, Waldermar de Almeida, ed. *Dicionário histórico-geográfico de Minas Gerais.* Editora Saterb, 1971.

Barman, Roderick J. *Brazil: The Forging of a Nation, 1798–1852.* Stanford University Press, 1988.

Barman, Roderick J. *Citizen Emperor: Pedro II and the Making of Brazil, 1825–91.* Stanford University Press, 1999.

Barroso, Hayeska Costa. "A produçao do gênero na/da cultura popular: problematizando um habitus de gênero junino." *Caminhos da História* 24, no. 1 (2020): 9–27.

Bayly, C. A. *The Birth of the Modern World, 1780–1914: Global Connections and Comparisons.* Blackwell, 2004.

Bayly, C. A. *Imperial Meridian: The British Empire and the World, 1780–1830.* Longman, 1989.

Bazin, Germain. *Aleijadinho et la sculpture baroque au Brésil.* Le Temps, 1963.

Bell, Stephen. *Campanha Gaúcha: A Brazilian Ranching System, 1850–1920.* Stanford University Press, 1998.

BIBLIOGRAPHY

Bergad, Laird W. *Slavery and the Demographic and Economic History of Minas Gerais, Brazil, 1720–1888.* Cambridge University Press, 1999.

Bernardino-Costa, Joaze. "Opening Pandora's Box: The Extreme Right and the Resurgence of Racism in Brazil." *Latin American Perspectives* 50, no. 1 (January 2023): 98–114. Translated by Heather Hayes.

Bernstein, Harry. *The Brazilian Diamond: Contracts, Contraband, and Capital.* University Press of America, 1986.

Bethell, Leslie. *The Abolition of the Brazilian Slave Trade: Britain, Brazil, and the Slave Trade Question, 1807–1869.* Cambridge University Press, 1970.

Bethell, Leslie, ed. *Brazil: Empire and Republic, 1822–1930.* Cambridge University Press, 1989.

Bethell, Leslie, ed. *Colonial Brazil.* Cambridge University Press, 1987.

Bethell, Leslie. "Politics in Brazil under Vargas, 1930–1945." In *The Cambridge History of Latin America*, vol. 9, *Brazil since 1930*, edited by Leslie Bethell, 3–86. Cambridge University Press, 2008.

Birchal, Sérgio de Oliveira. *Entrepreneurship in Nineteenth-Century Brazil: The Formation of a Business Environment.* Macmillan, 1999.

Blanc, Jacob. *The Prestes Column: An Interior History of Brazil.* Duke University Press, 2024.

Blasenheim, Peter Louis. "A Regional History of the Zona da Mata in Minas Gerais, Brazil: 1870–1906." PhD dissertation, Stanford University, 1982.

Bosi, Alfredo. *História concisa da literatura brasileira.* Cultrix, 2006.

Bowley, Arthur L. *Wages in the United Kingdom in the Nineteenth Century.* Cambridge University Press, 1900.

Boxer, C. R. *The Golden Age of Brazil, 1695–1750.* University of California Press, 1963.

Brant, Alice Dayrell Caldeira. *The Diary of "Helena Morley."* Translated by Elizabeth Bishop. Farrar, Straus and Giroux, 1957.

Britton, John A. *Cables, Crises, and the Press: The Geopolitics of the New International Information System in the Americas, 1866–1903.* University of New Mexico Press, 2013.

Brodie, Fawn M. *The Devil Drives: A Life of Sir Richard Burton.* W. W. Norton, 1967.

Brown, Sarah. "Organized Crime Drives Violence and Deforestation in the Amazon." *Mongabay*, 1 August 2022. https://news.mongabay.com/2022/08/organized-crime-drives-violence-and-deforestation-in-the-amazon-study-shows/.

Buckley, Eve E. *Technocrats and the Politics of Drought and Development in Twentieth-Century Brazil.* University of North Carolina Press, 2017.

Burton, Isabel. *The Inner Life of Syria, Palestine, and the Holy Land.* 2 vols. Henry S. King, 1875.

Burton, Isabel. *The Life of Captain Sir Richard Burton.* 2 vols. Chapman & Hall, 1893.

Burton, Isabel, and W. H. Wilkins. *The Romance of Isabel Lady Burton: The Story of Her Life.* Dodd Mead, 1904.

Burton, Richard F. *Abeokuta and the Cameroons Mountains.* 2 vols. Tinsley Brothers, 1863.
Burton, Richard F. *The Book of the Thousand Nights and a Night.* 10 vols. Printed by the Kama Shastra Society for private subscribers only, 1885.
Burton, Richard F. *The City of the Saints and Across the Rocky Mountains to California.* Edited by Fawn M. Brodie. Alfred A. Knopf, 1963.
Burton, Richard F. *First Footsteps in East Africa.* Longmans, 1856.
Burton, Richard F. *The Jew, the Gypsy and El Islam.* Edited by W. H. Wilkinson. Hutchinson, 1898.
Burton, Richard F. ed. *The Kama Sutra of Vatsyayana.* Introduction by Margot Anand. Random House, 2002.
Burton, Richard F. *The Lake Regions of Central Africa.* 2 vols. Longmans, 1860.
Burton, Richard F. *Letters from the Battle-Fields of Paraguay.* Tinsley Brothers, 1870.
Burton, Richard F. *A Mission to Gelele, King of Dahome.* Tinsley Brothers, 1864.
Burton, Richard F. *Wanderings in West Africa.* 2 vols. Tinsley Brothers, 1863.
Camargo, Aspásia. "Federalism and National Identity." In *Brazil: A Century of Change*, edited by Ignacy Sachs, Jorge Wilheim, and Paulo Sérgio Pinheiro, translated by Robert N. Anderson, 216–52. University of North Carolina Press, 2009.
Camelo Filho, José Vieira. "A dinâmica política, econômica e social do Rio São Francisco e de seu vale." *Revista do Departamento de Geografia* 17 (2005): 83–93.
Campbell, Courtney J. "Making Abolition Brazilian: British Law and Brazilian Abolitionists in Nineteenth-Century Minas Gerais and Pernambuco." *Slavery & Abolition* 36, no. 3 (2015): 521–43.
Carvalho, José Murilo de. *Teatro de sombras: a política imperial.* IUPERJ/São Paulo: Vértice, 1988.
Castelnau, Francis de Laporte de. *Expedições às regiões centrais da América do Sul*, 1850–1859. Translated by Olivério M. de Oliveira Pinto. Companhia Editora Nacional, 1949.
Castilho, Celso Thomas. *Slave Emancipation and Transformations in Brazilian Political Citizenship.* University of Pittsburgh Press, 2016.
Cavalcanti, José Adilson Dias, Marilda Santana da Silva, Carlos Schobbenhaus, Daniel Atencio, and Hernani Mota de Lima. "Geoconservation of Geological and Mining Heritage Related to Banded Iron Formation of Itabira Group, Quadrilátero Ferrífero, Minas Gerais, Brazil: A Complicated Issue." *International Journal of Geoheritage and Parks* 11 (2023): 118–48.
Chalhoub, Sidney. "The Politics of Ambiguity: Conditional Manumission, Labor Contracts, and Slave Emancipation in Brazil (1850s–1888)." *International Review of Social History* 60 (2015): 161–91.
Chalmers, Ian. *A Chalmers Miscellany.* Privately printed, 2008.
Chandler, Billy Jaynes. *The Bandit King: Lampião of Brazil.* Texas A&M University Press, 1978.
Chaves, M. L., J. Karfunkel, and D. B. Hoover. "Diamonds from the Espinhaço

BIBLIOGRAPHY

Range (Minas Gerais, Brazil) and Their Redistribution Through the Geologic Record." *Journal of South American Earth Science* 14 (2001): 277–89.

Chilcote, Ronald H. *Power and the Ruling Classes in Northeast Brazil: Juazeiro and Petrolina in Transition.* Cambridge University Press, 1990.

Comaroff, Jean, and John L. Comaroff. *Of Revelation and Revolution: Christianity, Colonialism, and Consciousness in South Africa.* Vol. 1. University of Chicago Press, 1991.

Cordiviola, Alfredo. *Richard Burton, A Traveller in Brazil, 1865–1868.* Edwin Mellen Press, 2001.

Costa, Emília Viotti da. *The Brazilian Empire: Myths and Histories.* Rev. ed. University of North Carolina Press, 2000.

Cunha, Ana Paula M. A., Marcelo Zeri, Karinne Deusdará Leal, et al. "Extreme Drought Events over Brazil from 2011 to 2019." *Atmosphere* 10, no. 642 (2019): 1–20.

Cunha, Euclides da. *Backlands: The Canudos Campaign.* Translated by Elizabeth Lowe. Penguin, 2010.

Cunha, Euclides da. *Os sertões (campanha de Canudos).* Edited by Leopoldo Bernucci. 2nd ed. São Paulo: Ateliêr Editorial, 2001.

Cunha, Euclides da. *Rebellion in the Backlands.* Translated by Samuel Putnam. University of Chicago Press, 1944.

Cyrino, Fábio. *Café, ferro e argila: a história da implantação da San Paulo (Brazilian) Railway Company Ltd. Através da análise de sua arquitetura.* Editora Landmark, 2004.

Daly, Jonathan. *The Rise of Western Power: A Comparative History of Western Civilization.* Bloomsbury, 2014.

Darwin, Charles. *"The Origin of Species" and "The Descent of Man."* 1859 and 1871. Reprint, Modern Library, 1960.

Darwin, John. *The Empire Project: The Rise and Fall of the British World-System, 1830–1970.* Cambridge University Press, 2009.

Davis, Wade. *Into the Silence: The Great War, Mallory, and the Conquest of Everest.* Vintage, 2011.

Dawsey, Cyrus B., and James M. Dawsey, eds. *The Confederados: Old South Immigrants in Brazil.* University of Alabama Press, 1995.

Dean, Warren. *With Broadax and Firebrand: The Destruction of the Brazilian Atlantic Forest.* University of California Press, 1995.

della Cava, Ralph. *Miracle at Joaseiro.* Columbia University Press, 1970.

Desmond, Adrian, and James Moore. *Darwin: The Life of a Tormented Evolutionist.* W. W. Norton, 1991.

Diacon, Todd A. *Millenarian Vision, Capitalist Reality: Brazil's Contestado Rebellion, 1912–1916.* Duke University Press, 1991.

Diacon, Todd A. *Stringing Together a Nation: Cândido Mariano da Silva Rondon and the Construction of a Modern Brazil, 1906–1930.* Duke University Press, 2004.

Disney, A. R. *A History of Portugal and the Portuguese Empire.* Vol. 2. Cambridge University Press, 2009.

BIBLIOGRAPHY

Dixon, Joy. "Havelock Ellis and John Addington Symonds, *Sexual Inversion* (1897)." *Victorian Review* 35, no. 1 (Spring 2009): 72–77.

Dorr, John Van N., II. *Physiographic, Stratigraphic and Structural Development of the Quadrilátero Ferrífero Minas Gerais, Brazil*. United States Geological Survey Professional Paper 641-A, US Government Printing Office, 1969.

Duncan, Julian Smith. *Public and Private Operation of Railways in Brazil*. Columbia University Press, 1932.

Eakin, Marshall C. *Becoming Brazilians: Race and National Identity in Twentieth-Century Brazil*. Cambridge University Pess, 2017.

Eakin, Marshall C. *British Enterprise in Brazil: The St. John d'el Rey Mining Company and the Morro Velho Gold Mine, 1830–1960*. Duke University Press, 1989.

Eakin, Marshall C. "Creating a Growth Pole: The Industrialization of Belo Horizonte, 1897–1987." *The Americas* 47, no. 4 (April 1991): 383–410.

Eakin, Marshall C. *A History of Latin America: Collision of Cultures*. Palgrave Macmillan, 2007.

Eakin, Marshall C. *Tropical Capitalism: The Industrialization of Belo Horizonte, Brazil*. Palgrave Macmillan, 2001.

Elliott, J. H. *Empires of the Atlantic World: Britain and Spain in America, 1492–1830*. Yale University Press, 2006.

Elliott, J. H. *The Old World and the New, 1492–1650*. Cambridge University Press, 1970.

Eriksen, Thomas Hylland, and Finn Sivert Nielsen. *A History of Anthropology*. 2nd ed. Palgrave Macmillan, 2013.

Eschwege, W. L. Von. *Pluto brasiliensis*. 2 vols. Translated by Domício de Figueiredo Murta. Editora da Universidade de São Paulo/Livraria Itatiaia Editora, 1979.

Evans, Chris. "Brazilian Gold, Cuban Copper and the Final Frontier of British Anti-Slavery." *Slavery & Abolition* 34, no. 1 (2013): 118–34.

Faoro, Raymundo. *Os donos do poder: formação do patronato político brasileiro*. Editora Globo, 1976.

Farwell, Byron. *Burton: A Biography of Sir Richard Francis Burton*. Penguin, 1963.

Faulkner, Walker. *Requiem for a Nun*. Random House, 1951.

Ferreira, Rodrigo de Almeida. *O descaminho de diamantes: Relações de poder e sociabilidade na demarcação Diamantina no período dos contratos (1740–1771)*. FUMARC, 2009.

Flory, Thomas. *Judge and Jury in Imperial Brazil, 1808–1871: Social Control and Political Stability in the New State*. University of Texas Press, 1981.

Fogel, Robert William. *Without Consent or Contract: The Rise and Fall of American Slavery*. W. W. Norton, 1989.

Franco, Maria Sylvia de Carvalho. *Homens livres na ordem escravocrata*. Instituto de Estudos Brasileiros, Universidade de São Paulo, 1969.

Freyre, Gilberto. *Casa-grande e senzala: Formação da família brasileira sob o regime da economia patriarcal*. 49th ed. Global Editora, 2003.

BIBLIOGRAPHY

Freyre, Gilberto. *Masters and the Slaves: A Study in the Development of Brazilian Civilization.* Translated by Samuel Putnam. A. A. Knopf, 1946.

Furtado, Júnia Ferreira. *Chica da Silva: A Brazilian Slave of the Eighteenth Century.* Cambridge University Press, 2009.

Furtado, Júnia Ferreira. *Chica da Silva e o contratador do diamantes: o outro lado do mito.* Companhia das Letras, 2003.

Furtado, Júnia Ferreira. *O livro da capa verde: o regimento diamantino de 1771 e a vida no Distrito Diamantino no período da real extração.* Annablume, 1996.

Gair, Jacob E. *Geology and Ore Deposit of the Nova Lima and Rio Acima Quadrangles, Minas Gerais, Brazil.* United States Geological Survey Professional Paper 341-A, US Government Printing Office, 1962.

Gama, José Basílio da. *The Uruguay (A Historical Romance of South America): The Sir Richard F. Burton Translation.* Edited by Frederick C. H. Garcia and Edward F. Stanton. University of California Press, 1982.

Gama, Rinaldo. "Biblioteca Nacional," *Veja*, 23 November 1994.

Gardner, George. *Travels in the Interior of Brazil.* 2nd ed. Reeve, Benham, and Reeve, 1849.

Garfield, Seth. *Indigenous Struggle at the Heart of Brazil: State Policy, Frontier Expansion, and the Xavante Indians, 1937–1988.* Duke University Press, 2001.

Giroletti, Domingos. *A industrialização de Juiz de Fora: 1850–1930.* Editora da Universidade Federal de Juiz de Fora, 1988.

Gonçalves, Alcindo e Luiz Antonio de Paula. *O grande porto: a modernização no Porto de Santos.* Realejo, 2008.

Graham, Richard. *Britain and the Onset of Modernization in Brazil, 1850–1914.* Cambridge University Press, 1972.

Graham, Richard. *Patronage and Politics in Nineteenth-Century Brazil.* Stanford University Press, 1990.

Gravatá, Hélio. "Viajantes Estrangeiros em Minas Gerais, 1809–1955." *Minas Gerais, Suplemento Literário*, 10 October 1970, 11–12.

Guenther, Louise H. *British Merchants in Nineteenth-Century Brazil: Business, Culture, and Identity in Bahia, 1808–50.* Centre for Brazilian Studies, University of Oxford, 2004.

Halfeld, Geraldo. *Henrique Fernando Guilherme Halfeld: Fundador da Cidade de Juiz de Fora.* n.p., 1970.

Halfeld, Henrique Fernando Guilherme. *Atlas e relatorio concernente a exploração do Rio S. Francisco.* Eduardo Rensburg, 1860.

Hanley, Anne G. *Native Capital: Financial Institutions and Economic Development in São Paulo, 1850–1920.* Stanford University Press, 2005.

Hanley, Anne G. *The Public Good and the Brazilian State: Municipal Finance and Public Services in São Paulo, 1822–1930.* University of Chicago Press, 2018.

Hardon, John A., S.J. *Catholic Dictionary: An Abridged and Updated Edition of Modern Catholic Dictionary.* Image, 2013.

Hartley, L. P. *The Go-Between.* Hamish Hamilton, 1953.

Herskovits, Melville J., and Frances S. *Dahomey: An Ancient West African Kingdom.* 2 vols. J. J. Augustin, 1938.

Holanda, Sérgio Buarque de. *Raízes do Brasil*. Editora José Olympio, 1936.

Holloway, Thomas H. *Immigrants on the Land: Coffee and Society in São Paulo, 1886–1934*. University of North Carolina Press, 1980.

Holston, James. *Insurgent Citizenship: Disjunctions of Democracy and Modernity in Brazil*. Princeton University Press, 2007.

Holten, Birgitte, and Michael Sterll. *Peter Lund e as grutas com ossos em Lagoa Santa*. Translated by Luiz Paulo Ribeiro Vaz. Editora UFMG, 2011.

Hoong, Yip Yat. *The Development of the Tin Mining Industry in Malaya*. University of Malaya Press, 1969.

Instituto Brasileiro de Geografia e Estatística. *Estatísticas históricas do Brasil, Séries Estatísticas Retrospectivas, vol. 3, Séries econômicas, demográficas e sociais, 1550 a 1985*. IBGE, 1987.

Instituto Estadual do Patrimônio Histórico e Artístico de Minas Gerais. "Conjunto Arquitetônico e Paisagístico da Fazenda de Jaguara." http://www.iepha.mg.gov.br/index.php/programas-e-acoes/patrimonio-cultural-protegido/bens-tombados/details/1/18/bens-tombados-conjunto-arquitet%C3%B4nico-e-paisag%C3%ADstico-da-fazenda-da-jaguara.

Instituto Estadual do Patrimônio Histórico e Artístico de Minas Gerais. *Guia dos bens tombados*. 2 vols. http://www.iepha.mg.gov.br/index.php/publicacoes/guia-dos-bens-tombados.

Instituto do Patrimônio Histórico e Artístico Nacional. "Santuário do Bom Jesus de Matozinhos-Congonhas (MG)." http://portal.iphan.gov.br/pagina/detalhes/46.

Ioris, Rafael R. *Transforming Brazil: A History of National Development in the Postwar Era*. Routledge, 2014.

Jensen, David. "Sivam Communication, Navigation and Surveillance for the Amazon." *Aviation Today*, 1 June 2002. https://www.aviationtoday.com/2002/06/01/sivam-communication-navigation-and-surveillance-for-wv-the-amazon/.

Jones, Raymond A. *The British Diplomatic Service, 1815–1914*. Wilfrid Laurier University Press, 1983.

Karasch, Mary. *Slave Life in Rio de Janeiro, 1808–1850*. Princeton University Press, 1987.

Kemper, Robert V., and Anya Peterson Royce, "Mexican Urbanization Since 1821: A Macrohistorical Approach," *Urban Anthropology* 8, no. 3/4 (1979): 267–89.

Kennedy, Dane. *The Highly Civilized Man: Richard Burton and the Victorian World*. Harvard University Press, 2005.

Kennedy, Dane. "Introduction." In *Reinterpreting Exploration: The West in the World*, edited by Dan Kennedy, 1–18. Oxford University Press, 2014.

Kennedy, Dane. *Mungo Park's Ghost: The Haunted Hubris of British Explorers in Nineteenth-Century Africa*. Cambridge University Press, 2024.

Kennedy, Dane, and Burke E. Casari. "Burnt Offerings: Isabel Burton and the 'Scented Garden' Manuscript." *Journal of Victorian Culture* 2, no. 2 (Spring 1997): 229–44.

BIBLIOGRAPHY

Kiddy, Elizabeth W. *Blacks of the Rosary: Memory and History in Minas Gerais, Brazil*. Pennsylvania State University Press, 2005.

Kiddy, Elizabeth W. "Militão and the Guerreiros: Local Feuds, Long Memories, and Brazil's Struggle to Control the São Francisco River." *The Americas* 70, no. 1 (July 2013): 23–24.

King, Charles. *Gods of the Upper Air*. Anchor, 2020.

Klein, Herbert S. *The Atlantic Slave Trade*. 2nd ed. Cambridge University Press, 2010.

Klein, Herbert S., and Francisco Vidal Luna. *Brazil: An Economic and Social History from Early Man to the 20th Century*. Cambridge University Press, 2023.

Klein, Herbert S., and Francisco Vidal Luna. *Feeding the World: Brazil's Transformation into a Modern Agricultural Economy*. Cambridge University Press, 2018.

Klein, Herbert S., and Francisco Vidal Luna. *Slavery in Brazil*. Cambridge University Press, 2010.

Klein, Herbert S., and Ben Vinson III. *African Slavery in Latin America and the Caribbean*. 2nd ed. Oxford University Press, 2007.

Klumb, R. H. *Doze horas em diligencia: guia do viajante de Petrópolis a Juiz de Fóra*. J. J. da Costa Braga, 1872.

Kraay, Hendrik. *Days of National Festivity in Rio de Janeiro Brazil, 1823–1889*. Stanford University Press, 2013.

Krause, James R., David P. Wiseman, and Faith Blackhurst. "The Boom Novel That Never Was." *Hispania* 103, no. 4 (December 2020): 603–20.

Langfur, Hal. *Adrift on an Inland Sea: Misinformation and the Limits of Empire in the Brazilian Backlands*. Stanford University Press, 2023.

Langfur, Hal. *The Forbidden Lands: Colonial Identity, Frontier Violence, and the Persistence of Brazil's Eastern Indians, 1750–1830*. Stanford University Press, 2006.

Lanna, Ana Lúcia Duarte. *A transformação do trabalho: a passagem para o trabalho livre na Zona da Mata mineira, 1870–1920*. Editora da UNICAMP, 1988.

Lanna, Ana Lúcia Duarte. *Uma cidade na transição, Santos: 1870–1913*. Editora Hucitec, Prefeitura Municipal de Santos, 1996.

Latrubesse, Edgardo M., Mario Cozzuol, Silane A. F. da Silva-Caminha, Catherine A. Rigsby, Maria Luca Absy, and Carlos Jaramillo. "The Late Miocene Paleogeography of the Amazon Basin and the Evolution of the Amazon River System." *Earth-Science Reviews* 99, no. 3–4 (May 2010): 99–124.

Leal, Victor Nunes. *Coronelismo: The Municipality and Representative Government in Brazil*. Translated by June Henfrey. Cambridge University Press, 1977.

Leão, Luciano de Souza. "A Double-Edged Sword: The Institutional Foundations of the Brazilian Developmental State, 1930–1985." In *State and Nation Making in Latin America and Spain: The Rise and Fall of the Developmental State*, edited by Augustin E. Ferraro and Miguel Centeno, 157–76. Cambridge University Press, 2018.

BIBLIOGRAPHY

Lengel, Edward G. *Colonial Williamsburg: The Story*. University of Virginia Press, 2020.

Lesser, Jeffrey. *Immigration, Ethnicity, and National Identity in Brazil, 1808 to the Present*. Cambridge University Press, 2013.

Levine, Robert M. *Father of the Poor? Vargas and His Era*. Cambridge University Press, 1998.

Levine, Robert M. *Vale of Tears: Revisiting the Canudos Massacre in Northeastern Brazil, 1893–1897*. University of California Press, 1992.

Lewis, Colin M. *Public Policy and Private Initiative: Railway Building in São Paulo, 1860–1889*. Institute of Latin American Studies, 1991.

Liais, Emm. *Hydrographie du haute San-Francisco e de Rio das Velhas*. B. L. Garnier, 1865.

Libby, Douglas Cole. *Transformação e trabalho em uma economia escravista: Minas Gerais no século XIX*. Editora Brasiliense, 1988.

Lima, Nísia Trindade. *Um sertão chamado Brasil: intelectuais e representação geográfica da identidade nacional*. Revan/IUPERJ-UCAM, 1999.

Lisboa, Apolo Heringer, Eugênio Marcos Andrade Goulart, Letícia Fernandes Malloy Diniz, orgs. *Projeto Manuelzão: a história da mobilização que começou em torno de um rio*. Instituto Guaicuy, 2008.

Lopez, Barry. *Horizon*. Alfred A. Knopf, 2019.

Lovell, Mary S. *A Rage to Live: A Biography of Richard and Isabel Burton*. W. W. Norton, 1998.

Lovell, Mary S. *A Scandalous Life: The Biography of Jane Digby el Mezrab*. Richard Cohen, 1995.

Loveman, Mara. "The Race to Progress: Census Taking and Nation Making in Brazil (1870–1920)." *Hispanic American Historical Review*. 89, no. 3 (August 2009): 435–70.

Lucas, Murilo Cesar, Natalya Kublik, Dulce B. B. Rodrigues, Antonio A. Meira Neto, André Almagro, Davi de C. D. Melo, Samuel C. Zipper, and Paulo Tarso Sanches Oliveira. "Significant Baseflow Reduction in the Sao Francisco River Basin." *Water* 13, no. 2 (2021): 1–17.

Luna, Francisco Vidal, and Herbert S. Klein. *An Economic and Demographic History of São Paulo, 1850–1950*. Stanford University Press, 2018.

Luna, Francisco Vidal, and Herbert S. Klein. *Social Change, Industrialization, and the Service Economy in São Paulo, 1850–1920*. Cambridge University Press, 2022.

Lyon, Michael John. *Like a Rolling Stone: The Life and Travels of George Francis Lyon, RN, FRS*. New Generation, 2017.

Macaulay, Neill. *Dom Pedro: The Struggle for Liberty in Brazil and Portugal, 1798–1834*. Duke University Press, 1986.

Machado, Fernando da Matta. *Navegação do Rio São Francisco*. Topbooks, 2002.

Malerba, Jurandir. *A Corte no exílio: Civilização e poder no Brasil às vésperas da independência (1808–1821)*. Companhia das Letras, 2000.

Maltby, William S. *The Rise and Fall of the Spanish Empire*. Palgrave Macmillan, 2009.

BIBLIOGRAPHY

Manchester, Alan K. *British Preeminence in Brazil, Its Rise and Decline: A Study in European Expansion.* University of North Carolina Press, 1933.

Maquine Mine, the Property of the Don Pedro Gold Mining, Limited. Joint Stock Companies Agency, Devonshire Chambers, 1888.

Maraux, Vincent. *Pierre Victor Renault: un pionnier français au XIXéme siècle, 1811–1892.* Virtual Books, https://doceru.com/doc/nvccn.

Marchant, Anyda. *Viscount Mauá and the Empire of Brazil: A Biography of Irineu Evangelista de Sousa (1813–1889).* University of California Press, 1965.

Marcus, Alan P. *Confederate Exodus: Social and Environmental Factors in the Migration of U.S. Southerners.* University of Nebraska Press, 2021.

Marques, A. H. de Oliveira. *History of Portugal.* 2nd ed. Columbia University Press, 1976.

Martins, Roberto B. *Crescendo em silêncio: a incrível economia escravista de Minas Gerais no século XIX.* ICAM, ABPHE, 2018.

Mattoon, R. H., Jr. "The Companhia Paulista de Estradas de Ferro, 1868–1900: A Local Railway Enterprise in São Paulo." PhD dissertation, Yale University, 1971.

Mattoso, Katia M. de Queirós. *Bahia, século XIX: uma província no Império.* Editora Nova Fronteira, 1992.

Mawe, John. *Travels in the Interior of Brazil.* 2nd ed. Longman, Hurst, Rees, Orme, and Brown, 1822.

Maxwell, Kenneth. *Conflicts and Conspiracies: Brazil and Portugal, 1750–1808.* Cambridge University Press, 1973.

Maxwell, Kenneth. *Pombal: Paradox of the Enlightenment.* Cambridge University Press, 1995.

McLynn, Frank. *From the Sierras to the Pampas: Richard Burton's Travels in the Americas, 1860–69.* Century, 1991.

McLynn, Frank. *Burton: Snow upon the Desert.* John Murray, 1990.

Mello, Suzy de. *Barroco mineiro.* Braziliense, 1985.

Meneses, José Newton Coelho, ed. *Nossa comida tem história.* Scriptum, 2020.

Mineração Morro Velho Ltda. *Morro Velho—História, fatos e feitos.* MMV Ltda, 1996.

Minutes of the Proceedings of the Annual Meeting of the Guinea Coast Gold Mining Company, Limited. Whitehead, Morris, and Lowe, 1883.

Mitchell, Margaret. *Gone with the Wind.* Macmillan, 1936.

Monteiro, Norma de Góis, ed. *Dicionário biográfico de Minas Gerais, Período Republicano 1889/1991.* 2 v. Assembléia Legislativa do Estado de Minas Gerais, 1994.

Morris, Jan. *Trieste and the Meaning of Nowhere.* Da Capo, 2001.

Moya, José. *Cousins and Strangers: Spanish Immigrants in Buenos Aires, 1850–1930.* University of California Press, 1998.

Moyen, François. *A história da Companhia Siderúrgica Belgo-Mineira: uma trajetória de crescimento consistente (1921–2005).* Acelor Brasil, 2007.

Nascimento, Lucigleide Nery. "The Long Journey to Become 'the River of National Unity': The São Francisco River Basin from the 1940s to 2008, and the Interactions of Environment, Government and Local Citizens." PhD dissertation, University of New Hampshire, 2010.

Nascimento, Lucigleide Nery, and Mimi Larsen Becker. "Hydro-businesses: National and Global Demands on the São Francisco River Basin Environment of Brazil." *IRSH* 55 (2010) Supplement: 203–33.

Needell, Jeffrey D. *The Party of Order: The Conservatives, the State, and Slavery in the Brazilian Monarchy, 1831–1871*. Stanford University Press, 2006.

Needell, Jeffrey D. *The Sacred Cause: The Abolitionist Movement, Afro-Brazilian Mobilization, and Imperial Politics in Rio de Janeiro*. Stanford University Press, 2020.

Needell, Jeffrey D. *A Tropical Belle Epoque: Elite Culture and Society in Turn-of-the-Century Rio de Janeiro*. Cambridge University Press, 1987.

North, Marianne. *Recollections of a Happy Life*. Edited by Mrs. John Addington Symonds. 2 vols. Macmillan, 1892.

Nozoe, Nelson Hideaki. *São Paulo: Economia cafeeira e urbanização*. Instituto de Pesquisas Econômicas, USP, 1984.

Oliveira, Januária Teive de, and Antonio Augusto Passos Videira. "As polêmicas entre Manoel Pereira Reis, Emmanuel Liais e Luiz Cruls na passagem do século XIX para o século XX." *Revista da SBHC* 1 (2003): 42–52.

Onnekink, David, and Gijs Rommelse. *The Dutch in the Early Modern World: A History of a Global Power*. Cambridge University Press, 2019.

Osterhammel, Jurgen. *The Transformation of the World: A Global History of the Nineteenth Century*. Translated by Patrick Camiller. Princeton University Press, 2017.

Pang, Eul-soo Pang. *In Pursuit of Honor and Power: Noblemen of the Southern Cross in Nineteenth-Century Brazil*. University of Alabama Press, 1988.

Pereira, Luiz Carlos Bresser. "From the Patrimonial State to the Managerial State." In *Brazil: A Century of Change*, edited by Ignacy Sachs, Jorge Wilheim, and Paulo Sérgio Pinheiro, translated by Robert N. Anderson, 141–73. University of North Carolina Press, 2009.

Pettitt, Clare. "One-Man Multidisciplinarian." *Nature* 525 (17 September 2015): 319.

Pierson, Donald, ed. *O homem no Vale do São Francisco*. 3 vols. Superintendência do Vale do São Francisco, Ministério do Interior, 1972.

Pinho, Wanderley. *Cotegipe e seu tempo: primeira phase: 1815–1867*. Nacional, 1934.

Pinson, Bobby, Eric Church, Clint Daniels, and Jeff Hyde. "Some of It." Sony/ATV Tree, Longer and Louder Music, Little Louder Songs, Mammaw S Fried Okra Music, 2018.

Platt, D. C. M. *The Cinderella Service: British Consuls Since 1825*. Archon, 1971.

Porter, Dale H. *The Thames Embankment: Environment, Technology, and Society in Victorian England*. University of Akron Press, 1998.

Pratt, Mary Louise. *Imperial Eyes: Travel Writing and Transculturation*. 2nd ed. Routledge, 2008.

Randall, Robert W. *Real del Monte: A British Silver Mining Venture in Mexico*. University of Texas Press, 1972.

Rangel, Alberto, and Emanuel Araújo, eds. *Cartas de D. Pedro I à Marquesa de Santos*. Editora Nova Fronteira, 1984.

Ribeiro, Gustavo Lins. "Learning from Minas Gerais: Flows of Capital, Production, and Managerial Models Within the Steel Industry." In *Industry and Work in Contemporary Capitalism: Global Models, Local Lives?*, edited by Victoria Goddard and Susana Narotzky, 91–104. Routledge, 2015.

Rice, Edward. *Captain Sir Richard Francis Burton: A Biography*. Da Capo, 2001.

Riedel, Augusto. *Viagem de S.S.A.A. Real Duque de Saxe e seu augusto irmão D. Luis Philippe ao interior do Brazil no anno 1868*. n.p., n.d.

Rippy, J. Fred. *British Investments in Latin America, 1822–1949: A Case Study in the Operations of Private Enterprise in Retarded Regions*. University of Minnesota Press, 1959.

Rippy, J. Fred. "The Most Profitable British Mining Investments in the Hispanic World." *Inter-American Economic Affairs* 8, no. 2 (Autumn 1954).

Rodrigues, José Honório. *Conciliação e reforma no Brasil; um desafio histórico-cultural*. Editôra Civilização Brasileira, 1965.

Rodríguez Monegal, Emir, ed. *The Borzoi Anthology of Latin American Literature, Volume II, The Twentieth Century—from Borges and Paz to Guimarães Rosa and Donoso*. With the assistance of Thomas Colchie. Alfred A. Knopf, 1977.

Roman, Philippe. "The São Francisco Interbasin Water Transfer in Brazil: Tribulations of a Megaproject Through Constraints and Controversy." *Water Alternatives* 10, no. 2 (2017): 395–419.

Romo, Anadelia. *Selling Black Brazil: Race, Nation, and Visual Culture in Salvador, Bahia*. University of Texas Press, 2022.

Roosevelt, Theodore. *Through the Brazilian Wilderness*. Charles Scribner's Sons, 1914.

Rosa, João Guimarães. *Grande sertão: Veredas*. 2nd ed. José Olympio, 1958.

Russell-Wood, A. J. R. *The Black Man in Slavery and Freedom in Colonial Brazil*. Macmillan, 1982.

Saba, Roberto N. P. F. "Seeking Refuge Under the Southern Cross: The Causes of Confederate Emigration to the Empire of Brazil," *Traversea* 2 (2012): 30–42.

Sadlier, Darlene J. *Brazil Imagined: 1500 to the Present*. University of Texas Press, 2008.

Saes, Flávio Azevedo Marques de. *As ferrovias de São Paulo 1870–1940*. Editora Hucitec, 1981.

Said, Edward W. *Orientalism*. Vintage, 1979.

Saint-Hilaire, Augusto de. *Viagens pelo distrito do diamantes e litoral do Brasil*. Translated by Leonam de Azeredo Pena. 1833. Companhia Editora Nacional, 1941.

Sallas, Ana Luisa Fayet. "Narrativas e imagens dos viajantes alemães no Brasil do século XIX: A construção do imaginário sobre os povos Indígenas, a história e a nação." *História, Ciências, saúde—Manguinhos* 17, no. 2 (April–June 2010): 415–35.

BIBLIOGRAPHY

Salvador, Gilberto Nepomuceno, Cecília Gontijo Leal, Gabriel Lourenço Brejão, Tiago Casarim Pessali, Carlos Bernardo Mascarenhas Alves, Gustavo Ribeiro Rosa, Raphael Ligeiro, and Luciano Fogaça de Assis Montag. "Mining Activity in Brazil and Negligence in Action." *Perspectives in Ecology and Conservation* 18 (2020): 137–42.

Santos, Milton, and María Laura Silveira. *O Brasil: Território e sociedade no início do século XXI*. 12th ed. Editora Record, 2008.

Sargen, Ian. *Our Men in Brazil: The Hesketh Brothers Abroad*. 2nd ed. Scotforth, 2009.

Saunders, Robert. *Democracy and the Vote in British Politics, 1848–1867: The Making of the Second Reform Act of 1867*. Ashgate, 2011.

Sawyer, Donald R. "The Physical Setting." In *Brazil: A Country Study*, edited by Rex A. Hudson, 90–103. Library of Congress, 1998.

Schultz, Kirsten. *Tropical Versailles: Empire, Monarchy, and the Portuguese Royal Court in Rio de Janeiro, 1808–1821*. Routledge, 2001.

Schwarcz, Lilia Moritz. *As barbas do imperador: D. Pedro II, um monarca nos trópicos*. Companhia das Letras, 1998.

Schwarcz, Lilia Moritz. *The Spectacle of the Races: Scientists, Institutions, and the Race Question in Brazil, 1870–1930*. Translated by Leland Guyer. Hill and Wang, 1999.

Schwartz, Stuart B. *Sugar Plantations in the Formation of Brazilian Society: Bahia, 1550–1835*. Cambridge University Press, 1985.

Silva, Christiano Barbosa da. "Claude Henri Gorceix: The Man, Teacher, and Work." *Revista da Escola de Minas* 67, no. 3 (July–September 2014): 319–40.

Silva, Eduardo. "Integração, globalização e festa: A abolição da escravatura como história cultural." In *Escravidão, exclusão e cidadania*, edited by Marco Pamplona, 107–18. Access, 2001.

Silva, Fábio Carlos da. *Barões do ouro e aventureiros britânicos no Brasil*. Editora da Universidade Federal do Pará, 2012.

Silva, Graziella Moraes, and Marcelo Paixão. "Mixed and Unequal: New Perspectives on Brazilian Ethnoracial Relations." In *Pigmentocracies: Ethnicity, Race, and Color in Latin America*, edited by Edward Telles, 172–217. University of North Carolina Press, 2014.

Skidmore, Thomas E. *Black into White: Race and Nationality in Brazilian Thought*. Oxford University Press, 1974.

Skidmore, Thomas E. *Politics in Brazil, 1930–1964: An Experiment in Democracy*. Oxford University Press, 1967.

Skidmore, Thomas E. *The Politics of Military Rule in Brazil, 1964–85*. Oxford University Press, 1988.

Slavery at Gongo Soco in Brazil, 1826–1857. Printed by W. Cornish, 1864. https://play.google.com/books/reader?id=Cz5cAAAAcAAJ&pg=GBS.PA2.

Southey, Robert. *History of Brazil*. 3 vols. Longman, Hurst, Rees, Orme, and Brown, 1810–1819.

Spivak, Gayatri Chakravorty. "Can the Subaltern Speak?" In *Can the Subaltern*

Speak? Reflections on the History of an Idea, edited by Rosalind Morris, 21–78. Columbia University Press, 2010.

Staden, Hans. *The Captivity of Hans Stade of Hesse, in A.D. 1547–1555, Among the Wild Tribes of Eastern Brazil*. Translated by Albert Tootal and annotated by Richard Francis Burton. Hakluyt Society, 1874.

Staden, Hans. *Hans Staden's True History: An Account of Cannibal Captivity in Brazil*. Edited and translated by Neil L. Whitehead and Michael Harbsmeier. Duke University Press, 2008.

Stocking, George W., Jr. *Victorian Anthropology*. Free Press, 1987.

Stolf, Rubismar, Sonia M. de S. Piedade, Jair R. da Silva, Luiz C. F. da Silva, and Miguel Â. Maniero. "Water Transfer from São Francisco River to Semiarid Northeast of Brazil: Technical Data, Environmental Impacts, Survey of Opinion about the Amount to be Transferred." *Engenharia Agrícola* 32, no. 6 (2012): 998–1010.

Strachey, Lytton. *Eminent Victorians*. Chatto and Windus, 1918.

Summerhill, William R. *Order Against Progress: Government, Foreign Investment, and Railroads in Brazil, 1854–1913*. Stanford University Press, 2003.

Telles, Edward E. *Race in Another America: The Significance of Skin Color in Brazil*. Princeton University Press, 2005.

Théry, Hervé. *Le Brésil*. Armand Colin, 2000.

Thomas, Hugh. *The Slave Trade: The Story of the Atlantic Slave Trade: 1440–1870*. Simon and Schuster, 1997.

Thomas, Nicholas. *Cook: The Extraordinary Voyages of Captain James Cook*. Walker, 2003.

Thoreau, Henry David. *Walden, or Life in the Woods*. Ticknor and Fields, 1854.

Tibães, Maria da Conceição Duarte. *John Rose, um inglês em Diamantina: dos biribiri as casarões*. Edited by Alex Sander Dias Machado. UFJVM, 2018.

Torrens, Hugh S. "The Early Life and Geological Life of John Mawe, 1766–1829, and a Note on His Travels in Brazil." *Bulletin of the Peak District Mines Historical Society* 11, no. 6 (Winter 1992): 267–71.

Tredoux, Gavan, ed. *The Book of Burtoniana*. 3 vols. https://burtoniana.org/burtoniana/index.html.

Trinidade, Ana Laura Cerqueira, Katiane Cristina de Brito Almeida, Pedro Engler Barbosa, and Sílvia Maria Alves Corrêa Oliveira. "Tendências temporais e espaciais da qualidade das águas superficiais da sub-bacia do Rio das Velhas, estado de Minas Gerais." *Engenharia Sanitária Ambiental* 22, no. 1 (January/February 2017): 13–24.

Trouillot, Michel-Rolph. *Silencing the Past: Power and the Production of History*. Beacon, 1995.

Turrell, Robert Vicat. *Capital and Labour on the Kimberley Diamond Fields, 1871–1890*. Cambridge University Press, 1987.

"Viagem do Imperador D. Pedro I a Minas-Geraes em 1830 e 1831." *Revista trimensal do Instituto Historico e Geographico Brazileiro* 60, no. 1 (1897): 305–84.

Vida de Menina. Directed by Helena Solberg. 2003.

Villela, André. "The Nineteenth and Early Twentieth Centuries." In *The Oxford Handbook of the Brazilian Economy*, edited by Edmund Amann, Carlos Azzoni, and Werner Baer, 40–62. Oxford University Press, 2018.

Voigt, Lisa. "Writing Home: The Captive Hero in José de Santa Rita Durão's *Caramuru*." In *Writing Captivity in the Early Modern Atlantic: Circulations of Knowledge and Authority in the Iberian and English Imperial Worlds*, 208–54. University of North Carolina Press, 2009.

Weaver, Stewart A. *Exploration: A Very Short History*. Oxford University Press, 2014.

Weinstein, Barbara. *The Color of Modernity: São Paulo and the Making of Race and Nation in Brazil*. Duke University Press, 2015.

White, Richard. *The Organic Machine: The Remaking of the Columbia River*. Hill and Wang, 1995.

Williams, Christian A. "Decolonising Knowledge: Reflections on Colonial Anthropology and a Humanities Seminar at the University of the Free State." *Strategic Review for Southern Africa* 40, no. 1 (2018): 82–103.

Williams, Daryle. *Culture Wars in Brazil: The First Vargas Regime, 1930–1945*. Duke University Press, 2001.

Wills, Mary. *Envoys of Abolition: British Naval Officers and the Campaign Against the Slave Trade in West Africa*. Liverpool University Press, 2019.

Worger, William H. *South Africa's City of Diamonds: Mine Workers and Monopoly Capitalism in Kimberley, 1867–1895*. Yale University Press, 1987.

Wright, Thomas. *The Life of Sir Richard Burton*. 2 vols. Everett, 1906.

Xica. Directed by Carlos Diegues. Embrafilme, 1976.

Xica da Silva. Rede Manchete, 1996–1998.

INDEX

Note: References following "n" refer notes.

Africa and Africans: East, 40; at Morro Velho, 3–4, 110–20; geography, 32; in Brazil, 15–17, 44, 51, 52, 61, 62, 64–66, 79, 99, 100, 110, 112–19, 151, 166, 171, 247–48, 256–57, 261, 300; southern, 17, 215, 223; West, 15, 17, 29, 225. *See also* slavery; enslaved
Agassiz, Louis, 76, 77
Amazon River basin, 31–32, 48, 51, 55, 57, 185, 209, 216, 242, 252, 293–94, 297
Andes mountains, 7, 15, 31–32
Andrade, Carlos Drummond de, 99
Anglo American Corporation, 104, 127, 161
AngloGold Ashanti, 104, 109; Cuiabá gold mine, 135–36
anthropology, 6, 12, 19–20, 73–74, 80–81; Anthropological Society of London, 19, 33, 80, 90; Boas, Franz, 81
Argentina, 7, 9, 22, 31, 32, 55, 261, 279, 287, 293

Bahia (captaincy/province/state), 15, 17, 57, 79, 127, 196, 200, 216, 233, 237, 241, 250–51, 253, 255, 257, 260, 264, 271, 278
Bahia (Salvador da), 30, 50, 51, 150, 166, 171, 250–53, 272, 284, 298
Barbacena, 77, 83, 85, 86–88, 193
Batista, Padre Cícero Romão, 257–58, 264
Belém do Pará, 50, 51, 57
Belo Horizonte, 71, 105, 148, 156–57, 169, 188–89, 199, 202, 208
Blunt, Wilfred, 7, 9
Bom Jesus da Lapa, 233, 255–56
Bonaparte, Napoleon, 17, 41, 45, 50, 76, 292
Braganzas, 31, 41–42, 45; arrival in Brazil, 132, 292; Comte d'Eu, 33; Duke of Saxe-Coburg-Gotha, Luís Augusto, 114, 135, 207; João VI, 41–42; José I, 166, 215; Maria I, 167; Pedro I, 41–42, 68, 132, 133, 144, 285; Pedro II, 13–14, 41–45, 54, 63,

68–69, 70, 122, 196, 207, 247, 260, 293, 295; Princess Isabel, 33; Princess Leopoldina, 114; Tereza Cristina, 122. *See also* Brazil: monarchy

Brazil: British influence and power, 42, 44–45, 54–55; Catholic church, 44, 285; elections and voting, 42–44, 171–72, 294–96, 300; First Republic, 92, 168, 254, 278–80, 285–86, 293–95; geography, 31–32, 56–58; highlands, 32, 85, 215, 231, 250; independence, 13, 31; inequality, 66, 227, 297; military, 44, 167, 168, 241, 251, 254, 260, 271, 274, 278–80, 285, 286; monarchy, 13, 24, 31, 41–42, 168, 285, 292, 295–96; nobility, 42; Northeast, 15–17, 19, 41, 57–58, 82, 93, 114, 151, 166, 196, 232–33, 242, 248, 252, 257–59, 261, 278, 297; politics, 42–44; population, 44, 104, 297–98; social structure, 78–79; Southeast, 17, 57–58, 103, 166, 248, 255, 261, 282, 297

British communities abroad, 94, 102–28

Brown, James Pennycook, 134–35, 139, 145, 192

Burton, Isabel, 7, 195; arrival in Brazil and departure, 33, 51, 287; caretaker of Richard, 22, 24, 29, 286–87; death, 288; destruction of personal papers, 11, 29, 102, 288–89, 292; descriptions of, 24; editor, 22, 29, 56, 187, 301; expedition down São Francisco River, 186, 232–34; health, 34, 48, 186; home life in São Paulo, 34–39, 47; marriage to Richard, 24, 29, 39; Morro Velho gold mine descent, 120–23, 186; "pack, pay, and follow," 29, 287;

Portuguese language skills, 29, 39, 46; publications, 11, 288, 291–92; publicist for Richard, 22, 24, 29, 33, 291–92; religious views, 24, 25, 35, 91, 97, 178–79, 202, 229, 258, 288–89, 291; sex and sexuality, 28; social status, 24, 52; social views, 36, 46; trip from Morro Velho to Rio, 192–94; visit to Passagem gold mine, 159–60

Burton, Richard Francis: anti-semitism, 179, 248, 289; arrival in Brazil and departure, 29–30, 51, 287; biographers, 7n6, 9–11, 24, 28, 33, 39, 288n14; boosterism, 59, 213, 224, 231–32, 235, 237; consul in Fernando Pó (Bioko), 26–27; consul in Santos, 7, 9, 14, 19, 21, 22, 34, 47, 50, 53–56, 58, 64, 130–31, 287; consul in Damascus, 7, 9, 22, 179, 248, 287, 289; consul in Trieste, 7, 56, 131, 285, 287–89; cultural relativism, 27, 120, 146, 158, 180; death, 285, 288, 291; descriptions of, 24, 26, 33, 289; destruction of personal papers, 11, 29, 102, 288–89, 292; *Explorations in the Highlands of the Brazil*, 11, 19–20, 22, 59, 107, 113, 129–30, 174, 258, 263, 287; explorer, 6–7, 13–14, 19, 33, 47, 58–60, 199; finances, 25–26, 111, 290, 291; gender, sex and sexuality, 28–29, 176–80, 187, 202–3, 272–73, 290, 301; health, 22, 28, 199, 237, 284, 286–87; homosexuality, 28, 290; in Africa, 7, 9, 13–14, 18, 25–27, 58, 65, 80, 93, 119, 131, 196, 199, 237, 244, 255, 270, 286, 290, 292, 301; in South Asia, 28, 58, 292, 301; in Middle East, 9,

INDEX

13–14, 58, 131, 290, 292, 301; income and finances, 24–26, 56; in U.S., 20, 58; knighthood, 291; linguistic skills, 7, 13–14, 33, 163, 174, 289–90; marriage to Isabel, 24, 29, 39; military career, 24, 26; mining interests, 56, 58–59, 131; names, 7n6; Portuguese language skills, 29, 46; publications, 7–9, 11, 22, 27, 33, 82, 180, 288–90; sources for, 11, 288; travel advice, 87–88; views on architecture, 97, 169; views on Brazil and Brazilians, 46, 127, 129, 162, 163, 174–82, 228–29, 238–39, 262; views on Brazilian development, 181, 235, 237, 243–44, 253, 259, 268, 271; views on environment, 137–38, 142, 175, 237; views on Northeast and *nordestinos*, 250, 253, 255, 258–59, 265–66, 280; views on race, slavery, and abolition, 73, 78–83, 90, 113, 119–20, 138, 174–78, 246, 255, 262, 273, 276; views on religion, 22, 26, 89, 97, 120–21, 130, 157–58, 160, 169, 178–79, 256, 258, 259–60, 288; worldview, 19–20, 78–84, 89, 130, 146, 182, 214, 300

Caldeira Brant family, 224–26, 229–30
Cameroon, 26–27, 80
Camões, Luís de, 22, 150
Canada, 17n27, 31–32, 292
Canary Islands, 27, 28
Canastra mountains, 93, 216, 240, 241
Canudos, 175, 251–52, 257, 294–95, 298
Caraça mountains, 136, 145–49, 151, 164, 173
Caraça Sanctuary, 146–48

Caribbean, 14, 17, 55, 108, 175, 210
Castro, Domitila de (Marchioness of Santos), 42, 131, 133
Cata Branca gold mine (Brazilian Company, Limited), 100, 112, 140, 184; enslaved workers, 99–100, 113
Catas Altas, 146, 148; Baron of, 133
Catholicism, 25, 35, 43, 44, 55, 89, 97, 110, 157, 179, 202, 258, 285, 288, 291. *See also* Burton, Isabel: religious views; Burton, Richard, views on religion; churches
Chalmers, George, 124–26, 137, 204
Chico (Francisco), 36–37, 38, 60, 67, 69, 83, 87, 122, 136, 159–60, 193
Chile, 7, 9, 108, 110, 287
Christie Affair, 45, 52–53, 229
churches, 184, 201, 259; baroque style, 90, 169; Blacks church Morro Velho, 192; Bom Jesus de Matozinhos, 96, 239; Jaguara estate, 205; Our Lady of the Abbadia, 246; Our Lady of the Assumption, 85; Our Lady of Carmel, 34–35, 210; Our Lady of the Conception, 137, 149; Our Lady of Good Death, 35; Our Lady of Mercy, 91; Our Lady of Piety, 85; Our Lady of the Pleasures, 225; Our Lady of the Rosary, 85, 90–91, 106, 118, 149, 201, 246; Our Lord of the Good End, 148, 262; Santa Quitéria, 148; Santo Antônio, 92, 220; São Francisco, 90–91, 226
climate and weather, 231, 235, 246, 249, 254, 259, 267, 270, 273, 280; drought, 242, 268; seasons, 60, 71, 83, 93, 201, 219, 244–45, 253, 280
Cocais gold mine (National Brazilian Company), 76, 133–34, 140, 222

351

INDEX

coffee, 24, 44, 56, 70–71, 82, 261, 293, 300; export economy, 28, 39–40, 48–49, 54, 62–66, 151, 248, 278, 282, 285, 292, 296–97; harvest season, 71
Coimbra University, 150, 156, 226
Columbus, Christopher, 14, 18
communications: mail service, 7, 30, 34, 83; telegraph, 30, 181, 261, 293
confederados, 19, 54–55, 184–85, 190, 192, 194, 202–3, 210–11; Mr. Davidson, 211, 213, 218, 235, 245, 262, 265, 270
Congonhas do Campo, 94–98
Congonhas de Sabará, *see* Nova Lima
Cornish miners, 107, 111, 118, 122, 133, 138, 142, 152, 159–62; Piddington, Thomas, 221–22, 228; Rose, John, 221–22, 228
Costa, Cláudio Manuel da, 167, 170, 173
Costa, José Joaquim Xavier da, 92, 167–68, 170–72
Cuiabá gold mine (East del Rey Mining Company), 131, 133, 135
Cunha, Euclides da, 175, 209, 251–53, 260–61, 295n39, 298
Curral mountains, 98, 105, 187
Curvelo, 234–35

Dahomey (Benin), 27, 229
Darwin, Charles, 18, 206
Dayrell family, 221–24, 229–30
Diamantina, 20, 22, 61, 132, 148, 174, 195, 199, 203, 214–30, 234–36; landscapes, 219–20, 223
diamonds, 20, 22, 40, 69, 98, 131, 166, 180, 213–30, 258, 296–97; discovery, 56–57, 61–62, 148, 151, 166; South Africa, 215. *See also* mining: diamonds
disease and health, 48, 237, 265, 270

Dumont, Henrique, 112, 203–5, 243, 295

Eakin, Marshall C.: Confederado ancestors, 185–86; at Gongo Soco, 141–42; interpreting historical sources, 186–87, 285, 301–2; reflections, 19–20, 96, 102–4, 109, 118, 124, 126, 148; religion, 258
Earle, Arthur, 69, 83, 86–87, 121, 136, 187
economic development, 63, 260, 282–83, 286, 292–93; capitalism, 63–64, 79
Eliza. See riverboat (*ajôjô*) and crews
empires and imperialism, 14–19
environmental damage, 142, 144, 151–52, 199
Eschwege, Wilhelm von, 62, 107, 159
Espinhaço mountains, 85, 98, 214–17
expedition, 130–31; daily routine, 89, 269; dog (Negra), 91–92, 191–92, 265, 278; pace, 63, 67, 71, 83, 186, 193–94, 206, 219, 253; summary of route, 195, 232–33; supplies, 191

festas juninas, 93
Faulkner, William, 23–24
Fernando Pó (Bioko), 26–27, 30
First World War, 14, 82n9, 292
food and diet, 88, 191, 211–12, 249, 259, 269–70; *cachaça*, 100, 192
Foreign Office, 7–8, 11, 18, 29, 30, 54, 59, 287; consular and diplomatic corps, 50–56; George Buckley-Mathew, 69
forests, 48, 62, 67–68, 70–1, 137–39, 142, 147, 189
Freyre, Gilberto, 81, 176, 209, 253, 299

INDEX

Gama, José Basílio da, 92
geology, 262; caves, 206, 208; diamond zone, 215–17; dolomite, 89; Iron Quadrangle, 98–99, 131–32, 136, 142, 164, 199; Itabira Peak, 95, 98, 99, 100, 151, 184; Itacolomi Peak, 173–74, 202; Itambé Peak, 223; steatite, 85
Glennie, Charles Archibald, 50, 60, 287
gold, 20, 44–45, 54, 75, 96, 98, 131–32, 166, 296–97, 300; discovery in Brazil, 17, 40, 56–57, 61–62, 66, 74, 79, 85, 107, 166, 202, 214, 235, 239
Gongo Soco gold mine (Imperial Brazilian Mining Association), 76, 107, 112, 132–33, 138–42, 152; ruins, 141–42
Gonzaga, Tomás Antônio, 167, 172–73
Gordon, James Newell, 107–8, 110, 111, 115, 117, 119, 121–24, 131, 134–36, 149–50, 186, 191–93, 218, 277; British vice-consul, 50n12
Great Britain: abolition of slavery and slave trade, 100, 112, 113; civilizing mission, 82; empire, 14, 17, 292–93
Guanabara Bay, 30, 61, 62, 194; views of, 30, 68

Haiti, 31, 79
Halfeld, Heinrich Wilhelm Ferdinand, 76–77, 86, 196–99, 259, 273–74
historical cities (*cidades históricas*), 96, 148, 156–57, 165, 169–70, 188
history and historians, 5–6, 11–13, 20, 24, 126–27, 280, 285, 300–303; and digital sources, 160–62; and material culture, 72, 141–42, 170, 239–40; and

visual culture, 73, 109, 115–18, 122, 126, 217–18; silences in history, 73–74, 301–2
Horta, Florisbella da, 105, 193
housing, 220, 236; hotels and inns, 33, 69, 86, 88, 149, 155, 194, 207; ranchos, 88, 100, 142–43, 184

imagined community, 13, 168, 252, 261, 286, 292, 298–99
immigration, 40, 54–55, 83, 121, 184–85, 216, 261, 296, 299
India, 15, 18, 19, 26, 28
iron and steel industry, 143–44; ARBED, 144, 189–90; ArcelorMittal, 143–44, 189–90

Jaguara estate, 203–5, 218
Jaguar Mining Company, 138, 145, 184
Januária, 233, 247–48
Juazeiro/Petrolina, 233, 242, 243, 247, 269–73
Juazeiro do Norte, 257–58
Juiz de Fora, 69–77

Kieran, 35–36, 38, 48, 60, 194
Klumb, R. H., 71

labor: peasantry, 12, 73, 78–79, 82, 121, 219; skilled, 210; wage labor, 110. *See also* slavery and enslaved
Lage, Mariano Procópio Ferreira, 70–71, 75, 77, 134, 194
landowners and landed estates, 209–11, 215, 219, 263–64, 285, 294–95
Liais, Emmanuel, 196–98, 211–12, 259, 273–74
Lisboa, Antonio Francisco (Aleijadinho), 96–97, 169
London, 18, 21, 25, 29, 30, 45, 52, 91, 111, 124, 126, 134, 158, 160, 217, 288, 291

353

London Exchange, 132, 133, 140
Lund, Peter Wilhelm, 203, 205–8

Mantiqueira mountains, 84, 85, 193
Mariana, 155–62
Mawe, John, 132, 217–18, 223–24, 236
Mecca, 7, 33
Mello Vianna family, 190, 192
Mexico, 15, 31, 32, 51, 52, 55, 110, 132, 210, 293
Middle East, 9, 12, 13, 19, 27, 46, 80, 145, 180, 287, 288, 290, 292, 301
Milnes, Monckton (Lord Houghton), 27–28, 33, 46–47
Minas Gerais, 17, 20–21, 32, 61–62, 70–72; Burton's summary of, 174–82; food and drink, 88, 100; origins, 39–40, 56–57, 156, 214; *Inconfidência*, 92, 167–68, 170–72; population, 79, 104, 150–51, 176. See also geology; historical cities
mining: 1820s boomlet, 132; coal, 150; diamonds, 22, 56, 59, 62, 167, 214, 218, 222–24, 227–28, 262–63; global, 111; gold, 56, 61–62, 100, 102, 112, 123, 127–62; iron ore, 95, 99, 142–43, 148, 187–88. See also diamonds; geology; gold
Mississippi River, 59, 61, 190, 235
Moeda mountains, 98–99
Morro de Santa Anna gold mine (Don Pedro North Del Rey Mining Company), 152–55; Maquiné gold mine, 154–55
Morro do São Vicente gold mine (East Del Rey Mining Company), 183–84
Morro Velho gold mine, 20, 21, 60, 87; Anglo-Brazilians (*morrovelhenses*), 111–12; British cemetery, 3–5, 110, 119, 302; British community, 110–12; British vice-consulate, 50, 110; collapse and rebuilding, 123–25, 152; closure of mine, 127; Casa Grande, 104, 109, 113–17, 135, 161, 302; dimensions, 108–9, 121–23, 124–25, 137; enslaved cemetery, 3–5, 119, 192, 302; enslaved labor, 19, 109, 112–21, 136, 155; geology, 106–7; history, 104–28; name, 91; owners, 104, 107; *revista* (review of enslaved), 113–15, 119, 135; *senzala* (slave quarters), 109, 119. See also St. John d'el Rey Mining Company
music, 94, 246, 266–67

nation-building and nationalism, 6, 13, 22, 23–24, 168, 171–72, 176, 252–53, 260–61, 263, 279–80, 282, 286, 296–300
Native Americans, 15, 39–40, 48–49, 78, 89, 166, 196, 216, 248, 251, 255, 275, 298
Nigeria, 26–27, 80, 146, 158
North, Marianne, 72–73, 108, 109, 113, 118–19
Nova Lima (Congonhas de Sabará), 21–22, 91, 102–28; dimensions, 104–6; names, 104; population, 104, 106, 110

obscenity, 7, 288–90
Oliveira, João Fernandes, 225–26
Orgãos mountains, 62, 65, 293
Ouro Branco mountains, 95, 97–99
Ouro Preto, Vila Rica de, 57, 61, 96, 155–56, 162–74, 183; dimensions, 170–71; population, 169
Oxenford, Edward, 132–34, 144, 152, 184, 222

Paraguay, 7–9, 22; War of Triple Alliance, 51, 180, 252, 287

INDEX

Paraibuna River, 70, 72, 74, 76, 85
Passagem gold mine (Anglo-Brazilian Gold Mining Company, Limited), 136, 158–60
patronage, 64, 217, 263–64, 294–95
Paulo Afonso Falls, 22, 59, 61, 233, 240, 269, 272, 280–83
Pedro II. *See* Braganzas
Peru, 7, 9, 110, 210, 261, 287
Petraglia, Father, 115–17, 120–21
Petrópolis, 21, 33, 57, 62–63, 68–69
Pilão Arcado, 233, 264–65, 267, 269
Pirapora, 22, 196–99, 231–32, 240–41, 272
Pombal, Marquis of (José Sebastião Carvalho e Melo), 166–67
Portugal, 29, 43–45, 54, 226; empire, 15–18, 22, 166; in Brazil, 13, 15–18, 31, 39–40, 48, 51, 57, 107, 138, 150, 196, 214–15, 227, 275
Prestes Column, 278–80

race and racism, 19–20, 79–83; racial mixture, 39–40, 81, 129, 150–51, 174–77, 196, 226–27, 246–48, 251–52, 298–99
railways, 61, 72, 181, 231–32, 240–41, 272, 293; Dom Pedro II, 83, 93, 293; Mauá, 57, 63, 67, 293; San Paulo Railway, 34, 47, 48, 49–50, 272, 287. *See also* transportation
Recife, 29, 30, 50, 51, 57, 81, 151, 243, 260, 271–72, 297–98
regionalism and regional identity, 41, 51, 56–58, 75, 180–81
religion, 43, 97, 111, 120–21, 150; celebrations, 89, 245, 259; funerals, 160, 291; Islam, 7, 80; Jesuits, 48, 90, 150, 275; Macaúbas Convent, 202–3, 226; Mormons, 20, 33, 178, 233–34; mysticism, 251, 258; nuns, 148, 157–58, 203, 258; pilgrims, 96, 256–58; priests, 48, 55, 68, 107, 110, 115, 120, 121, 146–48, 156, 157, 229, 256; Vatican, 258
Renault, Victor, 86, 88, 193
Riedel, Auguste, 113–19, 203–4, 207–8, 227
Rio das Mortes, 85, 89, 92
Rio das Velhas, 22, 60, 100, 105, 108, 129, 137, 183, 195, 215–17; characteristics, 200; development possibilities, 188, 213; headwaters, 98, 112, 183, 196; rapids, 208–9, 212–13, 267, 275–77; zones, 198–200
Rio de Janeiro, 17, 19, 20, 21, 22, 29, 107, 186, 193, 247, 293; British community, 33, 52–54; geography, 64; importance, 28, 40, 52, 132, 166, 214; population, 52, 56, 297–98; province or state, 32, 57, 62, 72, 74, 79, 171, 196, 233, 278, 297; role in slave trade, 40, 44, 52, 64, 112, 248
Rio de la Plata, 31, 51, 85, 166, 209, 217
Rio Doce, 85, 144, 151
Rio Grande do Sul, 50, 51, 54, 57, 63, 151, 171, 278, 294, 297
Rosa, João Guimarães, 200, 209n37
Royal Geographical Society, 18, 29, 33
Russell, Lord, 26, 27, 29–30

Sabará, 61, 131, 187–90
Saint-Hilaire, Auguste de, 107, 110, 218
Santa Bárbara do Oeste, 55, 185–86
Santa Luzia, 200–201
Santa Rita Durão, José, 150
Santos, 7, 9, 19, 21, 34, 40–41, 44, 200; description, 27–30; in 1860s, 47–50; immigration, 54
Santos, Francisco de Paula, 112, 140, 159, 164, 168, 203, 295
São Francisco River, 9, 19, 20–22,

355

241–42; Burton's views on, 58–60, 237, 268; course, 241–42, 253–54, 275; dams and reservoirs, 231, 233, 241–42, 264–65, 267, 268–69, 274, 282–83; development plans, 231–32, 243–44, 268–69, 274; explorers, 196–99; Halfeld survey, 76, 196–99, 259, 273–74; history, 196; origins, 93, 196, 216, 240; population, 243; Renault survey, 86; Sobradinho Dam, 269, 270, 271
São João del Rei, 87, 89–93, 100, 106–7, 129, 156–57, 169, 174, 188, 191, 225
Maranhão, 51, 166, 216
São Paulo, 19, 21, 27–28, 47–48, 56–57, 156, 260, 282, 289, 298; in 1860s, 34–35; growth and expansion, 39–41; province or state, 32, 55–58, 79, 151, 171, 185, 233, 248, 254, 278, 297
sertão (backlands), 13, 196, 231–32, 255, 263–65, 269, 271, 279; defined, 200–201; *sertanejos*, 250–51, 261, 269, 273, 276
shattered mirror, 20, 286, 299, 303
Silva, Chica da, 223–27
Silva, Virgulino Ferreira da (Lampião), 264
slavery and enslaved, 12–13, 15–17, 261; abolition, 43, 66–67, 260, 261, 293, 296; Agostinho, 191, 218, 245, 259, 262, 272; Antonio, 87; economic importance, 44; demography, 62, 67, 78–80, 297–98; João Paraopeba, 136; labor, 63–66, 80, 154, 209–10, 214; Miguel, 87, 136, 155; Minas Gerais, 78–83; quilombos, 227; slave trade, 17, 40, 45, 52, 61, 64, 151, 196, 261, 300; United States, 62, 67, 78, 82

Sousa, Ireneu Evangelista de (Mauá, Baron), 49, 62–63
Staden, Hans, 48–49
Stanley, Henry Morton, 6–7
Stanley, Edward Lord (Lord Derby), 11, 22, 25, 59–60, 131, 289
state building, 13, 66, 78, 157, 168, 170, 252–53, 260, 264, 269, 279, 282, 286, 293–95
St. John d'el Rey Mining Company, 3–5, 21, 60, 102–28, 302; archives, 104, 109, 118, 161, 302; origins, 91; Cata Branca enslaved labor, 100, 113; demise, 127; English workers, 105, 107, 110; manumission practices, 119; real estate, 184. *See also* Morro Velho gold mine
sugar plantations, 15–17, 44, 51, 66, 70, 82, 151, 166, 210–11, 261, 296
Syria, 7, 9, 179, 248, 289

Texas, 30, 41, 236
Thornton, Sir Edward, 45, 52–54, 56, 59–60, 69, 131
Tiradentes (São José del Rei), 76, 91–92. *See also* Costa, José Joaquim Xavier da
transportation, 252, 293; boats, 245, 267; coastal, 34, 62; Estrada Real, 61–62, 70, 92, 95, 105, 148, 150, 152, 184, 214; highways, 71, 83, 184, 234–36, 241, 247, 259, 271; mules and horses, 34, 62, 67, 69–75, 87, 101, 174, 192–93, 230, 284; registers/ *registros*, 74–75, 217, 254; riverboat (*ajôjô*) and crews, 22, 183, 190–92, 195, 199–201, 208, 230, 235–36, 244–45, 248–49, 253, 262, 264, 267, 269, 272, 274–78; roads, 57, 62, 67, 72–73, 83, 148, 184, 218; routes to

INDEX

mining zone, 57, 61; steamships, 181, 194, 203–4, 243, 271–72, 284; transatlantic, 30; *tropeiros*, 80, 88, 177, 193, 280; União e Indústria toll road, 69–75, 134, 140, 193–94

travelers and travel accounts, 11–12, 72–73, 130, 300–301

Treloar, Thomas and Allarina, 133, 152–53, 158–61, 184, 194

Trieste, 7, 56, 131, 285

United States, 12–13, 17, 20, 31, 293; imperial reach, 55, 292–93; independence, 30–31; politics, 43–44, 82, 179, 200, 296; regions and regionalism, 58, 171–72, 178, 299; slavery and slave trade, 52, 62, 66–67, 120, 129

Vale do Rio Doce Company, 99, 142, 144, 151–52

Vargas, Getúlio, 121, 170–72, 176, 254, 286, 294, 299

Victoria, Queen, 26, 42, 217, 291

violence, 258, 263–65, 279, 294

Wanderley, João Maurício, 260–63

World War II, 171, 213

Xique-Xique, 233, 261–63